ST. JOHN'S GOSPEL

A COMMENTARY

ST. JOHN'S GOSPEL

A COMMENTARY

BY

R. H. LIGHTFOOT

EDITED BY

C. F. EVANS

WITH THE TEXT OF
THE REVISED VERSION

OXFORD UNIVERSITY PRESS

Oxford University Press, Amen House, London E.C.4

GLASGOW   NEW YORK   TORONTO   MELBOURNE   WELLINGTON
BOMBAY   CALCUTTA   MADRAS   KARACHI   KUALA LUMPUR
CAPE TOWN   IBADAN   NAIROBI   ACCRA

First published by the Clarendon Press 1956
Reprinted lithographically in Great Britain
at the University Press, Oxford
from sheets of the First Edition
1957
First issued in Oxford Paperbacks 1960

PREFACE

AMONG the miscellaneous papers which R. H. Lightfoot had preserved in connexion with his work on St. John's gospel was the following pencilled draft of a preface to his commentary, written some little time before his death.

This volume had its origin in an attempt to provide a commentary on St. John's gospel for the Clarendon Bible. In the course of years, however, it became clear to me that I could not confine it within the limits which the publishers find it necessary to impose upon contributors to this series. Since they are good enough still to wish to publish the volume, I have sought to align it, in outward appearance at any rate, with my earlier book, *The Gospel Message of St. Mark*, also published by the Clarendon Press, although the scale of this work is much larger.

I have learned much from continental writers, and to those who know the publications of these scholars my debt will often be apparent. Among recent writers in this country I owe most to Archbishop Bernard for the scholarship and accuracy of his two volumes in the I.C.C., to Professor C. H. Dodd, whose Speaker's Lectures at Oxford some twenty years ago, now at length, it is believed, about to appear in print, first pointed out a path which I have found most trustworthy towards the understanding of this gospel, and to the great work of Sir Edwyn Hoskyns and Mr. F. N. Davey. As my manuscript has grown, however, I have often found it desirable to strike out in directions which, to the best of my belief, are new; and this combination of material from many sources together with some contributions of my own, I nope may justify the publication of this volume.

Like his predecessors in the field of Johannine studies, Bishop Westcott, Canon Scott Holland, and Sir Edwyn Hoskyns, Light-foot did not live to give his book its final form. When he died the Commentary proper, that is, the Exposition and Notes, had been completed, and was ready for publication. Except for a few changes of wording of an altogether minor kind, it is here printed as he left it. In addition to the Commentary, however, Lightfoot left behind, as possible parts of an Introduction, a number of separate studies with the following titles: The Person of Christ, The Background of the Doctrine of the Logos, The Lord's Patris, St. John the Baptist, The Disciples, The Multitude and the Jews, The Contents and Plan of the Ministry. These were of varying length, and some of them were in more than one draft. No very clear indication was to be found whether they were intended to constitute together the whole of an Introduction, or in what order they were to be presented, or in what way, if at all, they were to be connected with one another. Only the first two, which he seems latterly to have wished to print, the first as an Introduction and the second as an Appendix, had been finally approved by Lightfoot; the rest appear to have been written at an earlier period, and to have been laid aside, either to be reconsidered in the light of more recent work on this gospel, or to be abandoned altogether. There was also other matter proper to an Introduction which was for the most part of a much more fragmentary nature.

Three courses seemed to the editor to be open to him when he was asked to prepare the book for publication. He could have attempted to write, with or without the help of Lightfoot's material, a complete Introduction of the type which is commonly expected in a full length commentary. Apart, however, from a strong disinclination to supplement another man's work to this extent, particularly the work of so individual and meticulous a scholar as Lightfoot, he felt that to proceed in this way was to run the risk of seriously altering the balance of the book as a whole. Lightfoot's primary, and almost exclusive, concern was with the exegesis of the text of the gospel. In his study, 'The Lord the true passover feast', which was also found amongst his papers, and which is printed as an Appended Note (pp. 349 ff.), he had originally written: 'It is a good rule for the student always to try to explain St. John by St. John, and for this purpose he can hardly have too exact or minute a knowledge of the book and its contents. It has, indeed, been said that this gospel is so complete and coherent in itself that for the careful student it will be found to answer all the questions which it raises, so far as such questions are answerable.' He was thus not greatly concerned with what the Germans call *Einleitung*, and he was very diffident about his capacity to deal adequately with such matters. An alternative course would have been to publish the Commentary without any Introduction, but, in the editor's judgement, this would have been to deprive the reader of valuable insights into the character of St. John's gospel as a whole which were to be found in Lightfoot's introductory studies, and which, by their nature, could not have found a place in the running exposition of the text. The editor has, therefore, adopted a third course of using Lightfoot's material to write what may, perhaps, be regarded as a single Introductory Essay with appropriate subdivisions. Since this has involved considerable re-arrangement and editing of what was in some cases fragmentary, it would not be possible to indicate typographically with any precision where the contributions of the editor begin and end. Suffice it to say that it has been his aim to make the maximum use of what Lightfoot had written, and to confine his editorial work, so far as he could, to providing the necessary connexions and transitions. It was his delight to discover, when he had finished, that he had been able to make use of all the material that was available, and that it had shaped itself, as he believes, into something of a unity. It is to be hoped that in this form the Introduction will not be found more repetitive of the Commentary than would have been the case had Lightfoot himself written it, or than the Commentary is repetitive of itself, and that both in what it includes and in what it omits it follows the main direction of Lightfoot's own mind and interests. For its final shape the editor is, of course, alone responsible, and that responsibility, as those will realize who had experience of Lightfoot's high standards of composition, is not inconsiderable.

The draft preface quoted above concluded with the words: 'I am greatly obliged to my friend Mr. P. M. Haynes, M.A., of St. Edmund Hall, Oxford, for his unwearying diligence in verifying my references, and for many valuable suggestions.' The editor would like to add an expression of his own obligations to Mr. Haynes for his constant and ready co-operation, for information about the manuscript which only he was in a position to supply, for his preparation of the Indexes, and for correcting the greater part of the proofs. Lightfoot would also certainly have wished to thank the Rev. K. G. Martin, who read the Commentary through for him with a view to making corrections and verifying references. Finally the editor would acknowledge his great indebtedness at every stage to the Clarendon Press and its readers for their advice and skill, their vigilance and patience.

C. F. EVANS

C.C.C. Oxon.

CONTENTS

II. 2^{12}–12^{50}. *The public manifestation of the Lord*

LIST OF ABBREVIATIONS

H.T.R.   *Harvard Theological Review*
I.C.C.   *International Critical Commentary*
J.T.S.   *Journal of Theological Studies*
R.V.   The Revised Version of the Holy Bible (1884)
R.V. mg   Revised Version marginal note
ZNW   *Zeitschrift für die neutestamentliche Wissenschaft*

INTRODUCTION

A. THE ORIGINS OF THE GOSPEL

THE purpose of this book is a religious and theological exposition of the text of St. John's gospel. It is not proposed to discuss at length such difficult and controverted questions as its date, authorship, and place of origin, or its relation to the other Johannine books of the New Testament, and to the other canonical gospels. Only a brief account of these matters will be attempted in this Introduction.

There is now evidence available from papyrus texts discovered in Egypt that St. John's gospel may have been in existence soon after, if not before, A.D. 100.[1] The gospel seems, however, to have won its way to full acceptance slowly, and to have been regarded with disfavour for a time in some (probably very conservative) quarters of the Church. It has been generally agreed throughout the centuries that of the four gospels it was the last to be written, and one reason why its greatness and importance were not appreciated at once may have been its strongly marked difference from the other three. Only in the latter half of the second century do we find it placed by the whole Church on a level with these other three, to form an essential part of the fourfold Gospel. From this time onwards, however, its position was assured, and it should be remembered that the Church has never been aware of any fundamental incompatibility between the portrait of the Lord in this gospel and that in the other three. This question has long ago been settled by the religious consciousness of Christendom. In the doctrinal controversies which filled so large a place in the life of the church during the third and fourth centuries, St. John's gospel played a most important part, becoming 'almost the cornerstone of the New Testament Canon'.[2] The authoritative formularies of the Church's faith are stamped with the impress of St. John's gospel.

From the latter part of the second century, if not earlier, the authorship of this gospel has been assigned in the tradition of the Church to an eye-witness of the Lord's ministry, one of the original

[1] C. H. Roberts, *An Unpublished Fragment of the Fourth Gospel in the John Rylands Library*, 1935; *Fragments of an Unknown Gospel*, ed. H. I. Bell and T. C. Skeat, 1935.
[2] *Cambridge Biblical Essays*, ed. H. B. Swete, 1909, p. 288.

twelve, the younger son of Zebedee, the beloved disciple himself, who is believed to have lived to a great age, and to have attained to a position of authority in the church of Ephesus. This traditional ascription still receives support, and has never been shown to be impossible. What can be gathered from the New Testament concerning John, the son of Zebedee, is as follows. In all the four lists of the twelve the New Testament gives he is found, with his brother James, among the first group of four names, made up of two pairs of brothers. Until the Lord called the sons of Zebedee they had followed the trade of their father, being fishermen; and the family employed a staff of servants. The mother Salome is found, at a later date, in the Lord's company, as one of the women who followed Him in Galilee, who went up with Him and His disciples to Jerusalem, and watched the last events at a distance from the cross. Whatever may be the precise meaning of the name Boanerges given by the Lord to James and John— St. Mark understands it as meaning 'sons of thunder'—the two brothers obviously shared an ardent and impulsive temperament. Thus John on one occasion seems to have taken the lead in censuring an exorcist who made use of the Lord's name, but was not a disciple [Mk. 9³⁸]; similarly on another occasion the two brothers, indignant that a Samaritan village would not receive their Master, suggest that they should invoke divine vengeance upon it [Lk. 9⁵⁴]. It is noteworthy that on both occasions the matter was referred to the Lord for His decision. Again, their request that they might have places of honour, and be nearest to their Master in His glory, in complete forgetfulness, it seems, of the claims of St. Peter and the remaining members of the twelve, and their confidence that they could share His cup and baptism, suggest the same traits of devotion and impulsiveness [Mk. 10³⁵⁻⁴⁵]; and it seems clear that the Lord could value and accept this passionate devotion, although as yet untrained and immature, when we recall that along with St. Peter they, and they only, were associated with the Lord on three momentous occasions, and also, this time with Andrew as well as Peter, on a fourth [Mk. 5³⁷, 9²⁻⁸, 14³³⁻⁴², 13³ᶠᶠ·]. In the early chapters of the Acts of the Apostles St. John seems to be closely connected with St. Peter, but after their joint visit to Samaria he disappears from our sight, except for the mention of him in Gal. 2⁹, from which it appears that, at the time of St. Paul's second visit to Jerusalem after his conversion, St. John was one of the three reputed 'pillars' of the Church who gave to him and Barnabas 'the right hands of fellowship' as the apostle of the Gentiles, they continuing their mission to the Jews.

If we owe the fourth gospel to St. John, it is clear that on this last point a change occurred with the lapse of time; for in spite of efforts to maintain the contrary, the fourth gospel cannot be regarded as an attempt to win the Jews. But in other respects does not the fourth gospel reveal some of the traits which we have just discerned in the younger son of Zebedee? There is the same absolute devotion to the Person of the Lord, the same tendency to sharp, clear-cut distinctions. In no book in the Bible does the contrast between light and darkness appear in such unrelieved sharpness as in this gospel. It sees no half-tones; indeed the Jewish scholar C. G. Montefiore was moved by its treatment of 'the Jews' to speak of 'the horrible dualism of the author of the Gospel of Love!'[1] It is perhaps surprising that, if St. John survived to a ripe old age and wrote this work towards the end of his life, nothing whatever is known of his ministry during the latter part of his life; but is not this true very largely of all the leaders of the early Church, with the single exception of St. Paul? We may also recall two further points; first, the accuracy shown in this gospel about the geography of Palestine, about Jewish customs, and about the social and other conditions of life there during the Lord's ministry has never been impugned; and second, that the evidence which shows that the gospel may have been in circulation soon after, if not before, the end of the first century makes it possible to hold that it could have been written in old age by a younger contemporary of the Lord. Moreover, it cannot be decisively urged that, since the character of the gospel shows its author to have been an original thinker and theologian, he cannot have been the John who is described in Acts 4[13] as an 'uneducated layman'; for this passage may only imply that, in the opinion of the judges, the two apostles belonged to the 'people of the land', and had not studied in the rabbinic schools, a criticism which is brought in this gospel against the Lord Himself [7[15]; cf. 7[49]].

The mature character of this gospel should by no means be overlooked. It is hardly a book for children in the sense in which the synoptic gospels are suitable for, and can be largely understood by, the young. The fourth gospel does not reveal an interest in

[1] *The Synoptic Gospels*, 1909, ii, p. 750.

youth as such, and its apparent simplicity may easily hide its maturity, profundity, and subtlety of thought. According to more than one early tradition this gospel was put forth not by an individual acting on his own initiative, but by one who was the representative of a group, which had both impelled him to the task, and also itself had some share in its accomplishment; and the concluding words of 21²⁴ perhaps lend support to this tradition. But internal evidence also suggests strongly that, in its present form, the book is, in the last resort, the work of a single writer; its language and style are similar throughout, and it bears the stamp of a single mind which, with whatever help from others, has left the marks not only of its own style, but of its own method of presenting the truth. No one is likely to study this very mature and profoundly religious book, with its careful links, interconnexions, and antitheses, which only reveal themselves to very patient study, without inclining to the belief that it was probably composed slowly, each separate scene and discourse having been the subject of prolonged reflection and arrangement, and the whole being very closely knit together, and that it reached its present form only after deep thought upon the themes with which it deals, and as the result of a Christian experience likely to have extended over many years. If, therefore, we hold to the apostolic authorship, we must suppose that in later life the evangelist, under the guidance and inspiration of the Holy Spirit, will have come to understand much that was beyond him when he followed his Master in Palestine, as, indeed, certain passages in the book itself suggest [2²², 7³⁹, 12¹⁶, 16¹²]. But we must also suppose that the son of Zebedee has shown a remarkable ability 'to move with the times'. If he was an eye-witness of the Lord's ministry, we might have expected that his gospel would be in character the most primitive and Jewish of the four; but this is not the case. In it he shows himself to be familiar not only with rabbinic, but also with gnostic, speculations, and with the attempts of writers like the Jew Philo to reconcile Jewish and Greek religious ideas. He plants the roots of his gospel most firmly in history and historical facts, following the general outline of the 'saving events', already familiar to us from other New Testament writings and often recalling sayings and incidents which are already known to us from the first three gospels. There can be no doubt that the evangelist believes himself to be giving the true interpretation not only of the Christian revelation, but of the historical Lord Himself. His purpose is to nourish his readers in their devotion to the historic Person, and all his efforts are directed to that end. But he regards his inspiration as given him chiefly in order that he may make clear, in language which religiously minded Gentiles, as well as Jews, can make their own, the deeper implications and the ultimate or permanent significance of the revelation brought by the Lord, as these were understood by the Church (according to tradition that of Ephesus) in, and no doubt for, which he wrote, towards the end of the first century. And he does so, not by a repetition of the words which he heard long ago in Palestine, but by a restatement of them designed to reveal their meaning.

The arguments which have been urged against apostolic authorship are of varying weight and diverse character. Instead of examining them at length and in detail, it may be more profitable to set forth the views on this subject of one who, while thinking it more than likely 'that there was someone called John at Ephesus and that he played an influential part in the life of the Church in Asia', finds himself unable to believe that 'this person was the Apostle John, the son of Zebedee'.[1] Dr. Manson suggests, very tentatively, that in considering the origin of this gospel we have to postulate a body of tradition, consisting of both matters of fact and teachings, which had its original home in Jerusalem, its primary source being 'an anonymous disciple of the Lord, not necessarily to be identified with John, the son of Zebedee, or any other of the Apostles'. This tradition found its way, first of all, to Antioch in Syria, which we know to have been a kind of headquarters of the early Church (cf. Acts 11[19-30], 13[1-3], 14[26-28]). Here it left its impress 'on documents which we have reason to connect with that centre, on the liturgical usage of the Syrian Church, and on the teaching both of the missionaries who went out from Antioch (e.g. St. Paul) and of those who subsequently had the leadership of the Antiochene community itself (Ignatius)'.[2] In this way Dr. Manson accounts for such phenomena as the agreement of St. Paul in 1 Cor. 5[7-8], 15[20], 'a letter written at Ephesus by a missionary whose home base was Antioch', with the Johannine rather than the Synoptic dating

[1] T. W. Manson, in the *Bulletin of the John Rylands Library*, vol. 30, No. 2, May 1947, p. 320 n. 1.

[2] Ibid., p. 327. A similarity of phraseology and outlook may be noted between St. John's gospel and the Odes of Solomon, which, there is reason to believe, had their origin in Syria in the first quarter of the second century.

of the last supper and the Lord's death, or the remarkable fact that, whereas the first Christian writer to show the influence of the Johannine terminology is St. Ignatius, bishop of Syrian Antioch in the second century, he nowhere shows certain knowledge by quotation or otherwise of St. John's gospel. From Antioch, Dr. Manson thinks, the tradition moved to Ephesus, which he suggests should be regarded as 'a second missionary base or advanced headquarters' of the Church, and so be classed with Syrian Antioch rather than with such places as Athens, Corinth, Philippi, and Thessalonica, which were simply scenes of St. Paul's missionary work. At Ephesus 'the final literary formulation was achieved in the Gospel and Epistles attributed to John'. But 'how much of this long road was travelled in person by the original custodian of the tradition; how much he (or his disciples) added on the way as the result of meditation on what was given, or of contact with other religious and philosophical ideas', these are questions, Dr. Manson adds, to which no cut-and-dried answer is possible; and he urges a detailed examination of St. John's gospel with a view to their solution.[1] It should also be remembered that the Septuagint translation of the Hebrew scriptures into Greek, and the works of the Jewish philosopher Philo, who made it the purpose of his life to commend his ancestral faith to the Gentile world, originated at Alexandria. Unfortunately the early history of Christianity at Alexandria is at present lost to us, but at a later date a theology prevailed there which has much in common with St. John's thought, and in view of the fact that one of the most remarkable features of St. John's gospel is its fusion of Jewish with Greek thought in the cause of Christ, it is not surprising that the suggestion should be made that its origin is to be sought in that city. Finally, it should be observed that the evangelist, to judge from certain features of his book, and especially from the place occupied in it by the anonymous figure of 'the beloved disciple', seems to wish to veil his identity. A certain mystery has wrapped itself around him from the first, and a century passes before it is

[1] Ibid., p. 328. Dr. Manson does not deal with the problem of the authorship of the Apocalypse. This work, in spite of the great differences between it and the rest of the Johannine books, is undoubtedly connected with them in certain respects of vocabulary, style, and theological thought. If the widely held view is correct, that St. John's gospel and the Apocalypse are not by the same author, there is none the less an affinity between the two books which requires an explanation.

dispelled, at least to the satisfaction of the Church of the second century.

It is a remarkable, but hardly surprising, feature of more recent study of this gospel that interest has shifted from the question of authorship to the questions of the evangelist's milieu and of the identity of the readers whom he had in view. In Westcott's commentary, reprinted from the Speaker's Commentary in 1881, no less than thirty-two out of ninety-seven pages of Introduction were given to the first section, which deals with authorship, while the question for what readers the gospel was designed receives no special treatment. Believing, as did Westcott, that in this gospel no less than in the synoptic gospels we have the *ipsissima verba* of the Lord as heard by a foremost disciple, and an account of His works as seen by an eye-witness, the scholars of two generations ago strove their utmost to establish the traditional authorship, and to connect the fourth gospel directly and immediately with one of the original disciples of the Lord. Since then detailed discussion has gone to show both how difficult the problem is, and how little light those who reject the traditional authorship are able to throw upon it; for whereas we have some slight reliable knowledge about John, the son of Zebedee, we have none whatever about John the presbyter or any other figure to whom the authorship has been assigned. Furthermore, it has been increasingly realized that the value and importance of the book within the fourfold gospel does not stand or fall with its authorship by the son of Zebedee; and with the growing conviction that not the fourth gospel only but all the gospels have been affected by the momentous events which took place in the development and expansion of the Church's life and thought in the first century, attention has inevitably been directed primarily elsewhere, i.e. to the structure of the book itself, to the problem of the evangelist's milieu, and to his relation both to the religious and philosophical thought of his own time and to the traditions contained in the other books of the New Testament.

B. THE TEXT OF THE GOSPEL

At the present time there is a widespread tendency to believe, in spite of a complete absence of evidence in the manuscripts to support the theory, that misplacement, either on a large or on a small scale, has occurred in the order of the text of this gospel.

Many authorities, for instance, think that ch. 6 should stand before ch. 5, and also that 7^{15-24} should be removed from its present position, and placed at the end of ch. 5. Other examples of a recommended rearrangement of the text could be given.

The traditional order is certainly at some points surprising. Thus, at the end of ch. 5 the Lord is addressing Jews at Jerusalem, but ch. 6 opens with the words, 'After these things Jesus went away to the other side of the sea of Galilee.' We should have expected some mention of His journey northwards and of His arrival in Galilee before we read the words of 6^1. On the other hand, if ch. 6 is placed before ch. 5, the Lord is in Galilee at the end of ch. 4, which will now immediately precede ch. 6, and at Cana, not far from the western side of the lake. For geographical reasons, therefore, the transposition suggested is attractive. Again, the Jews' question at 7^{15}, 'How knoweth this man letters, having never learned?', which in the text as we have it opens the Lord's controversies with them at the feast of tabernacles, may seem inadequately motived or explained by the reference in the previous verse to the Lord's teaching. On the other hand, the Jews' question would be entirely natural and in place at the end of ch. 5, where at the close of the Lord's address to the Jews in 5^{19-47} He refers to the writings of Moses.

It should not, however, be assumed that the reason for the maladjustments, if such they be, lies in dislocations of the text after it had left the evangelist's hands; and in the complete absence of textual evidence to support suggested rearrangements, it is reasonable to hold that no attempt should be made to alter the order of the text as we have it. The fact that the narrative appears to make a number of fresh starts may be due to the use by the evangelist of material which had previously stood on its own, or in different connexions from those with which he has provided it. Whether this be so or not, we certainly seem to be dealing with a writer who, in his endeavour to impress the truth upon his readers, regards what we may call the order of thought as more important than a strictly chronological order of events, and who is prepared on occasion to subordinate the latter to the former. Possible examples of this are the placing of the cleansing of the temple at the outset of the ministry for a theological purpose of his own, and the narrating of the anointing of the Lord at Bethany by Mary before the Lord's entry, next day, into Jerusalem. The geographical difficulty in the present position of chs. 5 and 6 is not insuperable, if we may suppose that between 5[47] and 6[1] the Lord's return from Jerusalem to Galilee, on the west side of the lake, is assumed, and that thereafter, from His normal location there, He crosses to the east side of the lake, where the feeding of the multitude takes place, as described in 6[5-14]. Since the disciples the same evening embark for Capernaum, which is on the north-west side of the lake, and the Lord, after rejoining them in the boat [6[21]], teaches there the next day [6[59]], this assumption may be justified. For theological reasons suggest strongly that ch. 5 should precede ch. 6. In ch. 5, in the Lord's first address to the Jews, the reader has learned of the absolute identity, in will and work, of the Father and the Son, through the love of the Father and the perfect obedience, in love, of the Son; and this teaching seems to prepare for, and should naturally precede, the teaching of ch. 6, which represents a great advance on anything found in chs. 2 to 4. It has been shown in chs. 2 to 4 that the Lord, in both word and deed, gives life, but the way in which He does so, and what is involved in His doing so, are not considered until ch. 6, where we reach the first of His self-declarations in this gospel, 'I am the living bread', or 'the bread which gives life', and learn for the first time that He Himself is the gift which He brings [6[35, 48]], and that the bread which He will give is His flesh, for the life of the world [6[51]]. And only because of the teaching already given in ch. 5 about the Lord's union with the Father is the reader in a position to know in ch. 6 that the Lord, whose every act and word reflect the act and word of the Father [5[17-23]], is Himself the Mediator, offering to men nothing less than the life which He eternally shares with the Father, subject always to the essential qualification that this life, which is His by nature and right, becomes theirs only in and through Him, and as a result of His action for their sakes (cf. 17[4, 19], 19[30]). A minor corroboration of the view that ch. 5 should precede ch. 6 is that certain verses in ch. 6, e.g. 38–40, 57a, teach the same truths as 5[23-30]; and if these passages are examined, it becomes clear that in ch. 5 these truths are being set forth for the first time, whereas in ch. 6 they are subordinate to the main theme of that chapter, which is that the Lord Himself is the life-giving bread, and now only recapitulate earlier teaching.

The second example which was given of an alleged displacement was the passage 7[15-24]. It is frequently suggested that these verses do not belong here, and should be inserted at the end of ch. 5 with which they certainly have a close connexion. Thus the same Greek word is translated 'writings' in 5⁴⁷ and 'letters' in 7¹⁵. The teaching in 7¹⁶, ¹⁷, ²⁴ recalls that of 5³⁰, and 7¹⁸ recalls 5⁴¹, ⁴⁴. Finally, 7¹⁹ seems to refer directly to 5¹⁸, and 7²³ to 5⁹. These are striking facts. But on the assumption that the existing order of the text is correct, are they not satisfactorily met when we realize that it is a characteristic of St. John, when he has passed from one occasion to a later, similar occasion, to disregard the interval of time which has elapsed meanwhile, and to take up the teaching or controversy of the previous occasion as though the earlier hearers were still present, and the circumstances identical with those which had gone before? Another example of this tendency on the part of the evangelist is when the officers sent at 7³², in the middle of the feast of tabernacles [7¹⁴], to arrest the Lord apparently do not return to the rulers until 7⁴⁵, on its last day [7³⁷].

Reference may also be made here to a sentence which, in its present context, is often regarded as difficult. In the last words of 14³¹ the Lord bids the disciples to arise and to go on their way with Him; but the words are followed by the further teaching of chs. 15 and 16, and the prayer of ch. 17, and only at 18¹ does He go forth with them across the Kidron. The difficulty has led to the suggestion that here also the text has suffered dislocation, or else— what is surely unlikely—that the contents of chs. 15–17 were spoken during the walk through the city. The last words of 14³¹ very closely resemble those spoken by the Lord to the disciples at Mk. 14⁴², just before the arrest. If we think that St. John knew Mark, is it perhaps possible, however strange it may seem to us, that by inserting these words here he reminds us that the Lord's words and works are one, and that the words of chs. 13–17 are the counter-part of His work in chs. 18–21? If so, the purpose of these words in 14³¹, recalling words spoken at a supreme moment (according to St. Mark) of His later action, may be to remind the reader, in the midst of the Lord's discourse, how great was the cost to Him of that which in chs. 13 to 17 He reveals to His disciples. In support of this view it may be pointed out, first, that the teaching of chs. 15 to 17 represents a great advance on that given in ch. 14—a fact which suggests that ch. 14 should precede these chapters—and secondly, that elsewhere in this gospel, in spite of St. John's apparent independence of the synoptists, hints seem to be given from time to time, by verbal parallels, that the earlier tradition is being interpreted and should be kept in mind. The following instances may be given. The Lord's words to the impotent man at 5^8 are very similar to those which He addresses to the palsied man at Mk. 2^{11}, and His words when He approaches the disciples on the lake [6^{20} if we omit 'Be of good cheer'] are identical with those found in the same connexion in Mk. 6^{50}, Mt. 14^{27}, while it is possible that the reference to 'the treasury' in 8^{20} is not unconnected with the reference to it in Mk. 12^{41-43}, Lk. 21^1.

More important, however, for our understanding of this gospel than the particular answers which we give to such questions is the fact that it is hardly possible to discuss such problems as these, which are raised by the order of the text, without at the same time taking into account both the extreme care with which this gospel appears to have been composed as a complete and coherent whole, with each section playing its part in the whole, and also its relation to the traditions contained in the earlier gospels. Some further treatment of these two matters, is, therefore, called for.

C. THE PLAN AND STRUCTURE OF THE GOSPEL

St. John's gospel falls into two principal parts. The first, 2^{12} to 12^{50}, contains the record of the Lord's public ministry, and the second, 13^1 to 20^{31}, the record of the final events, of which the central feature is the crucifixion of the Lord. The division between these two parts is more clearly marked in John than it is in the other gospels, but in none of the gospels must it be regarded as an absolute division; thus, in John, the Lord's 'hour' arrives before the ministry is over [$12^{23, 27}$].

To deal here only with the first part of the book, the contents of chs. 1 to 12, 1^{1-18}, usually called the prologue, is designed to enable the reader to understand the doctrines of the book. It is, therefore, more philosophical in character than any other part, and should be most carefully studied. $1^{19}-2^{11}$ deals with the preparation for the ministry (see pp. 92 ff.). It contains the Baptist's witness to the Lord, and an account of the way in which certain men are drawn into the Lord's company; it ends with His promise to them of 1^{51}, with their first sight of its fulfilment, and with their belief which arises therefrom.

The first considerable section of the public ministry seems to run from 2^{12} to 4^{54}. It describes the presence of the true and real light in the world, its nature, the conditions under which it is offered to men, and the circumstances in which it is received or rejected. At the beginning and the end are two contrasted scenes. The first is of negative character, and takes place in Jerusalem, when the Lord comes to His Father's house [2¹⁶] and finds that it has been made into a market. When challenged by the Jews for His action in clearing it, in mysterious language He declares His ability forthwith to replace the building, if and when it is destroyed. The second, positive in character, takes place in Galilee, when the Lord restores an individual to perfect health, with the result that a whole household believes [4⁵³; cf. 2¹¹]. In between these two actions are two conversations of the Lord: (*a*) the first, 3¹⁻²¹, with a man, Nicodemus, the teacher of Israel [3¹⁰], to which a supplement is added, 3²²⁻³⁶, conveying similar teaching to that of 3¹⁻²¹, in the form of the final witness of the Baptist; (*b*) the second, with a woman, a Samaritan. The two recipients may be regarded as representing, respectively, official orthodoxy and nonconformity, and on each occasion the teaching given throws light upon the actions of the Lord, i.e. on the nature and meaning of the wine granted at Cana, and on the worship and meaning of the new sanctuary which He will build [2¹⁹⁻²¹ R.V. mg.]. Throughout 2¹²⁻⁴⁵⁴, as already in 1¹⁹⁻²¹¹, the reader's thought is directed, openly or otherwise, to the fulfilment, and therewith the supersession, of the Jewish religion by Him who, although He came as Messiah to the Jews, is also the Word made flesh. Although the Lord is always the central figure, direct personal reference to Him as the bringer of life and light into the world is for the most part absent, e.g. 3¹³⁻¹⁵; only at the close of the conversation with the Samaritan woman does He point directly to Himself [4²⁶], and only in the last words of the section do the Samaritans recognize Him as the Saviour of the world [4⁴²]. In the next section this will still be the case, but in a lesser degree.

In the second section, 5¹⁻⁴⁷, the Lord again restores an individual to perfect health (cf. 7²³), but on this occasion in Jerusalem. As in the healing of the officer's son, we are not told explicitly of any religious reaction on the part of the patient himself, and again emphasis is laid on the effect of the Lord's bounty upon those connected with the patient. But in this second case, when the Lord in Jerusalem on a sabbath day grants full strength to one who perhaps all his life had been infirm, the Jews, after finding out with the help of the beneficiary the identity of the Benefactor, proceed to harry the Lord, and when the Lord justifies His action in the words of 5¹⁷, for the first time we learn explicitly that they are seeking to kill Him. Thereupon the Lord addresses them in a solemn monologue, the first and longest of its kind in this gospel. In the first part He alludes to Himself chiefly, though not solely, in the third person: in their perfect co-operation based on love [5²⁰] the Father has granted to the Son the supreme attributes (*a*) of giving life, and (*b*) of passing a final and unerring judgement; but in the second part the Lord speaks throughout of Himself in the first person, with reference to His incarnate life, and to the witness borne to Him from every side. This witness, however, His hearers reject, and the true reasons for this rejection of it are made clear.

In the third section, which comprises ch. 6, the reader is transported, and for the last time, to Galilee. On the far side of the sea of Galilee a great multitude of some five thousand people, attracted by the wonder of the Lord's works of mercy, follow Him; and He feeds them. Interpreting His wonderful action in accordance with, and by means of, their own aspirations for national liberty, they concert to force kingship upon Him; and the Lord withdraws to high ground, this time alone. In the evening the disciples, who previously [6³] had shared the Lord's session on the mountain-top, descend to the sea and embark, but at first find great difficulty in reaching Capernaum, which was their objective. When, however, they are roughly in the middle of their course, they become aware of the approach of their Master, walking on the sea; and after their initial fears have been quieted by His personal assurance, they are willing to admit Him into the boat, and the difficulty of which they had previously been conscious disappears. Part of the purpose of 6²²⁻²⁵ seems to be to contrast the new knowledge of the Lord which the disciples now have as a result of their experience on the previous night with the ignorance, in this respect, of the multitude, which, having next day with difficulty reached Capernaum, at once inquires how and when the Lord Himself came there. The Lord does not satisfy its curiosity, but, at once laying bare its true motives in following Him, seeks to raise it to the knowledge and belief now granted to, and enjoyed by, the disciples (as 6⁶⁸, ⁶⁹ will shortly show). He Himself, He now reveals, is the source of life to men; nor will anyone who resorts to, and believes on, Him hunger or thirst again. It is, however, made clear that His hearers, although they have seen Him and partaken of His bounty, do not believe, and at 6⁴¹ their place is taken, and they become represented, by the Jews, who thus now appear for the first and only time in Galilee. Proposing to know His human origins, the Jews demur to the Lord's description of Himself as being, in contrast both to Moses and to the manna which descended from the visible sky, the source and giver of life, including that of the unseen world itself. At the close of the Lord's reply, which reiterates and amplifies that already made to the multitude, He reveals [6⁵¹] that the food which He offers and will offer is His flesh, thus indirectly referring to His sacrificial death. When the Jews again express inability to understand His meaning, the Lord affirms in the strongest terms, with reference now not only to His flesh but to His blood, that the actual participation in these, as true or real eating and true or real drinking, is essential for those who have, or are to have, (eternal) life. He who partakes of these dwells in the Lord, and the Lord in him; and the relation between him, who so partakes, and the Lord is to be similar to the relation between the Lord and His Father. Of the Jews we hear no more in this chapter, and our attention is now directed to those many of the Lord's disciples, who themselves find the discourse, to which they have also been listening, too stern and rugged. The Lord points out that He has been speaking of His earthly life and death, and asks how, if His doctrine of these is too much for them, they are to be enabled to enter into His resumption of His heavenly life. In and by itself the fleshly or earthly is barren; it only becomes life-giving if and when it is penetrated by the spiritual or heavenly; and His words, spoken to them, are the appointed means for their entry into this spirit and this life. Unhappily some of them, He knows, do not believe; as He has already said, no one can come to Him except by the divine prompting. In consequence of this declaration the Lord appears to be left alone with the twelve. On His turning to them, Simon Peter, in a confession of enthusiastic loyalty, affirms their understanding of, and devotion to, both His Person and His doctrine. The confession, it seems, is accepted, although in silence, by the Lord; the twelve were indeed the object of His choice; but He reveals also that even in their number, in one quarter, evil is at work.

The fourth section certainly consists of chs. 7 and 8, and may

possibly extend further. After continued residence in Galilee [7¹],
and the repulse of His brethren's suggestion that He should stage
a signal demonstration in Judaea at the approaching feast of
tabernacles [7²⁻⁹], the Lord goes up privately to Jerusalem, and is
only found teaching in the temple when the feast is half over [7¹⁴].
Whereas in His last previous visit to Jerusalem He had succeeded
in avoiding notoriety [5¹³], now, even before His arrival, He is the
subject of animated debate and controversy. The Jews, as a whole,
have made up their minds to kill Him [7²⁵] and at the close of the
section make a vain attempt forthwith to do so (8⁵⁹); the multitude,
conscious of the greatness of His words and works [7¹², ³¹, ⁴⁰⁻⁴³;
cf. 7²⁶, ²⁷], is vacillating and divided in its assessment of His
Person, but has no inkling of the seriousness of the situation [7²⁰],
in spite of a general fear of the authorities. The controversy with
the Jews is resumed in 7¹⁵⁻²⁴ from the point where it was dropped at
the previous visit 5⁴⁷; but the chief issues in chs. 7 and 8 are the
problems of the Lord's origin [7²⁷, ⁴¹, ⁴², ⁵²] and destiny [7³⁵, 8²²];
and, before the section closes, He and the Jews are found, in these
respects, to be in the sharpest contrast. He is 'from above', and
'not of this world' [8²³], and can say, 'Before Abraham came into
existence, I am' [8⁵⁸]; but they are 'from below', and 'of this world'
[8²³]. His teaching is from God, not from Himself [7¹⁷], and He
speaks the things which He has seen with, and heard from, the
Father, even God [8²⁶⁻²⁸, ³⁸, ⁴⁰], having been sent by Him [7²⁸, ²⁹,
8¹⁸, ⁴²]; but they speak from themselves [7¹⁸], seeking their own
glory [8⁵⁰; cf. 5⁴⁴], and do the things which they heard from their
father the devil [8³⁸, ⁴⁴], their desire being to give rein to the crav-
ings for murder which are natural to him [8⁴⁴]. If it is correct to
confine this section to chs. 7 and 8, two features of it should be
mentioned here. In contrast with the other sections of the ministry,
the Lord's teaching is not accompanied by, or brought directly
into connexion with, the performance of a work or sign on His
part. And secondly, the disciples are not directly mentioned in this
section, apart from the reference in 7³. It seems likely, however,
that the reader should by no means forget them. For in the summary
of the last section it was suggested that great importance should
be attached to the influence which, in 6¹⁶⁻²¹, the disciples'
experience of their Master's presence and its results had upon
them, in strengthening their belief in Him, as attested in 6⁶⁸, ⁶⁹.
As we have seen, the chief subjects treated in chs. 7 and 8 are the

Lord's origin, destiny, and Person; but the import of these for believers is also strongly emphasized. Thus at 8^{12} the Lord, declaring Himself to be the light of the world, adds that His followers shall not move and act in the darkness (contrast 6^{17}), but shall have the light of life, and that those who abide in His word shall know the truth [8^{31-32}]. And in 7^{39} we read that, after the Lord is glorified, believers in Him are to receive the Spirit. Possibly, therefore, the reader may be meant to keep the story of 6^{16-21}, as followed by the confession of $6^{68,\ 69}$, steadily before him in these chapters also. In ch. 6 the disciples have been seen to be learning increasingly how to use the key offered to them by their Master's words and works; in chs. 7 and 8 the Jews, on the contrary, are shown to have now closed their eyes to His true nature, while the multitude is puzzled and divided.

As there is no obvious break in the narrative at 9^1 we may regard this fourth section of the ministry as extending on to 10^{39}; and attention may be called to certain parallels and contrasts between the narratives of 5^{1-16} (in the second section) and 9^{1-38} here (see p. 138). In 5^{1-9} the Lord on a sabbath grants perfect health and strength to one who almost all his life has been infirm; in 9^{1-7} He grants sight to one who hitherto has never seen at all. In 5^{10-13}, in the parleys between the Jews and the man, the Lord does not appear; and indeed neither party is at first aware of the identity of the Benefactor; this is only made known to the Jews by the action, first of the Lord [5^{14}] and then of the man [5^{15}], who appears to side with the authorities. In ch. 9, during the altercations of verses 8 to 34, the Lord is again absent, but the man born blind is aware, from the time of the first encounter with the Lord [$9^{6,\ 7,\ 11}$], of the identity of his Benefactor; and the more severely he is harried by the authorities the more stoutly he acknowledges Him. Finally, after he is cast out [9^{34}], the Lord finds him, as in 5^{14} He found the formerly infirm man in the temple; but whereas the latter, after being reminded of his present happy state, received a warning not to endanger it and so perhaps to incur even greater distress than before [5^{14}], in ch. 9 the man born blind, who has already received physical sight [9^7], now receives full spiritual illumination also from the Lord [9^{35-38}]. Reasons are given in the exposition (pp. 205 f.) for seeing a connexion between the contents of chs. 9 and 10; it will suffice here to notice the emphasis in 10^{11-18} on the voluntariness of the Lord's action, as the good shepherd, in laying down

His life for the sheep. Before the end of the section we shall reach the encaenia at Jerusalem [10²²], the last festival, three months only, before the (final) passover; and the Jews, after a last controversy with the Lord [10²⁴⁻³⁶], accompanied by a fresh threat of violence in 10³¹ (cf. 8⁵⁹), will seek again to seize Him, in spite of His final appeal [10³⁷⁻³⁹]. It might therefore seem that sooner or later He will certainly be helpless in their hands, and that in the end their will— the will of the devil—not His will—the will of the Father—will be carried out. Accordingly in 10¹¹⁻¹⁸, before the darkness—and therefore also the light—is revealed at its maximum, the Lord shows that His laying down of His life is in no way forced on Him against His will; it is a wholly voluntary action on His part; it is indeed, together with its sequel, the very expression of His being, and it is also the action which, performed by Him in obedience to His Father [10¹⁸], above all else makes Him the object of the Father's love [10¹⁷].

In the fifth section, 10⁴⁰ to 11⁵³, the Lord's journey to Peraea is not only a link with Mt. 19¹, Mk. 10¹, but recalls the first scene of the book in 1¹⁹⁻²⁸. From Peraea, with His disciples, He journeys not indeed to Jerusalem itself, but to its immediate neighbourhood, to Bethany, for the last and greatest work of His ministry, the bestowal of life on Lazarus, His friend, who has died. Of all the Lord's signs, there is none in which word and work, event and teaching, are so closely interwoven as they are here. This is sufficiently illustrated by the fact that the revelation in word [11²¹⁻²⁷] is placed in the centre of the narrative of the event. In the exposition (pp. 223 ff.) it is sought to show that, if the story is rightly understood, the Lord, in saving Lazarus His friend, Himself now enters the gates of death to give life to Lazarus. And since it has long been clear that the agents of the Lord's death will be the Jews, the reader is not surprised to learn that after, and in consequence of, the Lord's gift to Lazarus, a meeting of the Jewish authorities is held which, fearing the possible political results of the Lord's many signs, passes a formal resolution for His death [11⁴⁶⁻⁵³].

In any summary of the sixth and last section of the ministry 12¹⁻⁵⁰, it must be kept continually in mind that, if the interpretation of the previous section is correctly based, in a certain sense the Lord's death took place when He gave life to Lazarus, and in ch. 12 we are allowed to see how external events work out in consequence. The Lord has withdrawn into the country near the wilderness, and is residing there with His disciples. Meantime passover approaches. Once more, and of His own will and act, the Lord returns into a place of danger (cf. 11^8), and is present at a supper in which Lazarus shares. The reader's attention, however, is chiefly directed first to the action of Mary, and then to the objection raised to it by Judas Iscariot. In the exposition (pp. 236 f.) reasons are given for regarding Mary's action as a symbolical embalming of the body of the Lord for burial; she thus shows her devotion and love for Him; but her further action in at once removing the ointment with the tresses of her hair shows her realization that the grave has no lasting power over Him; if He lays down His life, He also takes it again [10^{17}], both His actions having their source in His love for mankind in obedience to the Father, and in that only. Judas Iscariot, however, both in his objection to the deed of Mary, and in the false motive which he alleges for his objection, stands in sharpest contrast to her. If we are right in tracing an inner interpretation in these last scenes of the ministry, the Lord in a symbol has now died, has been buried, and has risen again; and on the next day the Messiah enters His capital in triumph. The multitude indeed, composed of both Judaeans and Galileans, entirely mistakes the significance of His entry; and perhaps their waving of the palm branches in His honour, as a token of their expectation of the national liberty which He is to win for them, may have given an added opportunity later to the Roman soldiers in their mockery of Him at 19^2 (see p. 238). In this gospel it is frequently suggested, directly or indirectly, that as a result of the life and death of the Lord the national religion of the Jews, the chosen people of God, will be universalized; and in $12^{20, 21}$ we learn that some Greeks, who had come up to worship at the festival, desire to see the Lord. On hearing of their wish, He replies that the hour of the glory or triumph of the Son of man has now arrived [$12^{23, 31}$], but that both for Him and for His followers it can only come through self-sacrifice and death, and the sorrow and distress which are inevitable accompaniments of these. It is only if He Himself is lifted up from the earth that all men will be drawn to Him [12^{32}]. The ministry closes with a last reference to the multitude and its perplexity [12^{29-34}], especially with regard to the Son of man and the lifting up which He must undergo. Thereupon, after a final appeal to the multitude at $12^{35, 36}$, as to the Jews at 10$^{37, 38}$, the Lord is hidden from them, and the ministry is over.

The reader who familiarizes himself with each of these sections, both in respect of its contents and of its place in the narrative, will find that each section, with the exception of the sixth, contains both action and teaching, that is a work or works, and a word or words, of the Lord, usually but not always (we have just seen that the fifth section is in this respect a striking exception to the general rule) in the order of work followed by word. In each section the words attached to the works explain the significance, the inner or true meaning, of the work(s); and conversely, the work(s) in each section are not only illustrations, but (to use St. John's own word), signs or sacraments of the (truth of the) teaching in that section. All the sections deal in one way or another with the theme of life or light (and in one case, the fourth, with both together), offered to men through the incarnate Lord; cf. what is said about the Logos in 1^4. Although the content of some sections may seem to be more important than that of others, the reader should consider whether it is not the case that each section has an essential part to play in the sequence as a whole, and, so far as we can judge, in that place in the gospel where it is found (see pp. 7 ff.). From beginning to end this gospel is a compact whole. Again, although the story moves steadily forward to the climax of chs. 13 to 20, yet in each section the passion is not only referred to, directly or indirectly, but is itself already present in a measure in each section. The Lord is revealed as giving Himself, in smaller or greater degree, throughout; and His manifestation of Himself, in both work and word, becomes steadily clearer, greater, and more personal, in proportion as the opposition to Him and to His work and teaching increases. During the record of the ministry the reader's gaze is thus kept ever fixed upon the future; and even when he has reached its end, he will be aware how, owing to the imperfect elements in his belief, much is still escaping him; but at the same time he is made conscious, in each section, that all the truth, so far as he is at present able to comprehend it, is already present; the hour of revelation or manifestation is yet to come, but nevertheless this same hour already is (cf. 4^{23}); and he thus arrives, or should arrive, in this gospel at the climax without sense of shock; the whole Gospel, so far as he can receive it, has been placed within his grasp from the beginning.

Finally, each of the sections is connected, more or less closely, with a festival of the Jewish sacred year. From the first it was a recognized part of the tradition that the Lord's death had taken place at passover time, and in thus spreading the incidence of the Jewish feasts throughout the ministry, St. John not only does justice in all probability to frequent visits of the Lord to Jerusalem, but also invites the reader to see the Lord's whole work in close connexion with the Jewish festivals, especially the passover. Since He is the sacrificial Lamb of God [1[29, 36]], the thought of this last feast is especially prominent; it might almost be said to dominate the gospel (see Appended Note, pp. 349 ff.). In St. John's view all these festivals in different ways have pointed forward to the coming of the Lord, and in that coming they have now been 'fulfilled' (cf. Heb. 10[1-25]).

It is not proposed to attempt here a similar analysis of the structure of the second part of this gospel, chs. 13 to 20, which may be regarded as a seventh or final section; for its subject-matter apparently was either of so different a character, or sufficiently fixed in the tradition of the Church, to require a different treatment. The two parts of this gospel are related almost as promise to fulfilment. For not only, as we have observed, does each of the sections into which the records of the ministry can be divided contain, as it were, the Gospel in miniature, but in each of them the event which is being narrated and the truth which is being set forth in and through the event are at some point linked with the supreme event of the Lord's passion, which is yet to come. Nothing further remains to be narrated except the Lord's passion, and its sequel, His resurrection. In one respect, however, chs. 13 to 20 closely resemble chs. 2 to 12, in that they also consist of work and word conjoined, only now it is the single, supreme work of the Lord's redemptive and life-giving death and resurrection (chs. 18 to 20), and a single, supreme word, delivered by the Lord no longer in public but to His disciples in private, in exposition of the meaning, purpose, and fruit of that passion and resurrection (chs. 13 to 17). But in this case the word precedes entirely the work, and the significance of what the Lord is to accomplish in His death and resurrection is laid bare not, as generally in chs. 2 to 12, after it has taken place, nor in the course of it, as in ch. 11, but in advance of it. There is, for this reason, little movement in chs. 13 to 20, and both word and work are of a highly concentrated character. In the account of the passion and resurrection the scene is limited to Jerusalem and its environs, while the long conversation of the Lord with His disciples not only takes place without any temporal change of scene, but is so set forth as to seem almost independent of time and place. For a more detailed treatment of the successive stages of this long discourse and its internal development, as also of the relation of the separate incidents of the passion to the narrative of the passion as a whole, the reader is referred to the exposition (see esp. pp. 258 ff., 280 ff., 295 f., 306, 308 ff., 329 ff.).

The unity of this gospel is not only a unity of structure, it is also a unity of themes; and the attempt will be made in the exposition to show how the great themes of light and life, of witness, judgement, glory, and others, some of which are more prominent in particular parts of the book, run like threads throughout it. We may here, however, give some treatment of two which may be said to stand out, inasmuch as the evangelist himself draws attention to them in the highly important statement with which he concludes his book. When he writes: 'Many other signs therefore did Jesus in the presence of the disciples, which are not written in this book: but these are written, that ye may believe that Jesus is the Christ, the Son of God, and that believing ye may have life in his name' [20³⁰, ³¹], he sums up his work as a narrative of the 'signs' of the Lord, whose purpose was to evoke 'belief'.

(a) Sign

In Lk. 24¹⁹ the Lord is described as having shown Himself powerful in work and word 'before God and all the people'. St. John also uses the same Greek word for 'work', which occurs here in Luke, in his references to the Lord's actions [5²⁰, 9⁴, 10²⁵], which are also the works of His Father (10³⁷, ³⁸, 14¹⁰, cf. 9³); and His whole activity may be described as His work (4³⁴). More important, however, is his frequent reference to them as signs. It is true that on the four occasions when he refers to a particular action of the Lord as a sign [2¹¹, 4⁵⁴, 6¹⁴, 12¹⁸], that action is one which we should call miraculous; but neither in its Hebrew nor in its Greek equivalent does the word imply that the action must be of this nature. Indeed, it seems clear that St. John deprecates belief based on miracle as such, or on miracle alone; for only once [4⁴⁸] do we read of 'signs and wonders', an expression which as a whole no doubt denotes miracles, and there the Lord's words, 'Except ye

see signs and wonders, ye will in no wise believe', obviously
deprecate a belief resting on a basis of this sort.

In the Old Testament the word 'sign' is used by itself for a pledge
or token, between man and man, or between God and man;
sometimes for a token of things to come, an omen. It is applied in
particular to symbolic acts performed by the prophets. Thus in
Ezek. 24²⁴ the prophet tells the people, who have asked for an
explanation of his behaviour on the occasion of the death of his
wife, that he is a sign to them; 'according to all that he hath done
shall ye do'. As in the example here given, among the Jews a sign
usually symbolized, pointed forward to, an event destined to
happen in the future, and was therefore valued as throwing light
in the present upon the future. In St. John's gospel the contrast
in the end is not so much between present and future, as between
seen and unseen, external event and internal truth. Hence in this
gospel, to those who believed, a sign performed by the Lord is a
visible pointer to the invisible truth about Him who performs it;
and the teaching which often accompanies the signs is designed to
make this clear. For instance, in the last and greatest of the signs
performed during the ministry, the raising of Lazarus from death
to life, the external event is a sign of the internal truth revealed
by the Lord in His words to Martha in 11²⁵. On the other hand the
'temporal' aspect of the sign, valued so highly by the Jews, is not
forgotten in this gospel; for rightly understood, all the actions of
the Lord during the ministry point forward to, and are signs of,
the supreme sign, which is itself also the thing signified, that is, the
historical death and resurrection of the Lord.

The word 'sign,' therefore, in John usually implies more than the
word 'symbol'. This latter meaning, however, does occur. Twice,
in an editorial note, the evangelist uses the verb translated in
R.V. as 'signifying', which we might render as 'showing by a sign'.
After the Lord has said in 12³², 'I, if I be lifted up from the earth,
will draw (*or*, attract) all men to myself', the evangelist notes in
12³³, 'In saying this, he showed by a sign by what kind of death he
was to die.' And after the Jews in 18³¹ have said: 'It is not lawful
for us to put any man to death', he adds in 18³², 'that the word
of Jesus might be fulfilled, which he spake, showing by a sign by
what kind of death he should die'. In other words, the Lord is to
die not by a Jewish but by a Roman form of punishment; He is
not to be stoned, but is to be lifted up from the earth upon the

cross. In this gospel the lifting up of the Lord upon the cross is, in another sense, His exaltation; in the outward form of the manner of His death St. John sees a sign, a symbol, of His triumph: 'the Lord reigns from the tree'.

In the light of these considerations and of the fact that St. John often uses the word 'signs' in the plural in reference, it seems, to the Lord's actions generally [2^{23}, 9^{16}, 12^{37}], it would be a mistake to confine the word to those of His actions which are expressly so described. His whole life is a sign, in action, of the love of God. Nor is the word applicable only to the Lord's works; it may be applied also to His words. When He says to the Jews, 'Whither I go, ye cannot come' [8^{21}], He is using spatial language, applicable in the world of 'flesh', to describe, and as a sign of, a state of affairs in the world of 'spirit', where spatial terms do not apply. In that world harmony and affection can use the language of mutual inhabitation found in $15^{4, 5}$, a language inapplicable in the world of space. The religious philosophy of St. John, if we may so speak, regards that which exists or happens in this world as deriving its importance and value from the fact that it represents, or embodies, an invisible and eternal reality. The world of 'flesh' is a sign of the world of 'spirit', and the two are essentially connected. Only through a right use of the world of 'flesh', in obedience to the Lord's commandments, can a man retain and increase his contact with the world of 'spirit'.

(b) Belief

Both St. Luke and St. John tell us the governing purpose with which they write their respective gospels, but if we compare Jn. $20^{30, 31}$ with Lk. 1^{1-4}, it becomes clear that the objects of the two evangelists, although similar, were not identical. Each was concerned with both history and theology, but perhaps we may say that whereas St. Luke sets the theology in an historical framework, St. John sets the history in a theological framework. The difference is one of degree only; but it is a real difference. And St. John tells us that, with his particular object in view, he has selected certain historical actions of the Lord, done in the sight of His disciples, and by treating them as signs—that is, as actions which convey an inward meaning beyond their outward form—has sought, in some cases no doubt, to strengthen, in other cases, it may well be, to engender, in his readers the belief that Jesus is both (in Jewish parlance) the Christ, and also (in a wider religious phraseology) the Son of God. His purpose, he adds, in so doing is that his readers, holding this belief, may have life in and through the Lord, and thus, if we may refer here to $1^{12, 13}$, may themselves receive a new birth and become children of God.

Turning to consider the use and meaning in this gospel of the verb 'to believe', we recall that, as a result of the first sign recorded by St. John, when the Lord made His glory known at Cana, His disciples believed on Him [2^{11}]. It would be a mistake to understand these words as suggesting that the Lord's disciples were won to belief in Him by His astonishing action; wonder has indeed its place in religion (cf. 5^{20}, 7^{21}), but it was not the purpose of the Lord to arouse men's wonder and no more (cf. 3^7, 5^{28}). Rather the words of 2^{11} imply that His disciples understood this, the first, action of His ministry in changing water into wine as a sign of the revelation which He was now bringing, that is, of His glory or triumph, and of the union of God and man in and by His life and death. At a later stage, in 15^1, the Lord will reveal Himself as the true or real vine, from which the vineshoots draw their life.

In the course of the gospel the content of belief is variously described; we read, for instance, of belief in the scripture [2^{22}], or in Moses [5^{46}]; but at present we are only concerned with it in respect of its more frequent and important use in reference to the Person, the word, and the work of the Lord. In this connexion it implies obedience [3^{36}, 7^{17}], and wholehearted devotion; the believer is convinced that the Father has sent the Lord [17^8], that the Lord is in the Father and the Father in Him [$14^{10, 11}$; cf. 10^{30}; 12^{44}]; and the highest expression of belief in this book is the confession of Thomas, 'My Lord and my God' [20^{28}]. This belief is not to be distinguished from knowledge; we notice, for example, St. Peter's confession at 6^{69}, 'We have believed and know that thou art the Holy One of God.' And if the words just quoted should be thought to suggest that belief is a preliminary and lower stage, to be superseded in due course by knowledge, it must be pointed out that the order can be reversed. Thus in 16^{30} we read, 'Now we know that thou knowest all things . . . by this we believe that thou camest forth from God'; or still more strikingly the Lord's words in His prayer in ch. 17: 'They knew of a truth that I came forth from thee, and they believed that thou didst send me' [17^8]. Two points, however, must be noticed, the first of which may help to explain why knowledge is often regarded as a higher stage than faith. Firstly, belief, or faith, is never used of the Lord's relation to the Father; it is used only of the relation of the disciples to the Father and to the Lord. On the other hand, the term knowledge is used of the relationship existing between the Father and the Son; thus the Lord knows His own, and they know Him, even as the Father knows Him, and He knows the Father [10¹⁴, ¹⁵]; belief, however, is used not of the Son, but only of the disciples. For them, as long as they are in the flesh, knowledge and belief go, and must go, hand in hand; the unveiled glory of the Son is not for flesh and blood (cf. 1 Cor. 13¹², 15⁵⁰). And the second point to be noticed is probably not unconnected with the first. Strictly, we have no right when dealing with St. John's gospel to use the substantives belief and knowledge. In each case the evangelist carefully avoids the noun, but, on the other hand, in each case he uses the verb freely, in the case of the verb 'pisteuein', 'to believe', nearly a hundred times. He thus indirectly, but unmistakably, emphasizes that the religious belief which is set forth in this gospel, and to engender which he wrote it, is no passive or unchanging state, still less a formal adherence to a set of propositions: it is a life of energy and growth, in which, although the end is implicit in the beginning, there is always more in front of the believer than he has been granted, or has been able as yet to make his own; and in this process, which is throughout a matter of believing, knowledge itself can never dare to cease to learn; from time to time it also dies to live. We may recall the Lord's words in 10³⁸, 'that ye may know and come to know that the Father is in me, and I in the Father'. Both faith and knowledge are processes which cannot be more than partial and preliminary in human experience, and in the light of the Christian revelation nothing is too good to be true. The foundation of the truth has indeed been laid once for all [14⁶; cf. 1 Cor. 3¹¹], but the truth iself, although present, is always on in advance [16¹²].

There is no essential difference between believing God [5²⁴] and believing in or on God [12⁴⁴, 14¹]. In the same way, since the Lord is, in word and action, Himself the revelation which He brings, there is no essential difference between believing Him [5³⁸, 8³¹, 14¹¹], believing on Him [4³⁹, 8³⁰] or on His name [2²³, 3¹⁸], or even simply believing [6⁴⁷, 19³⁵, 20⁸, ²⁹]. Any difference which does exist may be thus expressed. Whereas it would be impossible for anyone who did not believe the Lord to believe on Him, it might be possible for a man to believe Him (in the reduced sense of giving Him a favourable hearing, or even crediting His word 2^{22}, 4^{50}), and yet not to offer Him the complete devotion and obedience implied in believing on Him.

The content of belief may be variously expressed:

8^{24} Except ye believe that I am (R.V. mg.); cf. 13^{19}.
11^{42} That they may believe that thou didst send me; cf. $17^{8, 21}$.
12^{36} Believe on the light.
12^{44} He that believeth on me, believeth not on me, but on him that sent me.
14^{11} Believe that I am in the Father, and the Father in me.

And the result or issue of belief is action, showing itself in nothing less than a repetition and enhancement of the works of the Lord [14^{12}]. It was a leading feature of Jewish religious belief that, since their God had not yet made Himself fully known, not only would the future, when He did so, be immeasurably better than the present, but that all the distresses and perplexities of the present world would be at an end. This forward-looking view was taken up into Christianity. Thus hope is the second of St. Paul's triad alongside faith [1 Cor. 13^{13}], and even in St. John the future is regarded as having much in store for us, which is as yet beyond our grasp [13^{36}, 14^{12}, 16^{12}]. But the primary emphasis in this gospel is upon the truth that, with the coming and the presence of Jesus Christ, the Word become flesh, Himself a man, the obedient believer has eternal life [5^{24}, 6^{47}, $20^{30, 31}$], and therefore nothing that the future may hold in store for him can be different in kind from that which is already his; it will be different only in degree. It is, however, essential that he must never regard this eternal life as an acquisition or possession (cf. Phil. $3^{13, 14}$), but always as something granted to him, not of his own, an energy that will show itself in ever more fruitful activity, in a faith that prepares itself for ever new ventures, and in a knowledge that must never cease to learn.

D. RELATION TO THE SYNOPTIC GOSPELS

To examine the contents and to analyse the structure of the fourth gospel, and to take note of the themes which run like threads through it and which give it its unity, is inevitably to raise the question of its relation to the tradition of the Church before, and at the time of, its writing, and in particular of its relation to that tradition as we now have it in the synoptic gospels. All four gospels purport to be accounts of the same event and earthly career, yet St. John's account differs so markedly in many respects from the other three, that, if those three are taken as the standard of the tradition of the primitive Church, it must be concluded that St. John has acted with great freedom and boldness towards that tradition.

It is important at the outset, however, not to over-emphasize the differences between the fourth gospel and the synoptists, great as they may be. For more than a century the adjective 'synoptic' has been applied to the first three gospels on the ground that their accounts of the Lord's ministry present much the same point of view. It was natural that this adjective should become specially common in the era of 'source criticism', when synopses were compiled, revealing the close resemblances in the text of the first three gospels, and the difficulty of bringing St. John's gospel into line with them. The synoptic gospels thus came to be spoken of almost as a unity. The adjective may become, however, misleading, and even dangerous, in so far as it tends to blind us to the important differences, many of them not immediately apparent, between one synoptic gospel and another, and in so far as it leads us to exaggerate the isolation of the fourth. It may be legitimate from a certain point of view to speak of St. Matthew's gospel as a revised and enlarged edition of St. Mark's, although even this description of it should be used with caution, since it omits, for instance, to draw attention to some important divergences between the two gospels in their treatment of the Person of the Lord; but St. Luke, although he also, as we believe, like St. Matthew used the second gospel, is in some respects nearer to St. John than he is to either St. Matthew or St. Mark, and yet in certain doctrinal respects he is farther from St. John than is St. Mark. Thus the close attention paid during the last hundred years to textual resemblances and affinities among the first three gospels has tended to a neglect of those differences distinguishing them which, to religion, may be of at least equal, if not of greater, importance. For while it seems that St. Matthew and St. Luke felt themselves bound to reproduce more or less closely the traditions and teachings in the forms and in the words in which these had come to them, at the same time they believed it to be important, by additions and omissions here, by alterations and modifications there, to place them in a setting which each evangelist thought to need emphasis at the time when he was writing, and in the church or churches for which he was writing. And if the student is on his guard against being excessively influenced, on the one hand, by the verbal similarities between the first three gospels and by their general adhesion to the earlier tradition, and by St. John's different phraseology and by his apparent departure from that earlier tradition, on the other hand, he may become less willing to regard the first three gospels as being, in other than a comparatively superficial sense, synoptic, or to separate St. John's gospel very sharply from them.

Fifty years ago it was widely accepted that the fourth evangelist was aware both of the existence of the first three gospels and of their contents. Of the various solutions to the problem why, in that case, he differed from them, none won more than a measure of support. The explanation which was perhaps most widely held, particularly in this country, was that St. John had written to supplement the other gospels by the addition of fresh primitive tradition concerning certain aspects of the ministry which had been neglected by, or were unknown to, the synoptic evangelists. While this explanation should not be overlooked, at least in reference to certain particular instances, its great weakness as a whole is that it fails to recognize, and to account for, what must be called the large interpretative element in the fourth gospel. In recent years, however, the belief itself that St. John knew the other gospels has been challenged. It is admitted on all sides that he was aware of traditions (such as the feeding of the five thousand, or the cleansing of the temple) which form part of the synoptic gospels, but it is thought unlikely that he knew these stories from these gospels, and it is suggested that we ought to look to some other source, such as oral tradition, for his information on these and many other points. This view received strong support in Mr. P. Gardner-Smith's book, *Saint John and the Synoptic Gospels* (1938). His method is to work through St. John's gospel, noting its most striking divergences from the other three, both in general and in detail, raising in each case the question whether the divergence is not best explained by the hypothesis of St. John's ignorance of the synoptists. Especially does he find it 'inconceivable that St. John was content wantonly to contradict the testimony of "standard works" in matters dogmatically indifferent',[1] and he ends with two tentative suggestions of far-reaching importance. Firstly he says,

If once it is admitted that the Evangelist shows no positive signs of acquaintance with the synoptic writers it can no longer be assumed that his is literally the *Fourth* Gospel. It is just conceivable that its later and more developed tone is due to the fact that it was produced in some locality in which development had been more rapid than in other parts of the Church.[2]

Secondly he says,

There emerges a new possibility of regarding the Fourth Gospel as an independent authority for the life of Jesus, or at least for the traditions current in the Christian Church in the second half of the first century. So long as it was believed that John knew Mark, and altered his account in an arbitrary and irresponsible manner, interest in him as a historian could never be great. But if in the Fourth Gospel we have a survival of a type of first century Christianity which owed nothing to synoptic developments, and which originated in quite a different intellectual atmosphere, its historical value may be very great indeed.[3]

Mr. Gardner-Smith believes that the influence of interpretation in the book is too obvious to enable us to treat St. John's account as 'historical in the narrower sense of the term'; but 'where the Fourth Gospel differs from the Synoptics it may henceforth be wise to treat its testimony with rather more respect than it has lately received, and perhaps in not a few cases it may prove to be right'.[4]

No student of Mr. Gardner-Smith's book is unlikely to feel that, on the evidence which he puts before the reader, he has made out a strong case for his thesis, and for some of his arguments there would seem to be no satisfactory solution which could be offered by those who approach the problems from a different point of view. Nevertheless this book is written in the belief that the evangelist knew not only the synoptic tradition, but the three synoptic gospels themselves. It is not proposed here to set out the evidence for this belief in detail. Attention is called in the course of the exposition to verbal resemblances which are unlikely to be accidental, and which suggest the dependence of St. John on the other gospels, and the relation between them is discussed there as it arises. Here we

---

[1] *Saint John and the Synoptic Gospels*, p. 92.   [2] Ibid., p. 93.
[3] Ibid., p. 96.   [4] Ibid., p. 97.

shall be concerned with the question in certain more general aspects.

Firstly, it is difficult for us, in this scientific age, to realize the contrast between the ancients and ourselves in regard to matters of historical detail. Some words of Dr. James Drummond are worth recalling in this respect.

To ask whether a work is historical or not, is not the same thing as asking whether it is true or not; for truth in regard to the past may be of two kinds. This is an age of research and scientific accuracy, and the truth which we demand in history is the truth of fact. There must be no error in a genealogy; nothing must be said to have happened on Monday if it really happened on Tuesday; no action must be ascribed to a man which we are not prepared to support in a court of justice. All this is perfectly right, so long as it does not blind us to a higher truth. The facts in themselves are utterly barren. In history, as in religion, it is the spirit that quickens, and unless we can penetrate the spirit of great historical transactions, interpret the principles out of which they sprung, and throw ourselves with sympathetic imagination into the passions which animated the great human drama, we miss the only truth which is worth receiving. Now it is possible, and it was far easier long ago than it is now, to think less of the facts than of the inner meaning of the facts, and to believe that the highest historical truth is not reached till the due impression is made upon the mind of the reader, even though the impression cannot be made until the facts are cast into the striking forms and tinted with the warm colours of historical imagination. . . . Men like Philo had no interest in inquiring whether an incident really occurred in this way or that, and what we regard as the exercise of the first duty of an historian, they would probably have viewed as learned trifling. If we would understand the narratives of this period, we must try to place ourselves within its mental atmosphere, and not yield to that narrowness of mind which judges the past by the current phrases of its own day.[1]

That St. John was altogether indifferent to historical fact is out of the question; no evangelist is more insistent than he on the historical truth which he regards as essential to the Gospel. The words of 1[14], 'The Word became flesh, and tabernacled among us' are sufficient proof of this, and we may recall also the appeal to the truth of the evidence of an eye-witness at 19[35]. It may be possible to believe that St. John knew, for instance, St. Mark's gospel, and yet not to be forced to hold that St. John 'altered' St. Mark's

[1] *The Character and Authorship of the Fourth Gospel* (1903), pp. 28–32.

account, to use Mr. Gardner-Smith's words, 'in an arbitrary and irresponsible way'. Is it certain that what we regard as arbitrary and irresponsible would have appeared so to St. John?

A second consideration will carry no weight if Mr. Gardner-Smith's suggestion is followed that St. Mark and St. John were contemporaries, and that St. John's gospel must no longer be assumed to be the latest of the four. We may, however, incline to regard the tradition preserved by Eusebius (*Hist. Eccl.* vi. 14) from the writings of Clement of Alexandria as much more probable. According to Eusebius, Clement, professing to give the tradition of the presbyters from the first, wrote, 'John, however, last, having observed that the bodily things had been exhibited in the Gospels, being exhorted by his friends, inspired by the Spirit, produced a spiritual Gospel.' It is widely agreed that St. Mark's gospel is to be dated between A.D. 65–70, and that it was known and used by both St. Matthew and St. Luke, whose gospels are usually dated shortly after A.D. 80. But St. Mark's gospel is usually located at Rome, St. Matthew's is often connected with Syria, and St. Luke's with some other centre; and yet these two later evangelists paid high regard to St. Mark's gospel in the composition of their own. Is it not therefore probable that St. John, if his is the latest of the four and was put forth towards the end of the century, would have known of his three predecessors' works and of the regard paid to them; and if so, is it not possible that some deeper reasons exist to account for the extent of his divergence from them? And if these reasons can be discerned, however partially, do they not carry some weight in support of the view that the difficulties of discrepancy in detail, to which attention has been called, are of altogether secondary importance in any attempt to estimate the relationship of the four gospels in the vital matter of their presentation of the truth of the Gospel? Once it is granted that St. John knew at least the general synoptic tradition, is it not likely that we must go farther and hold that he knew at least Mark, and probably also Matthew and Luke (as well, no doubt, as other traditions current in the Church about the ministry)? For the question does not seem to have been sufficiently considered whether, if, so far as St. John knew, his gospel would stand alone, over against a diffused, miscellaneous mass of earlier tradition, he would have been prepared to write a gospel in which, in order to explain the Lord's work, he reinterprets the tradition with the great freedom that he shows ('he regards everything on its divine side', B. F. Westcott). Would he not have realized the great danger of one-sidedness? Is it not more probable that, when he wrote, the position of the earlier gospels in the Church was strong enough to avert any danger that his gospel might supersede them, in the sense in which, at an earlier date, St. Matthew may have thought that his work would supersede St. Mark's? It seems that St. John's gospel, if considered by itself in isolation, is a riddle; but that if it is regarded as the crown and completion of our gospel records, it falls forthwith into place. It may indeed have become increasingly clear, at any rate in certain quarters of the Church, that such a gospel as St. John's was needed, and that an inter-pretation of the Person of the Lord chiefly in terms of the Jewish Messiah, although already supplemented in certain respects in the other gospels, was rapidly becoming inadequate as an interpreta-tion of Him who was now worshipped by Gentile even more than by Jewish Christians in the little churches fast taking root in the larger cities of the Roman Empire between Jerusalem and Rome. Let the reader attempt the almost impossible task of forgetting, for the moment, the existence of St. John's gospel and all that he has learned from it and by means of it in reference to the Lord's incarnate life, and then let him consider whether he would not find considerable difficulty in answering certain questions which might be put to him. How, for example, is he to answer the question, 'What think ye of Christ?' In what sense is he to regard the Lord Jesus as the Jewish Messiah? What is the relation between His coming as Jesus of Nazareth and the future coming of the Son of man? What is the meaning of the mysterious title, the Son of man? Above all, how does the Lord remain a living force in mankind, the fountain head of vital religion? Did his disciples only transmit a message about His life and death and work and teaching, or had they, and have they, a further, greater, and more vital task? It is to St. John that we owe the definitive answers to these questions. In reading his gospel we are not left to speculate or to form theories. He has his own view of the Incarnation, and of its place in the world's history, and the dominating idea of his gospel is that of the Son as the full and complete revelation of the Father. St. John's purpose seems to be to produce in his readers an im-pression and conviction about the Person of the Lord which, he is persuaded, is the true understanding and interpretation of it; for his readers' sake he writes what may be described as the verdict of history, or perhaps we should rather say the verdict of the Church, on the Lord's Person and work. It may be that the view here suggested is anachronistic, in the sense that the Church only realized later that the full expression of the truth needed the fourfold gospel to which we are accustomed. But if indeed St. John was already aware of the need of such a gospel as he has given to the Church, and interposed his powerful influence to avert the difficulties we have mentioned, not only is the greatness of his work enhanced, but certain features of his gospel, which otherwise might surprise us, are adequately explained. If, for instance, he was able to assume the existence and position of the earlier gospels in the Church, he may not have regretted that his task could not be accomplished without a measure of one-sidedness. Because of the way in which it was necessary for him to record the ministry, some of the most winning and lovely features of the Lord's character, as we know them from the earlier gospels, could not find a place in his account.[1]

Probably, therefore, the relation of St. John's gospel to the other three (or, if we prefer so to put the matter, to the earlier traditions) is most profitably expressed if we hold that he sought not simply to supplement them, still less to supersede them—for they are likely to have had too strong a position when he wrote to allow him to do this, even had he wished—but that he sought to interpret them, and to draw out the significance of the original events. But if this judgement is correct, it has important, and perhaps surprising, consequences for our understanding of the synoptic gospels themselves. When we speak of an interpreter we mean one who explains to us, by language or signs, or in some other way with which we are already acquainted, something which, without his explanation, we could not understand. He makes us familiar with ground on which, without his help, we should be lost. But if we consider this definition of an interpreter in connexion with our present subject, we find a situation which is full of paradox. For students of the gospels at the beginning of this century would have agreed that, apart from certain particular problems, the synoptic gospels were

---

[1] Thus it has often been noticed that the attraction which drew notorious sinners and outcasts to the Lord is less obvious in John than in the other gospels. Or compare what is said of the Lord in relation to the multitude in Mk. 6^{34} with His criticism of the same multitude in Jn. $6^{26, 36}$.

as a whole intelligible. The difficulties which they presented arose chiefly from their fragmentariness or incompleteness. The great variety of theories which were put forward in explanation of the Lord's mission and purpose, as these lie before us in the first three gospels, ought no doubt to have placed students more on their guard in this matter; but on the whole it was believed that what these gospels offered could be understood without further explanation. The real problem was St. John's gospel. This was the book which seemed to need a key and an interpreter; but no key, it seemed, was to be found in the many efforts made to place it alongside, or in relation to, the earlier gospels, so long as they were regarded as the standard. If, however, it is nearer the truth to say that without St. John's gospel the earlier gospels are largely a puzzle, an unsolved problem, to which his gospel is designed to offer the key, then the situation is much changed. On this view it will not be possible to hold that the cardinal problem in the study of this gospel is the amount or nature of its historical matter, and that efforts should be made to settle this question before we pass to any others. This question is of great importance, and in this century it is unlikely to be far from our minds, but it is possible to over-emphasize the importance of the historical question in connexion with this book. The fact that the evangelist holds the historical Incarnation to be vital does not appear to prevent him from sitting lightly to subordinate aspects of his subject, where to do so is either necessary or of assistance to his purpose. Nor is it possible to hold that the shoe pinches severely in a single chapter only of this gospel, chapter 11, since the various sections of the book from beginning to end are inter-connected, and it only begins to reveal its secrets when we consider all its parts together. And further, it is both the history and the theology, the actions and the teaching, which go to make up this single whole.

One particular question may here be considered in greater detail in the light of our hypothesis of St. John as the interpreter of the synoptists, and with special reference to St. Mark's gospel, to which St. John is theologically nearest—the question of the scene of the Lord's ministry. From Mk. 6$^{1-6}$ it seems clear that in the case of the Lord the Greek word *patris*, which means native place, or fatherland, is regarded by St. Mark as situate in Galilee, presumably at Nazareth, Mk. 1^9. But many think that in Jn. 4$^{43-45}$ the Lord's *patris* is regarded as Judaea; and if so, the meaning will be

that the Lord, after His stay of two days in Samaria, does not
return to His *patris*, Judaea (since, as He Himself said, no prophet
receives his meed of honour in his place of origin), but proceeds to
Galilee. Here He is made welcome, because the Galilaeans at the
recent passover in Jerusalem had seen all that He did there on that
occasion, having gone up, as He did, to the festival. If 4^{43-45} is
thus considered in isolation, the interpretation just given seems
compelling, and we shall conclude that this is one of St. John's not
infrequent apparent contradictions of the earlier record, and that
whereas in the other gospels the Lord's 'Heimat', to use a German
equivalent, is in Galilee (cf. Lk. 4^{16-30}), in John it is located in
Judaea, and in particular at Jerusalem. But other passages in this
gospel are likely to occur to us, which seem to throw doubt on the
correctness of this interpretation of 4^{43-45}. For from 4^1, when news
had reached the Pharisees that the Lord was outstripping the
Baptist in the number of His disciples, we should infer that He left
Judaea at the very moment when His work was becoming, as an
onlooker might have thought, markedly successful. Again, the
reason given in 4^{45} for the Lord's reception by the Galileans should
be noticed. We read that they welcomed Him because they had
seen all the things that He did in Jerusalem at the feast. But it is
made clear in 2^{23-25} that the belief which on that occasion the
Lord's signs aroused in many was far from being wholly welcome
in His sight; and the words in 4^{48} to the nobleman, in the immediate
context of 4^{45}, words which are clearly meant to have a wider
application than the nobleman's own case, obviously deprecate a
belief based on the sight of signs and wonders. Hence in ch. 6,
when the Lord is once more in Galilee and is asked [6^{30}] for a sign
of this very sort, if His hearers are to believe, we ought not to be
greatly surprised when at the end of this chapter the Lord is left
alone with the twelve. If this is so, can it be said that the Lord
received in Galilee an honour which Judaea, His own *patris*, had
failed to render to Him? Does not St. John perhaps wish to teach
that, if the Lord's *patris* is sought anywhere on earth, nowhere does
He receive the honour due to Him, even as a prophet? For He is
not of this world [8^{23}] and His *patris* is in heaven, in the bosom of
the Father [1^{18}]; thence He came [3^{13}, 13^3, 16^{28}] and there alone
He is at home [3^{13}]; and there He does receive the honour due to
Him [$5^{22, \ 23, \ 37, \ 41}$, 8^{54}]. And St. John may be teaching in his
elusive way that, whether outward recognition is accorded to the

Lord [4⁴⁵] or not [Mk. 6¹⁻⁴], neither Galilee nor Judaea nor any other place on earth can be regarded as His *patris*.

What has just been said, however, does not solve the further kindred problem that in Mark, followed on the whole by Matthew, and to a much smaller extent by Luke, the Lord's ministry seems to be placed almost entirely in Galilee, until His one and only visit in these gospels to Jerusalem, that at which he died; whereas in John the ministry takes place chiefly in the south. In John, at 2¹⁻¹¹, the Lord is indeed in Galilee, and Capernaum is mentioned at 2¹²; but almost at once the Lord leaves for Jerusalem, where He cleanses the temple, and His first encounter with the Jews takes place. Later the Lord returns, by way of Samaria, to Galilee [4¹⁻³, ⁴³⁻⁵⁴], but soon goes back to Jerusalem [5¹]. Chapter 6 is entirely given up to Galilee, the scene of this chapter being laid partly on the east, partly on the west, side of the lake. In ch. 7, as in Mark ch. 10, the Lord leaves Galilee finally for the south, and the rest of the ministry is spent there. Thus, as against the single sequence in Mark, Galilee, Jerusalem, we have in John the sequence Galilee, Jerusalem: Galilee, Jerusalem: a single chapter devoted to Galilee alone, and then Jerusalem and the south alone. Further, in Mark the disciples are called and the twelve appointed in the north, during the ministry; but in John some disciples become attached to the Lord in the south, before the ministry begins. Finally, in John the Lord and the Baptist work for some time in the south concurrently, before the latter is imprisoned [3²²⁻²⁴], although the Lord's ministry has now been in existence for some time; contrast Mk. 1¹⁴.

It seems probable that in some of these matters St. John may be giving us better historical guidance than that provided by St. Mark, and that St. Mark himself may have been influenced, more than we have hitherto realized, by other than purely historical considerations. It has often been noticed that both at the beginning and at the end of Mark Galilee—'Galilee of the nations', as we read in Isaiah 9¹, 'Galilee of the Gentiles (or, foreigners)', as we read in 1 Maccabees 5¹⁵—seems to be regarded as the land of salvation; there the Lord proclaims the good news of the Kingdom of God [1¹⁴, ¹⁵], and there, after His resurrection, His disciples are to see Him [16⁷; cf. 14²⁸]. On the other hand, on two of the three occasions when Jerusalem is mentioned during the ministry in the first eight chapters (in 3⁷, ⁸ it occurs in a geographical enumeration), it is mentioned in connexion with hostility [3²², 7¹]; and the Lord's only journey to the south is a *via dolorosa* [8³¹, 9³¹, 10³³]; and there, in Jerusalem, as the result of a disciple's treachery, the Jewish authorities' relentless opposition, and a Roman procurator's weakness, He dies. Galilee and Jerusalem are thus placed, in Mark, in the sharpest contrast (there is no mention of Samaria); and it is possible that St. John, both for historical and for doctrinal reasons, wishes to redress the balance.[1]

(a) Historical reasons

Attention is often called to passages in Mark which on the most natural interpretation suggest previous visits to the south by the Lord before the last; e.g. the friends at Bethany in 14³, the householder in Jerusalem in 14¹⁴, the action of Joseph of Arimathaea in 15⁴³; cf. also 11¹⁻⁶, 14⁴⁹, and Mt. 23³⁷, Lk. 13³⁴. It is less often noticed that nothing is explicitly stated in Mark, or indeed in Matthew or Luke, to lead us to think that, when the Lord finally left Galilee, He did so with the express purpose of attending the passover. Good reasons can be given for thinking that, according to St. Mark, six months or more may have elapsed between the Lord's final departure from Galilee [9³⁰, ³³, 10¹] and the passover in Jerusalem, when he died (chs. 14 to 16).[2] If this is so, chronologically St. Mark and St. John are in comparatively close agreement here, and the Lord's final departure from Galilee may have been connected, as St. John implies [7², ¹⁰, ¹⁴], with His attendance at the feast of tabernacles. Accordingly St. John may well be correct when he represents the Lord, first, as welcoming some disciples of the Baptist in the south [1³⁵⁻⁴²],[3] and also working with them for some time in Judaea before the Baptist's imprisonment [3²²⁻²⁴]; and secondly, as visiting Jerusalem several times during the ministry

---

[1] It is not intended to suggest that in Mark hostility to the Lord does not show itself from the first in Galilee; cf. 2⁶, ⁷, ¹⁶, ¹⁸, ²⁴, 3⁶ (see a note by the Rev. J. C. Fenton in *J.T.S.*, New Series, Vol. III, Part 1, April 1952, pp. 56–58). Here we are only considering the possible doctrinal aspect of a geographical problem.

[2] See an article by Dr. T. W. Manson in the *Bulletin of the John Rylands Library*, vol. 33, No. 2, March 1951, pp. 271–82. The only point which can be mentioned here is that Mk. 10¹, rightly understood, probably suggests a resumption of public teaching by the Lord (in contrast with the recent privacy in Galilee), first in Judaea, and then in Peraea, before the final journey to Jerusalem.

[3] This is not necessarily inconsistent with their subsequent 'call' in Galilee in Mark. In Mk. 1¹⁶⁻¹⁸ this call is so abrupt that, as has often been suggested, these disciples are likely to have become already acquainted, in some way or other, with the Lord.

in connexion with the Jewish festivals. Certainly, in this last respect, his seems the more reasonable account; and if we follow him, we may assume that St. Mark has mentioned no festivals except the last, the passover, because he wishes to concentrate attention upon it as forming, as it were, the dark tunnel through which the Lord must pass before He can be reunited with His followers in Galilee.

(b) Doctrinal reasons

It is no doubt true that in John the very first scene in Jerusalem during the ministry is negative in character, since dissension at once breaks out between the Lord and the Jewish authorities [2¹³⁻²²], and that the Jews, whose headquarters are naturally in the south, are throughout His bitterest opponents; and also that the first two scenes of the ministry in John which are laid in Galilee, the provision of wine at the wedding feast at Cana, and the healing of the nobleman's son at Capernaum, are by comparison positive in character. Yet already at 4⁴⁸ a negative note is sounded in the Lord's words, 'Except ye see signs and wonders, ye will in no wise believe.' This note appears again in ch. 6 where the great multitude is said to be attracted to follow Him because they saw His signs upon the sick. The Jews also play a part in this chapter [6⁴¹, ⁵²], and the curtain falls upon the scene in Galilee with the Lord deserted by all except the twelve, and the warning that there is unfaithfulness even amongst them. In spite, therefore, of great differences in the presentation of the Galilean ministry in Mark and John respectively, it may perhaps be claimed that as regards the happiness of its beginning and its very different final outcome the two evangelists take much the same position, and if St. Mark did regard Galilee as more worthy than Judaea of the Lord's ministry and salvation, it may be part of St. John's purpose to show that in truth there is little or nothing to choose between them; light and darkness are to be found in both alike. And if, as seems certain, it was originally intended to close this gospel at 20³⁰, ³¹, and ch. 21 is a subsequent addition, part of the reason for the addition may be that it was desired to record the manifestation of the risen Lord not only in Jerusalem, as in ch. 20, but also in Galilee, as in ch. 21.

Something further may perhaps be said about the place occupied by Judaea and Jerusalem in the fourth gospel. In St. Mark's gospel there is a single passage, as we have remarked, from

Galilee to Jerusalem, and it is a passage from life to death. This passage from life to death, moreover, is closely connected with the disclosure of the Lord's Person. However much His disciples listen to Him in Galilee or the multitudes throng Him [Mk. $1^{16-20, 33}$, $2^{14, 15}$, $3^{7, 13-19}$, 4^1, 5^{21}, 6^{31}, 8^1], they do not know Him for what He is. Only when the public ministry in Galilee is over, and the Lord with His disciples is at the foot of Hermon in the north, does St. Peter, in the name of the disciples, confess His Messiahship. A few days later, in the Lord's transfiguration, three of the twelve are granted a brief vision of their Master in glory, this being almost at once followed by the beginning of His journey with His disciples and others to the south. This journey, the only journey to Jerusalem in St. Mark's gospel, the ultimate purpose of which seems to be to attend the passover feast, is regarded as of great significance. Three times it is made clear that the Lord is well aware what it means and involves, and what its issue will be. It is nothing less than the journey of the Son of man to condemnation and death, and the Lord's three revelations of this have been compared to the solemn tolling of a funeral minute bell. The thoughts, however, of those who accompany Him are by no means attuned to His understanding of it, and we also read of fear and amazement on their part [Mk. 9^{32}, $10^{24, 32}$]. This bewilderment reaches its height with the arrival at the city, for whereas the Lord by His action in entering it upon the humble beast of peace seeks to show, to those with eyes to see, the nature and purpose of His coming, the actions and cries of those who surround Him are suggestive of a welcome given to a popular national hero, of whom great things are expected by His fellow countrymen. Some at least seem to have regarded His entry as messianic; but of what kind was this Messiah? His entry into the city and His first action there are closely connected. He takes drastic action in His Father's house which He finds to be a den of robbers rather than a house of prayer, and its grandeur makes no impression on Him; He warns a disciple that it will be utterly destroyed, and being privately questioned on the matter He tells four of His disciples on what, or rather on whom, they should seek, instead, to build their hope [Mk. 13^{3-37}]. Meanwhile His action in the temple and the reason which He gives for it have led to a rupture with the authorities, who seek to destroy Him [Mk. 11^{17-18}]; but it should particularly be noted that it is not the action itself, but His authority or right

to act thus, which is formally challenged next morning by the
chief priest and scribes and elders [Mk. 11²⁷⁻²⁸]. It is clear to them
that the Lord regards Himself as having authority, indeed divine
authority, to do what He has done. The thought that He could be
upon the side of God, and that, if so, they must be numbered
among the enemies of God, is intolerable to them. Accordingly,
when the Lord finally acknowledges and confirms the truth about
His own Person to the Sanhedrin [Mk. 14⁶²], His declaration is not
only regarded as blasphemy, but is made the ground of His
condemnation to death; and when application is made to the
occupying power for the infliction of the penalty, the charge
preferred is the Prisoner's personal claim, the claim to Jewish
Messiahship or Kingship.

It thus seems that in the earlier gospels, especially in St. Mark,
the journey to the south, the entry into Jerusalem, the cleansing
of the temple, and the Lord's condemnation, resulting in His
death and resurrection, are very closely linked; and that He was
condemned not for His action, as such, in the temple but for His
personal claims. This last point, that the Lord was condemned not
for His actions as such or His teaching, but because in the end
He allowed certain truths to be known about His Person, should be
kept constantly in mind when considering the connexion between
St. Mark's gospel and St. John's. We have already suggested, in
considering the structure of the fourth gospel, that the entire
course of events, from the witness of the Baptist to the Lord's
commission to His disciples and His bestowal on them of the
Holy Spirit, is a single whole, and also that the record of the
ministry is contained in six sections, in each of which is contained,
in greater or less degree, the whole of the Gospel. Each sign,
together with the word accompanying the sign, refers directly or
by implication to the Lord's whole work: His coming, His
ministry in word and deed, His death, resurrection, exaltation. All
these various works constitute together His one single saving
action, which is to give eternal life to men. May it not be for this
reason, at least in part, that a visit of the Lord to Jerusalem at
passover time and His momentous cleansing of the temple are
placed at the outset of the record, and that the majority of His
significant actions are performed in or near Jerusalem, and are
expounded as signs of the authority and Person of the Lord, since
Jerusalem was the actual scene of the Lord's death which was

consequent upon His declaration of His Person? Thus in St. John's second chapter certain features which combine in St. Mark's gospel to form a single crisis at its close—the cleansing of the temple, the Jews' reaction to His authority, the Lord's death at passover time and His resurrection—are, in the words 'Destroy this shrine, and in three days I will raise it ... but He spake of the temple of His body', brought together with reference to the Lord's Person. In ch. 5, when He is again at Jerusalem at a festival, the Lord is persecuted by the Jews for healing on the sabbath, and in reply sets forth in a long continuous address His personal relation to the Father, who has given Him the divine prerogatives of giving life and of judgement. This second scene at Jerusalem, even more definitely than the first, is concerned with truths about the Lord's Person and, like the first, alludes also to His death at the hands of the Jews, and to the gift of inherent life which He has received from the Father. At the beginning of ch. 7 the Lord again visits Jerusalem for the feast of tabernacles, and is there throughout the events narrated in chs. 8 to 10. These chapters are filled with bitterly polemical altercations between Him and the Jews, and with a hostility which threatens His death (7^{32}, 8^{59}, 10^{31}), and in proportion as this hostility develops, and it becomes more certain what the end will be, so the Lord proclaims the nature and truth of His Person ever more actively and openly [$8^{12, 58}$, 9^{35-37}, $10^{7, 11, 30}$], and speaks of His death, sometimes figuratively, as with reference to a lifting up of the Son of Man, or to 'a little while' after which He will go away [8^{28}, 7^{33}, 8^{21}], sometimes openly [7^{19}, 8^{37}]. And this death, howsoever it may be procured by the murderous intentions of the Jews, is His own voluntary laying down of His life in order that He may take it again, and may so give eternal life to men [10^{17}]. In ch. 11 the Lord does not visit Jerusalem itself, but in spite of the disciples' protest at His proposal to return to the sphere of danger in Judaea He comes from Transjordan to its neighbourhood, to Bethany, for the express purpose of revealing Himself in His highest endowment, as Conqueror of death, though not without the expression of extreme distress, which seems to indicate the cost to Him of giving life to men. And it is after this culminating revelation of Himself that the meeting of the authorities is held which resolves upon His death. Because the Lord has shown Himself to be the resurrection and the life, therefore He must die. Accordingly the Lord no more moves openly among the Jews, but goes into the country near the wilderness, into a city called Ephraim, where He remains with His disciples, until the passover. Finally, in ch. 12, the Lord undergoes a symbolical burial at the hands of Mary, enters Jerusalem to be hailed as the messianic king, but in truth coming rather as the unique Son who has now fulfilled the work entrusted to Him by the Father, announces, with the coming of the Gentiles and their wish to see Him, the arrival of the hour that the Son of Man should be glorified; and therewith, after a final appeal, no longer to the Jews, but to the vacillating and puzzled multitude, the ministry is over, the Lord is hidden from them, and the record of the passion follows, its meaning and purpose having first been explained to the disciples at His last meal with them.

It would, therefore, seem likely that the evangelist has been led to give us, in the light partly of the actual events or of the primitive tradition, and partly of the experience of the first two generations of disciples, as they were guided to perceive ever more clearly the true import of that which had happened in their midst, a searching and profound interpretation of the Christian mystery of the Lord's Person and of His life-giving death and resurrection. And in order to do so he has both presented the Lord as continually giving His life by laying it down, and on each occasion taking it again, that He might give eternal life to men, and has also located the greater part of the ministry in Jerusalem because, in the earlier gospels, Jerusalem was the scene of the final crisis of the Lord's death and resurrection.

E. THE BACKGROUND OF THE GOSPEL

In the previous section it has been sought to show that, while St. John may be historically more correct than St. Mark in narrating more than one journey of the Lord from Galilee to Jerusalem in the course of the ministry, his purpose is by no means only historical; he is concerned also with theological truth. We may now consider further what it means to claim for St. John that he is the interpreter of the other gospels, and with special reference to his exposition of theological truth.

Theologically he would seem to stand nearest to St. Mark, for in the first as well as in the last of the gospels the Lord's Person is of vital significance. Important as is the doctrine of the kingdom of God, it is not the centre of gravity of the Christian faith; still less is it true that the Christian Gospel has to do with the Father only and not with the Son. This the fourth evangelist makes clear, but he is not able to do so without producing a portraiture of the Lord which, in some important respects, stands in contrast to that which is to be found in the earlier gospels. It is possible to state this contrast in more than one way. It can be said that, compared with the synoptists, the figure of the Lord in the fourth gospel is almost static in character. Or it may be said that in the three earlier gospels the Lord's manhood is more conspicuous than His divinity, and that His divinity is more conspicuous than His manhood in the fourth. Or it may be said that in the synoptic gospels, on the one hand, the Lord is always portrayed as having a goal before Him, which during the ministry is not yet realized (such passages as Lk. 12^{50} and 13^{33} are forcible expressions of this), and that the relation of His future triumph and glory to His present activity on earth is not made clear. In the fourth gospel, on the other hand, while the future still has its part to play (the expression 'the last day'—curiously enough, a term peculiar to this gospel in the New Testament—occurs in reference to what we call 'the end of the world' six times, although it is now a distant future, which is never brought into direct connexion with the Lord's *parousia* or presence), the Lord is presented at the beginning, middle, and end of His ministry as unchanging and unchanged, and that which had been thought to belong to the future, and to be at present utterly beyond men's grasp, is shown to be already in their hands, if they can receive it and enter into it. It is, in any case, in considering their presentations of the Person of Christ, particularly in relation to the Jewish and Greek background of early Christian life and thought, that we are likely to come closer to an understanding of the similarities and differences between the fourth gospel and its predecessors.

The catholic doctrine of the Person of Jesus Christ now receives admirable expression in the *Quicunque vult*. Our Lord Jesus Christ, the Son of God, is both God and man. He is God, of the substance of the Father, begotten before the worlds: and He is man, of the substance of His Mother, born in the world. He is perfect God, perfect man; equal to the Father, as touching His Godhead: less than the Father, as touching His manhood. And this Person, although God and man, is not two, but is one Christ. Only after several centuries, however, was the Church able to formulate this classical expression of its faith, an expression based on the experience of the full and perfect salvation which believers found themselves to have received through the historic incarnation and redemption. The implications of the experience had been present in the life of the Church from the first; but prolonged debate was needed before a satisfying statement could be given of Him in whom, as the Church had reason to believe, the love of God had been completely manifested. In thus setting forth as a result of its religious experience the two truths about the one Person of its Lord, that He is perfect God and perfect man, the Church claimed with justice to be only interpreting the original revelation, not to be adding anything to it. No attempt, however, was made by the Church, as such, to show how this can be, and the history of doctrine is evidence of how difficult it has proved to preserve the balance between these two features of the creed, and to walk along the narrow path of faith without inclining dangerously to one side or the other. Having set forth the conditions for a right understanding of the Person of its Lord, the Church refers us to the four canonical accounts of His ministry, and invites us to find the truth there.

In all these four accounts the revelation brought by the Lord is set forth as something which cannot be received lightly, or by all. In the first three gospels, in Mk. 4^{11} for example, we read that the mystery of 'the kingdom of God', an important term which seems to have been often on His lips, had been granted to a small number only, and in St. John's gospel, in which this term occurs only twice, at $3^{3, 5}$, we learn there that 'rebirth' is essential for sight of, or entry into, it. It is also made clear in all the gospels that there is a mystery connected with the Person of the Lord (although the form of this mystery in the fourth gospel is different from that which it takes in the other three), and that the mystery of the kingdom of God is in some way bound up with the mystery of His Person. In His teaching our Lord seems always to have sought to start with that which was familiar to His hearers, and thus to guide them from the known to the unknown. His teaching was direct, simple, and concrete, often by means of homely illustrations and parables. He bade men look intelligently at the world of nature and of common life, which they knew well, and so to pass on from their observation and knowledge of these to the deeper lessons which, through this same nature and common life, could be imparted to them. A knowledge of earth could be the pathway to a knowledge of heaven. And in the same way He was willing, it seems, that His hearers should know Him as a man; that was the primary, most obvious thing about Him. To judge from the first three gospels, He appears to have said comparatively little about His own Person, although He did not refuse the boundless love and awe of His disciples, and it should be clear to any unbiased student of these gospels that He was more than a purely human teacher of righteousness, and that they present the portrait of one who is not as other men are. In this connexion the way in which, in the first three gospels, the Lord explains the nature of the kingdom of God by teaching that it is like this or that, should be compared with the way in which, in St. John's gospel, He compares Himself to some aspect of the natural world, such as bread or light or a vine.

(a) The Jewish background

The immediate background of the Lord's ministry and Person is the Jewish religion. The soil in which Christianity was planted was that of the pious Judaism which was 'waiting for the kingdom of God'. A very important feature of any religion is its teaching about the problem and mystery of time; and the religion of the Hebrews was, and always has been, a religion of hope, which laid great emphasis on the future, and upon what, as they believed, the future had in store for them. There is every reason to believe that the doctrine of messiahship was the way in which the Lord's earliest disciples sought to understand Him. To the non-Christian Jew the word Messiah would imply a purely future hope, based on divine promises given to his fathers in the past; but a Jewish Christian saw matters in a different light, because he believed himself to know who the Messiah was. The good news of the earliest Christian missionaries was that the divine promises had been recently fulfilled, and that the Messiah had come in an utterly unexpected way. He had been put to death, but had been raised up and manifested to His disciples. He was now in glory with the Father, and would very soon come to gather His elect to Him. Meantime the latter were conscious of a new life, due to the presence of the Holy Spirit, which was regarded as an earnest or first-fruits of the future consummation; but at first, and for the first two or three decades, the centre of gravity in the Christian faith seems to have been that part of it, inherited from Judaism, which concentrated on the future more than on the present or the past. It would be untrue to say that this concentration on a future hope led those who held it, apart from a few misguided disciples [2 Thess. 3[11]], to be careless of the present; present and future were vitally connected, but at a time when it was believed [1 Thess. 4[15], 1 Cor. 15[51]] that the majority of Christians would during their lifetime witness the Lord's return, present difficulties could be resolutely faced in the courage and resource which came from the prospect of a glorious future (cf. Rom. 8[18]). Whatever may have been the strength of the expectation of deliverance among the Jews at the time of the Lord's ministry, it is certain that among His disciples, as a result of their association with Him, the expectation was immeasurably increased. Not only had some of the divine promises already come true, but others were now coming true for them and their generation. Their minds were filled with a great hope [Lk. 19[11]], which had only been deepened by His resurrection [Acts 1[6-7]] and by their experience of the Holy Spirit, and they believed themselves to be on the verge of the very 'consummation of the age' [Mt. 28[20]]. Accordingly, when such people came to depict their Master as Messiah, they probably looked upon Him as, so to speak, His own forerunner, as a still uncrowned king, who had walked incognito among His subjects. His earthly ministry was preparatory; the real deliverance He had yet to bring. His life, death, and resurrection—to all outward appearance the life, death, and resurrection of 'the prophet, Jesus, from Nazareth of Galilee' [Mt. 21[11]]—were the prelude to His real 'Presence'; for this, and not 'Coming' or 'Return', is the meaning of the word *parousia* used in the New Testament for what we now usually speak of as the Second Coming. In all this they showed themselves true children of their ancestral faith.

When an intense expectation takes fire and burns with a living flame within the eastern mind, its realization, it is assumed, will take place in the immediate future; the greater the hope the more imminent the deliverance; 'after two days will he revive us'. And similarly the greater the sin the more immediate the judgement; 'yet forty days, and Nineveh shall be overthrown'. Experience may make havoc of this foreshortening, this boldly poetical or prophetic perspective, but if the hope is truly religious, it will matter little to a Hebrew prophet or his hearers what the course of events makes of his dating, which was only a vigorous manner of utterance; the hope which projected these forms of expression will find no difficulty in reconstructing them. It may indeed be laid down, although it is a hard saying, that a conversion usually begins, to some extent, with a misunderstanding. We are attracted, in the first instance, not by the reality itself alone, which at present is beyond us, but by the reality as seen through some preconceived ideas of our own, which must gradually fade, or perhaps rather be transformed, as we come more nearly to know the reality. It is a profound saying of a medieval writer, 'God speaks one word, but we hear two'. The second word is our echo; it makes God speak in our language, and leads us to expect the fulfilment of His promises as we have at first understood them. Such seems to have been the case as regards the forms of the earliest beliefs of the disciples. The fact that by the time St. John wrote it had become clear that the earliest form taken by the Christian hope would not be realized, that those who had assumed that the earlier scenes of the drama of redemption, the birth, life, death, resurrection, and ascension of the Lord, would be followed forthwith by His 'Presence' had been wrong, and the fact that the hope for the future, though it has not quite disappeared from St. John's gospel, occupies a very subordinate position in it, should not blind us to the Jewish background of this gospel. If the Jews, or the great majority of them, are the permanent opponents of the Lord in John, there is nothing but respect for the Judaism of the past and for the Old Testament. The Lord, in speaking to the Jews, seems indeed to adopt an attitude of aloofness when he uses the words[1] *your law* [8¹⁷, 10³⁴], *their law* [15²⁵]; but he also says that *the scripture cannot be broken* [10³⁵], that *Moses wrote of* Him [5⁴⁶], and that *Abraham* (with whom His hearers are unfavourably compared 8⁴⁰) *rejoiced to see* His *day* [8⁵⁶]. And John not only by his opening words recalls Gen. 1¹, but in his first piece of narrative 1¹⁹⁻²⁸, with its references to *priests and Levites, the Messiah, Elijah, the prophet, Isaiah*, apparently assumes in his readers a knowledge of the Old Testament writings.

But the Jewish colouring of the gospel goes deeper. Although it is written in the popular Greek of the day, and in a style which, while simple and employing only a limited vocabulary, sustains an elevation worthy of its theme, the language used shows a strong Semitic strain, so strong indeed that attempts have been made to

[1] Perhaps the best way to understand these expressions is to recall 1¹⁷ or Gal. 3. The Lord, although showing a deep regard for the Law, is, as the Logos incarnate, above and independent of it, as He is by nature above and independent of all things (cf. 3³¹), although all things point to Him and speak of Him.

prove that the work is a Greek translation of an Aramaic original. These attempts have hitherto not commanded wide assent, but they are sufficiently successful to prove that the writer, although he composed his book in Greek, was acquainted with, and at home in, Aramaic thought and idiom. Emphasis has further been laid by several writers on the familiarity shown by John with the thought and language of the Jewish rabbis of his time. Indeed, a great Jewish scholar, Israel Abrahams, speaks of 'the cumulative strength of the arguments adduced by Jewish writers favourable to the authenticity of the discourses of the Fourth Gospel, especially in relation to the circumstances in which they are reported to have been spoken'.[1] Thus it will become clear in the exposition of chs. 7 and 8 that the rites and associations of the feast of tabernacles help to explain the contents of these chapters. It is also possible to show, by quotations from the Talmud, that in ch. 9 the Pharisees' trial of the man born blind is in full agreement with rabbinic conceptions; and the same is said to be true of the controversies in this gospel about sabbath observance, and about the origin of the Messiah. More important still, it appears to have been rabbinic teaching about the study of the Torah, that it, the Jewish law—chiefly, although not exclusively, as contained in the Pentateuch—'gives life in the age to come'; and much light is thrown upon the contents of this gospel if it is kept in mind that the Rabbis were prone to speak of the Torah as water, bread, and light for the world.[2] It thus seems clear that when we read of the Lord in ch. 4 offering living water, in ch. 6 as the bread which gives life, or in ch. 8 as the light of the world, we are being invited to think henceforth of Him, rather than of the Torah, as the source of religious truth and life and light. An historical person, Jesus Christ, the Word become flesh, appearing within the confines of Judaism, fulfils and replaces the written law given through Moses [1 17].

While our Lord was worshipped as the Jewish Messiah before He was identified with the universal Logos, and while the keen expectations for the future were the inevitable result of this, the first doctrine to be formulated about His Person, namely that He was the Messiah, it had nevertheless become clear before two

[1] Cambridge Biblical Essays, p. 181.

[2] For a fuller statement, cf. C. H. Dodd, 'The Background of the Fourth Gospel', *Bulletin of the John Rylands Library*, vol. 19, no. 2, July 1935; *The Interpretation of the Fourth Gospel*, 1953, pt. I, ch. 4.

generations of the Church's life had passed, as perhaps it was becoming clear to those who, like St. Paul, lived through the period of transition, that the Lord's Messiahship was not the only, nor perhaps the greatest, truth about Him. The fact that He had been born a Jew and was Messiah of the Jews must indeed carry permanent significance; it not only linked Him with the divine purpose for the Jewish nation from the beginning of its history; it also implied that hope must always be an essential feature of the Christian life, even if the earliest form of that hope was not to be fulfilled, but was to change its shape. It has perhaps been insufficiently emphasized how remarkable is the absence from the Christian literature of the first century of any sense of disappointment, in spite of such strong statements as are found in Mt. 10²³, Mk. 9¹, 1 Thess. 4¹⁵, Heb. 10²⁵, statements, the retention of which does not seem to have caused any serious difficulty to those who valued the documents. It is thus clear that, although the promise in the form in which it had been first interpreted had not been, and could not now be, fulfilled, yet its recipients, far from being disillusioned, were before long rejoicing in 'some better thing', and there was no setback in the steady progress of the Christian communities. The life of the Church was to fill something more than a brief pause between the penultimate and the final scene, and its endowment, the Holy Spirit, was something more than a first-fruits [Rom. 8²³] or pledge [2 Cor. 1²², 5⁵] of the expected 'Presence' of the Lord. The office of Jewish Messiah had proved inadequate to account for the Person and work of the Lord, who was so much more than the Messiah, that the very word Christ, the Greek translation of the Hebrew word Messiah, signifying 'Anointed', had taken on a new meaning. The growth and experience of the Church had shown that the Lord's life was not only an event in Jewish history, but also in world history. Nor was it to be understood only, or chiefly, as a preparation for a future event; it was itself the manifestation in history of the spiritual Power through which the worlds were made, the power which had always been at work, but unseen hitherto, in the course of events. For the expression of these truths a different tradition from the Jewish was at hand.

(b) The Greek Background: The Doctrine of the Logos

Writing about A.D. 200, Clement of Alexandria says, 'The way of truth (i.e. the Christian religion) is one, but different streams from different quarters flow into it as into an ever flowing river'.[1] This is an important and permanent truth about the Christian religion, but here we need only notice that, if the source of the river is to be sought in Judaism, almost from the first its waters were joined by streams which had taken their rise elsewhere, and had gathered strength as they passed through other soils. Jewish religion and Greek religion each had an essential contribution to make to it. Neither was capable by itself of becoming an historic universal religion, able to satisfy the needs and aspirations of humanity, but after each had received a contribution from the other, and had also been brought into relation with the Person of the Lord Jesus, Christianity could make this claim. The reason for the continued progress of the Christian communities, and for the confident development of Christian thought and hope, must be found, above all, in the influence exercised, most unexpectedly but also decisively, upon belief about the Lord's Person and work by that other great stream which from the first began to mingle its waters with the Jewish stream.

It is necessary, therefore, to glance briefly at the religious beliefs and aspirations of the non-Jewish world, that hellenistic, Gentile world, in which within a generation or two the Gospel found the majority of its disciples. It was these men, above all, as seems likely, that the fourth evangelist, although himself by origin a Hebrew, was desirous to instruct and help. A considerable amount of evidence exists about the life of religion at this time in the Roman empire. It is believed to have extended over a wide and varied field, the desire to gain, and to have contact with, the divine embracing both high philosophical thought on the one hand, and also rites of popular magic on the other. None the less its forms, though widely different, exhibit certain features in common. Thus the divine tends to be conceived as life and light, and we read of two realms, those of light and darkness, the mystic or initiate being offered the means by which he may pass from the latter to the former. Again, there is emphasis on the necessity of mediation between these two levels of existence, and on the fact that such mediation exists and is available, however various its forms. And the idea is widespread that the goal of religion for man consists in knowing God, a knowledge which brings with it both the vision of God and union with God. The importance of the practice of

[1] *Stromateis* i. 5 (29. 1).

ethical virtues is not indeed forgotten, but in general the emphasis is on thought more than on practice, on detachment from the world than on vigorous action in it. Accordingly, a thoughtful Gentile reader of St. John's gospel, when it first appeared, is likely to have felt that, however strange its atmosphere, it at least included religious terms and conceptions with which he was already familiar. We have only to think, taking the above points in order, of $1^{4, 9}$, 8^{23}, 1^{51}, 3^{13}, 17^{3}, 14^{7}, 17^{23}. Even more important for our present subject is the fact that in the best contemporary religious teaching, teaching which was mainly that of the later school of Plato, the antithesis, necessary in some form or other to religion, between that which ought to be and that which is, was not found, as among the Jews, in the contrast of the future with the present, but in the contrast of substance with shadow, of reality with appearance, of mind and spirit with matter, and that if the religious Greek sought to envisage his heaven more concretely, he preferred the image of space to that of time, and spoke of the perfect world as existing 'yonder', not 'here below'. And this teaching, which had formed the basis and the presuppositions of the religious life of the Gentiles now in large numbers seeking admission to the Christian Church, was destined to exercise great influence upon the final expression of the doctrine of the Lord's Person. It could not be otherwise, since before the end of the first century, to speak very broadly, the Jews had rejected, and the Gentiles were accepting, the Christian Gospel. Nevertheless, the roots of the Christian faith had been planted, and remained, in Judaism; and this meant that Christianity, like Judaism, and unlike Gentile religion, became a faith in which history, and above all the historical ministry of its Lord, played an all-important part. It is probably true that in no book of the New Testament has the fusion of the two chief and very different elements in Christianity, the Jewish and the Greek, been achieved with a surer touch or with greater thoroughness than in St. John's gospel.

The word which St. John selects as best adapted to enable his readers to understand the Person of Jesus Christ is the Greek word 'Logos'. The importance of this word for his purpose is that in the Greek language it means both reason, i.e. something thought, something existing in the mind, and also speech, something expressed, something directed outward. Similarly in English the use of words is the means by which a person expresses the thoughts which are in his mind. To put the matter very simply, St. John uses the word 'Logos' to explain how God expresses His nature and purpose to His creatures, and, above all, to man. And although he only uses the word 'Logos' in this technical sense in the prologue, and there only at 1^1 and 1^{14}, its implications are never far from his mind. The people among whom this gospel circulated were all familiar with the Greek language, and the word 'Logos' had long been used in a religious sense by both Jews and Greeks; by the latter in their own language, and by the former, as the Greek translation of a common and important word in the Hebrew Bible. It is noticeable that St. John does not explain the word 'Logos'; clearly he assumes that his readers will understand the meaning which he wishes to convey by using it; but, as a result of its diverse origins, the word would no doubt convey different shades of meaning to different readers. Some of these meanings we must consider.

In Jewish thought the word of 'Yahweh' is an active force or power going forth from Him in fulfilment of His will, and having results such as creation, renewal, inspiration; e.g. Is. $55^{10, \ 11}$ 'For as the rain cometh down and the snow from heaven, and returneth not thither, but watereth the earth, and maketh it bring forth and bud, and giveth seed to the sower and bread to the eater; so shall my word be that goeth forth out of my mouth: it shall not return unto me void, but it shall accomplish that which I please, and it shall prosper in the thing whereto I sent it'; Ps. 33^9: (Yahweh) 'spake, and it was done; He commanded, and it stood fast'; Ps. 147^{15}: 'He sendeth out his commandment upon earth; His word runneth very swiftly'. Thus the word of Yahweh is the power by which He created the universe and sustains it in being [Ps. 33^6]; through His word, regarded as His commandment to men, the latter receive life [Ps. 119^{25}], strength [119^{28}], enlightenment [119^{105}], truth [119^{160}], and deliverance from evil [119^{133}]; and when Yahweh's word comes to the prophets, they are conscious of a compelling force, which they cannot but obey [Jer. 1^{4-10}, 15^{16}, Amos 3^8]. This conception of Yahweh's word is in accordance with the Jews' habitual emphasis on will and action. Believing that their God had made promises to their fathers of a glorious destiny, not yet fully revealed, in store for their nation, since in contrast to all the other peoples of the world they were, as their religious literature taught them, the special people of His choice, they always looked forward. The future, which would bring the full revelation, not yet made, of Yahweh's word, and therewith of His mighty and loving purpose for them, would compensate and more than compensate for the injustices and difficulties of the present. The Jews therefore always lived in hope, in an atmosphere of expectation, relying on the word of Yahweh, as yet only partially revealed and known.

The Greeks also attached significance to the word 'Logos', but their conception of a divine Logos was very different from the Jewish. Whereas the Jews valued, above all, will and action in the expression of life, the Greeks assigned the highest place to intellect and thought. Contemplation rather than action, the exercise of reason rather than the exercise of will, present insight rather than future hope, appealed to the Greeks. They were more actively concerned to understand the world than to change or reform it or to fashion it anew. Accordingly the Greeks, unlike the Jews, did not seek to meet the problems of life by recourse to the thought of time, by contrasting the (often sad and difficult) present with the (anticipated glorious) future, but by recourse to the thought of shadow and substance, or of appearance and reality, by contrasting the outward (appearance) with the inward (reality). Thus some Greek philosophers such as the Stoics taught that a divine principle of logos or reason is within and behind the universe, and maintains it in being and order, and that man, whose reason itself has affinity with the divine reason, can raise himself, by the practice of moral and intellectual virtues, to contemplate, and even to enter into union with, this principle. Other philosophers, of whom the greatest was Plato, taught that the visible universe is a copy or reflection of the perfect, unchanging order or world of invisible ideas, in the contemplation of which, by the methods mentioned above, man's highest good consists. In either case, therefore, the Greeks sought to satisfy their religious aspirations not, like the Jews, chiefly in the world of action, but chiefly in the inner realm of thought and contemplation. Speaking very generally, we may say that the Jews valued life principally for the possibility which it offers of effective energy and action, the Greeks principally for the possibility which life offers of rational thought and understanding.

It might well seem that these Jewish and Greek conceptions of 'Logos' were so different that they could not be fruitfully joined together in a single unifying conception, and least of all that they could be perfectly expressed in a single personal life. As a result, however, of the campaigns of Alexander the Great, and the consequent diffusion of Greek thought and the Greek manner of life throughout the oriental world, there developed a tendency to unite the two conceptions, which was to have very important consequences. For example, in some later Jewish writings Yahweh's word, which originally suggested, as we have seen, an active power proceeding from Him, is identified with Wisdom, poetically regarded as the medium or agent through which He works in the world, and therefore distinct though not separate from Him, and remaining entirely dependent on His will. Thus in Proverbs 8^{22-31} Wisdom is said to have been possessed or formed by Yahweh before all things, and to have been His counsellor and architect in the creation of the universe; see also Proverbs 1^{20-23}, Wisdom $7^{22}-8^1$. In this way, during the last three centuries B.C., the idea of a divine agency mediating between God and the universe became widely spread in the countries bordering on the Mediterranean and in the near East, and the word 'Logos' was available to describe this agency. The student of St. John's gospel, however, may well be advised to keep three points in mind about the use of this word, and of terms like it, in the pre-christian period.

(*a*) The conception of such an agency was poetical rather than personal, descriptive rather than factual; nor is any suggestion known that this divine Logos might conceivably assume human nature and live a human life.

(*b*) To the Jew it was axiomatic that the seat or home of this agency must be sought, and found, in Israel; and in Jewish belief the 'Torah', a word which means instruction or direction, and which was applied chiefly, though not exclusively, to the law of Moses, was the permanent embodiment of Yahweh's word. Thus in the picturesque language of Micah $4^{1, 2}$, which is parallel to Is. $2^{2, 3}$, we read that one day the temple mount at Jerusalem will overtop all other hills, and a multitude of nations will flock to it, because it is the house where the God of Jacob dwells, and the 'Torah' will proceed from Zion, and Yahweh's word from Jerusalem. It will be noted that the nations, in order to satisfy their religious aspirations, are to go up to Jewry; Jewry is not to go down to them. Cf. also Ecclus. 24^{6-23}, Baruch 3^{12ff}.

(*c*) Since Jewish belief had by this time become strongly monotheistic, it was natural for the Jew to conceive the divine agency, of which we are thinking, as also one and undivided; but Gentile religion with its gods many and lords many (1 Cor. 8⁵), and its strong tendency towards pantheism, was prepared to welcome almost all forms of religious belief, however diverse, as due to, and participating in, this agency. For this reason the conception of the Logos could be applied more easily and widely in Gentile religion than in Judaism; but on the other hand Gentile religion lacked the unifying element so prominent in Jewish religious thought.

Thus both Jewish and Gentile religion had a distinctive and necessary contribution to make to Christianity; but at the same time each had to undergo a certain transformation, and to be marked with the sign of the cross, before it could make its contribution.

The fact that the word 'Logos' is not unequivocally used of Jesus Christ in any New Testament writing earlier than those ascribed to St. John (cf. Rev. 19¹³) should not be allowed to conceal how quickly in the doctrine of the Church the office and functions associated with the conception of the divine Logos were applied to Him, the conception thus being no longer poetical and imaginative, but becoming in the highest degree personal and factual. It will suffice to give four examples of this tendency. In 1 Cor. 1²⁴ the Lord is described as the power of God (in action) and the wisdom of God (in thought); and in 1 Cor. 8⁶, after saying that, 'for us there is but one God, the Father, the Origin of all things, and the Goal of our life' St. Paul adds: 'and one Lord, Jesus Christ, through whom are all things, and we through Him'. In other words, the Lord is the Agent in creation, and also the Mediator between man and God. In Col. 1¹⁵⁻¹⁷ we read that the Lord is the 'eikon' or image of the invisible God, that in and through Him all things have been created, and that in Him all things hold together; He is the consistency of all things. (An 'eikon' is a copy not only resembling, but derived from, its original, which the copy represents as the visible manifestation of the original.) Finally, in Heb. 1² the writer, referring to Jesus Christ, says that God made the ages (i.e. as we, like the Greeks, should normally say, the world, the universe) through Him. Accordingly it seems that St. John, in using the term 'the Logos' of Jesus Christ in the prologue to his gospel, has only taken the final step along a

path which the Church had been treading from the first. This
Word, as God in essence, has an extra-temporal relation in closest
connexion with the Father. This Word is the Agent and quickening
Spirit in creation, the life of all that lives, and the light of all that
shines. This light has at all times enlightened men, but had passed
unrecognized by the majority. At length, when the time came, this
Word took our nature upon Him and dwelt for a time among us,
and revealed the glory of an only-begotten from the Father. It is
in the narrative of the gospel that we are to learn that this glory
consists, above all, in self-sacrificing love. Such was the motive
for this action by the Word, action which is thus seen to be the
supreme example of the divine love for the world, since as a result
of it men were to be enabled, in and through Him, to have eternal
life. True to the Jewish origins of Christianity, and therefore laying
great emphasis on history, St. John not only makes his prologue
serve as an introduction to an historical narrative of the earthly
ministry of the Lord, but also leads up in the prologue itself to a
decisive historical event in 1^{14}. This event was the inclosing of the
universal Logos in a single divine human personality; and it was
precisely this synthesis of the individual with the universal which
gave to Christianity the dynamic which enabled it to overcome the
world, and to win the religious allegiance of mankind. For to
bring the idea of the Logos into union with the personality of an
individual, who is represented as living and working (almost) under
ordinary human conditions, was to bring together the two poles
between which the human spirit always moves.

F. THE PORTRAITURE OF THE LORD

It is a corollary of what has been said above, that in any formulation of the Christian Gospel difficulty is inevitable in giving full
weight to both its temporal and its eternal aspects, and also in
doing justice to both the human and the divine nature of the Lord.
In each case one side is likely to receive a certain over-emphasis.
This may be illustrated by a comparison of St. John's gospel with
St. Mark's. Within the first eleven verses of St. Mark's gospel
we meet what, using the language of a developed theology, we may
call the doctrine of the Trinity. The Father, although not named
directly, in verse 11 addresses the Lord Jesus, who comes from
Nazareth of Galilee, as His beloved, or only, Son, in whom He
finds full pleasure; and in verse 10 we read of the descent of the

Spirit on the Lord, that Spirit which, according to the Baptist, the Coming One, the infinitely Mightier than he, would grant to those who had received his (John's) baptism. The same features appear in the opening verses of St. John's gospel. There the unique Son is said in 1^{18} to be (permanently) in the bosom of the Father and to have declared, or explained, Him; and in 1^{32} the Baptist bears witness to the descent of the Spirit on the Lord Jesus, with the added note that the Spirit abode, or continued to remain, upon Him, and that 'this is He who', as the Baptist learned by divine intimation, 'baptizes in Holy Spirit'.

Both gospels, therefore, from the outset teach the same theological doctrine. We may, however, use a very small difference in their opening narratives to illustrate an important truth. St. Mark approaches the doctrine of the Lord's Person chiefly from the human side by way of the Jewish messianic hope, and hope implies an attitude towards the future—cf. Rom. 8^{23-25}. It is therefore natural that in Mk. 1^{7-8} the Baptist, speaking of the purpose of the coming, after him, of an infinitely Greater, should use the future tense: 'He shall baptize . . . in Holy Spirit.' On the other hand St. John, who has emphasized in the prologue the eternity of the Logos, and His equality with God, approaches the doctrine of the Lord's Person chiefly from the divine side by way of the doctrine of the Logos, who in Jesus Christ has taken human nature upon Him [1^{14}]; and it is therefore fitting that in this gospel the Baptist should not only emphasize that the Lord, although 'coming after him', is already present, even if as yet unknown [1^{26}], but in speaking of the Lord's work should use the present tense: 'He that baptizeth (or, is baptizing) in Holy Spirit' [1^{33}]. In other words, the fourfold gospel encourages both an attitude of expectation of something yet to be or to come, and also a consciousness of a full reality or truth already present, the second feature being the especial contribution of St. John. It is important that the distinction between the gospels in this respect should not be pressed too hard; thus the earlier gospels are by no means devoid of emphasis upon a divine event already present (cf. Mt. 12^{28}, Mk. 1^{15}, Lk. 17^{21}), and at first sight it might seem that what St. John says about the Lord baptizing in Holy Spirit is directly contradicted by some editorial words at 7^{39}. Broadly speaking, however, this distinction holds, not only for the opening of the two gospels concerned, but throughout.

Thus St. Mark sets forth the Lord's work as accomplished in a series of distinct chronological events, the last of which, His 'Second Coming', is still unrealized. After His reception of the Spirit and the declaration of His Divine Sonship at His Baptism, the secret of which only the reader shares with the Lord, the ministry in Galilee and its neighbourhood follows. The Lord gathers disciples round Him and calls the twelve, and examples are given of His mighty works and, to a less degree, of His teaching. Both to the evangelist and to the reader these mighty works are evidence of the Lord's divine power, and His teaching is with divine authority; but to very few of those who saw the works or heard the teaching was an understanding given of the mystery in which they were enshrouded. The Lord forbids spiritual forces to make the truth about Him known [Mk. $1^{25, 34}$, 3^{12}], and in His acts of power He avoids publicity [Mk. 1^{44}, 5^{43}, 7^{36}, 8^{26}], at any rate on Jewish soil (cf. Mk. 5^{19}). The teaching given to the multitudes was always in parables [Mk. 4^{34}], the surface meaning of which could indeed be easily grasped and remembered, but which for those, such as the disciples, privileged to understand its true significance[1] contained nothing less than the mystery or secret of the Kingdom of God [Mk. 4^{11}], and the disciple's frequent inability to appreciate the significance either of their Master's acts of power or of His teaching, in spite of special opportunities given either to them as a body [Mk. $4^{10, 34b}$, 7^{17}] or, even more privately to their leaders [Mk. 5^{37}], is represented as a constant cause of concern to Him [Mk. $4^{13, 40, 41}$, 6^{50-52}, 7^{18}, 8^{14-21}]. Exactly halfway through the gospel, however, there is a change. As soon as St. Peter, in the name of the disciples, has confessed his Lord's Messiahship (a truth which they are forbidden to reveal), the coming suffering and rejection, with their sequel in resurrection, are openly proclaimed, and very soon the journey to the south begins. The journey is preceded indeed by a revelation of the Lord's divine glory; but this is given only for a brief moment, and only—and even so under the seal of secrecy—to the three foremost of the twelve. The curtain of the divinity, perhaps we may say, is

---

[1] It may also be noticed how in Mk. 3^{31-35}, immediately before the parable chapter, 4^{1-34}, in which a distinction is made between 'those who were about Him with the twelve' and 'those outside' [4^{10-11}], the Lord, when told that His brethren after the flesh are seeking Him, declares His true brethren to be those, whoever they may be, who do the will of God. In Mt. 12^{49} the reference here to the disciples is made explicit.

beginning to be raised, but with extreme reserve. In the course of the journey to the south emphasis is laid more than once on the inability of the disciples to grasp the meaning of that which their Lord teaches is about to happen; nor are we led to suppose that they understood any better His entry into the city or His drastic action in the temple. But before the detailed narrative of the passion begins, the evangelist in ch. 13 records two momentous utterances of the Lord. First, the coming destruction of the Jewish temple is foretold, and second, now once more only to a chosen few of the disciples, and in private, the future issue of events is described. These are represented as including crises of extreme distress, to be followed by the break up of the natural order, and finally the coming of the Son of man. Clearly St. Mark, by inserting this chapter at this point wishes his readers, as they prepare to face the story of the passion, to bear in mind that, although they are not to expect the experience of the Church to be different from the experience of its Lord, and although the natural order itself will be dissolved, yet the end and climax is to be His coming in glory, a glory to be shared by His elect. In the story of the passion itself two moments only need to be noticed here. First, the Lord, during His examination by the Sanhedrin, publicly, and for the first time, announces His Messiahship; at length the secret about His Person is out. And secondly, at the moment of the Lord's death the veil of the temple is rent in two from the top to the bottom; God has now made a full and complete revelation of Himself in the Person of His Son; and a bystander, the Roman centurion, is allowed to penetrate the significance of the death he has witnessed: 'Truly this man was the Son of God.' In proportion to the length of St. Mark's passion narrative his record of the discovery by the three women of the empty tomb is as brief as the reference to the resurrection at the end of the three proclamations of the coming passion [Mk. 8^{31}, 9^{31}, $10^{33, \; 34}$]. In the concluding verses of the book the reader is allowed to learn that the Lord's death and burial are not the end; but then the curtain falls, with the promise that the Lord leads the way for the disciples into Galilee. Although, therefore, in St. Mark's gospel the thought of the Lord's divine nature is never far away, the emphasis is chiefly on His human nature, and His work is portrayed as consisting in a series of separate successive events, and the culminating event of all is yet to be. His work in this gospel has a beginning, a middle, and an end; and as regards the finale, it is at present incomplete. Although the reader is given a key to unlock the mystery with which this gospel deals, namely the mystery of the Lord's Person, he is left looking to the future to explain, indeed to justify, the record of events up to the point at which the gospel ends, and if we try to place ourselves in the position of those who themselves took part in the events, we are likely to learn that the part to be played by the future must have seemed more important still. From other parts of the New Testament we gain intimations of how matters worked out for the immediate participants. They came to know that through their Lord's death, and His conquest of it for their sakes, they had received a new endowment which, so far as they were faithful to it in action, and frequently in action most unexpected by themselves (cf. Acts 10[28, 29], 26[19, 20]), went a long way to solve their problem. But not the whole way; the lamp which illumined their path was still not sight but faith [2 Cor. 5[7]]; and since the first members of the Church were Jews, they believed that at any moment a consummation might occur, when faith would vanish into sight.[1]

The fourth evangelist stands at a further stage along this development. Throughout his gospel the Lord is presented, to use the language of Heb. 1[3], as the effulgence of the Father's splendour and the full expression of the Father's being (cf. Jn. 10[30], 14[9]). It is hardly surprising that in this gospel 'the Son' is regarded as the most satisfactory title of the Lord, and that His work is set forth as throughout the activity of the Son who speaks and acts in relation to, and out of intimate union with, His Father. As such His knowledge of all men is complete, and He can read their hearts (cf. 1[47, 48], 4[17, 18], 5[42], 6[64]). If He questions a disciple, it is not to gain information, but to put him to the test (6[5, 6]). Introducing His words with a solemn assurance of truth, He can say, 'Before Abraham came into existence, I AM' [8[58]]. He knows all that is to come upon Him [18[4]]; that the Father has placed all things into His hands [3[35], 13[3]]; that from God He came and to God He goes [13[3], 16[28]]; and that at the end He has fulfilled the trust committed to Him [19[28]]. There is a corresponding majesty about His Person; when He confronts those who have come to arrest Him, they are

---

[1] The student of both the Old and New Testaments will probably find it of value to bear in mind a remark attributed to Edward Caird: 'To the Jew religious insight always took the form of foresight.'

helpless until He has made certain dispositions for the disciples; only after this has been done are the officers able to proceed [18$^{4-12}$]; and in His presence, at a certain moment, not only the disciples [6^{19}] but Pilate [19^8] are conscious of fear. Finally, the Lord's last and chief work, the passion, is present also, in a measure, throughout; this is clear from the Baptist's words at 1^{29}, the Lord's action at Jerusalem in 2$^{13-22}$, and the steadily increasing determination and efforts of the Jews to kill Him [5^{18}, 7^1, 8^{59}, 10^{31}, 11^{53}].

On the other hand, all through this gospel it is also emphasized that He, who is not only Son of God but also Son of man, has in obedience to the Father a mission to fulfil, which is to be worked out during the days of His flesh. He must be lifted up [3^{14}, 8^{28}, 12^{32}]; He and His must work, while daylight lasts, the works of Him who sent Him [9^4]; is He not to drink the cup which the Father has given Him? [18^{11}]. Although at any and every moment that which sustains Him is the performance of the work, and the fulfilment of the will, of the Father who sent Him [4^{34}], only at the close can He say that this work has been accomplished [17^4; cf. 19^{30}]. And even in this gospel we read of the Lord's weariness [4^6] and thirst [4^7, 19^{28}]. In all this St. John is in accord with the earlier evangelists. Thus in Mark the supreme hour does not arrive till 14^{41}; indeed, as late as 14^{36}, the Lord has prayed that, if it be possible, it may pass away from Him; and in John we are told three times [2^4, 7^{30}, 8^{20}] that the Lord's hour has not, as yet, come; it is at 12^{23} that we first learn of its arrival (cf. 13^1, 17^1). None the less, in two important passages during the ministry [4^{23}, 5^{25}] the Lord says, 'The hour cometh, and now is', and these words are true also of all that is narrated in this gospel. Every event in it from the beginning to the end, has a double aspect; up to a point it is in itself the hour; but it also points forward; and the forward aspect, as we should expect in a religion having its roots and origin in Judaism, claims priority.

It seems, then, that the Person of the Lord is set before the reader of St. John's gospel chiefly, although not exclusively, in the light of an inner truth or reality usually thought to be, if existent at all, at any rate concealed from mens' eyes, as long as they live in this world. The evangelist thus unfolds the secret or mystery which is a strongly marked feature of the Lord's ministry in the earlier gospels, especially St. Mark's. But the element of secrecy has disappeared (for an apparent exception to this, at 7^{10}, see p. 177). The Lord frequently throughout the ministry reveals the truth about His Person both in word and action.[1] Those who accost Him as Rabbi (1^{38}), or know Him as Jesus of Nazareth (1^{45}), also recognize at once His Messiahship (1^{41}), divinity, and kingship (1^{49}), and find in Him the Figure promised in the Jewish scripture [1^{45}]. At the beginning of the ministry it seems that for some time the Lord does not point directly to Himself. The truths conveyed in such verses as 2^{19}, $3^{13, 14}$ are indirect. At 4^{26}, however, the Lord makes Himself known to the woman of Samaria, and in 5^{19-47}, His address to the Jews, although in the first part [5^{19-29}] He uses chiefly the third person, speaking of 'the Son', yet in the rest (5^{30-47}) He passes to the first person (cf. 3^{14} in the third person with the similar teaching in 12^{32} in the first person). In ch. 6 He tells the multitude and the Jews plainly that they must look for sustenance to Him. From the period of the next visit to Jerusalem there is no reserve, and at 18^{20}, when questioned by the high priest about His disciples and His teaching, the Lord replies, 'I have spoken openly to the world; I ever taught in synagogues, and in the temple, where all the Jews come together; and in secret spake I nothing.' Since in the earlier gospels the Lord's teaching by parable is closely connected with the mystery or secret of the Kingdom of God, it may be for this reason that parables of the kind found in these gospels do not occur in John. Certainly, the only occasion when teaching of a somewhat similar sort is given in 10^{1-5} (though the Greek word used for it is different from that used in the other gospels), the evangelist adds a note in 10^6 that the teaching was not understood.

But it is not only the Person of the Lord Himself which is set before us in John in the light of a truth or reality thought to be, if existent at all, at any rate hidden from men's eyes as long as they are in the world. Those who come into contact with Him, although clearly men of flesh and blood, are also presented or revealed, especially when they are portrayed in groups (e.g. the disciples, the multitude, the Jews), in a new, or at any rate stronger, light as compared with that in which they appear in the earlier gospels, a light which in some cases shows them to be in darkness (9^{41}).

---

[1] In John the incarnation and passion are not regarded as a humiliation of the Lord, as they are regarded, for example, in Phil. 2^{6-8}. Rather, in and by them the Lord reveals His own and His Father's glory (1^{14}, 2^{11}, $17^{4, 5}$).

'The man who chooses his side is seldom so good or so bad as his cause.' This maxim should be kept in mind when we consider the severe strictures passed in this gospel on particular groups in connexion with their attitude to the Lord. In John the passage from one group to another is always open for the individual, e.g. 8^{30}, 11^{45} (and conversely 6^{66}), as also that from one state of belief to another—e.g. the ascending order in $9^{12, \ 17, \ 33, \ 38}$. Further, we have to remember the teaching of such passages as 6^{44}, 12^{39-41}. The choice by the individual is subject to influences we cannot estimate. St. John shows us the forces at work, good and evil, beneath the surface of human life, these forces being revealed with special clearness at the time, and by the fact, of the incarnation of the Lord; but it may be suggested that no attempt should be made, in our understanding of this gospel, or, if we follow its teaching, of human life itself, to draw final conclusions, in other words, to judge (cf. Mt. 7^1). If it is asked how, in view of the open revelation of Himself by the Lord, the multitude and the Jews can have played the parts assigned to them in this gospel, possibly St. John would have reminded the questioner that the world, as such, although it is the object of God's love [3^{16}] and the Lord was sent to save it [3^{17}, 12^{47}], cannot recognize or know the truth; as such, it cannot see or enter into the Kingdom of God [$3^{3, \ 5}$]. This feature of John will often come before us in the course of the exposition; it will suffice here to notice it briefly.

(a) The multitude

In Mark the reaction of those who form the multitude or crowd, both to the Lord's teaching and to His acts of power (on one occasion the fact of His arrival, 9^{15}), is astonishment [1^{22}], amazement [1^{27}, 2^{12}], stupefaction [7^{37}]; more than once their thronging tends to make His task impossible [1^{33}, 2^4, $3^{9, \ 20}$], and He has to avoid them [1^{35}, 7^{33}; cf. 9^{25}]. None the less, their need and shepherdless state evoke His compassion [6^{34}, 8^2]; and although, as we have seen, He normally uses parables when He teaches them [4^{1-34}], the teaching is sometimes more direct [7^{14}, 8^{34}], and in an important context it is asserted as a universal truth that what is hidden is hidden only in order that it may be revealed, and that what is kept secret is kept secret only in order that it may come to light; and the Lord's hearers are forthwith urged and bidden to exercise their understanding of His words. In John, a gospel in which no one is ever astonished (the strongest verb used in this connexion is 'to marvel', 3^7, 4^{27}, $5^{20, 28}$, $7^{15, 21}$), the Lord is indeed found avoiding the multitude at 5^{13}, but in ch. 6 He feeds it physically and spiritually, and such a passage as 11^{42} illustrates His wish to save it. Normally, however, in this gospel, the weaker features of the multitude are brought to light: its rash impulsiveness [6^{15}, $12^{12, 13}$], the diversity of its opinions [7^{12}, 12^{29}], its fear of the authorities [7^{13}; cf. 9^{22}], its perplexities [7^{31}, 12^{34}], its shallowness [$12^{9, 17, 18}$], its low ideals [6^{26}]. In John, unlike the synoptists, we do not hear of the multitude after the ministry is over. It appears for the last time in 12^{34}, asking a question which remains unanswered: in St. John's account of the passion only the two diametrically opposed forces appear, those of the Father and those of the prince of this world.

(b) The Jews

In Matthew and Mark the term 'the Jews' occurs only in the editorial contexts Mt. 28^{15}, Mk. 7^3; in Luke we meet it also at 7^3, 23^{51}, exceptions which only serve to test the general rule. In these gospels hostility to the Lord (in Mark though on a smaller scale than in John it is present almost from the beginning, cf. Mk. 2^{6-7}, 3^6), is normally expressed by particular parties, especially Pharisees or Sadducees, or both. But throughout John His opponents are 'the Jews', the term occurring some seventy times, while the Pharisees are mentioned barely twenty times, and the Sadducees not at all. In the first chapter it is a delegation from the Jews—more narrowly defined in 1^{24} as the Pharisees—which comes, not indeed to undergo John's baptism (contrast Mt. 3^7) but to inquire into his office and credentials. To the delegation, as to his own disciples, the Baptist offers his witness; but unlike his disciples, who through it gain acquaintance with the Lord (1^{35-39}), the members of the delegation show no interest in the momentous announcement made to them by John ($1^{26, 27}$). The Jews' first contact with the Lord Himself is at 2^{18}; after His purification of the temple they desire a sign to justify His action. In the view of the evangelist signs have their part to play in life; thus the Baptist was enabled by a sign to see, and so to give his witness to the Lord ($1^{33, 34}$); but it seems that a certain disposition in the recipient is essential if the sign is to be understood, and the Jews have not this disposition.

To one of their leaders, Nicodemus, the Lord in ch. 3 reveals the need of a new birth for him who would see or enter the kingdom of God. Not only is a baptism by water necessary; it must be accompanied or followed by a baptism by spirit; but before the Lord can point towards the source which makes this further baptism possible [3¹³⁻¹⁵], the bewildered Nicodemus can follow Him no longer [3⁹, ¹⁰]. In ch. 5 the Jews are found persecuting the Lord because He has cured an infirm man upon the sabbath—a cause of difference prominent also in the other gospels—and when He replies by a reference to His Father's unintermitted work and to His own action correspondingly, their search for ways and means to do away with Him increases. The Lord's address which follows reveals to the reader for the first time the deeper causes of the difference between Him and the Jews. The Lord Himself, as the object of the Father's love, has a full and immediate knowledge of the Father, who has delivered to Him, the Son, the supreme attributes of life and judgement; He, who is moving among men as one with them, already gives life to whom He will, and already judges righteous judgement, since His judgement is one with that of the Father, and He seeks not His own will but the will of Him who sent Him. It is not His task to bear witness of Himself, for the Father bears, and already has borne, witness to Him. But the Jews to whom the Lord is speaking have never heard the Father's voice nor seen His form. Like is discerned by like, and it is their own origin [8⁴⁴] which prevents the Jews from discerning the Father in the Lord. For a time they have been willing to sun themselves in the light of the Baptist [5³⁵, cf. Mt. 21²⁶], but his word and work were of necessity temporary and partial, and the word and work of the Lord are permanent, and the Jews' disbelief in the Lord shows that the Father's word does not remain in them. Whereas the Lord's measure is the Father's will, the Father's love, their measure is esteem and reputation among men; and Moses himself, the very man in whom they trust, condemns them here. Throughout the record of the ministry the Jews are presented as those who claim to sit in judgement on the Lord, and to examine those who are in any way connected with Him [5¹², 9¹⁵, ¹⁹, ²⁴, ²⁶]. But they are blind to the significance of His presence [8²⁵, 15²²⁻²⁴], and since they are not 'of the truth', they cannot hear His voice [18³⁷], they do not understand His speech because they cannot hear His word [8⁴³], and similarly they misinterpret His works [10²⁵, ³², ³³, ³⁷, ³⁸]. The Father, therefore, cannot draw them to the Lord [6⁴⁴]; they are not part of the Father's gift to the Lord [6³⁷]. In 8⁴⁴ the reader learns of their paternity, and in 8²¹, ²⁴ of the fate which lies before them if they persist in their unbelief. Thus the inability to hear, see, and understand, a characteristic especially of the disciples in the earlier gospels, is seen in John as the especial characteristic of the Jews; but whereas the mystery of the kingdom of God has been granted, in spite of their limitations, to the former [Mk. 4¹¹], the latter, unless they believe, will die in their sin.

(c) *The Baptist*

In Mark, and still more definitely in Matthew, the role assigned to the Baptist is that of Elijah, who in him returns, in accordance with the prophecy of Malachi 4⁵, as the immediate herald, divinely sent, of the coming Messiah. In Luke, the gospel which opens with a detailed account of the Baptist's wonderful conception and birth, the only specific reference to the Baptist in connexion with Elijah is in 1¹⁷, where we read that he is to go before *God*, (*B* reads 'he will approach'), in the spirit and power of an Elijah; and similarly at 1⁷⁶ he is to be called the prophet of the *Most High*; but in spite of this change of emphasis, by which in Luke a more independent function seems to be assigned to the Baptist in connexion with the Lord, St. Luke, quoting in 3¹⁶, ¹⁷ words drawn from the sayings of the Baptist in Mark and elsewhere, seems to accept the view which regarded John, who baptized with water, as the forerunner of the Mightier than he, who will baptize in Holy Spirit and fire; cf. also Lk. 7²⁷.

St. John follows his predecessors in that in his gospel the Baptist contrasts himself with One who, although coming after him, is immeasurably greater than himself [1²⁷], but the following divergences from them, or changes of emphasis, are of importance. In this gospel (*a*) John is never called the Baptist, nor is his baptism of the Lord mentioned, and his task as a baptizer is less strongly emphasized than his work of witness. (*b*) It is asserted much more strongly than in the earlier gospels that He who comes after John in the succession of time none the less takes rank before him [1¹⁵, ²⁷]; that He was when John himself was not [1¹⁵, ³⁰]. Nor will John accept for a moment the title of Elijah, or that of any other office [1²⁰, ²¹, ²⁵, 3²⁸]; he is but a voice [1²³], giving witness [1⁷, ¹⁵, ¹⁹, ³², ³⁴, 3²⁶, 5³³], and thus preparing the way of the Lord [1²³]. (*c*) We read in 3²²⁻²⁴ that the Lord and His disciples, and John, baptize concurrently, but that when the Lord learns that news of His increasing following, as compared with that of John, has reached the ears of the Pharisees, He leaves Judaea for His second visit to Galilee [4$^{1-3}$]. A note is added that the Lord Himself did not baptize, this task being committed to His disciples. (*d*) Before the Lord thus leaves for Galilee, we are told that John, on hearing of the increasing scope of the Lord's work (which began, it will be remembered, at a wedding in 2$^{1-11}$), testifies to the completion of his joy, since he, the friend of the Bridegroom, of Him who has the bride, has heard the Bridegroom's voice [3^{29}]. John himself is of the earth [3^{31}] and must henceforth decrease [3^{30}], whereas to the extension of the work of Him who comes from above, from heaven [3^{31}], there can be no limit, as also to the joy which is His and which He bestows [15^{11}], a joy of which those who receive it cannot be deprived [16$^{22, 24}$]. In the same strain John is later described as a lamp to show the way [5^{35}]; but a lamp, however serviceable at night, loses its brilliance and attractiveness, and is no longer needed, when the sun has risen; cf. 8^{12}.

In the exposition of the prologue (p. 81) it will be suggested that the Baptist, in addition to his own unique work as the immediate herald of the Lord, represents all those who at any time or place, thanks to their participation in the life of the Logos, are enabled to prepare His way. It may thus become possible to understand the presentation of the role of the Baptist in this gospel. In Josephus he is a preacher of righteousness, and baptizes; in Matthew and Mark he offers, along with a stern call to repentance, a baptism of purification in preparation for the coming of a Greater than himself; in Luke his message can be described, like that of the Lord, as good tidings [3^{18}]. But the last of the evangelists has become aware that prophecy itself, whether in the person of Elijah or of any other, is the gift of, and is due only to, the Logos, now incarnate in the Lord; the utmost therefore that any man, however great, can do— and there is no greater man than a great prophet—is to bear witness to Him; apart from Him even His disciples can do nothing (with 15^5 cf. 1 Cor. 3^7, 15^{10}, 2 Cor. 12^{11}, Phil. 2^{13}). Accordingly the Baptist is at best (cf. Mt. 11^{11}, Lk. 7^{28}) a voice, one whose mission is by word and deed to try to turn what, but for the presence and work of the Logos, is a wilderness [1^{23}] into the fruitful garden of the Lord. And therefore the Baptist's message is presented in this gospel as supremely and solely one of witness.

The reader will recall that when John is first mentioned in the prologue in 1^{6-8} it is emphasized that he was not the light, but was sent from God to bear witness of the light, a light having, like life itself, its origin and fount in the Logos [1^4], but as yet not identified with any human person. After 1^{14}, however, where we read that the Logos took our nature upon Him in a single human being, the Baptist's witness becomes personal [1^{15}], and he now bears witness, not only to the light, but to the Lord who, being the Logos, is Himself the light. Similarly in 1^{19-34} the Baptist twice makes clear that originally he did not know the Lord [$1^{31, 33}$]. At first he had to walk by faith, fulfilling the mission laid upon him to baptize in water, as yet not fully aware that his task was no less than to make the infinitely Greater than himself manifest to Israel. Only after he had been divinely enlightened by a sign, promised to him at the outset of his work [1^{33}] and now fulfilled [1^{32}], was he enabled to see clearly, and to bear witness to the Lord as Son of God [1^{34}].

In the last scene in which John appears in this gospel, that in 3^{22-36}, it is made clear that his work has been faithfully carried out (cf. 10^{41}); the influence of the Bridegroom, to whom he has borne witness, is steadily increasing (cf. 4^1), and therefore John's joy is complete [3^{29}]; as far as his own work is concerned, he can now depart in peace. Nor does he any more need the sign which before was necessary [1^{32-34}]; he has heard the Bridegroom's voice for himself.

(d) The disciples

We have already had occasion to notice, in the first part of St. Mark's record of the ministry, the Lord's concern with the slowness of the disciples and their lack of insight into the meaning of His teaching and acts of power (see p. 58). For, as compared with 'those outside' [Mk. 4^{11}], they are within; to them, that is to the twelve along with others of His entourage, the mystery or secret of the kingdom of God has been granted, and to them in private all things are explained [4^{34}]. We might have expected that in the latter half of St. Mark's gospel, from 8^{27} onwards, after St. Peter's declaration in the name of the disciples of his Master's Messiahship, there would be a change, especially since the charge of silence previously laid on those with a knowledge of His Person [Mk. $1^{25,}$ ^{34}, $3^{11, 12}$] is forthwith laid on the disciples in respect of their confession [Mk. 8[30]]. But this is not the case; for it is at once shown how little understanding St. Peter has of the import of his own confession, and the Lord now calls to Him the multitude as well as the disciples [Mk. 8[34]], and instructs it also in the doctrine of the cross. None the less, and although the disciples show themselves as little able in the latter half of Mark to grasp the doctrine of life through death [Mk. 9[30-32], 10[32-34]], and the implications which it involves [Mk. 9[33-37, 38-40], 10[13-16, 41-45]], as they were in the first half to grasp the doctrine of their Lord's Messiahship, it is made clear that the hope of the world is still to be regarded as, above all, in their keeping. When the teaching about the Son of man and His future is renewed a second time, it is given in private to the disciples [Mk. 9[30, 31]], and, on a third occasion, only to the twelve [Mk. 10[32-34]], while at Mk. 14[33-42], as previously at Mk. 5[37-43], three of the twelve are taken apart, and in even greater privacy than usual are allowed a special revelation of their Master. And in Mk. 13[3-37] the Lord makes known to four disciples the future working of the divine economy, teaching them that their part in the drama is (*a*) to rely upon the Holy Spirit as their mouthpiece [Mk. 13[11]], and (*b*) to be themselves, and all men with them, wakeful and alert [Mk. 13[35-37]]. Moreover, in Mk. 14[17-25], in the setting of the Lord's last meal with the twelve, they are warned that they, as a body, are not without responsibility for the death which is about to come upon their Master; one of themselves, one who is even now sharing the meal, will lead the way to His arrest [Mk. 14[17-21, 43]], but at the same time their Lord dedicates Himself to death as a sacrifice on behalf of those whom He came to save, and gives Himself to the disciples in a union which, although it is only to be achieved and maintained at the cost of His own life, is to issue in a new life (if we follow St. Matthew, we may add 'with them') in the kingdom of God [Mk. 14[22-25]]. As is revealed in the subsequent words, the last words addressed to the twelve as a body, they all, and their leader Peter more than any, are about to lose their confidence in Him and be scattered; and it must be so; and although they, one and all, protest their loyalty, the only ray of hope held out is the Lord's promise, that after He is raised up, He will lead the way for them into Galilee. And at the end of this gospel [Mk. 16[8]] the reader, who thus far has been admitted only to a knowledge of the triumph of his Lord, is left in expectation of the promised baptism in Holy Spirit [Mk. 1[8]], to descend upon the disciples presumably in Galilee, as a result of their Lord's achievement for them and for all men at Jerusalem.

The prologue to St. John's gospel has already taught the reader that, although creation, and mankind above all, owes its life and illumination to the Logos, yet when the Logos came to His own creation, those who were His own did not receive Him [1¹¹]. Happily, the rejection was never universal, and in 1¹²⁻¹⁴ the reader learns of some who, having welcomed the Logos, and believing on 'His name', were empowered to become children of God, and to receive a new divine birth. Among these were those of the Lord's contemporaries who, when the Logos assumed human nature and moved as man among men, not only welcomed Him, but had sight of His unique glory, and in this gospel these men are usually described, as in the earlier gospels, by the word 'disciples.'

Certain of them, before the ministry begins, are drawn into the company of the Lord, and forthwith ascribe to Him various religious titles and offices (including that of Messiah), all based on their existing Jewish faith and hope [1⁴¹, ⁴⁵, ⁴⁹]. But John is careful to make clear that only after the first sign of the ministry at Cana of Galilee, with its revelation of the Lord's glory, do the Lord's disciples as such come to believe on Him.[1] Among them there was indeed an inner circle called the twelve; but it seems as if St. John, like St. Mark (Mk. 4¹⁰ and Mk. 2¹⁴ compared with Mk. 3¹⁶⁻¹⁹) is concerned not to emphasize too sharply the line between the twelve and the rest of the disciples. For in St. John's gospel the twelve, as such, are mentioned only twice, and in each case the context should be noticed. First, at the end of ch. 6; when the Lord declares that the twelve were indeed the object of His choice, and asks if they, like many of His disciples, wish to leave Him, He proceeds at once to reveal that even among the twelve evil is at work. And secondly, in ch. 20, the first reunion of the Lord takes place with 'the disciples', and He bestows the Holy Spirit on them [20¹⁹⁻²³]; and we learn further in 20²⁴ in connexion with the event of a week later, that Thomas 'one of the twelve' was not present on

[1] In Jn. 1¹⁹⁻⁵¹ they show no certain evidence of the new birth from above, 3³, which through the coming of the Lord will, as it were, rebaptize these titles, as well as those who use them. This is emphasized in Philip's words at the end of 1⁴⁵; at present he can speak of the Lord, although, as he admits, the Lord was foretold in the law and the prophets, only in reference to the (reputed) place of His origin, and His (it is assumed, purely human) parentage. In this last respect Philip is still like the Jews, cf. 6⁴².

the first occasion. The same tendency may perhaps be seen in ch. 1. Of the five men who first become attached to the Lord's company, three, Andrew, Simon, and Philip, are familiar names among the twelve; but that of Nathanael, to whom the promise of 1^{51} is made, a promise applying to them all, is otherwise unknown to us.[1] On the other hand, the actual choice and appointment of the twelve are not recorded by John, any more than they are by Matthew, and possibly the reader is thereby reminded that the Lord's choice and appointment of them (as indeed of all disciples) are no mere events of a particular day; these are the men entrusted to the Lord in the eternal counsels of God [$17^{6, 11}$]; they belong to the Father, and therefore to the Lord [$17^{9, 10}$]; they have received His glory, that glory which He Himself received from the Father [17^{22}]; they are the especial objects of His [13^1] and the Father's love [17^{23}].

In the light of the above it is not surprising that as the result of the Lord's first sign the disciples are said to believe on Him [2^{1-11}], and henceforth, as we are perhaps to assume from 2^{12}, remain in more or less permanent attendance upon Him. Twice, however, the evangelist, after describing an incident in the ministry, adds a note, in the first case [2^{22}] suggesting, and in the second case [12^{16}] explicitly stating, that at the time when the incident occurred the disciples did not understand its significance, which only became clear to them after the Lord's ministry was over; in other words when, as a result of His glorification, they had received the gift of the Spirit.[2] This incomplete insight on the disciples' part

---

[1] The tendency to identify Nathanael with Bartholomew, a name which is only a patronymic, Bar Tholmai, is said to date from the Middle Ages. It rests on the fact that in three lists of the twelve in the synoptic gospels (though not in that of Acts 1^{13}) the name Bartholomew occurs immediately after that of Philip, with whom Nathanael is associated in Jn. 1^{43-45}.

[2] This function of the Spirit in reminding the disciples of the Lord's words and in making clear the meaning of both His actions and His words is strongly emphasized in 14^{26}, 16^{12-15} (cf. also 13^7); and it is permissible to think that the passages contain a lesson for all believers. At the moment when an event occurs or a word is spoken, its true import is unlikely to be, indeed often cannot be, completely apprehended; but just as the Lord had made known to His disciples all things that He heard from His Father (15^{15}), although they could not appreciate this at the time, and could enter into their heritage, under the influence of the Spirit, only by degrees, so it must and will be for the believer as regards his understanding of his own experience. And a further point emphasized in this gospel is that the particular word or event is sometimes seen in its relation to earlier events and words, particularly those of scripture or prophecy (2^{22}, 12^{16}, 20^9), only as a result of later enlightenment, the word or event in question thus

during the ministry is on the whole in accordance with the impression which we receive from elsewhere in the first twelve chapters of this gospel. At the cleansing of the temple they recall Ps. 69[9] and have an inkling of the passion [2[17]], although not as yet, it seems, also of the resurrection [2[22]; cf. 12[16]]. In 3[22-24] they and the Lord and the Baptist concurrently baptize, the Lord, it appears, supervising, but not Himself taking part in, the work of His disciples [4[1, 2]]. In ch. 4 they have gone away from their Master in order to purchase provisions during His important conversation with the Samaritan woman, and on their return fail to understand His teaching about that which gives Him sustenance [4[8, 27, 31-34]], but in 4[35-38] they are told that they have not only entered on their evangelistic work, but are already reapers as well as sowers; even now they are engaged in reaping a harvest which they did not sow. In ch. 6 the Lord's disciples are present with Him [6[3]], and although Philip proves completely at a loss as regards the task before them [6[5-7]], the Lord is able to make use of a half-hearted suggestion of Andrew for the feeding of the multitude. The same night, when the disciples are crossing the lake and see the Lord drawing near to the boat they are afraid, but although unnerved by their experience of the advent of the Lord [6[19]], they are willing to receive Him in their midst [6[21]]; and it may be partly as a result of this experience that when, after the Lord's words making clear that in the preservation of union with Him life itself must be sacrificed [6[51-65]], many of His disciples leave Him, the twelve, through Simon Peter, declare that they desire to come only to Him whose words confer eternal life, and whom they believe, and know, to be the Holy One of God—a title given to the Lord in the earlier gospels [Mk. 1[24], Lk. 4[34]] only by one who, being possessed, has an insight denied to other men into the nature of Him with whom he had to do. The Lord in reply makes clear that they, the twelve, were indeed the object of His choice, but by His veiled reference to an evil personality among them we are reminded of the coming passion, and of the part which they, the twelve, will and must have in bringing it about. In 9[2] they are found putting a typically Jewish problem to the Lord, who in His reply refers to the coming revelation of divine action, a task in which they also have a part to play [9[3, 4]]. In ch. 11 the disciples express concern at

becoming linked both with the foreshadowing of it in the past, and the understanding of it in the future.

their Master's intention to expose Himself again to danger, and two further utterances illustrate very well both their imperfect comprehension on the one hand, and on the other hand their dogged faithfulness. When the Lord says [11¹¹] that He is going in order to awake Lazarus out of sleep, they reply that if Lazarus is fallen asleep he will recover; while when the Lord tells them that Lazarus is dead, and adds 'Let us go to him', Thomas says to his fellow disciples [11¹⁶] 'Let us also go, that we may die with Him'— that is, with the Lord.

At 11⁵⁴ the disciples are with the Lord in His final period of retirement; and at 13¹, the Lord's hour having come, we learn that the disciples are, in a peculiar sense, His own, the objects not only of His choice [6⁷⁰], but of His love. During supper He cleanses them in a manner which, as He warns them, they cannot as yet fully understand [13⁷], but He also discloses that there is in their number one of evil intent, an intent which will issue in action [13², ²¹]. Judas, of whom we last heard in 12⁴⁻⁶, at the Lord's bidding now withdraws, and the Lord is able to reveal His triumph fully and without reserve to those that remain. In spite of their still imperfect understanding [14⁵, ⁸, ²², 16¹⁷, ¹⁸) and the still mis-guided action of 18¹⁰ (contrast 18³⁶), the Lord, who has from the Father the gift of the Spirit in full [1³²⁻³⁴], indeed in infinite, measure [3³⁴], proceeds in chs. 14 to 17 to raise the disciples, those given Him out of the world [17⁶] by the Father [17²], into the same sphere and unity of the Spirit, even while they remain in the world [17¹¹, ¹⁵]. In thus imparting His own self to the disciples, the Lord sees the glory or triumph of the Son of Man, and the triumph of God in Him [13³¹]; this is now an accomplished fact, although the final work of the passion, as an event, is yet to be [13³², ³³]. The characteristic features, then, of the picture of the disciples in this gospel are the Lord's emphasis on His choice of them [6⁷⁰, 13¹⁸, 15¹⁶, ¹⁹], the fuller knowledge and belief granted to, and shown by, them during the ministry in respect of their Master's Person [2¹¹, 6⁶⁸, ⁶⁹], in spite of their great slowness of apprehension, a slowness showing itself especially in the case of individual members of the college of the twelve; but, above all, the heights to which they are raised, as it were in advance, by the Lord's disclosure to them of His inner heart in the conversation and prayer of chs. 13 to 17.

(e) *The world*

It is in these same chs. 13 to 17 that the distinction is made most clearly and sharply between the Lord's disciples and what the evangelist calls 'the world'. At 13¹ the Lord's hour, which has now come, is described as that in which He is to 'transfer from this world to the Father', and indeed, before chs. 13 to 17 are ended, He will be found speaking as though He has already left it [16⁴, 17¹¹]. He now therefore concentrates on 'his own who are in the world' [13¹; cf. 17¹¹], and who will remain in it [17¹⁵], although they will not be of it [17¹⁴], any more than is their Master [17¹⁶; cf. 8²³]. In a few hours the world, which cannot receive the Holy Spirit [14¹⁷], will behold the Lord no more [14¹⁹]; for the manifestation to the world is now over, although Judas (not Iscariot) does not as yet recognize any great or inevitable distinction between the disciples and the world [14²²]. There is, however, such a distinction, and because of it the Lord is able to leave the disciples a gift, His peace, a gift peculiarly His own, because He has won it for them. And since He has been able to achieve this only at the cost of His death, the way in which He bestows His gift is different indeed from that of the world [14²⁷, 16³³]. We have learned at 12³¹ that the ruler of the world is to be expelled, and he is now said to be at hand. He has no part or lot in the Lord [14³⁰], who therefore will not speak much more with His disciples. None the less, the world is the ultimate object of God's love (cf. 3¹⁶) and purpose [17²³]; and therefore, in order that the world may know that the Lord loves the Father and is acting as He does because the Father so bade Him, the disciples are invited to rise and to go hence with Him, to action.

In 15¹⁻⁷ a big step forward is taken in the picture of the Husbandman, the Vine, and Branches, and at 15⁸ the disciples, who are the branches, learn that by bearing fruit it becomes possible to glorify the Lord's Father, and thereby to become disciples to the Lord. Indeed He no longer calls them slaves or emissaries [13¹⁶] but friends [15¹³ ff.], and 'in His name' [15¹⁶] and by abiding in His love [15¹⁰] they have the right to approach the Father directly. It therefore becomes possible for them in their mutual love [15¹⁷] to face the opposition of a hostile world [15¹⁸⁻²⁵], for the world loves 'its own', and therefore must inevitably hate those who are not of this world, but who have been chosen 'out of the world', as it first, and for the same reason [8²³], hated the Lord [15¹⁸]. But the Holy Spirit, whose spiritual coming to them will replace the Lord's external presence, will enable them to stand their ground in giving witness to their Master [15²⁶ᶠ·]; for in three ways the world will come under the judgement or condemnation of the Holy Spirit [16⁸⁻¹¹].

First, as regards sin. Whereas none of the Lord's enemies was able to find fault or flaw in Him and yet refused belief on Him, the Holy Spirit will show that the world's wrongdoing is due precisely to disbelief in the Lord. Secondly, as regards righteousness. The Lord has been in the world, and the world has not recognized Him [1¹⁰], although He was the express image of the Father [14⁹, cf. Heb. 1³], to whom He is now returning. And yet He is the standard of righteousness at which men should aim. In Jeremiah 23⁶ the name to be given to the Messiah is 'The Lord (is) our righteousness', and in Jeremiah 33¹⁶ the same name is promised to Jerusalem. This promise has now been fulfilled, but to the new Jerusalem, represented by the disciples. Their righteousness can never be of themselves [Phil. 3⁹]; it is a righteousness of faith [Rom. 9³⁰, 10⁶], resting on the righteousness of the Lord [1 Cor. 1³⁰], and this righteousness cannot be perfectly fulfilled by men as long as they remain 'in the world'. Thirdly, as regards judgement or condemnation. The devil is called the prince or ruler of this world, because, even to those who wish to do good, 'evil is present' [Rom. 7²¹]. He is not, however, truly its ruler, since the world came into being only through the Lord's creative activity [1³, ¹⁰, see pp. 79 ff.], and now, thanks to the Lord's death, he has been expelled from his position of apparent authority in it [12³¹]; and here [16¹¹], for the same reason, he is said to have been condemned or judged. The world, therefore, in so far as it is under the authority of its ruler the devil, falls under the condemnation of the Holy Spirit, and although the disciples remain in the world, of which the devil may seem to be the ruler, yet he does not, or need not, have dominion over them [Rom. 6¹⁴], since (as they know through the enlightenment given them by the Spirit) he already stands condemned.

The outlook of the disciples, therefore, is bound to be different from that of the world [16²⁰]. At the present moment, for example, the disciples have sorrow because their Master is leaving them [16²²], and of this sorrow the world has no experience. But whereas the happiness of the world is not based on the elemental law of life

(16²¹) that joy can only come by way of a sorrow given through pain, and life only by way of death, and is therefore always in danger of impermanence, the joy which is available to the disciples, their Lord's own joy [15¹¹], a joy which brings them with Him into the presence of the Father [16²³], is a gift of which they cannot be deprived [16²²]. Their Lord came out from the Father into the world, and, His work accomplished, leaves the world and goes to the Father [16²⁸]. His path in the world was difficult, and so will be that of the disciples [16³³]; but in Him they can find peace. He overcame the world, and if they have courage, so can they—in Him.

In ch. 17 (see pp. 295 ff.) the Lord, who now is no more in the world [17¹¹], prays not for it [17⁹], but for those who were given to Him by the Father out of it (17⁶), and who are to remain in it (17¹¹). He speaks in the world as He does in order that the fullness of His joy may be in them [17¹³]. And although they are the object of the world's hatred, because they, like their Lord, are not of the world [17¹⁴, ¹⁶], yet He does not ask that they should be removed from the world, but that they should be kept from its evil [17¹⁵], and consecrated in the truth for their mission to the world [17¹⁷ ᶠᶠ·]. Besides praying for them, the Lord also prays for all believers on Him through the disciples' word, that through their union in mutual love, a union recalling, indeed reproducing, that of the Father and the Son, the world may believe not only that the Father sent the Son [17²¹], but also (through the glory given to them by the Son) that the Father's love for them is no less than His love for His Son, a love which existed before the foundation of the world [17²²⁻²⁴]. In this prayer therefore the world, although ignorant of the righteous Father, is none the less the scene in which the Father's name and love have been, and are, and are to be, made known.

THE GOSPEL ACCORDING TO

S. JOHN

I

The Introduction

A. 1¹⁻¹⁸ THE PROLOGUE

1 In the beginning was the Word, and the Word was with God, and the
2,3 Word was God. The same was in the beginning with God. All things
were made ¹by him; and without him ²was not anything made that hath
4,5 been made. In him was life; and the life was the light of men. And the
light shineth in the darkness; and the darkness ³apprehended it not.
6,7 There came a man, sent from God, whose name was John. The same
came for witness, that he might bear witness of the light, that all might
8 believe through him. He was not the light, but *came* that he might bear
9 witness of the light. ⁴There was the true light, *even the light* which
10 lighteth ⁵every man, coming into the world. He was in the world, and
11 the world was made ¹by him, and the world knew him not. He came unto
12 ⁶his own, and they that were his own received him not. But as many as
received him, to them gave he the right to become children of God, *even*
13 to them that believe on his name: which were ⁷born, not of ⁸blood, nor
14 of the will of the flesh, nor of the will of man, but of God. And the
Word became flesh, and ⁹dwelt among us (and we beheld his glory, glory
15 as of ¹⁰the only begotten from the Father), full of grace and truth. John
beareth witness of him, and crieth, saying, ¹¹This was he of whom I said,
He that cometh after me is become before me: for he was ¹²before me.

---

¹ *Or* through   ² *Or* was not anything made. That which hath been
made was life in him; and the life, &c.   ³ *Or* overcame. *See* ch. 12. 35
(*Gr.*).   ⁴ *Or* The true light, which lighteth every man, was coming   ⁵ *Or*
every man as he cometh   ⁶ *Gr.* his own things   ⁷ *Or* begotten
⁸ *Gr.* bloods.   ⁹ *Gr.* tabernacled.   ¹⁰ *Or* an only begotten from a
father   ¹¹ *Some ancient authorities read* (this was he that said).   ¹² *Gr.*
first in regard of me.

16,17 For of his fulness we all received, and grace for grace. For the law was
18 given ¹by Moses; grace and truth came ¹by Jesus Christ. No man hath
seen God at any time; ²the only begotten Son, which is in the bosom of
the Father, he hath declared *him*.

> ¹ *Or* through   ² *Many very ancient authorities read* God only begotten.

EXPOSITION OF 1¹⁻¹⁸

These verses give the key to the understanding of this gospel, and
make clear how the evangelist wishes his readers to approach his
presentation of the Lord's work and Person; and equally the rest
of the book will throw light on the contents of these verses. The
reader therefore should constantly recall this prologue, when in
the course of the rest of this gospel he meets such words as life,
light, glory, and truth, here used with reference to the Logos or
Word, and there with reference to the Lord.

Much of the prologue is written in the rhythm and style of
Hebrew poetry. The thought starts from eternity, from the being
of the divine life [1¹, ²], and thence passes to time [1³]. No doubt
the opening words recall Gen. 1¹ and therewith illustrate at the
outset the strongly Jewish colouring of this gospel. But, whereas
Genesis begins with the creation, in Jn. 1¹, ² we are taken behind or
beyond history and learn of the eternal existence of the Logos or
Word, Himself fully divine, with, or in relation to, God (cf. 17²⁴
ᵉⁿᵈ). Again, the O.T. expression 'the word of God' is not used; we
read of the Word absolutely, without qualification.

Although the word 'Logos' is of great importance, since it forms
the philosophical basis of St. John's doctrine of the Person of the
Lord, it is only applied to Him twice, at 1¹ in reference to His
eternal, divine life, and at 1¹⁴ᵃ in reference to His incarnation;
thereafter it is dropped in favour of the word 'Jesus', the historical
Person, who is the Logos become flesh. But it has thus been made
clear at the very beginning that the Lord's Person, in this gospel,
will be approached primarily from the divine side, by way of
the Logos doctrine, not, as in the earlier gospels, by way of the
Jewish messianic hope. And since no human intelligence can really
effect a synthesis of the human and the divine, we must not expect
that in this gospel the portrait of the Lord will be found to be fully
and completely human, any more than, in the other gospels, it is

fully and completely divine. The two kinds of portrait very nearly meet, but not quite (p. 56).

If, returning to 1¹, ², we ask how the Logos can be said to be God, fully divine, and yet to be also in relation to God, we may compare with due caution the language here used with that of certain O.T. passages, which speak of 'the name' of God. In these passages the name of God seems to be conceived as a manifestation of the being of God, distinct from but not independent of Him (cf. Ex. 33²¹, Deut. 12⁵, Ps. 54¹, and especially Is. 30²⁷). The term usually signifies an action of God in self-revelation; and the first words of Jn. 1¹⁴ describe the full, complete action of God in the revelation both of His nature and of His character.

At 1³, following the R.V. marginal rendering, we pass from the thought of the divine life, with which alone we were confronted at the outset, to the thought of creation; and in Hebrew fashion the two halves of the verse express the same truth, first positively, and then negatively. As in 1¹, ² the emphasis is still on the Logos; He is the Agent or Instrument or Medium in creation; and the verse teaches that (*a*) the created universe, unlike the Logos, is not eternal; and (*b*) the Logos is the source of all that exists, whenever or wherever this may be; nothing whatever exists in its own right, or apart from Him.

In 1⁴ᵃ, especially if we follow the R.V. mg for 1³, ⁴, the word 'life' means the right and power to bestow activity, to make alive; and at 1⁴ᵇ our thoughts are directed from creation to one particular part of creation, namely, to mankind. The words show that the life given to creation by and through the Logos, for mankind, takes also the form of illumination, the possibility of seeing and understanding. And this kind of light is not something external, like a lamp, giving a man light from outside himself, but is part of his being or life (cf. 12³⁶ and especially the last words of 11¹⁰). For life only comes fully into its own when it truly understands itself; and this understanding, this light, no less than the life or activity bestowed in creation, is granted by and through the Logos (cf. 8¹²).

In 1⁵ᵃ the past tense, used throughout 1¹⁻⁴, is dropped in favour of the present tense, and we are thus reminded that the shining of the light, which was manifested in creation and explains to man his true nature, is also (and very emphatically, as will be shown in the course of this gospel) a present fact; and therewith we read, for the first time, of 'the darkness'. The questions how, in view of the teaching of 1³, there can be darkness, or why men chose or choose to identify themselves with the darkness rather than with the light, are not answered by St. John, and should not be raised. All that can be said is that in religion, whenever such a word as light is used in a metaphorical sense, the presence, or at least the possibility, of its opposite, darkness, is also always implied. The problem is perhaps eased to some extent, if we reflect that in the higher religions, and in none more than in Christianity, great emphasis is laid on the essential connexion between the religious and the moral life; and the moral life is always conscious, if not of a struggle, at any rate of the need for choice between possible alternatives. Accordingly if men are given the possibility of walking in the light, in accordance with the law of their origin through the Logos [1³], this very possibility implies also their ability to choose to walk in the darkness, in obedience not to the law of their origin, but to a law of their own making. For them life does not, as it should, also signify light.

In 1⁵ᵇ, according to R.V. text, we learn that, although enlightenment, along with life itself, had been offered to mankind, there had been failure to discern the light. Men were in fact in darkness and had lost their way (cf. 12³⁵˒ ⁴⁶), and accordingly were bound to stumble (cf. 11¹⁰). For, like the light, the darkness is not only something external, of which those involved in it are or can be independent; it is also something internal; indeed, it is possible for those, who say that they see, in fact to be blind, i.e. in darkness [9⁴¹].

Hitherto no particular historical fact has been mentioned; but now at 1⁶ we read of an historical figure, divinely commissioned, and of the purpose of his mission. This purpose is expressed in positive form in 1⁷, and in negative form in 1⁸ (as in the two parts of 1³). It was, that he might bear witness to the (presence of the) light (cf. 1²⁶). [For the sake of clarity, in order to distinguish the John, now to be mentioned, from the evangelist, he will be described as the Baptist; but it should always be kept in mind that this title is not given to him in this gospel, in which at least as strong an emphasis is laid on his function as witness to the Lord as on his work of baptism.] There is no reference here to John the Baptist's work of baptism, but solely to his commission to bear testimony. The Baptist himself was not the light (he is described as a 'lamp' in 5³⁵), but the purpose of his testimony was that 'through him all men', not a few only or those of a single generation, 'might come to belief'; and therewith, at the outset of the book, as at its original close [20^{31}], we meet the important word belief, or rather the act of believing, on which great stress is laid in this gospel. This act of believing is men's response to the divine illumination offered in, by, and through the Logos; and we shall return to the thought of this illumination in 1^9.

But, before we do so, it may be felt that a pressing question should be answered; viz., at what point in this prologue do we pass from the thought of the work of the invisible Logos to that of the work of this same Logos incarnate in the Lord? On the one side 1^{1-5} certainly, and possibly also 1^{9-13}, are best understood as describing the relationship of the Logos to God, to creation, and to mankind, in the period before the Logos took our nature upon Him in the person of the Lord; and we are thus led up to the crowning historical event of 1^{14}. But on the other side 1^{6-8}, which separates 1^{1-5} from 1^{9-12}, unquestionably refers to the Baptist's work in bearing witness to the light, the function which will be ascribed to him, in relation to the incarnate Lord, throughout $1^{19}-12^{50}$; and further, does not 1^{11-13}, if not also such earlier verses as 4, 5, 9, 10, lead us instinctively to think of the historical ministry of Jesus Christ? 1^5, for example, would form an admirable summary of the Lord's ministry and its reception, as described in 2^1-12^{50}.

The solution to the problem may be that, although the incarnation of the Logos is not explicitly mentioned until 1^{14}, yet St. John wishes his readers to understand several of the earlier verses as a description both of the permanent work and functions of the Logos and of the Lord's historic life and work, since His historic life and work, as St. John will show in the course of his book, reproduce these permanent relations of the Logos with the world. Rightly understood, the Lord's ministry is, as it were, the relations, written small, of the Logos with mankind. It may be therefore for this reason that we encounter the Baptist and his work of witness as early as 1^{6-8}, because, although witness to the Logos is to be found always and everywhere, the Baptist uniquely represents this permanent, universal witness (cf. the reference in 1^7 to 'all men'), since this was his historical task at the time of the full, complete revelation of the Logos. It will be seen later that St. John frequently writes a passage or a narrative which is to be understood in more than one way.

At 1⁹ we return to think of the Logos, at the same time bearing in mind His coming historic manifestation in the Lord. Following R.V. mg in 1³, ⁴, we learned that the life which came into being in the Logos was the illumination of mankind; and we now read of the Logos as being Himself the true, genuine light, to whom the Baptist's (permanent or representative) task was to bear witness; and further, that He is the light of every human being born into the world, i.e. that He (and, it is implied, He only) can make clear to every individual the meaning and purpose of his life (cf. 8¹²). Just as in 1⁵ᵃ we read that the light shines in the darkness, so here in 1⁹ the present tense is again used of the illumination granted by the Logos. The illumination is in fact always and everywhere present, and witness is always and everywhere being given to it, but pre-eminently and uniquely in the early gospel-story about to be unfolded.

In 1⁵ a warning was given both of the existence of the darkness, and of its failure to grasp or understand the light. This dark side of the story is now [1¹⁰] developed more fully, and especially the part played in it by 'the world', a frequent and important term in John, used for the first time at the end of the preceding verse 1⁹. Every human being, we there learned, must live his life in the world (cf. 17¹⁵); and since the world originated in, and is the work of, the Logos, who enlightens every man from his birth onwards, it is open to man to live and understand his life in the light of this his origin, and in obedience to the Author of his being. From this point of view therefore the world may be regarded as the object of God's love [3¹⁶] and in the course of the book we shall learn that the Lord, who has come into the world [12⁴⁶] and gives it life [6³³, ⁵¹] and light [8¹²], is its Saviour [4⁴²] (cf. 1²⁹, 12⁴⁷). But in fact the world has not thus recognized its Maker; it has turned away from Him and refused the enlightenment offered, in the false belief that it owes its origin and obedience not to Him, but to itself; and in consequence the world will later be said 'not to know the Father' [17²⁵] and indeed 'to hate' the Lord [7⁷, 15¹⁸], who is not, any more than His kingdom [18³⁶], 'of the (this) world' [8²³, 17¹⁴, ¹⁶], and to have the devil as its 'prince' or ruler. The work of the incarnate Lord, however, will be shown to have resulted in the condemnation [16¹¹] and expulsion [12³¹] of this false ruler of the world; and at the end His prayer will be that through His disciples the world itself may be led to believe in His divine mission and credentials [17²¹, ²³].

1^11 repeats in a different form the teaching of 1^10. The Logos 'came to His own creation', this expression being parallel to 'the world' in 1^10a, b; but 'His own people', this expression now corresponding to the world in 1^10c, 'did not receive Him'. From 1^10a, b therefore we see what the response of the world should have been. It ought to have welcomed and received Him, in other words, believed on Him (cf. 2^11, 3^18, 36), but it was unwilling to follow the law of its origin and being [1^3] in obedience to the Logos, and so made itself into 'the world' of 1^10c, which opposes and resists Him. It is this lack of belief in the Logos which constitutes the sin of the world [1^29, 16^9]; and for this reason it becomes the subject, indeed the offspring [8^44], of the devil, who 'rules the world'. Some, however, in spite of the fact that they were 'in the world' (cf. 13^1, 17^11), did receive the Logos [1^12, 13]; they did not remain in the darkness and therefore had the light of life (cf. 8^12, 12^46); and to them was granted the 'right' or 'authority' of a new, divine birth, whereby they might become sons of the light (cf. 12^36), and thereby understand both their origin and its purpose. The nature and conditions of this divine gift, as it becomes available to mankind through the incarnation of the Logos, will be set forth in 3^1-21; at present only two points are made about it: (*a*) for this divine birth belief on the Logos is essential [1^12end]; this is indeed the supreme characteristic of those who receive it (cf. 9^38); and (*b*) the gift itself is not to be identified or confused with the gift of physical life; it originates solely and directly from God, and is not dependent on any action or desire of men [1^13].

At 1^14 we become conscious of a new note in the prologue; the first person plural, for example, is used, as also at 1^16; the event and truth expressed in the words 'the Word became flesh' are clearly something which concern the writer and his readers even more closely and directly than the events and truths of 1^1-13. And yet it is in line with, and a continuation of, the truths already mentioned; the word Logos, first used in 1^1, is now, for the second and last time, used once more. What then is implied in the words just quoted?

In John the word 'flesh' is used to describe the realm of the (merely) human, in contrast to the realm of the divine; the (merely) earthly, as opposed to the heavenly; the (merely) material, as opposed to the spiritual (cf. 3^6, 6^63); and it is therefore in danger of kinship with 'the darkness' of 1^5, or with 'the world' of 1^10c.

From this point of view humanity can be described as 'all flesh' [17²; cf. Is. 40⁶], in its transitoriness, weakness, and purposelessness. 'The flesh' is thus the sphere of the apparent, of that which at first sight seems to be (the fact or the truth), of that which is immediately obvious to the senses; and if a man lives his life at this level, if he thinks that this (partial) life is truly or true life, he is said to judge 'after the flesh' [8¹⁵], or 'according to appearance' [7²⁴].

If, however, the Logos 'becomes flesh' and thereby enters this visible order of things, 'the flesh' no doubt still has the characteristics just described, but the situation is greatly changed. St. John's teaching is that in 'the fullness of the time' (cf. Gal. 4⁴), i.e., as we should more naturally express ourselves, at the earliest possible moment, He who was the Agent in creation, and sustains and upholds the universe in being (cf. Col. 1¹⁷), by Himself becoming part of His creation, showed what is the purpose and what are the possibilities of this realm or order of 'flesh', which should be but has not been subject to its Maker. And this purpose, identical with the purpose which led to the foundation of the world, and these possibilities, now to be realized in the incarnate Word, are that the holy will of the Creator should be done in and by His creation, in this realm of 'flesh'. How the divine will can and should be done is now to be shown by the incarnate Word, partly by His teaching, still more by His manner of life, and above all by the manner of His death and its results. Nor is it only or chiefly a matter of showing. Through His incarnation and its results He will Himself enable those who, like Himself, are 'in the flesh' to realize this purpose and these possibilities.

The words 'the Logos . . . dwelt among us' [1¹⁴ᵇ] are St. John's description of the Lord's ministry, the subject with which the book will be occupied. The Greek verb implies that the Lord's stay, like the stay of every human being, was temporary only, a point emphasized also in the course of the book [7³³, 12³⁵, 13³³]. And yet, short as it was, it was adequate to enable the evangelist and those in fellowship with him—the 'we' of 1¹⁴—to see the glory of His revelation; 'we beheld his glory'. In the last sentence the speakers are obviously not merely eye-witnesses, in the obvious or legal sense of this word. The Jews were such, but they saw in the Lord only an opponent [6³⁶]. The sight—and this includes, but must not be confined to, physical sight—is sight of the Logos 'become flesh', become historical; and the last words must always be borne in mind. The seeing is neither physical only, nor spiritual only, but the seeing which arises from belief.

It must, however, never be forgotten that, by becoming flesh, that is, by taking humanity upon Him not as a vesture or as a disguise but as His very being, the Logos has necessarily abandoned, during the days of His flesh, all those qualities, such as universality or unbounded power, which are usually associated with the thought of the divine. It is indeed the measure of His greatness, and that which constitutes His glory, that He has been prepared to stoop so low and in fact has done so; but unless this fact is grasped by those who come in contact with Him, they will altogether fail to understand Him. For He is now a man, and they will see Him as a man, and are therefore in danger of seeing Him only as such (cf. 10³³, 19⁵). They may therefore claim to know His parentage [1⁴⁵, 6⁴²] and origin [7²⁷, ²⁸]; if He is 'a man who has told them the truth' [8⁴⁰], and the truth is unpalatable to them, they may seek to put Him out of the way [7¹, ¹⁹, 8³⁷⁻⁴⁰]; and His claim to divinity will be dismissed by them as blasphemy [10³³; cf. 5¹⁸].

It is true that He is still the Logos, and therefore still the author of every man's being [1³], and the light offered to enlighten and guide every man [1⁴, ⁵, ⁹] and to reveal to him that which he truly is (cf. 1¹¹; this truth is worked out fully in ch. 9), and thus to bring him out of the encompassing darkness [12⁴⁶] into the light both of true vision and of fruitful activity [8¹²]; but since He is not the embodiment of those ideas of divinity which are commonly held among men and are natural to them, much will depend on men's ability to abandon in His presence their preconceived notions of greatness; they must in fact become as open and receptive in His presence as little children (cf. Mt. 18³), if they are to understand the truth and so to become free [8³²]. Not indeed that they can ever become independent of Him (cf. 15⁵), as a pupil, when his education is complete, may become independent of his teacher; for He remains and must remain the Logos, the source and fount of all their life and light; but they can be enabled to 'walk in the light, as He is in the light', and to be at one with Him and with their fellows (cf. 17²¹⁻²³), and to be cleansed by Him from sin (cf. 1 Jn. 1⁷).

Thus the 'glory' of the incarnate Word may be said to have been not only His unique union with His Father, but also His fulfilment, in and through His thought and word and action, in other words in and through His human life, of the divine will, of the work which had been given Him to do (cf. 17⁴). Thereby He made Himself known for what He was and is, to those who had been given to Him [17⁶] and had received Him and His words [17⁸; cf. 1¹², ¹⁶]; thus they 'saw His glory'. And this sight, discernible only in and by the act of believing (for the belief is one which grows and deepens, and can therefore never be fully or finally expressed in words), involved for them a new birth (cf. 3¹⁻²¹), whereby they became members of the family of God [1¹², ¹³], and had as its result a radically changed outlook in the direction of their lives.

In 1¹⁴ᵈ the glory of the incarnate Logos is described as that of an, or the, 'only begotten' (i.e. a unique offspring) 'from the Father'; and thereafter, as has been noted, St. John leaves behind him the use of the word Logos, in order henceforth, throughout the book, to use not only the historical name 'Jesus', but also the more personal terms of 'Father' and 'Son'. The description, it should always be remembered, is of the glory of the Word incarnate, and implies therefore, in the later language of this gospel, that he who has seen this Word incarnate 'has seen the Father' [14⁹], and that this Word incarnate is 'the door' [10⁷], through which alone can be gained access to the Father [14⁶].

Finally, the Word incarnate is described [1¹⁴ᵉ] as 'full of grace and truth'. The combination 'grace and truth', which occurs in this book only here and 1¹⁷, corresponds to an O.T. expression (especially frequent in the Psalms), the first term of which is variously translated, e.g. kindness, loving-kindness, mercy, favour. It implies not only the graciousness and goodwill of the giver, but also the proof, or evidence of these, which he grants; the word occurs in John only here and at 1¹⁶, ¹⁷. The second term, as applied to Yahweh in the O.T., emphasizes His unswerving fidelity to His promises, His reliability. The Jews believed that their Law or Torah, regarded as God's word, revealed the divine grace and truth, thus understood. But St. John in 1¹⁴ transfers the two terms 'grace and truth', applied by the Jews to their Law, to the incarnate Word, and in 1¹⁷ pointedly denies them (no doubt we should add, in the fullest meaning of the words) to the Law given through Moses, and affirms that they came into being through Jesus Christ. At best, therefore, the Law was no more than a *praeparatio evangelica*; and this is indeed the doctrine of St. John. It should, however, be noticed that 'truth', as the word is used in this gospel, where it occurs twenty-five times, is nearer to the meaning which its Greek equivalent had acquired in the first century, viz. 'reality', the knowledge of which is eternal life, than to the meaning of its Hebrew equivalent, 'reliability'. Here therefore, as throughout this book, we have an important and far-reaching fusion of religious conceptions found, but with different nuances and shades of meaning, both in Hebrew and in Greek thought.

In 1⁶⁻⁸ the references to the Baptist's activity and work were all in the past tense; and it was suggested that the reason for this, and for the mention of the Baptist at that point, was that the thought of 1³⁻¹³ is primarily, though not exclusively, of the being and work of the Logos before His incarnation, so that the Baptist in 1⁶⁻⁸ stands not only for himself but for all those who at any time or place have borne witness to the Logos. From 1¹⁴ᵃ onwards, however, we have been thinking of the Logos as incarnate, and the Baptist's witness is therefore here [1¹⁵] introduced in the present tense, just as in the book itself he appears for a time as working alongside of the Lord [3²²⁻³⁰]. In his work we now see not only his own witness but also that of all those believers who bear witness to the Lord; and the witness here is to the Lord's pre-existence. Whereas, in respect of time, the Lord came after the Baptist, yet in respect of rank and office He is superior to him, because (again using human language, in respect of time) He 'was before' him, in the same sense that He was 'before Abraham' [8⁵⁸].

At 1¹⁶ we return to the first person plural; the believers thankfully acknowledge and bear witness to their reception of an overflowing divine grace, the reception of one gift or grace preparing the way for the reception of a yet greater grace or gift. In the two concluding verses the revelation brought by the incarnate Lord is contrasted, first with the earlier divine law imparted through Moses and secondly with the claim made by any person or religious system to have or to be able to impart a knowledge of God, apart from that brought and given by the incarnate and unique Son of God, Jesus Christ. We now for the first time meet the word 'Jesus'; and only here and at 17³ are the Lord's proper name and His historic title as Christ or Messiah thus joined together in this book; but cf. also 20³¹.

1¹⁸ᵃ asserts that God cannot be directly seen by man as an object of sight. Only he, who has seen Jesus, has seen the Father [14⁹]. At the time when St. John wrote, various forms of current religious belief did put forward claims to be able to provide the vision of God; thus ecstasy, it was believed, might conceivably give sight of Him, or He might become known to the purified intelligence and life. It was believed that man could see God, and still live, a belief which is already denied in the O.T., e.g. Ex. 33²⁰, Jdgs. 13²². St. John accepts the Jewish view of man as God's creature, as dependent absolutely upon His will and pleasure, and therefore as having no right or liberty, however much he may wish it (cf. Ex. 33¹⁸⁻²³), by his own will or in order to satisfy his own desire, to make God the direct object of his sight or knowledge. A desire of this sort, to see God, to know Him and therewith to have life, implies a misunderstanding by man of himself and of his creatureliness; it suggests that he is free to undertake and even to succeed in such a quest, independently of the will or good pleasure of God. The thought here is not of seekers after God, who are aware of their blindness; rather, it is of the blind who think that they see (cf. 9³⁹), but are in fact false guides (cf. 10⁵, ⁸). As against all such independent claims to the sight or the knowledge of God, this last verse of the prologue points to the Person of the incarnate Revealer, who is also Redeemer [1²⁹], and to Him only. If men will come to (know) Him [5⁴⁰], they will understand why God is invisible; for the Lord's revelation will make clear to them their own ignorance [8¹⁹, 14⁷] and helplessness [15⁵ᵉⁿᵈ], and will thus bring them to belief in Jesus, and therewith, for the first time, to a true knowledge both of themselves and of God [17³], which is eternal life.

To the words 'only begotten', already used in 1¹⁴ and used again, together with the word 'Son', not only here but also at 3¹⁶, ¹⁸, are now added the words 'He who is in the bosom of the Father'. The words suggest, as at 3¹⁶, that the motive for the revelation, about to be described, is the divine love; and further, since love is not content to impart anything less than itself, that only in the forthcoming revelation are the divine truth and the divine or eternal life made possible and available to men. The only Son, whom during His incarnate life the Father does not leave alone [8¹⁶, ²⁹, 16³²], in His ministry not only has done the Father's work [14¹⁰], but has declared the Father's word [7¹⁶, 12⁴⁹, ⁵⁰, 14²⁴]; and that word is, in the last as in the first [1¹] resort, Himself.

NOTES TO 1¹⁻¹⁸

1³⁻⁴. The punctuations in R.V. text and R.V. mg are equally possible, but the latter is to be preferred, as suiting the rhythm of the clauses better. The meaning is that all life, both seen and unseen, had its origin in, and derives its continued existence from, the eternal life of the Logos.

1⁵. 'apprehended it not'. St. John is prone to use words which include two meanings. The R.V. text, in the sense of 'did not understand', or 'did not appropriate, grasp it', is perhaps supported by the 'knew not' of 1¹⁰ and the 'received not' of 1¹¹. On the other hand, the verb here used occurs again at 12³⁵, where it certainly means 'overtake' or 'overcome'. If then we follow R.V. mg, we are reminded that religion, although regarding the conflict between light (good) and darkness (evil) as very real and far from being an illusion, yet has no doubt at all about the relative strength of the combatants, or the final issue. The devil is God's enemy, not His rival.

1⁶⁻⁸. Whereas the Logos 'was' (eternally) 1¹, John the Baptist, His greatest witness, 'came into being', 'arose' (like one of the Hebrew judges or prophets).

1⁹. In the exposition it has been assumed that the words 'coming into the world' qualify 'every man'. Both the form of the verse in Greek, and a close Hebrew parallel (implying 'every mortal man') to its last six English words, suggest that this is the correct interpretation. It is, however, possible to translate the verse according to R.V. mg, in which case the thought is that the coming of the Logos, who is the true light and lightens all men, is not only repeated or continuous, but increases in intensity, as men are enabled to receive the light; cf. Heb. 1¹⁻².

The adjective 'true' implies here perfection and completeness. The Baptist and all men may share in, partake of, the light, and to that extent be 'true'; but their light is partial and incomplete, compared with the perfect light, the Logos. In the words 'every man', emphasis is laid on the universality of the work of the Logos as light.

1¹⁰. Here the function of the Logos as the one and only Agent in creation is once more emphasized, as in 1³; but henceforth this feature of His work naturally falls into the background, since the book will be concerned with the Logos as incarnate.

1¹², ¹³. The strong and unqualified, typically Jewish language of 1¹¹ (cf. 3³²) might seem to suggest a universal, complete ignorance and rejection of the Logos; but in 1¹³ (cf. 3³³) we learn that there were some who did not reject the presence and work of the Logos, and therefore received the right, authority, privilege of a divine, spiritual birth, in addition to their natural birth. The three phrases in 1¹³, all referring to natural, physical birth, seem designed to heighten the contrast with the new or second birth, by which alone a man can 'see' or 'enter into the kingdom of God' [3³, ⁵]. 'Them that believe on his name': see pp. 23–24 and 115.

1¹³. An Old Latin version, instead of 'which were born', has here 'who was born', in clear reference to the manner of the Lord's birth as narrated in Matthew and Luke; and this reading was known before 200 A.D.; but it should certainly be rejected.

1¹⁴. However true it may be that 1¹⁰⁻¹³ can apply not only to the work of the immanent Logos throughout the ages, but also to the Lord's historic ministry, yet only now do we read that the Logos took human nature upon Him. Everything hitherto mentioned leads up to this decisive fact, the inclosing of the Logos in a Divine–human personality.

The word 'tabernacled', R.V. mg, closely connected here with the word 'glory', would recall to readers of the O.T. the 'shekinah' or visible dwelling of Yahweh among His people in the form of the glory seen in the tent or tabernacle of meeting [Ex. 40³⁴, Num. 14¹⁰]. St. John implies that the O.T. revelation is now made perfect, realized in its fullness, in the incarnation of the Logos.

In speaking of the glory of the incarnate Logos as that of an 'only begotten from the Father', St. John emphasizes two complementary truths. A son, since he derives his being from his father, is to this extent inferior, subordinate to him; and there is a sense in which this is true of the Lord's relationship to the Father (cf. 14²⁸), 'The Father is greater than I'. But in this case the Son is 'only begotten', unique (which is probably the meaning of the word 'beloved' applied to the Lord in the earlier gospels, e.g. Mk. 1¹¹, 9⁷, in respect of His relationship to the Father), and reveals fully the Father's glory (cf. 10³⁰), 'I and the Father are one'.

'full'. In spite of the bracket in R.V., this adjective may agree with either 'the Word' or 'his glory'.

1¹⁸. The reading of R.V. mg is quite possible (cf. 1¹, 20²⁸, and 1 Jn. 5²⁰) and perhaps has stronger textual support than that of R.V. text; but the latter is to be preferred, as being more in accordance with St. John's usage in a context of this sort; cf. 3¹⁶, ¹⁸ and 1 Jn. 4⁹.

B. 1¹⁹–2¹¹. THE INTRODUCTION (CONTINUED)

19 1 And this is the witness of John, when the Jews sent unto him from
20 Jerusalem priests and Levites to ask him, Who art thou? And he
21 confessed, and denied not; and he confessed, I am not the Christ. And
they asked him, What then? Art thou Elijah? And he saith, I am not.
22 Art thou the prophet? And he answered, No. They said therefore unto
him, Who art thou? that we may give an answer to them that sent us.
23 What sayest thou of thyself? He said, I am the voice of one crying in the
24 wilderness, Make straight the way of the Lord, as said Isaiah the prophet.
25 ¹And they had been sent from the Pharisees. And they asked him, and
said unto him, Why then baptizest thou, if thou art not the Christ,
26 neither Elijah, neither the prophet? John answered them, saying, I
27 baptize ²with water: in the midst of you standeth one whom ye know

¹ Or And *certain* had been sent from among the Pharisees.   ² Or in

not, *even* he that cometh after me, the latchet of whose shoe I am not
28 worthy to unloose. These things were done in ¹Bethany beyond Jordan,
where John was baptizing.

29   On the morrow he seeth Jesus coming unto him, and saith, Behold,
30 the Lamb of God, which ²taketh away the sin of the world! This is he
of whom I said, After me cometh a man which is become before me:
31 for he was ²before me. And I knew him not; but that he should be made
32 manifest to Israel, for this cause came I baptizing ³with water. And John
bare witness, saying, 'I have beheld the Spirit descending as a dove out
33 of heaven; and it abode upon him. And I knew him not: but he that
sent me to baptize ³with water, he said unto me, Upon whomsoever
thou shalt see the Spirit descending, and abiding upon him, the same is
34 he that baptizeth ³with the Holy Spirit. And I have seen, and have
borne witness that this is the Son of God.

35   Again on the morrow John was standing, and two of his disciples;
36 and he looked upon Jesus as he walked, and saith, Behold, the Lamb of
37 God! And the two disciples heard him speak, and they followed Jesus.
38 And Jesus turned, and beheld them following, and saith unto them,
What seek ye? And they said unto him, Rabbi (which is to say, being
39 interpreted, ⁴Master), where abidest thou? He saith unto them, Come,
and ye shall see. They came therefore and saw where he abode; and
40 they abode with him that day: it was about the tenth hour. One of the
two that heard John *speak*, and followed him, was Andrew, Simon
41 Peter's brother. He findeth first his own brother Simon, and saith unto
him, We have found the Messiah (which is, being interpreted, ⁵Christ).
42 He brought him unto Jesus. Jesus looked upon him, and said, Thou art
Simon the son of ⁶John: thou shalt be called Cephas (which is by
interpretation, ⁷Peter).

43   On the morrow he was minded to go forth into Galilee, and he findeth
44 Philip: and Jesus saith unto him, Follow me. Now Philip was from
45 Bethsaida, of the city of Andrew and Peter. Philip findeth Nathanael,
and saith unto him, We have found him, of whom Moses in the law,
and the prophets, did write, Jesus of Nazareth, the son of Joseph.
46 And Nathanael said unto him, Can any good thing come out of Nazar-
47 eth? Philip saith unto him, Come and see. Jesus saw Nathanael coming
to him, and saith of him, Behold, an Israelite indeed, in whom is no
48 guile! Nathanael saith unto him, Whence knowest thou me? Jesus
answered and said unto him, Before Philip called thee, when thou wast
49 under the fig tree, I saw thee. Nathanael answered him, Rabbi, thou
50 art the Son of God; thou art King of Israel. Jesus answered and said
unto him, Because I said unto thee, I saw thee underneath the fig tree,

---

¹ *Many ancient authorities read* Bethabarah, *some* Betharabah.   ² *Or*
beareth the sin   ³ *Or* in   ⁴ *Or* Teacher   ⁵ *That is* Anointed.
⁶ *Gr.* Joanes: *called in* Mat. 16. 17, Jonah.   ⁷ *That is* Rock *or* Stone.

51 believest thou? thou shalt see greater things than these. And he saith
unto him, Verily, verily, I say unto you, Ye shall see the heaven opened,
and the angels of God ascending and descending upon the Son of man.

2 And the third day there was a marriage in Cana of Galilee; and the
2 mother of Jesus was there: and Jesus also was bidden, and his disciples,
3 to the marriage. And when the wine failed, the mother of Jesus saith
4 unto him, They have no wine. And Jesus saith unto her, Woman, what
5 have I to do with thee? mine hour is not yet come. His mother saith unto
6 the servants, Whatsoever he saith unto you, do it. Now there were six
water-pots of stone set there after the Jews' manner of purifying,
7 containing two or three firkins apiece. Jesus saith unto them, Fill the
8 waterpots with water. And they filled them up to the brim. And he
saith unto them, Draw out now and bear unto the ¹ruler of the feast.
9 And they bare it. And when the ruler of the feast tasted the water ²now
become wine, and knew not whence it was (but the servants which had
drawn the water knew), the ruler of the feast calleth the bridegroom,
10 and saith unto him, Every man setteth on first the good wine; and when
men have drunk freely, *then* that which is worse: thou hast kept the
11 good wine until now. This beginning of his signs did Jesus in Cana of
Galilee, and manifested his glory; and his disciples believed on him.

¹ *Or* steward   ² *Or* that it had become

EXPOSITION OF 1¹⁹–2¹¹

Witness is borne by the Baptist to the Lord, 1^{19–36}. One result of
his witness is that disciples join the Lord and in turn bear witness
to Him; and they themselves receive a promise from the Lord,
1^{37–51}. Finally at a wedding at Cana the Lord changes water into
wine, thus manifesting His glory; and His disciples believe on
Him, 2^{1–11}.

The prologue is ended; but we do not at once pass to the Lord's
ministry; and reasons will be given for thinking that 1¹⁹ to 2¹¹
should be regarded as still introductory, although a change now
takes place in the character of the narrative. For the prologue,
although it deals with certain historical events, has made large use
of philosophical language. This language, however, is now dropped,
and we pass to a narrative entirely historical in form. Indeed, all
the paragraphs in 1¹⁹ to 2¹¹ are closely linked by careful notes of
time, which together amount to a continuous record of six, if not
of seven, days; and on each of the first four (or five) witness is
borne to the Lord. On the first, in 1^{19–28}, the Baptist gives witness,

negative as regards himself, positive as regards the Greater than he, in answer to an official deputation from the Jews. On the second, in 1^{29-34}, he gives direct witness to the Lord, at this, their first, meeting in this gospel. On the third, in 1^{35-42}, he renews his witness before two of his disciples, who thereupon follow the Lord. One of them, Andrew, in turn himself bears witness to the Lord and brings his brother Simon to Him. (In 1^{41}, however, instead of the word 'first', there is a variant reading 'in the morning'. If this latter reading is accepted as original—though this is unlikely—we pass in 1^{41-42} to the fourth day.) On the following day, in 1^{43-51}, Philip receives a direct summons from the Lord to follow Him, the Lord being about to leave for Galilee. Philip, having found Nathanael, bears witness to him of the Lord, and brings him into the Lord's presence. And to these men who, partly as a result of the Baptist's witness, partly as a result of a direct call, and partly owing to kinship and friendship among themselves, have become attached to the Lord's company and forthwith bear witness to Him, the Lord in 1^{51} gives a solemn assurance. It is to be their privilege to see an unveiling of heaven (the sight longed for by the writer of Is. 64^1), and a perfect contact between heaven and earth, because of the presence with them of their Lord, the Son of man.

It is usually thought that 1^{51} completes the introduction, and that St. John's account of the Lord's ministry begins at 2^1; but it is questionable whether the chapter-division is not misleading here, and whether we should not do better to regard 1^{19} to 2^{11} as a single section, preparatory to the ministry, which only begins after 2^{11}. The following considerations may be urged. (1) We have already noticed how the paragraphs of 1^{19} to 2^{11} are linked together by successive, detailed notes of time. It is therefore at least likely that the last paragraph [2^{1-11}] should be taken with its predecessors, rather than with the paragraphs which follow. (2) The Baptist's witness has led two of his disciples to follow the Lord. The messianic titles which one of them, Andrew, and soon afterwards Philip and Nathanael ascribe to Him show that belief has indeed been aroused in them; but, as is implied in the Lord's words in 1^{50} to Nathanael, companionship with Him is to deepen their belief immeasurably (cf. $6^{68, 69}$). And His promise in 1^{51} begins to be fulfilled in 2^{11}, the verse which forms the climax of the story of the wedding at Cana, where His disciples, we read, as a result of His manifestation of His glory, 'believed on Him'. Accordingly just as in Mk. 1¹⁶⁻²⁰ the Lord attaches four disciples to His company before the first scene in the synagogue at Capernaum [Mk. 1²¹⁻²⁸], so here the disciples—represented by the five of whom we read in 1³⁵⁻⁵¹—are not only called but forthwith admitted to a knowledge of their Lord deeper than that at present vouchsafed to others. For it should be noticed that the Lord's work in changing water to wine is (almost) private. Only the servants, who perform His bidding [2⁹], and the disciples [2¹¹] know how the good wine came to be. (3) According to St. John, the Lord works His first sign, a change of water into wine, at a wedding; and His disciples, seeing in His action a manifestation of His glory, believe on Him. We cannot forget that according to the earlier tradition the Lord compared the happiness of His presence with His disciples to that of a wedding party [Mk. 2¹⁹], or that in the same context [Mk. 2²²], under the figure of the wineskins, He emphasized not only the newness of His message, but the need also of a new life in those who received it.

Thus in this gospel, before the ministry opens, disciples are found with the Lord, and already form a company apart from those around them. From the outset they have been 'chosen out of the world'.

We must now return, to examine each paragraph more closely.

a. 1¹⁹⁻²⁸. At 1¹⁹ we meet for the first time the term 'the Jews', who here send an official delegation (naturally enough belonging to the religious orders, since the Baptist's work was obviously prompted by religious motives), to inquire into his person, office, and credentials. It is noteworthy that the first question treated, when the historical narrative of this gospel begins at 1¹⁹, is the personality of the Baptist. In Mark and Matthew he is identified with Elijah, as being the expected immediate forerunner of the Messiah and therefore the final herald of the consummation believed to be imminent. But in John, in which gospel the reader is to be taught to place the Lord's work and Person in a far larger framework than that of the Jewish Messiahship (although he will not by any means be allowed to forget this, the first and earliest, interpretation of the Lord's Person), and to see in Him the true life and light of every man at all times and in all places, such an explanation of the Baptist's work would be out of place, if not misleading; and the latter therefore disclaims not only the office of Elijah, but all offices suggestive of a messianic connexion.

Indeed, the Baptist will not call himself a person (we recall that he is outside the kingdom of God [Mt. 11^{11}, Lk. 7^{28}, Jn. 3$^{3, 5}$]); his task is solely, by his witness and his water-baptism, to make known to Israel One who, although unknown to his hearers, is already present; and great indeed as this task is, he himself is content to recall the words of Is. 40^3, and to identify himself with the voice of one unnamed.

Again, whereas in Mt. 11^3, Lk. 7^{19} the Baptist sends to inquire of the Lord whether He is indeed the One expected, the Lord's personality in this case being the uncertain quantity, in Jn. 1$^{19-23}$ the tables, as it were, are turned, the uncertain quantity being now the Baptist. He who is present but unknown is, as the reader is aware, the universal Word; now incarnate in the Lord; and although in time He may come after the Baptist, the latter is unworthy to carry out the lowliest menial task on His behalf [1^{27}].

The interview of the Baptist with the priests and Levites ends abruptly; we do not hear of their reaction to his words or of their departure or of the report which they presented at Jerusalem. This tendency to introduce characters who almost at once disappear is a feature of this gospel; other obvious examples are Nicodemus [3$^{1-12}$] and the Greeks [12$^{20-28}$]. Possibly, by adopting this method, St. John wishes the reader in every such case to place himself, as it were, alongside the character or characters upon the stage, and to consider, in the light of the context, what part he (the reader) is playing in the matter, and what is his reaction to it. In the present context, for example, if the reason suggested for the mention of the Baptist in 1$^{6-8}$ was correct, viz. that in this gospel the Baptist has a representative and universal, as well as an individual and particular, function and office, the reader might ask himself whether he finds that everyone and everything around him, all that goes to make up his experience, is a voice bearing witness to the Lord Jesus, and pointing to Him. Does the reader find that, if John the Baptist in this sense is not present, he is indeed in a wilderness; but that, if and when he is present, the way of the Lord is being prepared, is being made straight?

b. 1$^{29-34}$. The scene now changes; the deputation has withdrawn; when the Baptist sees the Lord coming to him, no audience is mentioned at this, the Lord's first appearance in this gospel on the stage of history, any more than on the similar first occasion of His appearance in Mk. 1$^{9-11}$; the reader alone is brought into the presence of Him to whom the Baptist now bears witness. This witness is threefold. First, Jesus is the Lamb of God, who takes away all human sin. Secondly, John, who was sent to baptize in water (only), and who of himself did not know the Lord, now having seen the Spirit descending on Him from heaven and remaining on Him, knows by divine intimation that He it is who brings baptism in Holy Spirit. And thirdly, He is the Son of God. Thus whereas in Mark the Lord at His baptism sees the Spirit descending upon Him and hears a voice sealing His divine Sonship, in John the Lord's baptism is not mentioned, and it is the Baptist who sees the descent of the Spirit upon the Lord and can therefore testify to His divine Sonship. In John that which takes place occurs not for the sake of the Lord (it is valuable to compare 11⁴² and 12³⁰), but for the sake of the Baptist and his witness to the Lord.

In view of the subordinate place assigned to messianic doctrine in this gospel it seems unlikely that the great words of the Baptist's witness to the Lord in 1²⁹ should be simply a messianic title,[1] without deep religious significance. Mr. C. K. Barrett has shown[2] that St. John is prone to embrace various strands of O.T. thought in a single phrase, which goes beyond any one of these strands, taken separately, and indeed also beyond them, taken altogether; and the Baptist's words in 1²⁹ may be a case in point. Thus the attempt to see here an identification of the Lord *sans phrase* with the paschal lamb of Ex. 12 or Num. 9 is not free from difficulties; to mention one only, it was not the function of the paschal lamb to remove sin. Others have seen an allusion to Is. 53⁷⁻⁸ (which is quoted, in reference to the Lord, in Acts 8³²), the same Greek word being used for lamb as here, which is not the case in the LXX version of Ex. 12 or Num. 9. On the other hand, in Is. 53⁷⁻⁸ (LXX) the reference is to the shearing, not the killing, of the lamb, though we should not forget Is. 53¹² in the same context. Again, the daily sacrifice in the Jerusalem temple consisted of a lamb; but this was not regarded as an atoning sacrifice. The most satisfactory explanation of the Baptist's words may therefore possibly be found along these lines: (1) St. John is drawing upon the O.T., in so far as the sacrificial language there used, whether in reference to a lamb or other animal, was available for use in

[1] As is maintained by Dr. C. H. Dodd, *The Interpretation of the Fourth Gospel*, pp. 230–8.

[2] *J.T.S.* July–October 1947, pp. 155–7.

reference to the sacrifice of Christ. (2) We know from 1 Cor. 5⁷ that at an early date in the history of the Church the Lord's sacrificial death, commemorated at the Christian Eucharist, was compared to that of the lambs slain for the paschal feast. St. John may have been strongly influenced by this Christian application of the Jewish passover, and to the comparison of the Lord with the paschal lamb has added a reference to His work in removing the world's sin. (3) This interpretation is in accordance with the teaching of this gospel as a whole, in which not only does the Jewish passover play an important part (see pp. 176 f. and Appended Note), but great stress is laid on the self-oblation of the Lord [6⁵¹, 10¹⁵, 15¹³, 17¹⁹].

It should be added that the Lord is compared to a lamb elsewhere in the New Testament at Acts 8³², 1 Pet. 1¹⁹, and frequently in the Apocalypse (e.g. 5⁶), though in this book the Greek word is different from that used here.

It was suggested above that St. John, while making use of Old Testament thought and phrase, also extends or goes beyond these; and in the Baptist's reference to the Lamb of God taking away the (collective) sin of the world we may be right to see a contrast between the universal redemptive work of the true paschal Lamb and that of the passover lambs, whose death benefited the children of Israel only. (Is it possible that we may find here an explanation why, whereas at 1²⁹ the Baptist's witness includes the relative clause 'which taketh away the sin of the world', thus emphasizing the universality of the Lord's work, these words are omitted at 1³⁶, when the Baptist bears witness to the Lord before two of his disciples, who obviously are Jews? In 1²⁹⁻³⁴, on the other hand, at the first encounter of the Baptist with the Lord, no audience is mentioned, and the evangelist seems to have the reader especially in view.)

But the Baptist's witness to the Lord is not confined to the good news of His sacrificial life and death and their results. Before giving his further witness, the Baptist emphasizes in 1³⁰, as in 1¹⁵, that He, whom he preceded in time, now takes precedence of him, for He existed first. His greatness was at first unknown to the Baptist; but the purpose of the latter's water-baptism was to make Him manifest to Israel; and, as a result of that which the Baptist has now heard and seen, he can bear witness that the Spirit has descended and remains upon the Lord. And the purpose of this descent is that the Lord, unlike John, may baptize not, or not only, in water, but in Holy Spirit, a baptism which, as we shall learn later, gives rebirth and therewith admission to the kingdom of God [3³, ⁵]. And finally, the Baptist adds, he who thus baptizes in Holy Spirit, is the Son of God. It is clear from this gospel as a whole that this title, for the evangelist, emphasizes, above all, the Lord's unique relation to the Father. The correct reading here, however, is not quite certain; see the note on 1³⁴.

c. 1³⁵⁻⁴². The scene again changes, in so far as now two of the Baptist's disciples are present, who on hearing their master's witness to the Lord, as He now moves among men, leave him in order to follow the Lord. These two disciples seem to illustrate the teaching of 6⁴⁴ᵃ; the Father has drawn them to come to the Lord. The story of 1³⁷⁻⁴⁰ is told very simply; but since we have here the Lord's first words to be recorded in this gospel and also learn how His first disciples join Him, we are perhaps meant to read much between the lines, especially as 1⁴¹ shows how great was the result of this first contact. A good way to do this is to consider how words and expressions which occur here are used elsewhere in John. When, for instance, we read that, in response to the Lord's invitation, the two disciples came and saw where He dwelt, and abode with Him that day, we should recall both the teaching of 1¹⁸ that the seat of the Lord's dwelling is in the bosom of the Father (cf. 8²⁹, 16³²), and also the promises held out to disciples in 12⁴⁶, 14², ³, 17²⁴.

Andrew, one of the two disciples of the Baptist who have thus followed the Lord, forthwith brings his greater brother Simon to Him, on the strength of the momentous announcement that they have found the Messiah; and Simon receives from the Lord his new name (cf. Rev. 3¹²ᵉⁿᵈ).

d. 1⁴³⁻⁵¹. Whereas the two disciples of 1³⁵ were led to the Lord by means of the witness of the Baptist, Philip now receives a direct call from the Lord to follow Him. Philip bears his witness to Nathanael and overcomes the latter's incredulity by persuading him to come and see for himself; we may compare the Lord's words at 1³⁹ to the Baptist's two disciples. Nathanael does not indeed, like Simon Peter, receive a new name; but he seems to be contrasted with Jacob. Jacob's new name was Israel [Gen. 32²⁸], but he remained to the end a man of guile. Nathanael, in whom is no guile [1⁴⁷], is more truly an Israelite than Jacob; and the introductory section of this gospel culminates in a solemn assurance given to him by the Lord [1⁵¹] that he, with other disciples, is to see, through the Lord's work and their association with Him in it, that which Jacob saw foreshadowed at Bethel [Gen. 28¹⁰⁻²²], this being the only allusion in the N.T. to the story of Jacob's dream of the ladder which reached from earth to heaven.

The Lord's own designation of Himself, 'the Son of man' (as opposed to the titles ascribed to Him in 1⁴¹⁻⁴⁹; see below), is here used for the first time in John; and the meaning of this important verse is like that of 1¹⁴ and 1¹⁸; it is a description of the coming ministry in which His disciples will witness their Lord's unbroken communion with the Father and will themselves partake in it. This unrestricted commerce (cf. 5¹⁷, 8²⁹) between the Father and the Son of man is here pictured as a never-ceasing activity. It is a 'work' [4³⁴], or a series of 'works' [5³⁶], which, in obedience to the Father's will and command [9⁴, 10³⁷], the Son, as the Son of man, carries out on earth [17⁴]; and it is here set forth under the form of a ladder, joining heaven and earth. On this ladder are actively engaged, in both directions, angelic ministrants. This figure of an angelic ministry is not used in John during the Lord's ministry; we read only of His life of communion with and obedience to the Father, and of the Father's love and work for Him. Possibly therefore it is significant that, when all is completed [17⁴, 19³⁰], when the ladder which in and by the work of the Son of man has joined heaven and earth in an indissoluble union is removed, then only do we read once more of angels [20¹²], occupying the place where the Lord's body, the instrument of His work on earth, had lain [19⁴²].

Part of the purpose of 1³⁵⁻⁵¹ is no doubt to show the different ways in which certain men came into the Lord's company; but we should notice also that, while regarding Him as their contemporary, they forthwith give witness or testimony to Him, ascribing to Him various messianic titles [1⁴¹, ⁴⁵, ⁴⁹]. In the course of this gospel we shall learn that some of these titles, although they played an important, even an essential, part in enlightening those who came to know the Lord at first through them, soon proved inadequate to describe His Person. It seems as though, in these introductory verses, St. John enumerates these titles at the outset, in order that, while not allowing them to be forgotten (cf. 4²⁵, ²⁶, 5⁴⁶, 12¹³), he may pass beyond them and impart to his readers, in the chapters which describe the ministry, the deeper and fuller understanding, which he wishes them to have of the Lord and of His work.

We notice too that twice in this introductory section a disciple brings a relative [1⁴¹] or a friend [1⁴⁵] to the Lord, who at once shows His knowledge of, and insight into, the circumstances, characters, and possibilities of those thus brought into His presence [1⁴², ⁴⁷, ⁵⁰; cf. 10¹⁴, ²⁷].

In these various ways, although with great reserve, St. John prepares his readers for the record of this gospel, and shows how he wishes them to approach it and to understand it and, like the original disciples, to share in it. For the Word has taken humanity upon Himself, and therewith the messianic age, and much more than the messianic age, is present.

e. 2¹⁻¹¹. On the third day after the giving of the promise in 1⁵¹, its fulfilment begins. From whatever source St. John derived this story, he probably selected it for his purpose (cf. 20³⁰, ³¹) because of its value as a 'sign' [2¹¹], that is, an event which is both a symbol and a channel of something greater than itself. For the story tells of water placed in six vessels of stone, which were connected with Jewish methods of purification (cf. 3²⁵), and relates how this same water, when the Lord's word is carried out by the servants, becomes wine of a surpassing quality. It thus sets forth, for him who is willing so to read it, the relation of the old order and the new, of the Law and the Gospel; the latter is seen as the perfecting and transformation of the former. And this positive work of the Lord takes place in Galilee.

At 2³, as at 6⁵, a crisis occurs, which in each case seems at first sight to be connected only with matters of drink and food. On both occasions the Lord shows Himself able, and more than able, to meet the need; but He does not have recourse to the methods of the market-place; cf. 6⁷⁻¹¹ and Is. 55¹. He makes use, indeed, of existing resources [2⁶⁻⁸, 6⁸, ⁹]; but the significance of His action lies elsewhere. The Jewish dispensation, here represented by water, is now through the word and work of the Lord to be superseded by and transformed into the wine of the Gospel, which alone can satisfy men's need; and the Lord's mother, who, apart from 6⁴², is mentioned in this gospel only in the opening and in the closing scene of the ministry [2¹⁻¹², 19²⁵⁻²⁷], unconscious of the deeper meaning of her words, draws her Son's attention to the need. The Lord's reply, including His address of her as 'Woman', where we might have expected 'Mother', can only be rightly understood, if the events at the cross, described in 19²⁵⁻³⁰, are borne in mind. That which at present He and His mother have in common [2⁴ᵃ] is their physical nàture, which of itself is not what St. John understands as the deepest bond of union (cf. 3⁶, 6⁶³ᵃ, and Mk. 3³¹⁻³⁵); and further, the hour when He will give the true wine, i.e. unite men indissolubly with Him through His self-consecration in the passion (cf. 17¹⁹⁻²³), the hour of His glorification [13³¹, ³², 17⁵] and of the dispensation of the Spirit (cf. 7³⁹), is not yet; contrast 12²³. When that hour is come, the Lord and His mother will indeed have much in common; for as a result of His word and action [19²⁵⁻²⁷] she, who of all mankind is the most closely linked with Him on the physical side, and he, who bears the unique title 'the disciple whom Jesus loved', are to become united, not so much by their common love for Him, as by His love for them, which will now become their life.

Again, the Lord does not act as a result of human prompting, however closely related to Him, on the physical side, the prompter may be; He acts only in accôrdance with the will of the Father [5¹⁹, ³⁰, 8²⁹]. After hearing His reply, His mother is prepared to leave the issue in His hands, only warning the servants to carry out her Son's bidding, whatever that may be.

In the order which He gives, the Lord shows His readiness to make use of the old order, so far as may be; it is His purpose, whenever possible, not to destroy, but to fulfil [Mt. 5¹⁷]. When He can do so, human need is fully met [2¹⁰], and the imperfection of the old order more than made good by His word and work (with 2¹⁰ᵉⁿᵈ cf. Gal. 4⁴, ⁵), although St. John notes that the master of the ceremonies remained unaware of the origin and source of the wine. His ignorance is similar to that of the Samaritan woman [4¹¹] or the Jews [8¹⁴, 9²⁹] or Pilate [19⁹], and is contrasted with the knowledge of the servants, who had performed the Lord's bidding; their knowledge thus prefigures that of His obedient disciples [17³, ⁶, ⁷].

No difficulty should be raised about the large quantity of wine here said to have become available towards the end of the marriage feast; the explanation is in 1¹⁶ (cf. also 6¹³).

At 2¹¹ we have the first of the evangelist's editorial comments, as it were, upon the events which he describes. If it is asked how his statement that the Lord 'manifested His glory' is to be reconciled with the statement in 7³⁹ that 'Jesus was not yet glorified', the answer may be given that any action of the Lord, the Word become flesh, is of necessity a manifestation of His glory; but that a full revelation of that glory is only made with the completion of His work, upon the cross. Hence, in our thought of the Lord's one work, His life and His death cannot be separated. As the reader was reminded at the outset in the proclamation of the Baptist, 'Behold, the Lamb of God, which taketh away the sin of the world' (if these words have been rightly interpreted on pp. 96 f.), each must be seen in relation to the other. As regards the nature of the Lord's glory, it is enough at present to say that it is His revelation of the Being and the character of the Father; it may be summed up in the words 'God so loved the world that He gave his only begotten Son' [3¹⁶].

As a result of this manifestation by the Lord of His glory, His disciples, we are told, 'believed on Him'. For the meaning of this phrase see pp. 24 f. and 115. As used here, it will imply that the disciples were enabled to penetrate beyond their Master's outward action, and to grasp its significance in respect of His work and Person.

NOTES TO 1¹⁹–2¹¹

1²¹. The term 'the prophet' occurs in three contexts in this gospel, here, 6¹⁴, and 7⁴⁰. In the first and last of these the office is clearly distinguished from that of the Messiah, and is perhaps to be explained in the light of the expectation illustrated by such passages as 1 Macc. 4⁴⁶, Mk. 8²⁸.

1²⁴. In John no section of the Jews is represented as more strongly opposed to the Lord than the Pharisees.

1²⁸. A Bethany beyond Jordan is not otherwise known, but this reading is probably correct.

1³⁴. A variant reading, which may be correct, is 'the chosen one of God', with which cf. Lk. 9³⁵. St. John does not elsewhere use this term of the Lord, but its meaning, if we ought to read it here, is not essentially different from that of 'the Son of God'.

1³⁵. 'was standing'. In Matthew, apart from 27³⁶, a significant exception which tests the general rule, no one is ever found seated in the presence of the Lord; the evangelist would have regarded such a position as unfitting in His presence. Is it possible that the same explanation may apply here?

1³⁶. 'as he walked'. On this verb see the note on 6⁶⁶ (p. 170).

1³⁸. St. John often translates Hebrew terms into their Greek equivalents (cf. 1⁴¹). The word 'Rabbi' is to be understood as a title of respect, like the English 'Sir'.

1³⁹. In all the gospels the hours are counted from sunrise, i.e. from about 6 a.m., so that 'the tenth hour' is 4 p.m. If, as is likely, the notes of time in this gospel sometimes carry a significance beyond their surface meaning, in this case it is lost to us.

1⁴¹. 'first'. As has been stated in the exposition, the R.V. is probably correct, as against another reading 'in the morning'. The translation 'his own' may be too strong; the Greek may only signify 'his'.

In the N.T. the Hebrew word Messiah is transliterated into Greek only here and 4²⁵; elsewhere it is rendered by the Greek translation Christ, 'the anointed one'.

1⁴⁴. Philip and Andrew are also mentioned together at 6⁵⁻⁹, 12^{21, 22}. Since Philip's connexion with Bethsaida, which was at the north-east end of the sea of Galilee, is again emphasized at 12²⁰⁻²³, when certain Greeks approach him in the hope of securing an interview with the Lord, possibly St. John implies that Jew and Gentile mixed with especial freedom in this place; and here [1⁴⁴] it is noted that three of those whom the Lord called into His company, Philip, Andrew, and Peter, were natives of this place.

1⁴⁵. Nathanael appears again at 21²; he is otherwise unknown. The word may be translated 'the gift of God'.

Outside the N.T. Nazareth is said to be unmentioned, either in earlier or in contemporary literature.

The words 'the son of Joseph' are applied to the Lord again at 6⁴². The use of the words there may be regarded as a typical example of the Jews' misunderstanding of the truth about His origin. Here the words are used by one called indeed to be a disciple and prepared to see the promises of the O.T. fulfilled in Him, but as yet without the deeper understanding of His Person. St. John, no more than St. Mark, refers directly to the tradition of the manner of the Lord's birth as given in the first and third gospels. He may well have regarded the taking of humanity upon Himself by the Logos as, for him, a more valuable and significant expression of the truth of His Person, than the stories of His birth in Matthew and Luke; and certainly it was no part of his task or purpose to refer to the Lord's infancy, as that is described in Lk. 2^{40, 52}.

1⁴⁶. 'Come and see'. Bengel's comment, 'the best remedy for preconceived opinions', is very suitable here; but precisely the same Greek words occur at 11³⁴, and there the comment would be out of place.

1⁴⁹. The two titles ascribed by Nathanael to the Lord are to be understood as messianic. The title 'King of Israel' is found again in John at 12¹³, where it is given to the Lord by the multitude at the triumphal entry.

1⁵⁰. Nathanael's faith is at present based on wonder only. Through his coming intercourse with the Lord, it will gain a better foundation.

1⁵¹. The normal use of the word 'amen' (here translated 'verily') is to express full and formal agreement with words just uttered by some other speaker. In all four gospels, however, the Lord frequently uses the word at the beginning of a sentence, to strengthen the expression, 'I say unto you'; and in John the word is always duplicated. It is also noteworthy that in John the expression 'never introduces a new saying unrelated to what precedes'. This verse, for example, containing a promise of the Lord, together with His self-designation as the Son of man, may be regarded as His response to the witness borne to Him, and the ascription to Him of certain messianic titles, in 1⁴¹⁻⁴⁹.

Gen. 28¹² is usually understood to mean that the angels were going up and down the ladder, at the foot of which lay Jacob; and the LXX translation supports this view. If St. John understood Gen. 28¹² in this way, then his teaching is that the Lord, as the Son of man, is the true or real ladder, whose ministry joins heaven and earth. The Hebrew, however, can mean either 'upon it' or 'upon him'; and according to some Jewish explanations of Gen. 28¹² the angels were ascending and descending, not upon the ladder, but upon Jacob, regarded as both ancestor and embodiment of (the true) Israel, God's elect. The form of the Greek in Jn. 1⁵¹ suggests that Gen. 28¹² was understood by St. John in this way. By the interpretation, however, which he now gives to it, he wishes his readers to understand that the dream of Gen. 28¹² is to be fulfilled in the ascent and descent of the angels (not on the individual Jacob, nor on the nation Israel, but) on the Son of man; He it is who in truth and reality joins heaven to earth, and earth to heaven.

Jewish interpretation also connected Gen. 28¹² with Is. 49³, 'Thou art my servant: Israel, in whom I will be glorified'. In John God is glorified in and by the Lord's life and death [7¹⁸, 13³¹, 17⁴]. And just as in Is. 49 Yahweh's servant is thought by many to be partly identified with Israel, and partly as a messenger of God to Israel, so the term 'the Son of man' may have both a corporate and an individual reference.

In all four gospels the term 'the Son of man' is used only by the Lord Himself, Jn. 12³⁴ being no real exception to this rule. The term, as it is used in the earlier gospels, has its roots in Jewish thought, and has special reference to the function of judgement, e.g. Mt. 25³¹, Mk. 8³⁸. Its implications are certainly messianic, although it is constantly associated in the Lord's later teaching with suffering and death, e.g. Mk. 8³¹, 10⁴⁵; this was the novel Christian contribution to the meaning of the term.

St. John by no means forgets this function of judgement in connexion with the Lord as the Son of man; e.g. 5²², ²⁷, 9³⁵ (following R.V. mg),³⁹; but usually the term, as it occurs in his gospel, has more in common with Hellenistic than with purely Jewish thought. To Hellenistic readers the term would suggest an ideal humanity, existing independently of particular examples of individual men, as their perfect archetype. This archetype, according to St. John, was manifested in the Lord. As the Son of man, He has descended from heaven in His incarnation [3¹³], in order to give life to the world [6²⁷, ⁵³]; and He will ascend thither again [6⁶²], when His work is finished, although, even while on earth, He is not cut off from heaven [3¹³]. But His ascent must be by way of the cross [3¹⁴, 8²⁸, 12³⁴]; only so can His glory be completed [12²³, 13³¹]. Further, it is His glory, as the Son of man, to impart this perfect humanity of His also to believers on Him, who then do not come into judgement [5²⁴; cf. 3¹⁷, ¹⁸], but having passed out of death into life share in His work [17²², ²³] and His glory. Thus the glory of the Son of man is His revelation, promised in 1⁵¹ to disciples, of the being and the character of God; and it is manifested, above all, in the passion [8[28], 12[23, 32-34]], in which the glorification of the Son is also the glorification of the Father.

2[1]. 'the third day': that is, after the promise given in 1[51]. In the N.T. the expression 'the third day' or 'after three days' usually means what we should describe as 'the day following the morrow', or 'after two days'. Since four, if not five, successive days are mentioned in 1[19-51], the wedding takes place on either the sixth or the seventh day after the opening of St. John's narrative at 1[19]. But further, since in the earlier Christian tradition 'the third day', being that of the Lord's resurrection, was also the day of the revelation of His glory, St. John, who wishes the reader to discern the revelation of the Lord's glory—i.e. of His resurrection (cf. 11[25]) as well as of His passion—throughout this gospel (cf. 1[14], 2[11]), by the use of these words here may be indirectly reminding him to share this interpretation of the Lord's life and work.

2[4]. 'What have I to do (or, in common) with thee'? The same Greek words form the LXX translation in 1 Kgs. 17[18]; cf. 2 Sam. 16[10]; these passages show how the sentence here should be understood. In the earlier gospels the sentence is used several times by 'the possessed', on finding themselves in the presence of the Lord; e.g. Mt. 8[29], Mk. 1[24], 5[7], Lk. 4[34], 8[28].

2[6]. The measure mentioned implies that each waterpot would hold about twenty gallons.

II

The public manifestation of the Lord

SECTION 1. 2^{12}–4^{54}

The new order seen against the background of the old order

2 After this he went down to Capernaum, he, and his mother, and *his* brethren, and his disciples: and there they abode not many days.

13 And the passover of the Jews was at hand, and Jesus went up to
14 Jerusalem. And he found in the temple those that sold oxen and sheep
15 and doves, and the changers of money sitting: and he made a scourge of cords, and cast all out of the temple, both the sheep and the oxen; and he poured out the changers' money, and overthrew their tables;
16 and to them that sold the doves he said, Take these things hence; make
17 not my Father's house a house of merchandise. His disciples remembered
18 that it was written, The zeal of thine house shall eat me up. The Jews therefore answered and said unto him, What sign shewest thou unto
19 us, seeing that thou doest these things? Jesus answered and said unto
20 them, Destroy this ¹temple, and in three days I will raise it up. The Jews therefore said, Forty and six years was this ¹temple in building,
21 and wilt thou raise it up in three days? But he spake of the ¹temple of
22 his body. When therefore he was raised from the dead, his disciples remembered that he spake this; and they believed the scripture, and the word which Jesus had said.

23 Now when he was in Jerusalem at the passover, during the feast,
24 many believed on his name, beholding his signs which he did. But
25 Jesus did not trust himself unto them, for that he knew all men, and because he needed not that any one should bear witness concerning ²man; for he himself knew what was in man.

3 Now there was a man of the Pharisees, named Nicodemus, a ruler
2 of the Jews: the same came unto him by night, and said to him, Rabbi, we know that thou art a teacher come from God: for no man can do these
3 signs that thou doest, except God be with him. Jesus answered and said unto him, Verily, verily, I say unto thee, Except a man be born
4 ³anew, he cannot see the kingdom of God. Nicodemus saith unto him, How can a man be born when he is old? can he enter a second time into
5 his mother's womb, and be born? Jesus answered, Verily, verily, I say unto thee, Except a man be born of water and the Spirit, he cannot enter

¹ *Or* sanctuary ² *Or* a man; for . . . the man ³ *Or* from above

6 into the kingdom of God. That which is born of the flesh is flesh; and
7 that which is born of the Spirit is spirit. Marvel not that I said unto
8 thee, Ye must be born [1]anew. [2]The wind bloweth where it listeth, and
thou hearest the voice thereof, but knowest not whence it cometh, and
9 whither it goeth: so is every one that is born of the Spirit. Nicodemus
10 answered and said unto him, How can these things be? Jesus answered
and said unto him, Art thou the teacher of Israel, and understandest not
11 these things? Verily, verily, I say unto thee, We speak that we do know,
and bear witness of that we have seen; and ye receive not our witness.
12 If I told you earthly things, and ye believe not, how shall ye believe,
13 if I tell you heavenly things? And no man hath ascended into heaven,
but he that descended out of heaven, *even* the Son of man, [3]which is in
14 heaven. And as Moses lifted up the serpent in the wilderness, even so
15 must the Son of man be lifted up: that whosoever [4]believeth may in
him have eternal life.

16   For God so loved the world, that he gave his only begotten Son, that
whosoever believeth on him should not perish, but have eternal life.
17 For God sent not the Son into the world to judge the world; but that
18 the world should be saved through him. He that believeth on him is
not judged: he that believeth not hath been judged already, because
he hath not believed on the name of the only begotten Son of God.
19 And this is the judgement, that the light is come into the world, and
men loved the darkness rather than the light; for their works were evil.
20 For every one that [5]doeth ill hateth the light, and cometh not to the
21 light, lest his works should be [6]reproved. But he that doeth the truth
cometh to the light, that his works may be made manifest, [7]that they have
been wrought in God.

22   After these things came Jesus and his disciples into the land of Judaea;
23 and there he tarried with them, and baptized. And John also was baptizing in Aenon near to Salim, because there [8]was much water there: and
24 they came, and were baptized. For John was not yet cast into prison.
25 There arose therefore a questioning on the part of John's disciples with
26 a. Jew about purifying. And they came unto John, and said to him,
Rabbi, he that was with thee beyond Jordan, to whom thou hast borne
27 witness, behold, the same baptizeth, and all men come to him. John
answered and said, A man can receive nothing, except it have been
28 given him from heaven. Ye yourselves bear me witness, that I said, I
29 am not the Christ, but, that I am sent before him. He that hath the bride
is the bridegroom: but the friend of the bridegroom, which standeth
and heareth him, rejoiceth greatly because of the bridegroom's voice:
30 this my joy therefore is fulfilled. He must increase, but I must decrease.

---

[1] *Or* from above   [2] *Or* The Spirit breatheth   [3] *Many ancient author-*
ities omit which is in heaven.   [4] *Or* believeth in him may have   [5] *Or*
practiseth   [6] *Or* convicted   [7] *Or* because   [8] *Gr.* were many waters.

31 He that cometh from above is above all: he that is of the earth is of the
   earth, and of the earth he speaketh: [1]he that cometh from heaven is
32 above all. What he hath seen and heard, of that he beareth witness;
33 and no man receiveth his witness. He that hath received his witness
34 hath set his seal to *this*, that God is true. For he whom God hath sent
   speaketh the words of God: for he giveth not the Spirit by measure.
35 The Father loveth the Son, and hath given all things into his hand.
36 He that believeth on the Son hath eternal life; but he that [2]obeyeth
   not the Son shall not see life, but the wrath of God abideth on him.

4 When therefore the Lord knew how that the Pharisees had heard
2 that Jesus was making and baptizing more disciples than John (although
3 Jesus himself baptized not, but his disciples), He left Judaea, and de-
4 parted again into Galilee. And he must needs pass through Samaria.
5 So he cometh to a city of Samaria, called Sychar, near to the parcel of
6 ground that Jacob gave to his son Joseph: and Jacob's [3]well was there.
   Jesus therefore, being wearied with his journey, sat [4]thus by the [3]well.
7 It was about the sixth hour. There cometh a woman of Samaria to draw
8 water: Jesus saith unto her, Give me to drink. For his disciples were
9 gone away into the city to buy food. The Samaritan woman therefore
   saith unto him, How is it that thou, being a Jew, askest drink of me,
   which am a Samaritan woman? ([5]For Jews have no dealings with
10 Samaritans.) Jesus answered and said unto her, If thou knewest the
   gift of God, and who it is that saith to thee, Give me to drink; thou
   wouldest have asked of him, and he would have given thee living water.
11 The woman saith unto him, [6]Sir, thou hast nothing to draw with, and
12 the well is deep: from whence then hast thou that living water? Art
   thou greater than our father Jacob, which gave us the well, and drank
13 thereof himself, and his sons, and his cattle? Jesus answered and said
14 unto her, Every one that drinketh of this water shall thirst again: But
   whosoever drinketh of the water that I shall give him shall never thirst;
   but the water that I shall give him shall become in him a well of water
15 springing up unto eternal life. The woman saith unto him, [6]Sir, give
16 me this water, that I thirst not, neither come all the way hither to draw.
17 Jesus saith unto her, Go, call thy husband, and come hither. The
   woman answered and said unto him, I have no husband. Jesus saith
18 unto her, Thou saidst well, I have no husband: For thou hast had five
   husbands; and he whom thou now hast is not thy husband: this hast
19 thou said truly. The woman saith unto him, [6]Sir, I perceive that thou
20 art a prophet. Our fathers worshipped in this mountain; and ye say,
21 that in Jerusalem is the place where men ought to worship. Jesus

---

[1] *Some ancient authorities read* he that cometh from heaven beareth witness of
what he hath seen and heard.   [2] *Or* believeth not   [3] *Gr.* spring: *and
so in* ver. 14; *but not in* ver. 11, 12.   [4] *Or* as he was   [5] *Some ancient
authorities omit* For Jews have no dealings with Samaritans.   [6] *Or* Lord

saith unto her, Woman, believe me, the hour cometh, when neither in
22 this mountain, nor in Jerusalem, shall ye worship the Father. Ye
worship that which ye know not: we worship that which we know: for
23 salvation is from the Jews. But the hour cometh, and now is, when the
true worshippers shall worship the Father in spirit and truth: ¹for such
24 doth the Father seek to be his worshippers. ²God is a Spirit: and they
25 that worship him must worship in spirit and truth. The woman saith
unto him, I know that Messiah cometh (which is called Christ): when
26 he is come, he will declare unto us all things. Jesus saith unto her, I
that speak unto thee am *he*.

27   And upon this came his disciples; and they marvelled that he was
speaking with a woman; yet no man said, What seekest thou? or, Why
28 speakest thou with her? So the woman left her waterpot, and went
29 away into the city, and saith to the men, Come, see a man, which told
30 me all things that *ever* I did: can this be the Christ? They went out
31 of the city, and were coming to him. In the mean while the disciples
32 prayed him, saying, Rabbi, eat. But he said unto them, I have meat to
33 eat that ye know not. The disciples therefore said one to another, Hath
34 any man brought him *aught* to eat? Jesus saith unto them, My meat is
35 to do the will of him that sent me, and to accomplish his work. Say not
ye, There are yet four months, and *then* cometh the harvest? behold, I
say unto you, Lift up your eyes, and look on the fields, that they are
36 ³white already unto harvest. He that reapeth receiveth wages, and
gathereth fruit unto life eternal; that he that soweth and he that reapeth
37 may rejoice together. For herein is the saying true, One soweth, and
38 another reapeth. I sent you to reap that whereon ye have not laboured:
others have laboured, and ye are entered into their labour.

39   And from that city many of the Samaritans believed on him because
of the word of the woman, who testified, He told me all things that
40 *ever* I did. So when the Samaritans came unto him, they besought him
41 to abide with them: and he abode there two days. And many more
42 believed because of his word; and they said to the woman, Now we
believe, not because of thy speaking: for we have heard for ourselves,
and know that this is indeed the Saviour of the world.

43   And after the two days he went forth from thence into Galilee. For
44 Jesus himself testified, that a prophet hath no honour in his own country.
45 So when he came into Galilee, the Galilaeans received him, having seen
all the things that he did in Jerusalem at the feast: for they also went
unto the feast.

46   He came therefore again unto Cana of Galilee, where he made the
water wine. And there was a certain ⁴nobleman, whose son was sick at

---

¹ *Or* for such the Father also seeketh   ² *Or* God is spirit   ³ *Or*
white unto harvest. Already he that reapeth, &c.   ⁴ *Or* king's officer

47 Capernaum. When he heard that Jesus was come out of Judaea into
Galilee, he went unto him, and besought *him* that he would come down,
48 and heal his son; for he was at the point of death. Jesus therefore said
unto him, Except ye see signs and wonders, ye will in no wise believe.
49 The ¹nobleman saith unto him, ²Sir, come down ere my child die.
50 Jesus saith unto him, Go thy way; thy son liveth. The man believed
51 the word that Jesus spake unto him, and he went his way. And as he
was now going down, his ³servants met him, saying, that his son lived.
52 So he inquired of them the hour when he began to amend. They said
therefore unto him, Yesterday at the seventh hour the fever left him.
53 So the father knew that *it was* at that hour in which Jesus said unto him,
54 Thy son liveth: and himself believed, and his whole house. This is
again the second sign that Jesus did, having come out of Judaea into
Galilee.

¹ *Or* kings' officer ² *Or* Lord ³ *Gr.* bondservants.

EXPOSITION OF SECTION 1. 2¹²–4⁵⁴

*The new order, seen against the background of the old order in
reference both to the Lord's works and to His words.*

It seems possible that the purpose of the brief note in 2¹², by
which St. John links 1¹⁹ to 2¹¹ with the Lord's next action, the
cleansing of the temple at Jerusalem, is to remind the reader of the
earlier tradition, according to which the first and greater part of
the Lord's work was laid in Galilee, with Capernaum as a kind of
headquarters of it (cf. Mt. 11²³). In John, however, the main scene
of the Lord's work is, from the first, the south; and in 2¹³ we pass
forthwith to Jerusalem at passover time, and to the temple. This,
the centre of Jewish worship and national hope, itself an obvious
symbol of the existing order, is the scene of the Lord's first public
work; and that work is at once manifested in a negative way. For
His action in the temple is not now the completion and perfection
of the Jewish order, like His action in changing water to wine in
the comparative privacy of 2¹⁻¹¹; it is in opposition to the old order,
and (in consequence of the attitude and future action of those who
now accost Him [2¹⁹, ²⁰]), is destined to lead to its replacement.

For this event we have parallel accounts in the earlier gospels;
and in the Marcan context [11¹² to 12¹²], the withering of the fig-
tree, the mountain cast into the sea (contrast Micah 4¹), and the

allegory of the wicked husbandmen all foreshadow the rejection of Israel. We may also recall actual or alleged references by the Lord to the coming destruction of the temple in Mk. 13¹, ² and its replacement [14⁵⁸, 15²⁹]. The setting of the event in the first three gospels, very soon after the Lord's arrival at the capital towards the end of His ministry, is more likely to be historically correct than that in John. One reason for the position assigned to it in John may be that it is part of his purpose to represent the judgement or discrimination effected by the presence and work of the Lord among men as in operation from the outset of His activity; and 'the cleansing of the temple', understood as the purgation or judgement of Judaism which He effected, is a suitable means of calling attention to this aspect of His work (see pp. 40 ff.). This belief is likely to be strengthened, when we notice that in the story, as told here, emphasis is laid on the expulsion from the building not only of all those occupied in the sacrificial traffic (the reader will recall that such traffic will soon be needed no more), but also of the sacrificial animals themselves, a detail peculiar to John; and further that in 2¹⁵, although not in 2¹⁴, the sheep and the oxen are mentioned in the order in which they occur in Ps. 8⁷. It is clear from Heb. 2⁶⁻⁸ and other N.T. passages that this psalm, with its reference to 'man', or 'the son of man', played an important part in early Christian thought about the Lord's Person; and we shall read in Jn. 5²⁷ that the Lord has received 'authority to execute judgement, because He is the Son of man', or, possibly, 'a son of man'; cf. R.V. mg. We shall learn later that this judgement is completed or fulfilled at and by the Lord's passion [12³¹]; and reference, direct or indirect, to the Lord's coming death and resurrection will dominate the latter part of the story which we are now considering [2¹⁷, ¹⁹⁻²²].

'The Jews', whom hitherto we have only met in indirect contact with the Baptist [1¹⁹], now come into direct contact with the Lord. In Mk. 11²⁸ they ask to know His authority for acting thus in the temple; and the question which they put in Jn. 2¹⁸ has the same implication; but it is expressed here in a particularly Jewish form. For the Jews, as St. Paul very soon found (cf. 1 Cor. 1²²), were prone to demand a sign or miracle if they were to be persuaded of the presence or reality of divine truth or revelation (cf. Ex. 4¹⁻⁸, Jdgs. 6¹⁷, ³⁶⁻⁴⁰, 2 Kgs. 20⁸⁻¹¹). On the present occasion they fail to see that the Lord's action in 2¹⁴⁻¹⁶ is itself a sign, viz. of the coming destruction of the temple worship; and they presumed to ask for that which, in truth, has just been granted. In reply the Lord, in ambiguous language [2¹⁹⁻²¹], offers the supreme sign of the Gospel, namely, His resurrection, in other words, Himself and His work, since He is the resurrection [11²⁵]. Let the Jews destroy the shrine of the Word become flesh, in a very short time He will raise it up (cf. 10¹⁷, ¹⁸). Any other kind of sign, such as that which the Jews implicitly demand, is refused. The Lord's reply may be an example of semitic parataxis, i.e. the placing, side by side, of two sentences joined by 'and', where we should subordinate one sentence to the other, 'Though you may destroy this shrine, in three days I will raise it up'. But some think that His reply is an example of the ironic imperative, used by the prophets, e.g. Amos 4⁴, 'Come to Bethel, and transgress' (cf. Is. 8⁹, ¹⁰). In either case, the reply in veiled language conveys the truth that the Jews in their unbelief will themselves become the instruments in bringing about the sign which the Lord now offers them; for it is they who will 'lift up the Son of man' [8²⁸]. Thus the sign given will also be their judgement and their condemnation.

The Jews, as we should expect in this gospel, in which from first to last they fail to comprehend the Lord, understand Him to refer to the building of stone, and they express incredulity; and therewith the conversation, and the description of the incident (which must have been one of great excitement), are brought abruptly to a close. Only to the reader is the meaning of the Lord's words revealed [2²¹], with a further note that only the Lord's resurrection brought the saying itself to the disciples' remembrance and gave them a true understanding both of the O.T. and of the Lord's words here. St. John's note at 2²², like that at 12¹⁶, teaches in positive language the same truth which St. Mark constantly expresses in negative language, when the latter emphasizes the disciples' lack of understanding during the ministry. Only when the Lord's work is finished, are the disciples enabled, through their endowment by Him with the Spirit, sent to them by the Father in His name [7³⁹, 14²⁶, 15²⁶, ²⁷], to understand the events of His ministry in accordance with their true meaning.

For the statement in 2²¹ that the temple or shrine of the Lord's body would replace the Jewish temple of stone must have carried great significance for St. John's readers, because the conception of the community of believers as a 'temple' or 'shrine', which is 'the body of Christ' [1 Cor. 12²⁷], is prominent in 1 Cor. 3¹⁶, 2 Cor. 6¹⁶, Eph. 2²¹. Thus the temple which the Lord will raise up is 'the church' [Eph. 1²², ²³], in which God is worshipped 'in spirit' [Eph. 2²²] and 'in truth' [Eph. 4¹⁵ R.V. mg]; cf. Jn. 4²³⁻²⁴.

But the temple mentioned is also the Lord's human body, the shrine of the incarnate Word, which was laid in a tomb [19⁴²] and raised within three days. Indeed, the Church is the Lord's body only because it is united with Him in His ministry, death, and resurrection [Rom. 6³⁻⁵, Col. 3³]; and St. John, by his citation at 2¹⁷ of words from Ps. 69, which is quoted in all the gospels and in other parts of the New Testament in reference to the passion, has already brought the Lord's cleansing of the temple into connexion with His death. The self-oblation of the true paschal Lamb must precede His resurrection; and the life of the Church derives from this twofold event. It is true that St. John, unlike St. Paul, does not use the expression 'the body of Christ' in reference to disciples; but the union of the glorified Lord with those who believe on Him is a cardinal doctrine of this gospel; in fact this union is compared in 17²², ²³ to nothing less than the perfect and permanent union of the Father and the Son.

Accordingly there is in this story, thus set before us here, a triple depth of meaning. First, the Lord performs an act by which He condemns the methods and the manner of the existing Jewish worship. Secondly, this act, as set forth by St. John, is a sign of the destruction of the old order of worship, that of the Jewish Church, and its replacement by a new order of worship, that of the Christian Church, the sanctuary or shrine of the living God. And thirdly, intermediate between the old order and the new order is the 'work' —the ministry, death, and resurrection—of the Lord, which alone makes possible the inauguration and the life of the new temple.

It will be found to be a conspicuous feature of this gospel that those, who in it come into contact with the Lord, *ipso facto* come also into judgement; by their attitude to Him, and to His works and words, they pass judgement on themselves, a judgement either of acquittal or of condemnation. To speak generally, in the case of groups who come into contact with Him, the final attitude seems to be implicit from the outset; we may instance the disciples on the one hand [1¹⁴, 2¹¹], and the Jews on the other [2²⁰] (see pp. 68–73 and 64–66). In the case of individuals, the judgement is apt to appear as a process, in which we read, on the one hand, of an increasing enlightenment (e.g. in 4^{1-29} or 4^{46-53}), or, on the other, not yet indeed of a definite unbelief, but at least of an imperfect response to the Lord (e.g. 3^{1-12}), which will probably never come fully to the light.

We are now to be shown, partly by conversations of the Lord with individuals—in ch. 3^{1-15}, with its appendix 3^{16-21}, with a man, the Rabbi Nicodemus, a member of the Sanhedrin, and in ch. 4^{1-42} with a Samaritan woman—partly in 3^{22-30}, with its appendix 3^{31-36}, by further witness given, now for the last time, by the Baptist, and partly in 4^{46-54} by a work of the Lord within a Gentile household, what is the significance, for mankind, of His action in the Jewish temple at Jerusalem.

In 2^{23-25}, before proceeding to the Lord's conversation with Nicodemus, St. John notes that the sight of the Lord's signs during the passover festival at Jerusalem led many to believe on His name. The Lord Himself, however, it is pointed out, was able to assess the interest thus aroused at its true value and therefore did not seek to build on it; Himself the Word become flesh, and therefore the source of life and light [1^4], He had immediate knowledge of the heart of every man (cf. $1^{42, 47, 48}$).

The verb 'to believe', as used in 2^{22}, does not necessarily imply more than to give credence to a passage of scripture, or a statement, or a person; but 'to believe on the name' of the Lord [2^{23}], an expression which has already occurred in the prologue [1^{12}] and will recur at 3^{18}, is equivalent to the strong expression 'to believe on' Him (cf. 2^{11}), the only difference being that 'to believe on His name' expresses more precisely a recognition of the significance of His Person, e.g. that He is 'the only begotten Son of God' [3^{18}]. Here, however, verses 24 and 25 of ch. 2 show that an allegiance evoked by the evidence of signs is of doubtful worth, for in the last resort belief should not stand in need either of signs [20^{29}] or of another's evidence [$4^{41, 42}$]. Not that such an initial faith is of no value; but it is only a first attraction to the Lord (cf. $4^{45, 48}$), and does not yet know Him as the Son of man, still less as the unique Son of God, and is therefore imperfect and liable to be overthrown; and of this He, the Word become flesh, is well aware. An example of the growth and flowering of a perfect faith will be given in ch. 9; but an illustration of the imperfect type of belief here evoked by the Lord's signs (with 2^{23}; cf. 3^2) is given forthwith by the case of Nicodemus.

We meet Nicodemus three times in this book; here alone with the Lord; at 7^{50} attending a meeting of the Sanhedrin; and at 19^{39} when he helps Joseph of Arimathaea to remove the Lord's body from the cross. It is noticeable that, whereas he does vainly attempt to uphold justice at the meeting in 7^{45-52}, no similar word is recorded as coming from him during the crucial meeting in 11^{47-53}. The passages, taken together, give a tolerably clear picture of his character, as containing a definite but limited measure of strength, and a definite but limited measure of perception of the truth. His words in 3^2 show him to represent those who see both in the teaching and in the signs of the Lord unmistakable evidence of divine origin; his interest is aroused, and he seeks a fuller understanding. He therefore approaches the Lord out of the darkness (in which his colleagues and fellow-Jews are immersed), just as Judas on the other hand finally forsakes the Lord, in order to join the Jews, and thus identifies himself with the night [13^{30}]; and in courteous speech he indirectly invites the Lord to expound His teaching.

Forthwith the Lord, with a solemn assurance occurring three times [$3^{3, 5, 11}$] in this short conversation, affirms the necessity of a rebirth for him who wishes to see (varied in 3^5 as 'to enter into') the kingdom of God. (In accordance with the general teaching of this book, that which is here called rebirth is no longer solely a future matter, but is said to be a present necessity. The student should contrast the language used of 'the regeneration' in Mt. 19^{28}, and also compare Lk. 22 $^{29, 30}$.) When Nicodemus understands the Lord's words in their most literal sense (see p. 130), the Lord defines the rebirth as one by means of water and spirit. (It is characteristic of St. John to refer unmistakably, but none the less always indirectly, to the two Christian sacraments of baptism and the eucharist; and at 3^5 the instructed reader cannot fail to think of the rite of initiation into the Christian Church, a rite issuing in the endowment of its members with the Holy Spirit.) It is thus at once made clear that man as such, being 'of the earth' [3^{31}], 'of this world' [8^{23}], cannot see or enter the kingdom of God. For the gulf between flesh and spirit is absolute [3^6]; and therefore the doctrine of the universal necessity of rebirth should not cause surprise, because the kingdom of God belongs to the realm or order of spirit (cf. $4^{23, 24}$). And whereas the things of the flesh can be precisely measured and calculated, it is otherwise in respect of the things of the Spirit. The Greek word *pneuma*, which means both spirit and wind, itself suggests this. For, whichever meaning it may have in any context, its origin and action are mysterious and unpredictable, but also undeniable; whether as spirit or as wind its presence is shown in its activity and its results; and such will be the characteristics also of him who is spiritually reborn. The final remark of the bewildered Nicodemus [3⁹], who judges 'according to sight' or 'appearance' [7²⁴] or 'according to the flesh' [8¹⁵], shows that the conversation has been lifted into a region which he at present cannot enter. Judaism, even learned Judaism [3¹⁰], is found at a loss in this vital matter of rebirth. The conversation, however, is continued by the Lord; and just as Nicodemus at the outset had included others with him ('we know' 3²) so in 3¹¹ the Lord speaks, not only as Himself the Word become flesh, but also, it seems, on behalf of those who received Him [1¹²] and believe on Him [2¹¹]; and Nicodemus is regarded as the representative of others also [3¹¹, ¹²]. They are warned that the truths about to be revealed must be received on the ground of testimony which can only be verified, as it were, from within; they cannot be established by external evidence, and are therefore unacceptable to the natural man [3¹¹ᵇ]; the sight promised in 1⁵¹ is not visible to him as such. If the necessity of rebirth does not find credence [3¹²ᵃ], it is even less likely that a welcome will be given to the revelation of the divine act, which makes possible the rebirth. None the less, this revelation is now given. The gulf between flesh and spirit can only be spanned from above. Of himself man cannot gain the height of heaven; but, in order to enable him to do so, One has descended from heaven as 'the *Son of man*' (we here meet this expression for the second time), whose destiny it is to be lifted up. Just as Moses, in order to save the Israelites from plague [Num. 21⁹], lifted up or exalted a bronze serpent on a pole or stake, like a condemned criminal, for all to see, so there must be a lifting up or exaltation of the Son of man, in order that through Him and through belief in Him men may have eternal life (this term is here used for the first time in John); thus and thus only is the necessary rebirth made possible—and, to the believer, actual.

It should be noticed that the revelation is at present made in veiled language. The Lord does not refer expressly to Himself, as He will in the later chapters, e.g. in the repeated 'I am . . .' of chs. 6 to 15. We hear only of Him 'that descended out of heaven'

[3¹³], 'the Son of man' [3¹³, ¹⁴], 'the Son' [3¹⁶, ¹⁷, ¹⁸]; nor is the nature of the descent from heaven or of the lifting up, explained as yet, although the instructed reader no doubt has the key. He will also remind himself that the doctrine of rebirth, which has just been set forth, explains the significance of the Lord's action, at the beginning of this section, in the temple at Jerusalem, and is also explained by it. The Jewish temple, as such, is doomed to destruction; but the promise is given of its reconstruction in another form.

3¹⁶⁻²¹ may be regarded either as a continuation of the Lord's words to Nicodemus, or (more probably, in spite of the 'comfortable words' in the Book of Common Prayer) as an elaboration, by the evangelist, of the import of that conversation. We have learned that the possibility of rebirth for man is conditioned by the descent of the Son of man from heaven, and also that the Son of man must be exalted or lifted up, in order that in Him the believer may have eternal life. In 3¹⁶, ¹⁷ this action of the Son of man is explained as being due to the love of God for the world, a love which led Him to give His only Son. God's purpose herein is declared [3¹⁷] to have been solely positive, not negative; salvation, not condemnation (cf. Rom. 8³²⁻³⁴). On the other hand, since the Son of God, Himself love, life, light, and truth, has come into the world, and there is no love, life, light, or truth which does not take its origin from Him [1³], acceptance of His witness and consequent devotion to Him are essential [8³¹, 15²², 16⁹]; and rejection of Him or disbelief in Him is therefore acceptance of and identification with hatred, death, darkness, and falsehood [8⁴⁴, ⁴⁷, 15²³]. Thus in the presence of the incarnate Word, or Son, every man is bound to reveal himself as what indeed he is; either he ranges himself on the side of the realities embodied in the Lord, or against them, and therefore against Him. Hence the manifestation of the Lord, if rejected, is bound to have a very dark side, not as its object, but as its inevitable result; and this aspect of the truth, which will be emphasized in subsequent chapters, is here [3¹⁸⁻²⁰] mentioned for the first time, in the form of judgement or condemnation. There is no book of the N.T. in which the contrast of love and hatred, life and death, light and darkness, truth and falsehood appears in such unrelieved sharpness as in this gospel. Nor is it only a matter of spiritual acceptance of the witness offered; thought and action, word and work, are inseparably connected [3¹⁹⁻²¹]. Truth therefore is not only to be perceived and welcomed; it is also to be 'done' [3²¹], carried out in action; and conversely an action 'wrought in God' will lead to manifestation of the truth.

In 3²²⁻³⁰ the Baptist gives his final testimony to the Lord. In the first three gospels the imprisonment of the Baptist takes place before the Lord opens His ministry in Galilee; but in this passage and at 4¹ we read that for a time both baptized simultaneously in the south, though the reference to the Baptist at 5³⁵ in the past tense suggests that this period was brief and that, before ch. 6 opens, John's activity was over. Jn. 3²², ²⁶ and 4¹ are the only passages in the gospels which state that the Lord baptized, and the statement in 4¹ is at once qualified in 4² by an explanation that in fact not the Lord, but His disciples, baptized. Since in 3²²⁻³⁰ the whole emphasis is on the contrast between the Baptist's work and that of the Lord, and of the supersession of the former by the latter, we seem to be invited to contrast the two baptisms in question. If we do so, we remember that, whereas the Baptist in ch. 1 emphasizes [1²⁶, ³¹, ³³] that his baptism is a baptism in water (only), the baptism brought by Him, to whom he bears witness, is, as John has learned by divine revelation [1³³], a baptism in holy spirit. It is true that the Baptist was sent, and had his authority, from heaven [1³³, Mk. 11³⁰]; but he himself, although pronounced by the Lord to be as great a man as ever lived, was not a member of the kingdom of God [Mt. 11¹¹, Lk. 7²⁸], which can only be entered by means of the rebirth—by water and Spirit—set forth in 3³, ⁸; and of this entry the Lord, and He only, is the door [3¹³⁻¹⁵, 10⁷⁻⁹]. In 3²²⁻³⁰, therefore, the Baptist is the representative of the old order, as Nicodemus was in 3¹⁻¹⁵.

To judge from 3²⁵, an inquiry seems to have arisen into the whole matter of the administration and efficacy of the various contemporary Jewish rites of purification by water; and the Baptist's disciples are concerned at the increasing notoriety of the Lord, in contrast to that of their master. The Baptist replies that the events now occurring are in accordance with the divine will [3²⁷], and also with his own earlier witness [3²⁸]. His task, as 'the friend of the bridegroom', was solely to put all in order for the union of the Bridegroom with His bride, Israel; and he has now been allowed to hear the Bridegroom's voice. Hence the joy assigned to him, the joy of making the preparations for the new order and of standing on its threshold, although not within it, is completed (with $3^{29\text{end}}$ contrast 15^{11}, 16^{24}, 17^{13}); and the greater the Bridegroom is seen to be, the less does he himself become.

At 3^{31-36} the same uncertainty arises as at 3^{16-21}; the passage may be regarded either as a continuation of the Baptist's words or, more probably, as a short, reflective supplement to 3^{22-30}. It is closely related to thoughts already expressed in 3^{1-21} (cf., for example, 3^{31-33} with $3^{6,\ 11,\ 13}$, and $3^{35,\ 36}$ with $3^{16,\ 18}$); but it also forms a suitable appendix to 3^{22-30}. For the Baptist was, after all, 'from the earth', and therefore could only speak 'from the earth' [3^{31}; cf. 8^{23}]; and we now pass to the thought of the testimony borne by Him who (and who alone, as we learned in 3^{13}) 'comes from above' and is 'above all'; whom God has sent; who speaks the words of God; to whom God gives the Spirit without limit; the Son of the Father's love, into whose hand the Father has given all things (cf. 13^3). He is now bearing witness of that which He has seen and heard in the presence of the Father (cf. 8^{38}); and although the great majority of men decline His testimony, he who has received it is able, thanks to it, to guarantee both the reality and the reliability of God. And the result for him, the believer, is eternal life [3^{36}]; whereas he who disbelieves and disobeys the Son remains outside the circle of the divine energy of life and love (cf. $3^{19,\ 36}$, 12^{46}).

Both at the beginning and at the end of the Lord's conversation with the woman of Samaria, there is a contrast between the old order and the new order now coming into being [4^{23}]: first, water drawn from Jacob's well is not to be compared with the water brought by the Lord [4^{7-15}]; and secondly, both the Jewish worship in the temple at Jerusalem, and the Samaritan worship on Mount Gerizim, are to be, indeed are being, replaced by a worship which will have its seat neither in Jerusalem nor in Samaria. Thus the different symbolisms of water, the mention of which, as will be shown in a moment, is very frequent in the first three chapters, and of the temple-worship, which we encountered in 2^{13-22}, are now brought together in 4^{1-26}, and the meaning of each is explained. The advance of the thought of 4^{1-15} on that of 3^{3-8} is that in 3^{3-8} water gives initial admission to eternal life by a new birth; in 4^{1-15} the water offered is a continuous and unfailing supply, ever welling up afresh in the recipient [4^{14}] and satisfying all desire. And the advance of the thought of 4^{21-26} on that of 2^{13-22} may perhaps be expressed in the words of Rev. 21^{22}, 'And I saw no temple therein; for the Lord God the Almighty, and the Lamb, are the temple thereof.'

Like the note of witness, the theme of water runs like a silver thread through the early chapters of this gospel. Thus the Baptist baptizes in water [1²⁶, ³¹, ³³]; water becomes wine in 2¹⁻¹¹; water is needed for rebirth [3⁵]; both the Lord and the Baptist baptize, the latter where there is much water [3²²⁻²⁶]; the Lord will give living water [4⁷⁻¹⁵]; and in 5²⁻⁹ the impotent man had been hoping to regain his health in the water of the pool of Bethesda. Thereafter water is only mentioned or implied in certain important passages 7³⁷⁻³⁹, 9⁷, ¹¹, 13⁵⁻¹⁴, 19²⁸, ³⁴.

Water, especially in hot countries, is one of the most compelling needs of man. In many parts of the world the word 'thirst' suggests the most passionate and painful craving that a man can undergo; it is the agonized protest of the human body against being deprived of its most vital need; and if unslaked, it is the prelude to the most dreadful of deaths. In the O.T., and in the literatures of other nations, man's desire for God is often compared to desire for a draught of water which will quench his thirst, e.g. Ps. 42¹⁻²; and in Jer. 2¹³ Yahweh describes Himself as 'the fountain of living waters', yet forsaken by His people in favour of 'cisterns, broken cisterns', hewed out by men themselves.

The R.V. mg at 4⁶ should be noticed. It is true that in the LXX the two Greek words found here, like their Hebrew originals, are sometimes used interchangeably, and this may be the case here also; but elsewhere they are apt to be distinguished. For the word in 4⁶, ¹⁴, *pēgē*, usually denotes a natural well or spring, whereas that in 4¹¹, ¹², *phrear*, more often describes a well constructed artificially, and may be used of a cistern or reservoir. Is it possible, therefore, that in St. John's thought Jacob's Well can be described by the more living word until the coming of the Lord, but that with His arrival it becomes no better than a cistern, in contrast to the fount of springing water which His coming brings?

4¹⁻⁴² describes the Lord's first contact in this gospel with others than Jews, and in this connexion certain features of the narrative may carry more than their surface significance. For it is repeatedly emphasized in John, especially in the later chapters, that the universal religion, which is to be the result of the Lord's completed word and work, as opposed to the particularity and nationalism of the Jewish religion, can only come into being after and because of the Lord's death. For example, 12^{20-22} records the desire of certain Greeks or Gentiles (a word which by origin denotes the peoples of all nations other than the one, chosen, Jewish nation) to see the Lord; and in 12^{23-32} this desire is brought into immediate and vital connexion with His death, through which the invitation to salvation will be offered to all men. And if the record in 4^{1-42} of the Lord's contact with Samaritans is carefully compared with St. John's record of the passion, a certain parallelism reveals itself, and it may be thought possible that ch. 4 itself contains hints of the cost to the Lord in achieving this result. Thus His weariness [4^6] should be compared with His greater physical suffering described in the words of $19^{1, 2}$; His desire for a draught of water [4^7] with 19^{28}, these being the only two passages in John which allude to thirst on His part; and His words in 4^{34} with His final word from the cross at 19^{30}, the Greek verb being from the same root in both places. It is perhaps also noteworthy that 4^{26}, the Lord's first direct personal self-declaration in John, is quickly followed by the Samaritans' confession of Him as 'the Saviour of the world' at 4^{42} (cf. 3^{14-17}, 12^{32}). But possibly the most remarkable similarity is the exact verbal parallelism, strangely neglected in both authorized and revised version reference Bibles, in the note of time at both 4^6 and 19^{14}. Doubtless those who do not think that St. John invites his readers to discern religious teaching in his apparently artless notes of time can give a satisfactory reason for the reference at 4^6 to 'the sixth hour' (that is, noon), as designed solely to explain why the Lord should now rest, because of the midday heat. But, as has just been pointed out, precisely the same words—in the original Greek as in the English—occur at 19^{14} in a particularly important context, immediately before the Lord is handed over to be crucified; and there the explanation just offered cannot apply.

At the outset of the story He, who has come in order to be to the believer the source both of living energy [10^{10}] and of living water [$7^{37, 38}$], is found wearied [4^6], athirst [4^7], and alone [4^8]. For the disciples have gone away to procure material provisions in the market-place (cf. 6^{5-7}, where the same Greek word *agorazein* is used; cf. also Is. $55^{1, 2}$, Lk. 10^{38-42}), and so the Lord cannot look to them for refreshment. In consequence, not they, but a woman, a Samaritan, receives the coming revelation of a source of life and energy to be had 'without money and without price'. On her arrival, the Lord asks for a draught of water. The woman, thinking instinctively of current quarrels and divisions, expresses surprise. The Lord, tacitly declining to continue the conversation at the level she has chosen, suggests in mysterious language that she, not He, did she know the true facts of the encounter, would be the one to crave the gift. (It is true that the Speaker Himself, a tired and thirsty Traveller, has just asked for relief; but in fact the hearer's need is far greater than His.) It is therefore essential, if she is not to miss her opportunity, that, to use language drawn from elsewhere in the gospels, she should not judge 'according to appearance' [7²⁴], or 'after the flesh' [8¹⁵]; otherwise she will be 'caused to stumble' [Mt. 11⁶, 13⁵⁷]. That for which she would have asked, did she understand the situation, is described as living water [4¹⁰], a Hebrew expression the surface meaning of which is flowing, as opposed to still, water (cf. Lev. 14⁵); and this, as we should expect, is the sense in which at present the Lord's words are understood by the hearer [4¹¹]; of their deeper meaning, to be explained by the Lord in 4¹³, ¹⁴, only the reader is aware at present.

In 4¹³, ¹⁴ the Lord, contrasting the water of the well with that which He will give, says that the latter will quench thirst permanently, and will become in the recipient an internal fount of springing water, issuing in eternal life. The hearer now makes an advance, in so far as she becomes prepared to be the recipient, rather than the giver, of a bounty; and she in her turn now asks for water, the water mentioned by the Lord, which she regards as likely to be a useful means, not only to quench thirst, but also to lighten daily toil [4¹⁵]. It was her hope to avoid, in this way, all future journeys to the well; but the Lord forthwith lays a task upon her; she is, after all, to return to the well, but with a new purpose; she is to bring another with her to Him there [4¹⁶]. To her rejoinder that He has asked what is not possible, the Lord in 4¹⁷, ¹⁸ reveals His full knowledge of her life (cf. 2²⁴, ²⁵); and she, in consequence, begins to have a faint inkling of the remarkable situation in which, all unexpectedly, she now finds herself, and (whether or not from a desire to change the subject) uses the opportunity to put to the Stranger, Himself a Jew, the controverted question of the right place where worship should be offered, Gerizim or Jerusalem. As a prophet, He should know. The Lord is now prepared to answer her directly (contrast 4¹⁰), and, giving her a strong assurance, He rules out the problem as no longer relevant. Very soon the day of local and differing, as opposed to universal and united,

worship is to pass; indeed the hour of the new worship is already
come. It is a worship, no longer to be offered by non-Jews in
ignorance (cf. Acts $17^{23, 30}$), or in accordance with Jewish rites,
although it is true, having its source and origin in Judaism; and it
will be offered to 'the Father in spirit and truth'. For the worship
here in view is that of men sought by the Father, above all through
His gift of His Son [3^{16}]; hence it is essentially connected with Him
who, and who only, has bridged the gulf between earth and heaven
[3^{13}]. By thus opening the way to the Father, indeed by being
Himself the way to the Father [14^6], and making known all things
that He heard from His Father [15^{15}], the Son is making this
worship possible for men. Just as the living water offered by the
Lord in 4^{10}, springing up unto eternal life in the recipient [4^{14}],
differs from and surpasses the water of Jacob's well, so this worship
differs from and surpasses earlier forms of worship in its life-
giving and creative power; for it is to be a worship 'in spirit and
truth'. These two words imply much more than the sincere and
honourable character and dealing implied in Ps. 15 as a condition
of true worship. For the Speaker, who is Himself the truth no less
than the way [14^6], is come, precisely in order to raise men into
the sphere of that truth or heavenly reality to which He by right
belongs; and in $17^{17, 19}$ He will pray that, through His self-
consecration for the sake of His disciples, they also may be consecrated or sanctified in truth.

The teaching thus given, although largely unintelligible to the
hearer, especially that at 4^{23} with regard to the present hour, none
the less is enough to arouse her messianic expectations. She is still
unable to discern in the Traveller the Word become flesh, the Son
of man; but she is able to express her conviction that One will
come and, having come, will make all things clear; and this
enables the Lord to direct her forthwith to the Object of her hope.
He, of whom she has spoken, is even now present, and is talking
with her.

At 4^{26} the conversation has reached a suitable conclusion, and
at this moment the disciples return, and silently marvel at the
scene before them. Whereas in Mark the Lord's words and actions
often arouse such violent emotions as astonishment, e.g. 1^{27}, 7^{37},
and fear, e.g. 4^{41}, 9^{32}, St. John in this connexion, except at 6^{19}, 19^8,
never uses any stronger term than wonder, surprise, e.g. 7^{21}; but
we are perhaps right to link with this word in John the same

associations that we connect with the stronger terms in Mark. If so, we are thus taught that here [4²⁷] we are indeed in the presence of revelation, of an unveiling of the divine activity and nature; and, as often in Mark, e.g. 6⁵¹, ⁵², 10³², so here, in the presence of these, human inquisitiveness and curiosity are at once felt to be wholly out of place [4²⁷]. The woman, in leaving her waterpot behind her (the Greek word only occurs elsewhere in the N.T. at 2¹⁻¹¹), although it had been the essential article in her original motive for coming to the well, now, in her changing outlook, unconsciously obeys the behest, not only of Hebrews 12¹, to 'lay aside all cumbrance' (R.V. mg), but also of Mark 6⁸, where the Lord insists that the disciples on their mission tour are to travel absolutely light. She too now has, or rather is beginning to have, that within her, which will quench all thirst [4¹⁴] (cf. Gal. 4¹⁹). Of her we henceforth hear, and need to hear, no more than that she forthwith carries out the duty that always accompanies new knowledge of God; she goes out on her mission to others, and now brings to the Lord, not one man [4¹⁶] but many [4²⁸, ³⁹]; and this, even although, as the reader is aware, her religious equipment or perception is at present immature and incomplete [4²⁵, ²⁹]; contrast 9³⁸.

Meantime the disciples who, having gone away on business [4⁸], were absent during their Master's revelation of Himself and so know nothing of the details of the recent conversation, try to persuade Him to avail Himself of the provisions they have brought [4³¹]. He explains His mysterious reply of 4³² by telling them in 4³⁴ of a spiritual refreshment unknown, as yet, to them, but available to Him in and through His late activity; and clearly, as a result of His activity, He is even now receiving it. For St. John constantly emphasizes that the Lord has been sent by and from His Father to carry out the Father's will, which consists in the fulfilment and completion, by the Lord, of a work, namely, the salvation of the world [3¹⁷]; and the importance of 4³⁴, occurring at this place in the narrative, is that, although there will indeed be a moment when the Father's 'work' [5¹⁷, ¹⁹], as carried out by the Son, will be complete [17⁴, 19³⁰], yet it is also complete at every step and stage of His obedience to, and fulfilment of, the Father's will and purpose; and one such step has just been taken in the conversation of 4⁷⁻²⁶ and its results, which are even now in train [4²⁸⁻³⁰, ³⁹⁻⁴²]. Hence the Lord is receiving 'meat', or nourishment, in and through the accomplishment of the work for which He has been sent.

Accordingly we are here taught that, looking at the Lord's life and work on earth, we may regard these, at any moment, as complete and perfect; but, looking at 19^{30}, we may also say that, until the moment of His death, they were not complete. Nor is it only a matter of the Lord's work on earth, of His performance of a solitary task in the days of His flesh. That work was indeed unique, and all that is now to be said derives from and is dependent on His perfect and complete performance of His work. But He is also the Logos or Word, and therefore the Lord passes at once in 4^{35-38} to the thought of the work of others, since they derive all their being and activity from Him [$1^{3,\,4}$]. By the use of what may have been two proverbial sayings of the time, He reminds His disciples that in connexion with the sowing and reaping of the fields we rightly speak of a process which has a beginning, a middle, and an end; in other words, the time interval is an essential factor. (We are told that in Palestine 'four months' would be the shortest possible time between sowing and harvest.) Again, it may well happen that those who reap are not the same as those who sowed [4^{37}]. Both sayings are familiar truths; and yet the Lord, knowing what the woman is at this moment doing [4^{28-30}], sees the harvest ready to be reaped, and bids the disciples share His vision. Let them look upon the fields, and see the work as God's work, whenever and wherever it takes place, carried out for Him by His labourers, whosoever they may be. Then they will see the results of the beginning in the end, and the promise of the end in the beginning; and there will be no need to speak, in this connexion, of a before and after, of this man or of that, since the work will be seen as one (cf. 17^{20-23}), so that all, whatever the nature of their work, and whatever their place upon the roll of time, may equally rejoice together. For not only are all, in their degree, reapers, and therefore gathering fruit, the issue of which is eternal life [4^{36}]; but all, in so far as they are reapers, owe the reward, which are receiving, to the labours of others [4^{38a}].

If we confined ourselves to the teaching of chs. 13 to 20, we might suppose that only with the completion of the Lord's work [17^{4}, 19^{30}] did that of His disciples begin [$17^{11,\,18}$, 20^{21}]; and there is here a most important truth. But at 4^{38} they are reminded that they have been already sent, in the very fact and from the moment of their being brought into their Master's company; they themselves are reapers as well as sowers, since (to change the metaphor, as St. Paul does in 1 Cor. 3[6, 7, 10]) they are building on the work of their forerunners.

In 4[39-42] we read of the result of the invitation in 4[28, 29] of the Samaritan woman to her fellow countrymen; and the teaching of the preceding paragraph is carried one step farther. It is now shown that, although the missionary's work is an essential and god-directed stage, in order that others may receive the knowledge of God (cf. 1 Cor. 3[5]), yet in and by himself (or, as in this case, herself), apart from the charge and commission laid upon him, he is nothing, cf. 1 Cor. 3[7], 2 Cor. 12[11]; his greatness consists solely in that which, for a particular purpose and a brief moment, has been entrusted to him (cf. 1 Cor. 15[10]). In the present case, for example, without or apart from the woman, the Samaritans would not have been brought into contact with the Lord. She spoke a word, the word, to them; and we have already noticed that this confession or *word* [4[25, 29, 39]] was very far from perfect; but such as it was, for its purpose and at the moment it was adequate; and it brought many of her countrymen to belief in Him [4[39]] (cf. 17[20]). On the other hand, having come themselves, they beg the Lord to remain with them, and many more are now brought to belief, as a result, not of her word, but of the Lord's. The woman's word, if now prolonged, would become mere 'talk' [4[42]] and would bear no fruit; but her countrymen, thanks to her, have now been enabled to hear for themselves, and know that their Visitor is truly 'the Saviour of the world' (cf. 3[17]).

It is thus made clear that belief on the testimony or evidence of others, however right and necessary at first, should be but temporary, and that the hearer should himself come to grips with that which he at first receives upon the witness of another (cf. 1 Jn. 5[10]). If he continues to believe only on the witness of another, this witness will become to him 'a tale of little meaning, tho' the words are strong'.[1] We recall that St. Augustine heard the Lord say to him, 'Ego sum cibus grandium',[2] 'I am the food of the mature, of the full grown'; and those who wish to become full grown should not rest, beyond a certain point, on intermediaries.

Passing to 4[46-54], we notice that both at the beginning and at the end of this episode there is a reference to the Lord's earlier work at Cana. This seems to invite us to compare the two 'signs'. Whereas in 2[1-11] the Lord, by changing water into wine, relieved the momentary

---

[1] Tennyson, *The Lotos-eaters*.   [2] *Confessions* 7. 10.

embarrassment of those responsible for the ordering of a happy marriage-feast, in 4⁴⁶⁻⁵⁴ He restores to life one who was already at the point of death. Since in the greatest sign of the ministry, that in ch. 11, we shall read of the restoration of the dead Lazarus to life, we should perhaps discern already in 4⁴⁶⁻⁵⁴ a development in the Lord's work of bringing salvation, and in the consequent manifestation of His glory.

If, as is often suggested, the story of the officer in 4⁴⁶⁻⁵⁴ is another version of the story of the centurion in Mt. 8⁵⁻¹³ = Lk. 7¹⁻¹⁰, the inference will be that he was a Gentile. In that case we may trace the following sequences in 2¹³ to 4⁵⁴. The Lord begins His ministry in Jerusalem with the cleansing of the temple, and follows this up by His conversation with the Jewish rabbi Nicodemus. In neither case, it seems, does He win active welcome or sympathy, though no doubt we should not forget such incidental passages as 2²³, 4¹. We next find Him outside Judaea, in conversation with the nonconformist Samaritan woman; and here His words fall on good soil. Not only does she raise the question whether He may be the Messiah, but her countrymen are led to see in Him the Saviour of the world. Finally, a Gentile in Galilee, whose importunity is not to be quenched by the Lord's words in 4⁴⁸ (cf. 2⁴), and his whole house believe. Thus, before in ch. 5 opposition becomes open and avowed, the seed is beginning to bear fruit (cf. 1¹²); but not chiefly in that quarter where it should have found its greatest welcome (cf. 1¹¹).

If the Lord's reply in 4⁴⁸ to one in desperate need of help seems strange, it is to be remembered that the purpose of both the Baptist's and His own ministry was that men should 'believe' [1⁷, 12⁴⁴]. According to all the gospels the Lord, from time to time, did 'signs and wonders'; and in certain cases, as here, these had the happiest results; but such actions were incidental and subsidiary to His main work, and by no means always led men to belief—cf. the question put to the Lord at 6³⁰, in spite of His bounty to this same multitude on the previous day;—sometimes indeed they resulted in an increased opposition to Him as at 11⁴⁶⁻⁵³. The Lord's words in 4⁴⁸ clearly express His distress at the general unreadiness to believe, in the absence of external and exceptional or marvellous evidence. When, however, the official undeterred (cf. Lk. 18¹) renews his request as a matter of the utmost urgency, it is granted; and the official forthwith shows that the Lord's general criticism in 4^{48} at any rate applies to him no longer. Placing implicit confidence in the Lord's word he starts upon his homeward way, soon to learn, when he meets his servants, that his trust and confidence have been justified. The belief which in consequence he and his now share is clearly of a deeper and more lasting kind than that to which allusion is made in 4^{50}.

Attention may be drawn to the threefold emphasis in this story on belief [$4^{48, 50, 53}$] and on life [$4^{49, 50, 53}$]. It may also be remarked that he who brings his great need to the Lord becomes progressively more human, as we say. As late as 4^{49} he is still 'the official'. Having accepted in faith the Lord's word, he becomes 'the man' [4^{50}], and finally we see him, in union with his household, and with a deepened faith, as 'the father' [4^{53}].

NOTES TO SECTION 1. 2^{12}–4^{54}

2^{12}. Brief transitional notes, such as that here, are a feature of this gospel (cf. 4^{43-45}, $11^{45, 46}$).

Capernaum is mentioned five times in John; at 2^{12}, 4^{46}, $6^{17, 24, 59}$.

The Lord's mother, His brethren, and His disciples are said to have gone together with Him on this visit to Capernaum. A distinction, however, will before long become apparent in the response made to Him by His brethren and His disciples respectively; contrast 7^5 with 2^{11}; and we recall the Lord's saying in Mk. 3^{31-35} that His brethren are to be found in those who do the will of God. This consideration may explain certain textual variations, especially in the order of the substantives, in this verse.

2^{13}. 'the passover of the Jews'. See Appended Note, pp. 349 ff.

2^{15}. It is said that clubs and sticks were not carried in the temple courts; and the mention of the corded scourge used by the Lord may be thus accounted for. But it may also be explained on the ground that punishment and suffering were deserved by and are now inflicted on those who, for their own purposes, had dishonoured God's house; and that this punishment and suffering are later undergone, on men's behalf, by the Son of God Himself [19^1].

2^{16}. The word 'merchandise' suggests a reference to the messianic passage Zech. 14^{21end}, if it is translated 'In that day [the day of the Lord] there shall be no more a trafficker in the house of the Lord of hosts'.

2^{17}. The Lord's consuming zeal for His Father's house recalls Ps. 69^9 to the disciples' minds, and they see in His action the fulfilment of this verse, regarded as prophecy; but not till after His resurrection do they understand to what His action and words in the temple point [2^{22}].

2^{19}. It has been shown on pp. 19 f. that reference is made, directly or indirectly, to the Lord's death and its results, throughout this gospel. In the other records of the temple cleansing no such reference is found; but since in fact the earlier gospels suggest that it was His action then which led the authorities to plan His death, it is appropriate that St. John, in accordance with his method, should have this veiled allusion to it here, at the Lord's first encounter in this gospel with the Jews.

There is a clear connexion between His words here and those ascribed to Him in Mk. 14^58 = Mt. 26^61, Mk. 15^29 = Mt. 27^40 (cf. also Acts 6^14).

2^20. In this gospel the Jews are frequently represented as sitting in judgement on the Lord and submitting His words and works to a kind of judicial scrutiny. Here, for instance, they demand His credentials, and at 8^25 they ask Him, as their deputation asked the Baptist at 1^19, 'Who art thou?', and as Pilate asks the Lord at 19^9, 'Whence art thou?' And St. John is careful to make clear that those who put such questions and act in this way show themselves to be blind, since the truth is that, so far from being His judges, men are and must be on their trial in His presence, He being the Logos, as described in 1^1, ^14. Accordingly, in seeking to assess or to pass judgement on Him, the Jews reveal their inability to understand His mission.

According to Josephus, *Ant.* xv. 380, the building of the temple was begun in the eighteenth year of Herod the Great, i.e. about 20 B.C. It is said to have been completed in A.D. 63; only to be utterly and finally destroyed in A.D. 70.

2^22. 'they believed the scripture'. Since both here and in 20^9 we read of 'the scripture' (not 'the scriptures' which is the more usual term in the N.T. generally, and at Jn. 5^39, when the reference is to the O.T. as a whole) it is usually thought that the reference, both here and in 20^9, must be to a definite passage of the O.T. And since Ps. 16^10 is cited in Acts 2^31, 13^35 as a prophecy of the Lord's resurrection, this is usually regarded as the verse which St. John in both places may have had in view. If, however, it is possible that in 2^22 and 20^9 he is thinking of the whole O.T., we may remind ourselves that the Lord Himself founded His doctrine of resurrection on the fact that God is described in the O.T. as the God of Abraham, and the God of Isaac, and the God of Jacob (Mk. 12^18-27), and that therefore those who have once formed the object of God's care do not, owing to death, pass beyond the compass of that care.

3^3. In this verse St. John brings together the Greek idea of rebirth and the Jewish idea of the kingdom of God.

'anew'. The R.V. text is justified, since the reply of Nicodemus shows that he understands the Greek word as equivalent to 'a second time'. Nicodemus, being 'of the earth' (cf. 3^31) and comprehending only 'earthly things' [3^12], can only understand the word in this way; but it will not escape the reader that the word can also mean 'from above' (cf. R.V. mg); and this is certainly its meaning on the three other occasions of its use in John [3^31, 19^11, ^23].

'the kingdom of God'. This term, frequent in the earlier gospels (though St. Matthew usually substitutes 'heaven' for 'God'), occurs in John only here and at 3^5. The term which St. John forthwith substitutes for it in 3^15-16, and uses seventeen times altogether, is 'eternal life'. The theme of the

Lord's kingship is prominent in His trial before Pilate [18³³⁻³⁸], where the Lord uses the words, 'My kingdom is not of this world'.

3⁴. At 2²⁰ we have already had the Jews' misunderstanding of the Lord's utterance in 2¹⁹; and we now have another example of the way in which, if His words are understood solely in a material or superficial way, they are altogether misunderstood. Other instances may be found in 4¹⁰⁻¹⁵, ³¹⁻³⁴, 7³³⁻³⁶, 8⁵⁶⁻⁵⁸, 11¹¹⁻¹³, 14⁴⁻⁶. Since not only the Jews but disciples misunderstand in this way, the method is probably to be regarded as a means by which St. John seeks to train the reader in a right approach to an understanding of the Lord's words; it cannot be regarded as solely an illustration of the blindness or dullness of the Jews.

3⁵. The meaning of this verse must be the same as that of 3³; to be born of water and Spirit is equivalent to being born anew or from above. The language of 3³, however, is now stated in a more definite form. To understand St. John's meaning in any context, it is always valuable to compare his method in a parallel matter. Thus in ch. 6, where the Lord speaks of eating the flesh and drinking the blood of the Son of man, no instructed reader could fail to think of the Church's eucharistic rite; but none the less the allusion is indirect. Similarly here an indirect allusion to the rite of Christian baptism cannot pass unnoticed; but the direct reference in the present context seems to be to the cleansing properties of water in its religious use, already much emphasized in this gospel, especially in connexion with John's baptism. That baptism had been one of preparation for a supreme event believed to be imminent, the coming of the kingdom of God. In 3³, ⁵, however, it is implied that sight of and entry into this kingdom are no longer solely future: through the coming of the Lord (though this is not directly stated here), entry is now possible for him who is reborn by water and Spirit. In 1²⁶ John, speaking of his preparatory baptism in water, by implication contrasts it with the baptism in the holy Spirit brought by the Lord [1³³]. We are indeed to learn at 7³⁹ that only with and by the Lord's glorification, which has still to be consummated in His passion, is the dispensation of the Spirit granted; but that glory is already being manifested [1¹⁴, 2¹¹], and since the Spirit is abiding in full measure on the Lord [1³³, 3³⁴] throughout His work, the new dispensation is here regarded as already present and available [1³³].

3⁸. One and the same Greek word, already used in 3⁵, ⁶, is translated in this verse as both 'wind' and 'Spirit'. St. John, according to his custom, probably means the word to be understood in both these senses in the first half of the verse. One who has received the new birth is said to be like both the Spirit and the wind, whose coming and going, though unmistakable, are always mysterious and inexplicable.

3⁹. The Jew Nicodemus asks, 'How can these things come to pass?' The thought of spiritual rebirth, although Ezekiel comes very near to it in Ezek. 36²⁵⁻²⁷, was indeed unfamiliar in Jewish thought at this time; in this doctrine we may see Greek thought making its contribution to the Christian religion.

3¹². At 6⁶¹ the Lord, who has been speaking of the need for men to feed upon His flesh and blood, which He took upon Him in the incarnation, asks, 'Doth this cause you to stumble? What then if ye should behold the Son of man ascending where he was before?' If we may regard this language as largely parallel (at a later stage) to that of 3^{12}, it seems that the 'earthly things' of this verse, in speaking of which the Lord does not win credence, may be man's condition as needing the rebirth made possible for him by the Lord's incarnation, and that the 'heavenly things' will be the result of the rebirth, namely, eternal life [3^{15}; cf. $6^{57, 58}$].

3^{13}. It is often said that the Lord's ascension is here regarded as an event already in the past. It would perhaps be truer to say that St. John wishes the reader always to keep in mind two complementary truths, however difficult it may be to reconcile them: first, that the Lord's incarnate life and work form a real succession of events in time; and second, that His Person includes in itself, at all times and in all places, incarnation, crucifixion, resurrection, and ascension; and it is this second truth which is emphasized in this verse.

The textual evidence throws some doubt on the last four English words; but they are not at variance with St. John's doctrine, which is that the Lord did not cease to be with the Father, and therefore in heaven, while He lived on earth [1^{18}, 8^{29}, 16^{32}]. Indeed, wherever He is, there is heaven.

3^{14}. 'lifted up . . . must be lifted up'. The Greek word, when it occurs elsewhere [8^{28}, $12^{32, 34}$] in this gospel, is always used, as here, in reference to the Son of man, and always also in connexion with the Lord's crucifixion and His exaltation, the two events being inseparable in John.

'must'. Cf. the use of this word in Mk. 8^{31}, in the first proclamation of of the coming passion.

3^{15}. Since only 'eternal life' is 'life indeed', the noun is often used without the adjective in John; e.g. 3^{36}, 5^{40}. In so far as a difference exists between the terms, eternal life is always the 'life indeed', whereas life is also the power or source which gives or results in eternal life. Hence eternal life is never predicated of the Father or the Son, whereas 'the Father has life in himself' and has granted this same life to the Son [5^{26}] who is Himself 'the life' [11^{25}, 14^6] and came that men 'may have life' [10^{10}].

3^{16}. In later Judaism the Logos doctrine was especially valued because of a growing emphasis on the transcendence of Yahweh, an excessive emphasis which removed Him ever farther from direct contact with the world and left the Logos as His only or at least His chief means of contact with it, the Logos thus becoming a kind of plenipotentiary of an absent monarch. But in John, in spite of the great importance assigned in this book to the Logos doctrine, God Himself acts directly in relation to the world [5^{17}], which He loves [3^{16}] and desires to save [3^{17}]. Although uniquely [$1^{14, 18}$] Father of the Lord (cf. 20^{17}), He is also the Father of all men [4^{21}] and is seeking them [4^{23}]. St. John's doctrine of the absolute union of the Father and the Son [5^{19}, 10^{30}] prevents any difficulty from arising in respect of Their, as it were, double operation.

3^{19-21}. Belief and disbelief in this gospel are vitally connected with a corresponding ethical practice; and he who loves and comes to the light is said to 'do the truth', i.e. to live and act in harmony with that which is truly real, since indeed it is the divine activity itself.

3^22. The Lord now leaves Jerusalem for the neighbourhood of Jordan.

3^23. The sites cannot be identified with certainty.

3^31. Although the terms 'the earth' and 'the world' are of kindred meaning in John, 'the earth' is less heavily weighted with the unsatisfactory associations attached in this gospel to 'the world'; cf. 12^32, 17^4.

3^33. The subject in this verse is probably the Baptist (cf. 3^26); but he is not mentioned by name, perhaps because that which is here said (primarily) of him is also applicable to all those who receive and embrace the witness given by the Lord.

3^34. 'he whom God hath sent' is the Lord; and the meaning is that God does not give the Spirit (or the divine life, cf. 5^26) partially, but fully, to the Lord, who therefore speaks the words of God, the same truth being expressed in different language in the next verse.

3^36. Just as belief and obedience are inseparably connected (cf. 8^30, 31), so disbelief will inevitably show itself in disobedience; the verb used here expresses both these qualities. That disobedience incurs 'the wrath of God', an expression found in John only here, is emphasized also in Eph. 5^6 (cf. 1 Thess. 1^10, 2^16).

It is noticeable that in this last verse of ch. 3, the chapter in which the chief subjects to be treated in this gospel have been briefly sketched for the first time (cf. especially 3^13-21), the final note is an already existing division of mankind into two classes. As always in this gospel, the reader is invited to see temporal actions and attitudes not so much (as in the earlier gospels) in the light of the fruit which they will one day bear and reveal, but in the light of the immediate, eternal significance which they carry.

4^1. 'the Lord'. In narrative St. John, like St. Matthew and St. Mark but unlike St. Luke, normally uses the proper name 'Jesus' in reference to the central Figure. In chs. 1 to 12 the title 'the Lord' is used only in three passages 4^1, 6^23, 11^2, all of which may be called editorial notes.

'the Pharisees'. Their motive appears to be jealousy (cf. Mt. 27^18) or at least anxiety because of the Lord's increasing popularity (cf. 3^26). But the small value of their judgement is revealed in their remark at 12^19, a few days before the crucifixion.

4^2. This correction of 4^1 and 3^22 is thought by some to be a later addition to the text; and two small points of style in the Greek perhaps support this view.

4^3. As at 7^1, Galilee in this gospel appears to be a place of withdrawal from the (southern) Jews, and therefore of temporary security.

4^4. St. Mark does not mention Samaria or Samaritans. In Matthew, when the twelve are sent out on a mission, they are bidden to avoid Samaritan towns [10^5]. In Luke, the scene of the central part of the Lord's ministry seems to be laid in Samaria [9^51, 52, 17^11]; but it should be noticed that this happens only because the Lord is on a journey southwards from Galilee to Jerusalem, which is His goal [9^51]. Similarly in Jn. 4^1-42, which describes the Lord's only encounter in this book with Samaritans, the Lord is on a journey, this time northwards, from Judaea to Galilee. In no gospel, therefore, does He deliberately go to Samaria as a sphere of His work; He only visits it in passing.

4⁶. 'thus': probably with reference to the weariness just mentioned.

4⁹. The last words of this verse are an editorial note and do not form part of the woman's words to the Lord. It is not certain (see R.V. mg), but likely, that they are part of the original text. As 4⁸ suggests, commerce between Jews and Samaritans took place without difficulty, and at 4²⁷ the disciples are surprised, not so much that the Lord is speaking with a Samaritan, as that she is a woman. Hence recent research may be correct in suggesting that the words should be translated, 'For Jews do not use [(in this case) a waterpot (cf. 4²⁸)] along with Samaritans', *sc.* for fear of incurring uncleanness. If so, the woman will be expressing surprise, in the first part of this verse, at the Lord's readiness to disregard a Jewish custom or regulation.

4¹². Cf. 8⁵³, 'Art thou greater than our father Abraham?' St. John's purpose in each case is no doubt to emphasize the measureless superiority of the new order to anyone or anything representative of the old order.

4¹⁸. Jewish opinion reprobated the repetition of marriage more than three times at most; hence the woman's past married life was already a discredit, apart from her present illegitimate connexion.

4²⁰. The patriarchs had set up altars in the neighbourhood [Gen. 12⁷, 33²⁰]. After the return from the exile, the Jews excluded the Samaritans from any share in the worship of the temple at Jerusalem; and the latter subsequently erected a temple on Mount Gerizim.

4²². The Lord here identifies Himself with the historic Jewish race (contrast His language in 8¹⁷, 10³⁴, 15²⁵), and confirms the truth that 'the commonwealth of Israel', to quote the words of Athanasius (*De incarnatione Verbi*, 12. 5), 'was the school of the knowledge of God to all nations'.

4²³. 'and now is'. In 4²¹ the Lord gave an assurance of the coming of an hour when recourse would not be had either to Jerusalem or to Gerizim for the worship of the Father. The reader, who has grasped the teaching of 2¹⁹⁻²¹, will naturally and rightly think of the Church's worship of the Father after the coming of the Holy Spirit. But in 4²³ the Lord says that this hour 'cometh and now is'; and the same words recur in 5²⁵. This expression is not found elsewhere in John; but it could be applied with truth throughout this gospel. In His life and work, endowed as He is with the fullness of the Spirit [1³³, 3³⁴], that is already realized which in believers will only become effective after they, as a result of His completed work, receive the Spirit, which was His.

4²⁴. 'God is spirit : cf. 'God is light' 1 Jn. 1⁵, 'God is love' 1 Jn. 4⁸, ¹⁶. These expressions should not be regarded as so many definitions of the being of God, but rather as describing the nature of His relation to the world, and of His activity within it.

4²⁶. The two Greek words for 'I am', on the Lord's lips, without a predicate actually expressed (as here), are a feature of this gospel, and the correct translation must be decided in each case by the context. Here and at 6²⁰ the R.V. translation is probably correct; but at 8²⁴, ²⁸, ⁵⁸, 13¹⁹ we should probably translate simply 'I am' (as indeed the R.V. does at 8⁵⁸), and see a reference to the Lord's divinity. For the two words in the Greek are the same as those of the LXX in certain O.T. passages, e.g. Deut. 32³⁹, Is. 46⁴, where Yahweh is the Speaker, and thus emphasizes His Godhead. And in such cases as 18⁵, ⁶, ⁸ the reader, while accepting the R.V. translation, since the hearers of the words would understand them in this way, is himself no doubt meant to perceive the deeper meaning which is latent in them.

4³¹. Two points may be noticed here. First, the Lord's teaching to His disciples in 4³¹⁻³⁸ is inserted between His conversation with the woman and its results on her [4⁷⁻³⁰] and its further results on others, through her word and work [4³⁹⁻⁴²]. In this way the past (4⁷⁻³⁰) and the future (4³⁹⁻⁴²) are seen to be a unity, a single whole, and the teaching of 4³¹⁻³⁸ explains and illustrates this unity. Secondly, although the disciples were present when the conversation ended [4²⁷], their surprise [4²⁷] and lack of insight [4³³] show that they do not, cannot, as yet receive and share their Master's mind; owing to the exceptional, indeed unique, task which is reserved for them [17¹⁸], only the completion of the Lord's work on earth [7³⁹, 19³⁰, ³⁴] will avail to equip them adequately for their mission [20²¹]; and until His work on earth is complete, they continue to show the same lack of comprehension which is implied here (cf. 11⁸, ¹², 13³⁶, ³⁷, 14⁵, ⁸, ²²).

4³⁴. 'him that sent me'. This is the first of the twenty-four occasions in John, in which the Greek verb here used refers to the 'sending' of the Son by the Father; see note on 5³⁶.

4³⁵. The thought in 4³⁴⁻³⁸ is not easy to follow, because of the various factors involved: the Lord's, the woman's, the disciples', others' work. With regard to 4³⁶, the woman may be said to be both sowing [4²⁹] and reaping [4³⁰, ³⁹⁻⁴²]; and, as we have seen [4²⁸], she is already gathering fruit to issue in eternal life. The Lord during His ministry sowed much seed [Mt. 13³⁷], as in the story just told in 4⁶⁻²⁶; and on these widely scattered seeds the disciples will begin their work, a work to which in 4³⁸ they are regarded as having been already sent, since He, their Master, has been sent, and has associated them with Himself in the work [17¹⁸]. They themselves therefore never lay a new foundation; it is already laid [1 Cor. 3¹¹]; in the present case, for example, a woman is already building on it.

4³⁵, ³⁶. The word 'already' in 4³⁵ should probably be read as the first word of 4³⁶, as R.V. mg (cf. 7¹⁴, 9²², 15³). With the thought of 4³⁶ᵇ cf. Lev. 26⁵, Amos 9¹³.

4⁴². The confession, to which belief leads, that 'this is truly the Saviour of the world', recalls the teaching of 4²⁰⁻²⁶, and is appropriately said of the Lord in Samaria. The term 'the Saviour of the world' occurs here only in John (but cf. 3¹⁷, 12⁴⁷); it is found also in 1 Jn. 4¹⁴.

4⁴³⁻⁴⁵. On these verses see pp. 34–36.

4⁴⁶. This 'King's officer' (R.V. mg) was probably in the service of Herod Antipas, tetrarch of Galilee at this time, who is given the courtesy title of king in the first two gospels.

4⁴⁸. The expression 'signs and wonders' is frequent in the O.T., e.g. Ex. 7³, Deut. 4³⁴, 34¹¹ (cf. Joel 2³⁰), and is found also in the N.T., especially in Acts, but occurs in John only here.

The New Order and the Old Order in Conflict

5 After these things there was ¹a feast of the Jews; and Jesus went up to Jerusalem.

2 Now there is in Jerusalem by the sheep *gate* a pool, which is called in 3 Hebrew ²Bethesda, having five porches. In these lay a multitude of 5 them that were sick, blind, halt, withered³. And a certain man was there, 6 which had been thirty and eight years in his infirmity. When Jesus saw him lying, and knew that he had been now a long time *in that case*, 7 he saith unto him, Wouldest thou be made whole? The sick man answered him, ⁴Sir, I have no man, when the water is troubled, to put me into the pool: but while I am coming, another steppeth down 8 before me. Jesus saith unto him, Arise, take up thy bed, and walk. 9 And straightway the man was made whole, and took up his bed and walked.

10 Now it was the sabbath on that day. So the Jews said unto him that was cured, It is the sabbath, and it is not lawful for thee to take up thy 11 bed. But he answered them, He that made me whole, the same said unto 12 me, Take up thy bed, and walk. They asked him, Who is the man that 13 said unto thee, Take up *thy bed*, and walk? But he that was healed wist not who it was: for Jesus had conveyed himself away, a multitude being 14 in the place. Afterward Jesus findeth him in the temple, and said unto him, Behold, thou art made whole: sin no more, lest a worse thing befall 15 thee. The man went away, and told the Jews that it was Jesus which had 16 made him whole. And for this cause did the Jews persecute Jesus, 17 because he did these things on the sabbath. But Jesus answered them, 18 My Father worketh even until now, and I work. For this cause therefore the Jews sought the more to kill him, because he not only brake the sabbath, but also called God his own Father, making himself equal with God.

19 Jesus therefore answered and said unto them,

Verily, verily, I say unto you, The Son can do nothing of himself, but what he seeth the Father doing: for what things soever he doeth, these 20 the Son also doeth in like manner. For the Father loveth the Son, and sheweth him all things that himself doeth: and greater works than these

---

¹ *Many ancient authorities read* the feast.   ² *Some ancient authorities read* Bethsaida, *others*, Bethzatha.   ³ *Many ancient authorities insert*, *wholly or in part*, waiting for the moving of the water: 4 for an angel of the Lord went down at certain seasons into the pool, and troubled the water: whosoever then first after the troubling of the water stepped in was made whole, with whatsoever disease he was holden.   ⁴ *Or* Lord

21 will he shew him, that ye may marvel. For as the Father raiseth the dead and quickeneth them, even so the Son also quickeneth whom he
22 will. For neither doth the Father judge any man, but he hath given all
23 judgement unto the Son; that all may honour the Son, even as they honour the Father. He that honoureth not the Son honoureth not the
24 Father which sent him. Verily, verily, I say unto you, He that heareth my word, and believeth him that sent me, hath eternal life, and cometh
25 not into judgement, but hath passed out of death into life. Verily, verily, I say unto you, The hour cometh, and now is, when the dead shall hear the voice of the Son of God; and they that hear shall live.
26 For as the Father hath life in himself, even so gave he to the Son also to
27 have life in himself: and he gave him authority to execute judgement,
28 because he is ¹the Son of man. Marvel not at this: for the hour cometh,
29 in which all that are in the tombs shall hear his voice, and shall come forth; they that have done good, unto the resurrection of life; and they that have ²done ill, unto the resurrection of judgement.

30   I can of myself do nothing: as I hear, I judge: and my judgement is righteous; because I seek not mine own will, but the will of him that
31 sent me. If I bear witness of myself, my witness is not true. It is
32 another that beareth witness of me; and I know that the witness which
33 he witnesseth of me is true. Ye have sent unto John, and he hath borne
34 witness unto the truth. But the witness which I receive is not from man:
35 howbeit I say these things, that ye may be saved. He was the lamp that burneth and shineth: and ye were willing to rejoice for a season in his
36 light. But the witness which I have is greater than *that of* John: for the works which the Father hath given me to accomplish, the very works
37 that I do, bear witness of me, that the Father hath sent me. And the Father which sent me, he hath borne witness of me. Ye have neither
38 heard his voice at any time, nor seen his form. And ye have not his word
39 abiding in you: for whom he sent, him ye believe not. ³Ye search the scriptures, because ye think that in them ye have eternal life; and these
40 are they which bear witness of me; and ye will not come to me, that
41 ye may have life. I receive not glory from men. But I know you, that ye
42 have not the love of God in yourselves. I am come in my Father's
43 name, and ye receive me not: if another shall come in his own name,
44 him ye will receive. How can ye believe, which receive glory one of another, and the glory that *cometh* from ⁴the only God ye seek not?
45 Think not that I will accuse you to the Father: there is one that accuseth
46 you, *even* Moses, on whom ye have set your hope. For if ye believed
47 Moses, ye would believe me; for he wrote of me. But if ye believe not his writings, how shall ye believe my words?

---

¹ *Or* a son of man   ² *Or* practised   ³ *Or* Search the scriptures
⁴ *Some ancient authorities read* the only one.

EXPOSITION OF SECTION 2. 5¹⁻⁴⁷

THE Lord restores an impotent man to perfect health (cf. 7²³) on a sabbath. The Jews' opposition becomes open and avowed, whereupon the Lord, by setting forth His relation to the Father, explains the ground of His authority as Giver of life and as Judge [5¹⁹⁻³⁰], and points to the various sources of witness to Himself [5³¹⁻⁴⁷].

The Lord is once more in Jerusalem; and just as it seemed possible to trace a development between His first and second sign at Cana, so now, if we compare His first [2¹³⁻²²] and second [5¹⁻¹⁵] work at Jerusalem, we find that in this second work the Jews' opposition has increased; it now becomes outspoken, and they desire His death. Throughout this gospel the greater His work for men, the greater the cost to Himself, and the greater the manifestation of His glory.

The story in 5¹⁻⁹ has points of resemblance with the story in ch. 9 of sight bestowed on one born blind (see p. 16). There, as here, we learn (it might seem almost accidentally, and at a late stage) that the Lord's work was wrought on a sabbath [5⁹, 9¹⁴]; there, as here, the recipient of the Lord's bounty has a question put to him about his Benefactor, and neither recipient can at first answer the question [5¹², ¹³, 9¹²]. But whereas in ch. 5 he who was formerly infirm is found 'in the temple' [5¹⁴], and appears at the first opportunity to link himself with the Jews [5¹⁵] rather than with his Benefactor, an action which leads forthwith to a conflict between the Jews and the Lord, in ch. 9 he who was formerly blind is 'cast out from the synagogue' [9³², ³⁴], is in consequence found by the Lord, and is led by Him into a full and deep expression of belief [9³⁵⁻³⁸].

At first the Jews' criticism is directed against the impotent man's action (not against the Lord), the offence being, not his restored health, but his carrying his pallet on the sabbath; and for the present he shelters himself behind his unknown Benefactor. Later, however, when both he and the Jews have ascertained who healed him, the Jews' criticism changes both its direction and its motive. It now becomes aimed against the Lord, and is caused by His actions, of which that in 5⁸ is presumably typical, upon a sabbath. (In John therefore, as in the earlier tradition, the Lord's actions on the sabbath are recorded as giving rise to controversy.) The Lord replies in a sentence [5¹⁷] which must be considered carefully.

1. In the earlier gospels the Lord usually justifies His apparent indifference to and breach of sabbath ordinances by claiming a right, tacitly or openly, to overrule them, when works of mercy are concerned (cf. Mk. 3^{1-5}, Lk. 13^{10-17}). In Mk. 2^{23-28}, however, in defence of His disciples' action on a sabbath, He reminds their critics, the Pharisees, how David and his companions, whose action is clearly compared with that of His disciples, on one occasion broke the law; and the section ends with the claim that the Son of man is lord even of the sabbath. In the parallel record in Mt. 12^{1-8} a further reference is made to the priests who in the temple break the sabbath with impunity, and the Lord adds, 'A greater matter than the temple is here'. In these passages we discern a claim that with the arrival of the Lord a new order, indeed the new age itself, is present, and that therefore much, previously regarded as essential, is no longer binding. Hence the Lord's defence in Jn. 5^{17} may be said to be present, up to a point, in the earlier tradition; but in John the claim is far more definite, and is now explicitly made on the ground of the Lord's equality with His Father, as the Jews forthwith perceive [5^{18}]. Because of the Lord's unique relationship to His Father, since the Father never ceases from activity, neither does His Son.

2. The reader at once understands, as do the Jews themselves [5^{18}], that the Lord's words 'My Father' express on His part a unique relationship to God. For in none of the gospels is God regarded as the Father of all men, whether believers or not, in the same way in which He is the Father of the Lord. This is made sufficiently clear in 20^{17}, where the Lord's message to His 'brethren', after He has completed His work, is that He is ascending to His Father and their Father, to His God and their God. Although they are His 'brethren', the distinction is still kept.

3. Unlike the reader, however, the Jews do not understand that the Lord utters these words, because He is the Logos become flesh, and therefore 'he that hath seen' Him 'hath seen the Father'. Accordingly, as the Father is in Him, and He in the Father [10^{38}; cf. 14^{11}], He cannot but set forth His oneness with the Father [10^{30}]. But to the Jews, who cannot recognize Him [8^{19}], except as a man [5^{12}, 9^{16}, 19^5], this claim of His appears to express independence of God and therefore to be blasphemy [10^{33}]; whereas, as the Lord proceeds to show in 5^{19-30}, His relationship to the Father, rightly understood, is one of absolute dependence.

4. In this verse the Father's work and that of the Son are said to be in union 'until this present moment'. For, the Word having become flesh, there is a beginning, a middle, and an end to His work, and that end has not yet come. Throughout, He must work the works of Him that sent Him, while it is day [9⁴]; the night, the period of rest from work, will come, and then the light of the world will be withdrawn [9⁴, ⁵, 12³⁵, ³⁶]. At present the union in activity has been and is absolute; but it has to be preserved to the end (cf. Lk. 12⁵⁰), and the safeguard of the preservation is not in the human nature assumed, but in the Person assuming it. Hence the future must not, as it were, be mortgaged; and the union in activity is described as existing 'until now'. We might indeed have expected that the words 'until now' would be predicated rather of the Son, the Word become flesh, than of His Father; but the fact that they are predicated of the Father emphasizes not only the absolute union in activity of the Father and the Son, but also the Father's part or share in that activity: as we have already learned, the Father Himself loves, gives [3¹⁶], sends [3¹⁷], seeks [4²³].

5. Jewish teaching is said to have tended to make an exception, in respect of the sabbath rest of God emphasized in Gen. 2²⁻³, Ex. 20¹¹, 31¹⁷; it was held that He ceased indeed from His work of creation, but is still unceasingly active as Upholder and moral Governor or Judge of the world, blessing the righteous, and condemning the wicked. The lesson of 5¹⁷ is that the sabbath rest of the Father, rightly understood, is the unimpeded activity of love, so that in deeds of mercy wrought on the sabbath the work of the Father and the Son is at one; and in the Lord's monologue which now follows in 5¹⁹⁻³⁰, we are to learn that in respect of the judgement, the outcome of which is either life or death, Their work. is also one.

There is, however, a striking difference between the Rabbinic conception of the divine judgement and that set forth in Jn. 5; for the issue of the judgement is depicted in John as completely unforeseen and also unforeseeable (cf. Mt. 25³¹⁻⁴⁶, Rom. 11³³ᵇ). The impotent man, for example, is chosen for restoration not only after his infirmity has lasted for thirty-eight years, but from among a large number of others in like case; and it is made clear in 5¹⁴ both that the selection was by no means in consequence of his past exemplary conduct (cf. Mt. 5⁴⁵ᵇ), and also that he must be careful for the future 'to make his calling and election sure' [2 Pet.

1^{10}]. 5^{14} contains the first reference to sin since 1^{29}, where the Baptist proclaims that the Lord, 'the Lamb of God, takes away the sin of the world'; and we are thus reminded that He who is Judge [$5^{22, 27}$] is also Saviour.

St. John clearly attaches great importance to the long address, which extends from 5^{19} to 5^{47}. It may be regarded as an exposition of the relation between the Father and the Son (in preparation for the claims put forward by the Lord in the succeeding chapters), and therewith a defence of Christian monotheism. Its importance is indicated by the duplicated terms 'answered and said', and by the solemn introductory words, twice repeated in the course of the address [$5^{24, 25}$]. Again, there is now an increasing disclosure, by the Lord, of the significance of His Person. Whereas in 3^{1-21}, for example, the references to 'the Son of man' and 'the Son' were not directly explained as relating to the Speaker Himself, here the use of the third person [$5^{19-23, 25-29}$] alternates with the use, by the Lord, of the first person, already used in 5^{17} and now again in 5^{24} and in 5^{30}, the verse which concludes the first part of the address. The Speaker is revealed to be very much more than He is thought to be by those whom He is addressing. He is the Son, who shares the Father's inherent life [5^{26}]; but this, although it is the truth about Him [$1^{14, 18}$, 14^6], they neither see nor understand.

In 5^{17} the Lord had expressed, in a positive form, the complete union in action between the Father and Himself. He now in 5^{19} shows that the union is due to the absolute dependence, in all things, of the Son upon the Father; and this is expressed first negatively and then positively. His actions, we read, have their origin, not from Himself, but from His sight of the actions of the Father; and all that the Father does is done also by the Son. The union, therefore, is absolute. It is not, for instance, as though the Son reveals the Father in certain particular ways or in certain remarkable actions; no moment of His life, and no action of His, but is the expression of the life and action of the Father [12^{45}, 14^9]; and, we may add, the same is true of His words [3^{34}, 8^{26}, 12^{49}]. Accordingly the works and the words of the Father and of the Son are identical; and by the substitution of the first for the third person in $5^{24, 30}$ it is shown that we are here dealing primarily, not with the eternal relations of the Father and the Son, but with the present moment, with the historical revelation made in Jesus

Christ, whose works and words are therefore those of God. Hence the great stress laid in this gospel upon the necessity of belief in the Lord. Since He is the only way to light and life [1⁴, 14⁶], not to believe in Him must be synonymous with death [8²¹, ²⁴] and darkness [12³⁵, ³⁶, ⁴⁶].

The basis of the union on the Son's side was said in 5¹⁹ to be absolute dependence (which expresses itself in obedience; cf. 8²⁸, ²⁹); and in 5²⁰ the basis of the union on the Father's side is shown to be love, which holds back nothing from the Son. The reference here is not to knowledge, on the part of the Son, of such mysteries as those mentioned in 2 Cor. 12¹⁻⁵; the Lord's words in this gospel are never concerned with revelations of this sort. The promise given in 1⁵¹ to disciples was that they should see the heaven opened, and the unbroken activity or commerce which joins earth and heaven in and through their Lord—this and nothing else. That therefore which the Lord reveals in John is no particular fact or piece of knowledge, without reference to Himself, nor is it any exceptional or temporary illumination; that which He reveals and imparts, both in word and in action, is a life; and the life which He reveals is the life of God, as made known in Himself, the Word become flesh.

In considering 5¹⁷ we saw that, as regards the union in action of the Father and the Son, 'the future was not mortgaged', and a reference to Lk. 12⁵⁰ was suggested; and in the last part of 5²⁰ it is made clear that, although the Logos has become flesh, His revelation has not yet reached its zenith. No limit indeed can be placed to the revelation, since it is infinite, being the revelation of the life of God; but within the historic life of the Word become flesh, with which we are here concerned, there is a goal to be reached; the Lord's work of mercy in 5¹⁻⁹ (cf. 7²¹) is to be by no means the last or greatest of His works; and the purpose of the Father in showing these greater works to the Son, which the Son will forthwith carry out, is to excite the wonder, and therewith the adoration, of those who hear and see.

In Jewish thought the bestowal of life and death was regarded as the especial and indeed sole prerogative of Yahweh: 1 Sam. 2⁶ 'The Lord killeth and maketh alive'; 2 Kings 5⁷ 'Am I God, to kill and to make alive?'; and in 5²¹ the union in action of the Father and the Son is described with reference to this prerogative, although the explicit thought here is at present positive only, that of giving life. But it is at once made clear in 5^{22} that we are not here concerned with the bestowal of physical life, as in the quotations just given; we are primarily concerned with a judgement, which issues in either life or death. In this matter of judgement also, the Jews clung with remarkable tenacity to the thought of the justice of their God: Gen. 18^{25} 'shall not the Judge of all the earth do right?' Deut. 32^4 'All his ways are judgement; a God . . . just and right is he'; and it was one of their chief difficulties that true justice, as far as they could see, or what in their opinion justice should be, was not awarded in this life.

This right of judgement, we read, has been given by the Father to the Son. The teaching of $5^{19, 20}$ should prevent us from any danger of understanding $5^{21, 22}$ to mean that the Father has, as it were, abdicated His sovereign right of judgement in favour of the Son (cf. also $12^{48, 49}$); in this matter, as in all else, the union is absolute; and a further safeguard is given in 5^{23}. The Father's purpose in assigning the right of judgement to the Son is here said to be that all men may give to the Son the same honour or reverence which they give to the Father. The Father therefore remains Judge, but exercises His function of judgement in and through the Son; and accordingly if honour is not given to the Son, the Father, who sent Him, is not honoured. The last words of 5^{23}, 'which sent him', show that the judgement is even now taking place in and through the Lord's historic ministry; and we are thus prepared for the teaching of 5^{24}, preceded, like the whole address, by a solemn formula, and now given in the first, not the third, person. Everyone who hears (i.e. in obedience; contrast 8^{43b}) the Lord's word and believes the Father who sent Him—he has eternal life; he has passed out of the state of death into the state of life (cf. 1 Jn. 3^{14}), and he is not judged (cf. 3^{18}). Thus to hear and see the Lord is itself the judgement; for to do so leaves no man where he was before; in the Lord's presence every man is seen and shown and known, whether he himself realizes it or not, for what he truly is.

The nature of eternal life is not here defined; but 17^3 shows it to be that men should know the Father, the only true God, and Him whom He sent, Jesus Christ. (This is the knowledge, as we learned in ch. 4, which will quench all thirst.) Since this life is declared to be a possibility, indeed a fact, of the present, it is unnecessary to refer to physical death; the death mentioned in 5^{24} is the state out of which a man has passed when he hears and obeys

the word of the Lord, in other words, believes on Him. This prepares us for the equally important next verse, which states as both
a future and a present truth that the dead, those, that is, who do
not know [1¹⁰] or receive [1¹¹] the Logos, the Son of God, shall
hear His voice; and those that hear—i.e., in this case, those who both
hear it and obey it—shall live. This latter hearing is possible for all
those who are of the truth [18³⁷]; it is not possible for those whom
the Lord is addressing [5³⁷, 8⁴⁷]; they only hear His speech, which
they do not understand [8⁴³].

In 5²⁶ we learn that the Father, who is said to have life in Himself,
gave to the Son also to have this inherent life; and in 5²⁷ that the
Son has received the right or authority to pass judgement, because
He is the Son of man. It was pointed out in the note on 1⁵¹ that in
Jewish thought and in the earlier gospels judgement is an essential
feature of the work and office of the Son of man, and the translation
of 5²⁷ in R.V. text, which can be justified on grammatical grounds,
is probably correct; but it should not be overlooked that this verse
is the only passage in the gospels where neither of the two Greek
nouns used in this term has the article; so that the term could be
translated here simply 'a son of man' as in R.V. mg. Possibly
therefore St. John wishes his readers to remember that their Judge
is not only One who in virtue of His office as the Son of man
exercises this prerogative, but is also truly human, one of themselves; and on this interpretation the prerogative of judgement
may be regarded as belonging to the Lord's humanity. And just
as at 3⁷ Nicodemus was bidden not to marvel at the Lord's teaching
on the necessity of rebirth, since he should consider the twofold
nature of man [3⁶, ⁸], so here the Jews are told that they should not
be surprised at the teaching of 5²⁴⁻²⁷, if they recall their own traditional doctrine of the resurrection of the dead, and a future judgement, with its separation of those who have done good from those
who have done evil. That which is now added to this doctrine is
that their future Judge already stands before them (5²⁸, 'His
voice'); and in 5³⁰, with a return to the first person singular, the
teaching thus far given is summed up. The Lord is absolutely
dependent on the Father; His verdicts are those which He hears
from the Father; and the judgement pronounced by Him (the
Son) is righteous, being directed solely to the fulfilment of the
good pleasure of the Father who sent Him.

The reader will observe that, whereas in 5²⁴, ²⁵ eternal life is mentioned not only as a future, but also as a present possibility ('an hour cometh, and now is'), in 5²⁸, ²⁹ the reference is only to a future resurrection; in 5²⁸, ²⁹ physical death is presupposed. This twofold conception of eternal life appears again in 6⁵⁴, with its reference to 'the last day', and is treated at length in ch. 11, in which the Lord calls Lazarus forth from the tomb. In ch. 5, however, in which the Jews' opposition to the Lord is only in its initial stages [5¹⁶, ¹⁸], the emphasis is chiefly on His present work as giver of eternal life; not until the Lord's passion is close at hand do we learn more fully of His work as the vanquisher of physical death, a work only to be carried through at the cost of His own life.

In the Lord's utterance 5¹⁹⁻³⁰ it has become clear, especially by His use of the first person in the verbs of 5³⁰, that in His words about the Son and the Son's relation to the Father He is referring to none other than Himself, the Word become flesh. The truths of 5¹⁹⁻³⁰, therefore, are put forward by One who seems to be and indeed is (5²⁷ R.V. mg) speaking as a man to men. It is, however, laid down in Deut. 19¹⁵ᵇ that for the establishment of a 'word' at least two witnesses must give evidence; and further, both Jewish and Greek law deprecated the acceptance of a man's evidence about himself (cf. 8¹⁷). Accordingly the Lord, forestalling in 5³¹ an objection which will be raised on this ground against Him (cf. 8¹³), passes in 5³¹⁻⁴⁰ to the nature of the evidence or 'witness' which He offers; and from this, by a natural extension, to the thought, in 5⁴¹⁻⁴⁷, of repute or reputation or 'glory'. He cannot, however, offer evidence which His hearers with their present outlook and presuppositions will accept or find convincing (cf. 3³). Since His mission and work are from above, it is in the nature of things impossible to expose them to such scrutiny and evidence as would be in order in a legal matter. The immeasurable gulf between earth and heaven [1⁵¹, 3¹³], flesh and spirit [3⁶], man and God [1¹⁸], cannot thus be overcome. Hence the Lord who, alone of all flesh, knows whence He came and whither He goes [8¹⁴], must of necessity [5³⁴] decline all human evidence on His behalf (cf. 5⁴¹); He alone can give the evidence required, and He knows that it is true [8¹⁴]. The present context 5³¹, ³² accepting the principle of Deut. 19¹⁵ᵇ, states the same truth in another way. Granted that if He bears witness of Himself, as the world must understand these words, His witness is invalid or untrue. In fact it is Another, the Father, who bears witness of Him [5³²]; and the Lord, who *ex hypothesi* alone is in a position to know and express the truth about the matter [7²⁹, 8⁵⁵], knows that the Father's witness to the Son is true.[1]

Before, however, the nature of the witness given by the Father is considered, the Jews are reminded that they themselves have sent a delegation to inquire of the Baptist [1¹⁹⁻²⁸]—thereby showing that they were prepared or at least felt bound to assign some weight and authority to his activity and evidence—and that he has 'borne witness to the truth'. And although no merely human witness would be in place, or indeed possible, when given in the Lord's behalf, yet since John both acted and spoke by divine mandate [1³³, ³⁴, 3²⁷, ²⁸], his witness, for the sake of the welfare and salvation of the Lord's hearers, is recalled [5³³, ³⁴]. In some degree indeed the Baptist did enlighten the surrounding darkness [5³⁵]; and the Jews were willing 'for an hour' to sun themselves in the illumination which he gave; but it is now becoming very clear that their joy in the Baptist and his witness was not lasting (cf. Lk. 8¹³).

For the Lord has a witness greater than that given by the Baptist; 'the works' given to Him by the Father to accomplish, and accomplished by Him in obedience to the Father's will, bear witness of Him, that the Father has sent Him [5³⁶]. These 'works' are the sum of the Lord's activity on earth, and form His food [4³⁴]; they include His words, and such works as that of 5¹⁻⁹ (cf. 7²¹), but can best be expressed as His activity in judging and in giving life (cf. 5²⁰⁻²³). In the results of these two activities belief is able to discern the lordship of Jesus; and therefore the activities, with their results, bear witness of and to Him; nor is there need, or indeed possibility, of other forms of witness.

It is remarkable that, when in 5³⁷ the direct witness of the Father to the Lord is at length explicitly mentioned, the allusion to this witness is made in the past tense; contrast 8¹⁸. This suggests that witness to the Lord is to be found not only in His present activities, but also in a witness in the past. We may compare the thought of 5¹⁷, that the Father is and has been working up to the very moment

---

[1] The requirement of two witnesses other than the subject of the witness cannot be fully satisfied during the Lord's ministry, because His work is not yet over; it is satisfied, so far as is at present possible, in the words of 8¹⁸. But when the Lord's work is finished, in other words when He is glorified, the Holy Spirit, who forthwith becomes active on the completion of that work [7³⁹], will join with the Father in bearing witness of the Lord [15²⁶; cf. 16¹⁴]; and therewith also the disciples (in whom He, the Holy Spirit, will be active), because they have been with their Lord from the beginning [15²⁷].

when the Lord is speaking. In other words, all life, in and from the beginning onwards, when rightly understood, has borne witness, as the activity of the Father, to the Lord; and of this activity the ministry of the Baptist [5³³; cf. 1⁶⁻⁸, Mt. 11¹¹ᵃ] and the scriptures [5³⁹, ⁴⁵⁻⁴⁷; cf. Lk. 16³¹, 24²⁷] are only two, although the most conspicuous, examples. But the Jews throughout have proved deaf and blind to the Father's revelation of Himself. His word does not 'abide' in them; did it so abide (cf. 15⁷), they would give credence to His Emissary, the Lord.

Again, the witness of the scriptures of the O.T. [5³⁹] should lead them to the Lord, and so to life [5⁴⁰]; for they always point, like Moses [5⁴⁶], to a goal beyond themselves; of themselves they do not, as the Jews believe, afford eternal life. And what has been the result of this study of the scriptures? Not, as it should have been, the love of God, but pride of self for a literal and rigid fulfilment of the letter of the scripture, a treatment of it which, as St. Paul found [2 Cor. 3⁶], so far from giving life, brings death. And this pride is now inevitably showing itself in opposition to One who, in the matter of sabbath observance, for example, gave the first place to judgement and the love of God (cf. Lk. 11⁴²).

We thus pass to the thought of reputation, honour, or 'glory', in the eyes of men, a glory which the Lord does not accept [5⁴¹], but which, in the form of Pharisaism or self-righteousness, one type of religious observance, unlike that of Ps. 119⁹⁷, ¹⁶⁵, is always in danger of seeking, and thereby of loving, the glory of men more than the glory of God [12⁴³]. Those who are thus minded are unlikely, are indeed unable, to receive One who comes with no other credentials than that He is the Father's Word, become flesh; if and when another comes, offering his own credentials, the Jews will welcome him [5⁴³], because of his likeness to themselves. For he will speak from himself and thereby seek his own reputation (cf. 7¹⁸), thus making himself dependent on those to whom he speaks; and they to their ruin will ally themselves with him.

In the final verses 5⁴⁵⁻⁴⁷ the Lord disclaims the office of Accuser of the Jews. It is not His part, whose judgement is the judgement of the Father, to arraign His hearers to the Father. Their hope is that, owing to their devotion to Moses as a final authority, they will find in him their representative and advocate. On the contrary, they must learn that it is Moses who is even now accusing them. For he was the author of the law, which always looks beyond itself to the glory of God; and therefore Moses, rightly understood, is a witness to Him who is addressing them, whose glory is that of an only begotten from the Father. Hence the Jews show that they do not truly believe Moses, since they do not believe the Lord; and if they do not believe Moses' writings, assuredly they will not believe the Lord's words, of whom he wrote.

NOTES TO SECTION 2. 5¹⁻⁴⁷

5¹. In John the Lord is never found at Jerusalem, except in connexion with a festival. The reading of R.V. text is more likely to be correct than that of R.V. mg; and, if so, this is the only occasion when St. John does not define the festival mentioned; and the reference is probably to one of the minor feasts, in contrast to the three great festivals of passover, pentecost, and tabernacles. Mr. H. St. J. Thackeray (*The Septuagint and Jewish Worship*, pp. 80–111) thinks that the book of Baruch may deal indirectly with the events which befell Jerusalem in A.D. 66 to 70. If so, the Hebrew original of the book, which was early lost, may have been written not long before or after this gospel; and possibly those may be right who detect certain connexions between the book of Baruch and Jn. 5. In the request which the former contains, that it should be read at 'a feast' (the same Greek word, without the article, as here) the reference is, Mr. Thackeray believes, to the festival, in the Jewish calendar, of New Year's day (*Rosh hashanah*), which fell in the autumn, before the feast of tabernacles. If we may assume the right reading in Jn. 5¹ to be 'a feast', the reference here too may well be to this New Year Festival.¹ In that case St. John, who bases the chronology of his book upon the Jewish festivals, gives us the following order of events:

2¹³. The Lord visits Jerusalem at passover (spring).

5¹. The Lord visits Jerusalem for the New Year festival (early autumn). [The evangelist does not mention the feast of tabernacles, this year.]

6⁴. The Lord feeds the multitude near the sea of Galilee at passover time (spring).

7². The Lord visits Jerusalem at the feast of tabernacles (autumn). [Thus rather more than a year will have elapsed since His previous visit at 5¹, and will have been spent, according to St. John, in Galilee; see 6¹, 7¹.]

10²². The Lord, who has resided continuously at Jerusalem since the feast of tabernacles [7², ¹⁰, ¹⁴, ³⁷], is still there at the encaenia, or dedication festival (winter).

11⁵⁵, 12¹, 13¹. The Lord after the encaenia visits Peraea. He returns thence to Bethany, near Jerusalem [11⁷, ¹⁸], and then withdraws to

¹ See also A. M. Farrer, *A Study in St. Mark*, pp. 210 to 215.

the neighbourhood of the wilderness, to a city called Ephraim [11⁵⁴]. Finally, He once more returns to Bethany six days before the passover (spring), and on the next day enters Jerusalem [12¹²⁻¹⁹].

5². Recent research suggests that the R.V. text may be correct. The name 'Bethzatha' (R.V. mg) is thought to be identical with the Bezetha mentioned by Josephus.

5⁴. This verse, probably a later addition to the text, explains what is assumed in 5⁷. The belief that angels or spirits are attached to particular springs and at certain times bestow curative properties on their waters, was widespread in antiquity. If the pool in question was fed by an intermittent spring, possessed of healing power, the contrast between the inadequate or impermanent water of the pool and the life-giving word and work of the Lord is similar to that which we have already met in other forms at 2⁶⁻⁸, 3²⁵⁻³⁰, 4¹³, ¹⁴.

5⁷. Possibly the 'first come, first served', as described in this verse, and the impotent man's lack of help at the critical moment, should be contrasted with the Lord's universal and permanent invitation, as described in 6³⁵, ³⁷.

5⁸, ⁹. Cf. the very similar expressions in Mk. 2⁹, ¹¹, ¹².

5¹³. Whereas the blind man of ch. 9, on the first occasion when he looks upon the Lord, seeks also to know Him [9³⁵⁻³⁸], it seems that the impotent man of ch. 5, when cured, makes no such attempt.

The withdrawal of the Lord, owing to the presence of a crowd, may be compared with His action at 6¹⁵.

5¹⁶, ¹⁸. The Greek verbs in these verses are in the imperfect tense, suggestive of continuance; and therefore the particular episode narrated in 5¹⁻¹⁸ should probably also be understood as representative of various conflicts of the Lord with the Jews, arising from His disregard of sabbath ordinances. This disregard is thus a ground of offence in this, as in the earlier gospels; but St. John unveils the true and deeper ground of conflict. This lies in the Lord's words in 5¹⁷, ¹⁸ ᵉⁿᵈ, which claim to justify His action. Hence the Jews' desire to kill Him, here first mentioned, is a result of His self-revelation; and as the story proceeds, it will be found that the more He reveals Himself, the more resolute do they become to destroy Him; and conversely, that the more resolute they become, the more fully He reveals His nature and being.

5¹⁹, ²⁰. In Rabbinic teaching a rebellious son was said 'to make himself equal with his father'; cf. 5¹⁸ᵉⁿᵈ. In 5¹⁹⁻³⁰, therefore, the Lord shows that He is not, as it were, a second God over against the Father, still less a rebellious son. Owing to the Father's love for the Son [5²⁰], and the Son's perfect obedience [5¹⁹, 8²⁹], the interaction between Father and Son is complete and perfect. As the Son does not act of Himself [5¹⁹, 8²⁸], so He does not speak from Himself [12⁴⁹, 14¹⁰; cf. also 16¹³, of the Holy Spirit], but only as the Father teaches [7¹⁶, ¹⁷] or has taught [8²⁸] Him (the present and the past tenses can be used interchangeably in respect of that which the Son sees, hears, receives from the Father; cf. 6³⁷ with 10²⁹). Similarly He has not come 'of Himself' [7²⁸, 8⁴²] or 'in His own name' [5⁴³], but the Father has sent Him [5³⁰, ³⁶]; and He does not seek or do His own will, but the will of Him that sent Him [5³⁰, 6³⁸].

When therefore we are told that the Son only does what He sees the Father doing, and conversely that the Father shows the Son all that He, the Father, does, the purpose is to emphasize the absolute union, in thought and will and action, of the Father and the Son, the incarnate Logos; cf. 1¹⁴, ¹⁸, ⁵¹.

5³⁵. It has been suggested that the right translation here is, 'He was the lamp that is kindled and shines'; i.e. John's light was derivative, not self-originated (cf. 1⁸). In any case, the words about him here should be contrasted with the Lord's words in 8¹², 'I am the light of the world'. A lamp is invaluable in darkness (cf. 1⁵⁻⁸); but as soon as the sun rises, the usefulness of the lamp is over. The use of the past tense in reference to John and his work suggests that his ministry is to be regarded as now over; in other words, by this time he has been imprisoned; contrast 3²⁴.

5³⁶. 'the Father hath sent me'. The Greek verb here, different from but of the same meaning as that in 4³⁴, is used seventeen times in John of God (or, the Father) 'sending' the Son. Altogether, therefore, the emphasis on this 'sending', occurring in one form or another in John forty-two times, an average of twice a chapter, is a fundamental trait of the book.

5³⁷ᵇ. There is no contradiction of 1¹⁸. Just as the Jews do not hear God's voice [8⁴⁷], but the disciples, who keep the Lord's word, hear it [14²³, ²⁴], so the Jews do not see God's form [8¹⁹], but disciples, who truly see the Lord, have in Him seen the Father [14⁹]. Voice and form are the means whereby a person is made known to and discerned by another person.

5³⁸ᵃ. Contrast 15⁷.

5³⁹. The R.V. text is probably right. It was rabbinic teaching that in the torah eternal life was made available for Israel.

5⁴². 'the love of God', that is, love for God, the genitive being objective.

5⁴⁴. Cf. Mt. 23⁵, Jn. 7¹⁸, 12⁴³, Rom. 2²⁸, ²⁹.

Grecians will perceive how easily the word for God could fall out of the text after the words for 'the only', and the R.V. text should probably be followed. The thought of 'the only God', in contrast to the 'gods many and lords many' of paganism [1 Cor. 8⁵, ⁶], is found in 17³, Rom. 16²⁷, 1 Tim. 1¹⁷, 6¹⁵, ¹⁶, Jude²⁵; but here [5⁴⁴] the contrast is different; it is between the one and only Source to which men should look for recognition (cf. 1 Cor. 3⁸, 4⁴, ⁵, 2 Cor. 10¹⁸), and the various and varying estimates which men are apt to form of their own and their neighbours' conduct (cf. 1 Cor. 4³, 2 Cor. 10¹²). That a man should desire recognition is both natural and right; for as a created being he is not his own master and, in order to find security and therewith happiness, must have regard to the commands and will of Another. The danger is that he may seek recognition in the wrong places; he may try to find security either in himself or in the esteem of others; and both these sources, sooner or later, will prove broken reeds. Only so far as he lets these go, and, as a child of God, seeks to honour God, and God only, does he build upon a rock, which will not fail him; and only so can he 'believe'.

The Lord as Life-giving Bread

6 After these things Jesus went away to the other side of the sea of
2 Galilee, which is *the sea* of Tiberias. And a great multitude followed him,
because they beheld the signs which he did on them that were sick.
3 And Jesus went up into the mountain, and there he sat with his disciples.
4,5 Now the passover, the feast of the Jews, was at hand. Jesus therefore
lifting up his eyes, and seeing that a great multitude cometh unto him,
saith unto Philip, Whence are we to buy ¹bread, that these may eat?
6 And this he said to prove him: for he himself knew what he would do.
7 Philip answered him, Two hundred ²pennyworth of ¹bread is not
8 sufficient for them, that every one may take a little. One of his disciples,
9 Andrew, Simon Peter's brother, saith unto him, There is a lad here,
which hath five barley loaves, and two fishes: but what are these among
10 so many? Jesus said, Make the people sit down. Now there was much
grass in the place. So the men sat down, in number about five thousand.
11 Jesus therefore took the loaves; and having given thanks, he distributed
to them that were set down; likewise also of the fishes as much as they
12 would. And when they were filled, he saith unto his disciples, Gather
13 up the broken pieces which remain over, that nothing be lost. So they
gathered them up, and filled twelve baskets with broken pieces from
the five barley loaves, which remained over unto them that had eaten.
14 When therefore the people saw the ³sign which he did, they said,
This is of a truth the prophet that cometh into the world.
15 Jesus therefore perceiving that they were about to come and take him
by force, to make him king, withdrew again into the mountain himself
alone.
16 And when evening came, his disciples went down unto the sea; and
17 they entered into a boat, and were going over the sea unto Capernaum.
18 And it was now dark, and Jesus had not yet come to them. And the sea
19 was rising by reason of a great wind that blew. When therefore they had
rowed about five and twenty or thirty furlongs, they behold Jesus
walking on the sea, and drawing nigh unto the boat: and they were
20 afraid. But he saith unto them, It is I; be not afraid. They were willing
21 therefore to receive him into the boat: and straightway the boat was at
the land whither they were going.
22 On the morrow the multitude which stood on the other side of the
sea saw that there was none other ⁴boat there, save one, and that Jesus

¹ *Gr.* loaves.　　² *See marginal note on* Mat. 18. 28.　　³ *Some ancient
authorities read* signs.　　⁴ *Gr.* little boat.

entered not with his disciples into the boat, but *that* his disciples went
23 away alone (howbeit there came ¹boats from Tiberias nigh unto the
24 place where they ate the bread after the Lord had given thanks): when
the multitude therefore saw that Jesus was not there, neither his disciples,
they themselves got into the ¹boats, and came to Capernaum, seeking
25 Jesus. And when they found him on the other side of the sea, they said
26 unto him, Rabbi, when camest thou hither? Jesus answered them and
said, Verily, verily, I say unto you, Ye seek me, not because ye saw signs,
27 but because ye ate of the loaves, and were filled. Work not for the meat
which perisheth, but for the meat which abideth unto eternal life,
which the Son of man shall give unto you: for him the Father, *even*
28 God, hath sealed. They said therefore unto him, What must we do,
29 that we may work the works of God? Jesus answered and said unto
30 them, This is the work of God, that ye believe on him whom ²he hath
sent. They said therefore unto him, What then doest thou for a sign,
31 that we may see, and believe thee? what workest thou? Our fathers
ate the manna in the wilderness; as it is written, He gave them bread
32 out of heaven to eat. Jesus therefore said unto them, Verily, verily,
I say unto you, It was not Moses that gave you the bread out of heaven;
33 but my Father giveth you the true bread out of heaven. For the bread
of God is that which cometh down out of heaven, and giveth life unto
34 the world. They said therefore unto him, Lord, evermore give us this
35 bread. Jesus said unto them, I am the bread of life: he that cometh to
me shall not hunger, and he that believeth on me shall never thirst.
36 But I said unto you, that ye have seen me, and yet believe not. All that
37 which the Father giveth me shall come unto me; and him that cometh to
38 me I will in no wise cast out. For I am come down from heaven, not
39 to do mine own will, but the will of him that sent me. And this is the
will of him that sent me, that of all that which he hath given me I should
40 lose nothing, but should raise it up at the last day. For this is the will of
my Father, that every one that beholdeth the Son, and believeth on him,
should have eternal life; and ³I will raise him up at the last day.
41   The Jews therefore murmured concerning him, because he said,
42 I am the bread which came down out of heaven. And they said, Is not
this Jesus, the son of Joseph, whose father and mother we know? how
43 doth he now say, I am come down out of heaven? Jesus answered and
44 said unto them, Murmur not among yourselves. No man can come to me,
except the Father which sent me draw him: and I will raise him up in
45 the last day. It is written in the prophets, And they shall all be taught
of God. Every one that hath heard from the Father, and hath learned,
46 cometh unto me. Not that any man hath seen the Father, save he which
47 is from God, he hath seen the Father. Verily, verily, I say unto you,

¹ *Gr.* little boats.   ² *Or* he sent   ³ *Or* that I should raise him up

48
49 He that believeth hath eternal life. I am the bread of life. Your fathers
50 did eat the manna in the wilderness, and they died. This is the bread
which cometh down out of heaven, that a man may eat thereof, and not
51 die. I am the living bread which came down out of heaven: if any man
eat of this bread, he shall live for ever: yea and the bread which I will
give is my flesh, for the life of the world.

52 The Jews therefore strove one with another, saying, How can this
53 man give us his flesh to eat? Jesus therefore said unto them, Verily,
verily, I say unto you, Except ye eat the flesh of the Son of man and
54 drink his blood, ye have not life in yourselves. He that eateth my flesh
and drinketh my blood hath eternal life; and I will raise him up at the
55 last day. For my flesh is ¹meat indeed, and my blood is ²drink indeed.
56 He that eateth my flesh and drinketh my blood abideth in me, and I in
57 him. As the living Father sent me, and I live because of the Father; so
58 he that eateth me, he also shall live because of me. This is the bread
which came down out of heaven: not as the fathers did eat, and died:
59 he that eateth this bread shall live for ever. These things said he in ³the
synagogue, as he taught in Capernaum.

60 Many therefore of his disciples, when they heard *this*, said, This is a
61 hard saying; who can hear ⁴it? But Jesus knowing in himself that his
disciples murmured at this, said unto them, Doth this cause you to
62 stumble? *What* then if ye should behold the Son of man ascending
63 where he was before? It is the spirit that quickeneth; the flesh profiteth
nothing: the words that I have spoken unto you are spirit, and are life.
64 But there are some of you that believe not. For Jesus knew from the
beginning who they were that believed not, and who it was that should
65 betray him. And he said, For this cause have I said unto you, that no
man can come unto me, except it be given unto him of the Father.

66 Upon this many of his disciples went back, and walked no more with
67 him. Jesus said therefore unto the twelve, Would ye also go away?
68 Simon Peter answered him, Lord, to whom shall we go? thou ⁵hast the
69 words of eternal life. And we have believed and know that thou art
70 the Holy One of God. Jesus answered them, Did not I choose you the
71 twelve, and one of you is a devil? Now he spake of Judas *the son* of
Simon Iscariot, for he it was that should betray him, *being* one of the
twelve.

¹ *Gr.* true meat.   ² *Gr.* true drink.   ³ *Or* a synagogue
⁴ *Or* him   ⁵ *Or* hast words

EXPOSITION OF SECTION 3. 6¹⁻⁷¹

The Lord's works: 1. He feeds the multitude, 6¹⁻¹⁵.
             2. Walking on the water, He rejoins the disciples, as they cross the lake, 6¹⁶⁻²¹.

The Lord's words: 1. He gives teaching in the Capernaum synagogue on the meaning of the bread of life, 6²²⁻⁵⁹.
             2. The twelve alone remain faithful, but are warned that one of their own number is evil, 6⁶⁰⁻⁷¹.

This section is confined to Galilee and its neighbourhood.

From this point to the end of the gospel, in connexion with the Lord's declarations about Himself (especially in the seven times repeated 'I am . . .', to the first of which we come in this chapter), the reader should always bear in mind the revelation, given by the Lord in ch. 5, of His Person in its combination of greatness and humility. While on the one hand His union with the Father is absolute, and what the Father wills and does, that the Son wills and does, and that only, on the other hand the union, realized on the Father's side in love, is realized on the Son's side not only in love, but in complete obedience to and dependence on the Father.

Before the reader passes to the exposition of this section, four features of it should be mentioned.

1. This is the only considerable section of this gospel devoted entirely to the neighbourhood of the sea of Galilee. Previous brief visits of the Lord to Galilee have alternated with His visits to Jerusalem, and early in ch. 7 He will finally leave Galilee.

2. The three groups which are constantly in contact with the Lord during the ministry, the multitude, the Jews, and the disciples, (see pp. 62 ff. and 69 ff.), all appear and play important parts in this section. The multitude, prominent in 6¹⁻⁴⁰, seems to merge into the Jews at 6⁴¹, ⁵²; and possibly the disciples of 6⁶⁰ are reduced to the twelve at 6⁶⁶, ⁶⁷.

3. All through this chapter, except for St. Peter's confession at 6⁶⁸, ⁶⁹, emphasis is laid on the inability of those addressed by the Lord to rise to what we may describe as a spiritual understanding, an understanding not bounded by material, physical considerations. Thus at 6⁷ Philip deals with the Lord's question solely at the economic level; at 6¹⁵, as a result of the Lord's wonderful gift, there is danger that the multitude will use violence, in order to make Him an 'earthly' king, whereas the instructed reader knows

that His kingdom has its origin and authority elsewhere [18³⁶]; at 6¹⁹ the disciples are afraid, when the Lord, using means which they cannot understand, approaches their boat in the middle of the lake; in 6²²⁻²⁵ St. John is at pains to make clear the inability of the multitude also, relying solely on the evidence of the boats, to understand how the Lord could have reached Capernaum. At 6⁴² the Jews' difficulty consists in the knowledge, which they think they have, of the Lord's (solely) natural origin; and at 6⁵² they take His words in the most external sense which the latter can carry, and in that only. And finally, at 6⁶⁰, ⁶¹, when many of the Lord's disciples prove unable to assimilate His teaching about the bread which came down out of heaven, and their participation in it, with the results for them (in other words, about the descent of the Son of man and its purpose), He asks how they are to understand the meaning of the ascent of the Son of man, His return, when His work is completed, to the Father. We recall how, in Mk. 6⁵¹, ⁵² also, the disciples fail to understand the significance of the Lord's actions, and for this reason, shortly before St. Peter's confession near Caesarea Philippi, are strongly rebuked in Mk. 8¹⁴⁻²¹; but here in John the twelve, through St. Peter, at 6⁶⁸, ⁶⁹ forthwith make a full confession.

Throughout this chapter therefore, as indeed in this gospel as a whole, the reader is reminded of the Lord's words in 3³ to Nicodemus about the necessity of a rebirth from above for vision of, and entry into, the kingdom of God, and thereby for an understanding and reception of the Lord's Person and His gifts; in a word, for belief on Him.

4. Whereas the first few verses of this chapter [6¹⁻¹⁴], which describe the feeding of the multitude, are closely parallel to Mk. 6³⁴⁻⁴⁴ (cf. also Mk. 8¹⁻¹⁰), in that part of the chapter [6²⁵⁻⁷¹], in which the Lord, starting from the feeding of the previous day, points to Himself as the bread of life, teaching is given which in the earlier gospels is associated with the Lord's actions (not narrated in John) at His last meal with His disciples [Mk. 14²²⁻²⁵ and parallels]. Thus a connexion already traceable in certain similarities of language in the earlier gospels between the feeding of the multitude and the events of the last supper becomes more explicit in John, especially when we notice that the first reference by the Lord to the part to be played by one of the disciples in betraying Him, a part revealed by Him in the other gospels at the

last supper, is made in John for the first time in this chapter [6⁷⁰, ⁷¹].

Further, the two events narrated in the earlier gospels, the Lord's feeding of the multitude and His last meal with His disciples, were regarded in the Church from an early date as foretastes of the anticipated banquet in the kingdom of God. It is therefore note-worthy that in this chapter which, as we have seen, includes a narrative [6¹⁻¹⁴] of the feeding of the multitude and an almost direct reference [6⁵¹⁻⁵⁹] to the Eucharist, the Church's continued memorial of the last supper, St. John emphasizes that the Lord is the Giver of the food at each, at the cost of His own life and death.

It will be remembered that the Lord's purging of the temple, which occurs near the close of the other gospels, and in them is a link in the final chain of events leading to His death at passover time, is found in John at the outset of His ministry, again at pass-over time, and is combined with teaching by Him on His death and resurrection [2¹⁹⁻²²]. Just so, it seems, the sacramental teach-ing, which in the other gospels is given privately in connexion with the Lord's actions at the last supper in Jerusalem, is given openly in John in ch. 6, in close connexion with His feeding of the multitude during His ministry in Galilee, again at passover time [6⁴], and includes references to His death and ascension. It seems to be part of St. John's purpose to show that the Lord's redemptive activity is universal and also is achieved throughout His ministry and life, and not solely, as perhaps might be thought by a reader of the earlier gospels only, for His disciples, and in and by His death.

At the outset of this chapter the Lord, having left the western for the eastern shore of the lake, is followed by a great multitude impressed by His ability to cure the sick, a note which recalls many scenes in the other gospels. He now ascends the hill country and is seated there with His disciples, the evangelist adding that the Jewish passover-feast was not far off. The reader knows that at the next passover-feast the Son of man will be exalted, lifted up [3¹⁴, 8²⁸, 12³²]; on this, the immediately preceding passover-feast, He is seated, as on a new Sinai, with His disciples round Him. The immediate task, however, is not to deepen and fulfil the old coven-ant by instructing His disciples in the sermon on the mount (cf. Mt. 5¹, ²), nor is it to grant mass restoration to health (cf. Mt. 15²⁹⁻³¹); it is to satisfy the needs of a mighty crowd [6⁵; cf. 6³⁵];

and the Lord, taking the initiative (contrast Mk. 6³⁵, ³⁶), puts the question of 6⁵ to Philip. St. John's note in 6⁶ prevents us from any danger of thinking that the Lord is indeed adopting the level of the disciples' thought, as they have revealed it in 4⁸, ³¹⁻³³. Philip forthwith takes the Lord's words at their surface value and deals with the problem at the level of the market-place, at the same time admitting that the solution he suggests will prove inadequate. Andrew, of whom we hear little in comparison with his greater brother Peter, but whose interventions are always valuable and to the point [1⁴¹, 12²²], draws attention, but without much confidence, to a small local source of help which could be used. The matter now passes solely into the hands of the Lord, nor do we hear (contrast Mk. 6⁴¹) that the disciples take part in the distribution. At His word all recline upon the springing grass (the note of 6⁴ is evidence of the time of year), and He serves them (cf. Lk. 12³⁷), the result being that they have as much as they wish; and when the disciples are once more mentioned, being bidden to collect the broken pieces that remain, the amount is still prodigious. As a result, those who have enjoyed the bounty see in the Lord the prophet of their expectation, and concert to thrust royalty forthwith upon Him, in order to achieve their own purposes. The Lord, however, perceiving their design, leaves both the disciples and the multitude, and withdraws again into the high ground, alone.

In the evening the disciples—on their own initiative, it seems (contrast Mk. 6⁴⁵)—descend to the sea and seek to return in a boat to the western shore. For a short time therefore they do not see their Lord (cf. 14¹⁸, ¹⁹, 16¹⁶), and it has already become dark, and also the sea is rising by reason of a mighty wind. But when they have succeeded in reaching the centre of the lake, they see their Master mysteriously approaching the boat, and are seized with fear. Here and here only do we meet in John a frequent and notable feature of the Marcan record—fear on the part of the disciples with reference to their Master. If we consider St. John's doctrine of His Person, it becomes clear that such a reaction is, initially, inevitable and right; but it is a sign of immaturity, and should be overcome [1 Jn. 4¹⁸]; nor is there any desire on the part of the Lord that His disciples should be subject to it [6²⁰]; and as soon as they are willing, on receiving His personal assurance, to admit Him into the boat, they are at the haven where they would be (cf. Ps. 107³⁰). We seem to have here the teaching of 14⁵, ⁶, 15⁴, ⁵, in another form.

Like 4^{1-3} and 11^{1-2}, 6^{22-24} is a curiously involved passage, in which also various readings occur; thus some texts omit the last six English words of 6^{23}. Its purpose, however, is plain; it is to make clear how the Lord and the multitude come together next day in a different place, and why His movements since the previous day, although known to the disciples, are inexplicable to it (6^{25}).

The next day, we read, the multitude which now once more stood (or perhaps, had stood, if we take the reference to be to its assemblage on the previous day) on the eastern shore, having noticed on the previous evening that the disciples in their boat had gone away alone, without their Master (cf. 6^{15}), and now seeing that He obviously had not made use of the only other means of transport by water, since the boat in question was still there, avails itself, in its search for Him, of boats which had arrived from Tiberias, and so comes to Capernaum. Therewith we pass to a conversation which, by means of a series of questions put by the multitude, leads up to the Lord's words in 6^{33}, followed by His self-declaration in 6^{35}. This is succeeded by a short monologue on His part in 6^{36-40}, which recapitulates some of the truths taught in the long unbroken discourse of 5^{19-47}. The difficulty which the Jews (the term 'the multitude' does not occur again in this chapter) then raise about His self-declaration, a difficulty put in the form of a question about His Person [$6^{41, 42}$]—since the reader must always keep in mind that the Lord, 'the Word become flesh', is speaking to His hearers as a man to men,—leads to a warning against dis-obedience to the divine initiative and invitation, and to a renewed exposition of the teaching, ending with the momentous further declaration in 6^{51} that the Speaker, the living and life-giving bread which descended from heaven, will give His flesh for the life of the world.

We now return to consider 6^{25-51} in detail.

The question of the multitude at 6^{25}, like that of the Jews at 6^{42}, is 'after the flesh' [8^{15}] or 'of the earth' [3^{31}], and receives no direct reply. Instead, the Lord solemnly warns His hearers that their interest in Him is now based on nothing better than hope of material benefit. Their thoughts must be raised to a higher level, and in 6^{27} they are bidden to work or give service, in order to secure not perishable food, but lasting food which issues in eternal life; this food it is the purpose and in the power of the Son of man, the accredited Representative of the Father, to impart to them.

The hearers ask what is required of them, if they are to work or give services which God can reward, and learn that only one service is required (itself, however, only to be accomplished with divine help), namely, belief on Him whom God has sent.[1] The hearers perceive that the Lord is referring to Himself, and the conversation begins to turn, as often in this gospel, on the nature of His credentials. If His hearers are to give Him credence (contrast the much stronger term, belief on Him, which in 6²⁹ the Lord had described as the service desired by God), He must work a sign (cf. 4⁴⁸), and He is reminded, by a quotation, that their fathers in the wilderness were sustained by the gift of the manna, there called bread out of heaven.[2] (This reference is of great significance here, in view of a Jewish belief that 'in the last days' manna would again be given; the Messiah as a second deliverer would correspond to Moses, the earlier deliverer.) The brevity of the Lord's reply must be expanded, if it is to be fully understood; it is given in solemn assurance, and contains two truths. First, not Moses, but God, was the Giver of the manna; and secondly, He, the Lord's Father, is now giving them (in the Person of His Son) not manna which for a time descended from the sky and, itself perishable, satisfied their physical hunger only, but heavenly sustenance which is more than a matter of physical food. In the next verse this sustenance is called the bread of God, and is said to be 'He who (or, 'the bread which'—the Greek will tolerate both renderings—) comes down out of heaven, and gives life to the world'. The listeners, like the woman of Samaria at 4¹⁵, naturally understand the words of 6³³ in their impersonal sense and, their thoughts still running on the

[1] We learn in 6³⁵, ³⁷, 7³⁷, ³⁸ that belief on the Lord can also be described as 'coming to' Him; cf. 5⁴⁰, Mt. 11²⁸. Granted this form of service or work, namely belief, all other works would follow, being included in this one work and its results. Thus the task of man is shown to be, not so much a completion of anything, as an attitude of obedient service to God, and of devotion to that which God works, or reveals. And since God's supreme work or revelation is the sending of His Son, man's chief or only work should be to allow the Son's word to have free course (or, place) in him [8³⁷]. Then all the rest, in thought and word and deed, would follow.

[2] It is true that the Lord's hearers are said in 6¹⁴ to have understood His action on the previous day as a sign; but, to judge from 6²⁶, the expectations raised in them by that sign were limited to hopes of the bestowal of unlimited bounty by a wonder-worker; the sign was a portent, and no more. They did not see in it a symbol and channel of the true or real gift offered by the Lord, a gift which is in the last resort Himself. Hence their demand for a (fresh) sign in 6³⁰ is simply for a fresh portent and fresh bounty which, it is implied in 6³¹, must be even greater than that of the manna.

Lord's bounty of the previous day, beg that this gift of bread may become perpetual. But whereas in 4¹⁶ an abrupt change took place in the conversation at this point, here the subject is continued, and a great advance is made; for all possibility of understanding the Lord's words impersonally is now removed, and we reach the first of his seven self-declarations in this gospel. He reveals that He Himself is the life-giving sustenance or bread, of which He has been speaking. He does not merely impart a gift which He brings; He is that gift; and the recipient will no longer hunger or thirst.

At once, however, the Lord reminds His hearers that they are in danger of forfeiting His gift. They have had the unique privilege of seeing in the flesh the Fountain-head of life and truth (cf. Mt. 13¹⁷), but this has not led on their part to belief. Everything given to the Lord by the Father will come to Him, and be received, since the Lord's sole purpose is to do not His own but the Father's will, this will being that nothing given to Him by the Father should be lost by Him, but that it should be raised up by Him at the last day. In other words the Father's will is that all who behold the Son and believe on Him should forthwith have eternal life, and at the last day be raised up by the Lord.

The Lord has identified Himself [6³⁵] with the gift of the Father, the true bread out of heaven [6³²]; and the listeners, who at 6⁴¹ and 6⁵² are now described by the familiar title 'the Jews', resent His assertion, on the ground that they know His (physical) parentage. Believing themselves to be fully equipped with adequate knowledge of the facts of 'the world', their world, they assume that these are not, cannot be, the means of revelation. They are right, in so far as the divine could not be revealed in that which is only human and no more (cf. 3⁶); but they are far astray if they assume that the divine can only be revealed in a superhuman way, which they can themselves assess, and on which therefore they can pass judgement. Rather, as their religion should have taught them, revelation, the unveiling of the presence of God, makes all human judgement 'a very small thing' [1 Cor. 4³]; in God's presence man is reduced to silence, and cannot but abhor himself [Job 42⁶]. For this reason the Jews are bidden not to indulge, like their fathers, the Israelites, in the wilderness [Num. 14²], in inarticulate, suppressed resentment; the discourse must once more be raised, as at 6²⁷, from the earthly to the heavenly level (cf. 3¹²); and this the Speaker forthwith does [6⁴⁴], as He alone can do (cf. 3¹³). So long as a man remains, and is content to remain, confident of his own ability, without divine help, to assess experience and the meaning of experience, he cannot 'come to' the Lord, he cannot 'believe'; only the Father can move him to this step, with its incalculable and final results. It is indeed, as was foreseen long ago in prophecy [6⁴⁵], the divine purpose that all should thus be brought to the Lord, and there is thus no thought here of a limited number of selected individuals; it is open to everyone to hear the Father's voice (cf. 18³⁷ᵉⁿᵈ) and, in the discipleship which results, to come to the Speaker. He who has thus heard, and learned, comes to the Lord.

In 6⁴⁶ we are reminded of the Logos doctrine of 1³, ⁴; man by himself cannot hear or see God (cf. 3¹³); only He, who is from God [1¹, ¹⁴, ¹⁸], is capable of this; all other sight or knowledge of God is and must be mediated through Him.

This part of the teaching [6²⁶⁻⁵¹] now draws to a close, although one momentous statement remains yet to be made at the end of 6⁵¹, which will make clear that the Lord's language in 6³²⁻³⁵ is not to be understood in a sense which would imply that the true bread, the bread of life which He gives, costs nothing to the Giver. On the contrary, His gift involves His death. But first the truths set forth in the first part of the teaching are reiterated. The believer, he who is drawn to the Lord by the Father, who has listened to the Lord's voice and has learned, he has eternal life. And his food, that which ever nourishes his life, is the Speaker, Himself at the moment, it is true, a man among men. But the believer will always bear in mind the reason for which He came down from heaven and is thus present in the flesh. It is in order that men may share His life; and His hearers must never confound this eternal, heavenly gift which He brings with the solely temporary, physical gift of the manna, as enjoyed by their fathers. The latter partook of the manna and later, in the course of nature, died. But the Lord is now speaking of food which descends out of heaven, in order that those who partake of it may not die. He Himself has come down, as this living bread, out of heaven; and he who partakes of this food will live for ever; and indeed the food which the Speaker will give is His flesh, on behalf of the life of the world (cf. 17²¹ᵉⁿᵈ).

If for a moment we turn our thoughts back to the earlier chapters, it becomes clear that in John reference is made from the outset—at first, indeed, in veiled language, but more and more clearly—to the

spokesman protests that the Lord, and He only, is the object of their faith; in the words uttered by Him, which have proved too hard or harsh for others [6⁶⁰], they find eternal life. And further, this belief, which has become also knowledge, sees in Him 'the Holy One of God'. Jesus, the Word become flesh, is also and uniquely He who is separated from sinners [Heb. 7²⁶] and belongs to God; and He it is 'whom the Father sanctified and sent into the world' [10³⁶].

St. Peter had spoken in the name of the twelve ('we', 6⁶⁸, ⁶⁹), and the Lord in 6⁷⁰ answers them as a body. St. Peter's words have expressed a true faith, and it is sealed in the Lord's reply that they were indeed His choice (cf. 15¹⁶), and therefore were enabled to respond as they have. But He shows also that even those who, thus chosen, 'have left all and followed' Him [Mk. 10²⁸], can claim no security, still less presume upon His choice of them. One of themselves, one even of the twelve [6⁷¹], will be guilty of extremest perfidy, of utter breach of faith; he is indeed 'a devil'. Accordingly the higher the privilege, and the greater the knowledge, the deeper the possible fall; nor can or should any disciple be sure of himself or of his loyalty until the end (cf. Mk. 13¹³, 14²⁹⁻³¹, Jn. 13¹⁸, ²², ²⁸). Again, although in the Lord's presence men in truth range themselves forthwith on this side or on that, the distinction is not immediately apparent, nor can any line be visibly drawn, as it were, between two groups, since evil is present even in the inner circle of disciples, which is formed by the twelve.

NOTES TO SECTION 3. 6¹⁻⁷¹

6¹. 'the sea of Galilee': so also in Matthew and Mark; St. Luke always has 'lake'. In the N.T. the lake is called 'the sea of Tiberias' only here and at 21¹. Tiberias was a town on the west side of the lake (cf. 6²³), founded about A.D. 26 by the tetrarch Herod Antipas, who named it after the emperor Tiberius, to be the capital of Galilee; hence perhaps the double designation here.

6⁵. In the three earlier gospels, in their parallel accounts of this feeding of the 5,000, the disciples first raise the problem how the multitude is to be fed; here, as also in the further accounts in Matthew and Mark of the feeding of the 4,000, the Lord does so. It is a feature of John that the Lord takes the initiative (e.g. 5⁶, 9⁶), nor does He ever act forthwith as a result of human prompting; even at 2³ and 11³ He shows, by a delay before He takes action, His independence of others' suggestion—in other words, His complete dependence on His Father's will, and on that only.

6⁵⁻⁹. The characters of Philip and Andrew are lightly but clearly marked in John. For Philip cf. also 1⁴³⁻⁴⁶, 12²⁰⁻²², 14⁸⁻¹¹; he seems to be essentially a hard-headed, practical man, at home in matters of finance and organization, who distrusts his own understanding of the Lord's mind [12²²], which he finds difficult to grasp [14⁸]. For Andrew cf. also 1³⁷⁻⁴², 12²²; on each of these occasions he is instrumental in bringing others with him into the presence of the Lord; and here [6^{8, 9}] he is represented as ready to regard something, however small, as at any rate better than nothing, and therefore as worth bringing to the Lord's notice.

At 4⁸ the Lord was left at Jacob's well, because His disciples had gone away into the city 'to buy food', and were therefore absent during His conversation with the woman of Samaria about His gift of living water. The same verb is used here, in the Lord's question to Philip; and in the light of Is. 55¹ these verses provide a good example of the irony which is frequent in John and may indeed already be present in the parallel passage Mk. 6^{36, 37}. Philip's reply, like the disciples' words at 4³³, shows that his thoughts on these matters turn naturally to the methods of the market-place; an outlay even of some £10, he says, would be inadequate. A denarius, the coin here mentioned, was the normal wage for a day's labour (cf. Mt. 20²).

6¹¹. 'having given thanks': so in Mt. 15³⁶, Mk. 8⁶, the accounts of the feeding of the 4,000. The reference, as also in the case of the 'blessing', mentioned in the three earlier gospels at this point, is to the Jewish prayer of thanksgiving and blessing, offered by the head of the household, or by the host, before a meal. At an early date the Church began to use both verbs in connexion with the Eucharist.

St. John's gospel differs from the three earlier gospels in their parallel accounts of this feeding, and from the first two gospels in their second narratives of the feeding, in that here the Lord Himself makes the distribution; in the other accounts the disciples do so. Nor does this gospel mention the breaking of the bread, a feature common to all the other accounts.

6^{12, 13}. This collection of the broken pieces, 'that nothing be lost', is in accordance with Jewish custom. Conceivably there may be a veiled reference to 6³⁹ (cf. also 17¹²); in both verses the same verb is used as here.

6¹³. All four evangelists, in their accounts of this feeding, use the same Greek word to describe the stout wicker baskets which were filled with broken pieces, as opposed to the more flexible baskets of woven hemp mentioned as being used for the same purpose in the second accounts of the feeding in Matthew and Mark, and also in Acts 9²⁵ in connexion with the lowering of St. Paul from the city wall of Damascus.

6¹⁴. The 'great multitude', which was following the Lord because they saw His signs upon the sick [6²], now as a result of 'the sign' (the R.V. text should be followed) of the meal, which they have received, sees in Him 'the prophet'. Unlike the same term as used in 1²¹, 7⁴⁰, the words as used here may mean, in the light of the next verse, the Messiah. For it is now desired to make Him king, in a kingdom 'of this world' (cf. 18³⁶). The Lord indeed will make the meaning of His sign clear in His teaching next day in the synagogue at Capernaum [6⁵⁹] and, as a result, will be left alone with the twelve [6⁶⁶, ⁶⁷]. But at present the multitude, interpreting the sign at its own level and in the light of its own supposed advantage (as is made clear at 6²⁶), sees in Him one who, if sufficient pressure is brought to bear upon Him, will, as its leader, solve its national and economic problems. Hence its perception has now become even more selfish and dull than it was at 6². The multitude is indeed right in discerning in the Lord a deliverer, indeed the Deliverer; but it is very far astray as regards His office and His mission. In the Lord's conversation with Pilate He will show that royalty does in fact belong to Him, but that it is a royalty which does not have its origin from this world and is therefore not to be established by force [18³⁶]; for 'force', in the striking words of an early Christian treatise, *The Epistle to Diognetus*, 'is not a means of which God makes use'. The Lord therefore again withdraws, but this time alone (contrast 6³). According to St. Matthew and St. Mark, His purpose in doing so was to pray.

6¹⁹. The width of the lake, at its greatest, is between six and seven miles; and since the Greek word translated furlong is roughly equivalent to 200 yards, St. John's statement of the position of the boat at this time is similar to that of Mk. 6⁴⁷, 'in the midst of the sea'.

6²⁶. In 4⁴⁶⁻⁵⁴ the father, whose son was dying, 'believed' [4⁵³] as a result of the sign [4⁵⁴], which was granted to him. Here on the contrary the multitude, although it had witnessed the Lord's signs on the sick [6²] and also the sign [6¹⁴] of the previous day, as a result seeks only to make use of these in order to satisfy its physical needs. It is thus shown that signs in different cases lead to precisely opposite conclusions, according to the way in which they are regarded and received, and that in this case the multitude, although it has seen the Lord, does not believe [6³⁶].

6²⁷. Both the thought and the style of St. John are deeply Hebraic in character, and for the sake of emphasis the Hebrews often expressed a truth or, as here, a precept in the form of two directly opposed propositions, where Western thought finds it more natural to use the language of comparison. Thus the words in Hosea 6⁶, 'I desire mercy and not sacrifice', which are twice quoted in Matthew, should not be understood as a condemnation of all sacrificial rites, but as expressing Yahweh's desire that His people should rate merciful dealing even more highly than their sacrificial duties. Similarly here the Lord's meaning is that His hearers should make it their first aim to be able to receive that which He offers; He does not mean that they are to neglect material provision altogether. Mt. 6³³ expresses the same thought in another form, 'Seek ye first the kingdom of God, and his righteousness; and all these things shall be added unto you.'

The term 'the Son of man' has occurred previously four times in John, at 1⁵¹, 3¹³, ¹⁴, 5²⁷. In ch. 6 it occurs not only here but also in verses 53 and 62, and in later chapters at 8²⁸, 9³⁵ (see note there), 12²³, ³⁴ (twice), 13³¹. Confining ourselves at present to chs. 2 to 6, at 3¹³, ¹⁴ we learned that the

Son of man, and He only, has bridged the otherwise impassable gulf between heaven and earth, the visible and the invisible, and also that, if He is to accomplish His task of giving life to the believer, He must be lifted up, an expression which in John refers outwardly indeed to the physical elevation of the Lord's body on the cross, but inwardly to His 'exaltation' or return to the Father, which according to St. John that elevation effected. It is therefore fitting that the term should be emphasized in this chapter, which sets forth the Lord as life-giving bread and the source of eternal life to those who believe on and come to Him [6³⁵, ⁴⁰, ⁴⁷]. This gift, however, involves His own death [6⁵¹, ⁵³], and therefore will not be complete until His work is ended; hence the 'shall give' of this verse 6²⁷, as at 6⁵¹ (cf. 4¹⁴). (It is, however, equally possible to use the present tense, as in 6³², 'my Father is giving you'; in this case the Lord's work in the incarnation and the passion is regarded as an indivisible unity.) Finally, throughout this chapter, especially in verses 27 to 50, emphasis is continually laid, as in this verse 6²⁷, on the Father's action in the salvation of mankind. He it is, the Father, even God, who has 'sealed' or guaranteed the Son (cf. 1³²⁻³⁴); He, through whom the Son lives [6⁵⁷], has sent the Son [6²⁹]; He, the Father, gives the true, heavenly bread [6³²], and draws men to the Lord [6⁴⁴; cf. 6³⁷, ⁶⁵], and wills that they should have eternal life [6⁴⁰]. But throughout the chapter the Lord shows also what His own part is, and by the indirect reference to His sacrificial death in verses 51ᵇ to 59 reveals its purpose to be that both the world and those who eat His flesh and drink His blood may have life.

'shall give'. The hearers are to do their part and work; none the less, the result will be a gift, the gift of the Son of man, who has been attested by the Father.

6³¹. The quotation is probably made from Neh. 9¹⁵, but Ps. 78²⁴ is similar. The story of the manna may be found in Ex. 16 and Num. 11.

6³². 'It was not Moses that gave you'. The hearers are regarded as one with their forefathers in the unity of the Jewish race.

6³³. 'cometh down out of heaven'. It is noteworthy how often these words, the verb being either the present or the past participle, occur in this chapter. In the present participle [6³³, ⁵⁰], the thought is of the descent as characteristic of Him who descends; in the past participle [6⁴¹, ⁵¹, ⁵⁸], of the descent as an historical event.

6³⁵. The seven self-declarations of the Lord in John are: the bread of life 6³⁵, ⁴⁸ (cf. also 6⁴¹, ⁵¹); the light of the world 8¹², 9⁵; the door 10⁷, ⁹; the good shepherd 10¹¹, ¹⁴; the resurrection and the life 11²⁵; the way and the truth and the life 14⁶; the true vine 15¹, ⁵. All these similitudes are to be understood as descriptive of some aspect of the Lord's work as the Word become flesh.

The words 'I am the bread of life' reveal that the Lord Himself is the gift which He brings. The genitive is qualitative, as is shown by the synonym 'living bread' at 6⁵¹ᵃ (cf. 'living water' at 4¹⁰); but the expression should be understood as including the power to bring life into being; life proceeds from life.

6³⁹. 'the last day'. This expression, in the N.T. found only in John, occurs on the Lord's lips four times in this chapter, at verses 39, 40, 44, 54, and at 12⁴⁸. It is also used by Martha at 11²⁴; and, in the narrative, in a different connexion, of 'the last day' of the feast of tabernacles [7³⁷]. Just as at 1³, in the prologue, the universe is said, in accordance with fundamental Hebrew beliefs, to have been created at a definite time in the past, so here it is regarded as subject to a definite limit in the future. The doctrine expressed here may be summed up in the words of 1 Jn. 2¹⁷, 'the world passeth away . . . but he that doeth the will of God abideth for ever'.

The twofold teaching of this chapter (Jn. 6) on the present and the future aspect of eternal life is exactly parallel to that of 5²⁴⁻²⁹ (cf. also 11²³⁻²⁶). He who, drawn by the Father, comes to the Lord and believes on Him, he who eats the flesh of the Son of man and drinks His blood, he abides in the Lord and the Lord abides in Him; he has eternal life, and the Lord will raise him up at the last day. A distinction between the two aspects of eternal life, however, may be noted. Whereas the final paragraphs of this chapter seem to show that in spite of the Lord's choice of disciples and His present gift of eternal life to the believer, that choice may be annulled and that gift may be forfeited (cf. 17¹²), at the last day, we may assume, no such danger will remain.

6⁴⁰. 'beholdeth': the Greek verb 'may be used either of bodily vision or of mental contemplation, but always connotes intelligent attention'. It was obviously essential that the Lord should be seen and heard in the flesh by His contemporaries (cf. 1 Jn. 1¹⁻⁴); but physical sight and hearing do not of themselves produce belief. Such sight may have its part to play in engendering belief [20²⁹ᵃ]; but it may also have the opposite result [6³⁶, 15²⁴ᵇ]. In the case of those who believe, but did not see or hear the Lord in the days of His flesh, the equivalent of such sight and hearing is presumably the conviction that 'Jesus Christ is come in the flesh', 1 Jn. 4². If so, we may see here a good illustration of the great importance of the historical tradition, as it has been handed down in the Church through successive generations.

6⁴¹. Hitherto the listeners have been described as 'the multitude' [6²², ²⁴], which is clearly of Galilee [6², ⁵], whereas the term 'the Jews', which we now meet, is elsewhere in John for the most part used of the dwellers in the south, and especially of the Jerusalem authorities, who are hostile to the Lord from the beginning. St. John's purpose therefore, here and at 6⁵², may be to show that Galileans also stumbled at the Lord's teaching and ultimately were not different from those who opposed Him in the south.

6⁴². 'the son of Joseph'. See p. 103. Just as the food now offered was contrasted at 6²⁶, ²⁷ with the physical food provided for the multitude on the previous day, or at 6³¹⁻³³ with the manna temporarily provided in the wilderness, and just as the Lord's true kingship [18³⁶] is contrasted with the external kingship desired for Him by the multitude as a result of His gift to them of physical food [6¹⁵], so the 'outward' knowledge of the Lord is now to be contrasted with the true knowledge of Him as the heaven-sent Revealer of the Father, a knowledge promised, under the form of sight, to disciples in 1⁵¹, and necessary to belief in Him (cf. 6³⁶).

The question of the Jews should be compared with that put in Mk. 6³, 'how doth he now say?': i.e. what does He mean, when He says . . .? It is the same form of question as in Mk. 9¹², 12³⁵, Jn. 8³³, 12³⁴, 14⁹.

6⁴⁴ᵃ. The converse truth is expressed in 14⁶ᵇ, and that of 6⁴⁵ᵇ in 1¹⁸.

6⁵¹ᵉⁿᵈ. The doctrine of the Lord's incarnation now begins to be united, more definitely than hitherto, with that of His coming passion; such verses as 1¹⁴ᵃ, ³³ᵇ, ⁵¹ begin to join hands with 10¹¹, ¹⁵, ¹⁸.

6⁵⁴⁻⁵⁸. It is often suggested that the Greek verb used in these verses for 'eating'—and not elsewhere in John, except at 13¹⁸—may be deliberately chosen, in order to emphasize that there is here a definite reference to participation in the elements at the Eucharist; but this is by no means certain.

6⁵⁶. 'abideth in me, and I in him'. This language is not to be understood as merely figurative, but as describing a religiously true relationship which can only, or can best, be described in this way (cf. 14²⁰, 15⁴, ⁵, 17²¹⁻²³).

6⁵⁷. It is a basic thought in this gospel that the perfect relationship between the Father and the Son is to be reproduced in the relationship between the Son and His disciples (cf. 15⁹, ¹⁰).

6⁶⁰. 'saying': perhaps rather, 'discourse'. It is 'hard', in the sense that it is regarded as requiring more, both of insight and of sympathy, than the hearers are prepared to grant; and this is now the reaction of disciples, who hitherto have followed the Lord, and not only of the Jews. Thus this final scene in St. John's record of the Lord's work in Galilee is clearly of great significance, in revealing a judgement or separation or discrimination between true discipleship and the reverse. Indeed, the discrimination will penetrate even the ranks of the twelve [6⁶⁶⁻⁷¹]; and we are thus prepared for the transition from the early chapters of the book, the keynote of which has been witness or testimony to the Lord, to the central chapters, in which the chief theme will be the sifting, testing judgement effected by His presence among men.

6⁶¹. 'knowing in himself' (cf. 2²⁴, ²⁵, 6⁶⁴, 13¹¹).

6⁶². The Greek sentence, strictly, is incomplete; some such insertion as the R.V. 'What' is necessary. The meaning of the passage may perhaps be summarized in the words 'no cross, no crown'. In 6⁶¹ the Lord has perceived that His words, implying His death and also the necessity that His disciples should share in it, are giving them pause, and causing offence; and He reminds them that the death of the Son of man is not the last word in the matter; true, it involves, for Him and for them, 'the scandal of the cross'; but it is also the path of His exaltation, of His return to the glory of the Father, and of His resultant work, only made possible by the cross, in and for them through the lifegiving presence of the Holy Spirit.

6⁶³. Light is thrown on this verse if we compare Gen. 2⁷ or Ezek. 37⁵.

6⁶⁴. 'from the beginning': i.e. from the time of the Lord's choice of the disciples (cf. 6⁷⁰, 13¹¹, ¹⁸, ¹⁹).

6⁶⁶. 'Upon this', or perhaps 'as a result of this' (cf. 19¹²).

The two verbs in this verse convey practically the same meaning, although the first also hints that those who thus act are making 'the great refusal'. To 'walk with' a person (or in a district [7¹] or among certain people [11⁵⁴]) is a characteristic semitic expression for sharing the company of another, and can be used in both a literal and a metaphorical sense.

6⁶⁷, ⁷⁰, ⁷¹. Apart from 20²⁴, this is the only occasion when 'the twelve', as such, are mentioned in John. No doubt they are regarded as the constant companions of the Lord, e.g. 2², ¹², ¹⁷, ²², 3²², 4⁸, ²⁷; but neither St. Matthew nor St. John has any precise parallel to Mk. 3¹³⁻¹⁹, Lk. 6¹²⁻¹⁶, which record their appointment by the Lord; for Mt. 10¹⁻⁴ only records their names, not their appointment.

6⁶⁸ᵃ. Whereas the twelve as a body have no desire to 'go away' from the Lord to any other, Judas [Mk. 14¹⁰] did so (the verb in the Greek is the same), when he had resort to the chief priests.

6⁶⁸ᵇ, ⁶⁹. St. Peter's confession here is clearly a counterpart to the more primitive form of his confession in Mk. 8²⁹. There too the confession is made in answer to a question put by the Lord, and there too it contrasts strongly with the verdict (Mark) or the action (John) of others in regard to Him. In John, however, coming at the close of this chapter, in which the Lord has revealed the nature of His Person and His work much more clearly than hitherto, it emphasizes, more strongly than the confession of Messiahship in Mark, the capacity of the twelve, chosen by the Lord, to overcome the difficulties, felt so strongly by other disciples [6⁶⁰, ⁶⁶], as regards belief in Him.

The last five words of 6⁶⁹ are remarkable. In previous chapters the Lord has been called the Lamb of God [1²⁹, ³⁶], the Son of God [1³⁴, ⁴⁹], the Messiah [1⁴¹], the Saviour of the world [4⁴²]; but St. Peter's final words here ascribe to Him a new title, apparently not usually associated with the Messiah, and only to be found elsewhere in the gospels, with reference to the Lord, in the utterance in Mk. 1²⁴, to which Lk. 4³⁴ is parallel. The root idea of holiness is separation; and the confession therefore implies not only that the Lord is indeed by nature from above and not of this world [3³¹, 8²³], but also that in this respect He stands unique. He alone has descended out of heaven [3¹³, 6³⁸]; He alone speaks words which bestow eternal life [6⁶⁸]; and of these truths St. Peter and his colleagues are assured. The fire has been cast upon the earth, and is already kindling [Lk. 12⁴⁹]. What has proved to be an insuperable objection to others [6⁶⁰, ⁶⁶] has become to them the gate and means of life; and therefore the Lord's glory is already manifest. But the two following verses remind the reader of the cost to the Lord in thus fulfilling His work. Although on the one hand the twelve, through St. Peter, have confessed their belief and know that they owe their life to the Lord, and on the other hand the Lord has chosen them, yet even among them, regarded as a body, is an Achilles' heel.

It will be remembered that in Mk. 8²⁷⁻³³ St. Peter, although he has just confessed the Lord to be Messiah, is almost at once identified with Satan, because he, the disciples' leader and therefore having great influence upon them [8³³], seeks to divert the Lord from the path destined for the Son of man. In Jn. 6⁷⁰, however, the Lord speaks of Judas as a devil; and it seems probable that St. John thus shows, not Peter, but Judas to be that member of the body who truly and in deed allied himself with evil.

Note on a possible parallelism betweeen ch. 6 of this gospel and the narrative of the Lord's ministry in Mark.

Mk. 6^{35-52}, the first feeding of the multitude in Mark, is followed by a voyage across the lake, in the course of which the Lord rejoins His disciples; similarly Jn. 6^{1-21}.

Mk. 8^{1-13}, the second feeding of the multitude in Mark, is followed by a voyage, and this by the demand for a sign; similarly Jn. 6^{16-30}.

If, then, we omit Mk. 8^{22-26}, which is perhaps closely connected with Mk. 8^{27-30}, we reach Mk. 8^{27-33}, which includes St. Peter's confession, the first proclamation of the passion, and the identification of Peter with Satan. Similarly in Jn. 6^{66-71} we find a confession, in a new form, by St. Peter, and an allusion to the part of Judas in causing the passion. But whereas in Mk 8^{33} Peter is addressed as Satan, in Jn. $6^{70,\,71}$ it is made clear that the real root of evil among the twelve is Judas.

It must not be forgotten that Jn. $6^{51-58,\,70,\,71}$ also shows an unmistakable connexion with the two events narrated in St. Mark's account of the last supper, the prediction of the betrayal, and the Lord's sacramental gift to the disciples.

Note on a possible contrast between 6^{16-21} and such verses as 6^{42}, $7^{11,\,27,\,34}$, $8^{14,\,25}$, $9^{16,\,29}$, 10^{24}.

In both Matthew and Mark, as in John here, the feeding of the multitude is followed at once by the narrative which describes how the Lord the same night rejoined His disciples, as they rowed with difficulty across the lake. The story, as told in John, seems to invite a spiritual, as well as a literal, interpretation even more strongly than the same story as told in the earlier gospels; but no use of it in this respect is explicitly made by the evangelist in the teaching which follows in ch. 6. When, however, we consider how the Lord reveals Himself and His Person to the disciples in 6^{20} and what is the result, in 6^{21}, of His doing so, it becomes possible that we should contrast the knowledge gained in 6^{16-21} by the disciples with the ignorance, as regards the Lord's Person and true origin, shown by others in 6^{42} and such verses of chs. 7, 8, 9, and 10 as are mentioned above. In Ps. 77^{19}, where Yahweh's way is said to have been in the sea, and His paths in the great waters, the writer adds, 'And Thy footsteps were not known'. In Jn. 6^{16-21}, however, He who walks upon the waters makes Himself known to the disciples and thus brings them to the haven which they were trying to reach.

The Lord as giver of living water [7$^{37,\ 38}$], *the light of the world* [8^{12}], *the door* [10$^{7-9}$], *and the good shepherd* [10$^{11-14}$]

The Lord's word and work combined:

1. Word. (*a*) In Galilee controversy with His brethren, 7$^{3-9}$.
   (*b*) In Jerusalem at the feast of tabernacles controversy with the Jews, 7$^{14-52}$, 8$^{12-59}$.
   (*c*) Teaching on the work of the good shepherd, 10$^{1-18}$.
   (*d*) Final controversy with the Jews at the feast of the dedication, 10$^{22-39}$.

2. Work. The Lord gives sight to a beggar blind from birth, 9$^{1-12}$. Resulting judgement on the Pharisees, who have cast out the beggar, 9$^{13-41}$.

At 7^{10} the Lord leaves Galilee finally for the south.

In this section the Jews attempt repeatedly to arrest [7$^{32,\ 44}$, 10^{39}] and to kill [8^{59}, 10^{31}] the Lord.

At 10^{40} the Lord withdraws to Peraea.

7 And after these things Jesus walked in Galilee: for he would not
2 walk in Judaea, because the Jews sought to kill him. Now the feast of
3 the Jews, the feast of tabernacles, was at hand. His brethren therefore
said unto him, Depart hence, and go into Judaea, that thy disciples also
4 may behold thy works which thou doest. For no man doeth anything
in secret, ¹and himself seeketh to be known openly. If thou doest these
5 things, manifest thyself to the world. For even his brethren did not
6 believe on him. Jesus therefore saith unto them, My time is not yet
7 come; but your time is alway ready. The world cannot hate you; but me
8 it hateth, because I testify of it, that its works are evil. Go ye up unto
the feast: I go not up ²yet unto this feast; because my time is not yet
9 fulfilled. And having said these things unto them, he abode *still* in
Galilee.

10 But when his brethren were gone up unto the feast, then went he also
11 up, not publicly, but as it were in secret. The Jews therefore sought him
12 at the feast, and said, Where is he? And there was much murmuring
among the multitudes concerning him: some said, He is a good man;
13 others said, Not so, but he leadeth the multitude astray. Howbeit no
man spake openly of him for fear of the Jews.

14 But when it was now the midst of the feast Jesus went up into the
15 temple, and taught. The Jews therefore marvelled, saying, How knoweth
16 this man letters, having never learned? Jesus therefore answered them,

¹ *Some ancient authorities read* and seeketh it to be known openly.
² *Many ancient authorities omit* yet.

17 and said, My teaching is not mine, but his that sent me. If any man
willeth to do his will, he shall know of the teaching, whether it be of
18 God, or *whether* I speak from myself. He that speaketh from himself
seeketh his own glory: but he that seeketh the glory of him that sent
19 him, the same is true, and no unrighteousness is in him. Did not Moses
give you the law, and *yet* none of you doeth the law? Why seek ye to
20 kill me? The multitude answered, Thou hast a ¹devil: who seeketh to
21 kill thee? Jesus answered and said unto them, I did one work, and ye all
22 ²marvel. For this cause hath Moses given you circumcision (not that
it is of Moses, but of the fathers); and on the sabbath ye circumcise a
23 man. If a man receiveth circumcision on the sabbath, that the law of
Moses may not be broken; are ye wroth with me, because I made a
24 man every whit whole on the sabbath? Judge not according to appearance, but judge righteous judgement.

25   Some therefore of them of Jerusalem said, Is not this he whom they
26 seek to kill? And lo, he speaketh openly, and they say nothing unto
him. Can it be that the rulers indeed know that this is the Christ?
27 Howbeit we know this man whence he is: but when the Christ cometh,
28 no one knoweth whence he is. Jesus therefore cried in the temple,
teaching and saying, Ye both know me, and know whence I am; and I
am not come of myself, but he that sent me is true, whom ye know not.
29
30 I know him; because I am from him, and he sent me. They sought
therefore to take him: and no man laid his hand on him, because his
31 hour was not yet come. But of the multitude many believed on him; and
they said, When the Christ shall come, will he do more signs than those
32 which this man hath done? The Pharisees heard the multitude murmuring these things concerning him; and the chief priests and the
33 Pharisees sent officers to take him. Jesus therefore said, Yet a little
34 while am I with you, and I go unto him that sent me. Ye shall seek me,
35 and shall not find me: and where I am, ye cannot come. The Jews therefore said among themselves, Whither will this man go that we shall
not find him? will he go unto the Dispersion ³among the Greeks, and
36 teach the Greeks? What is this word that he said, Ye shall seek me, and
shall not find me: and where I am, ye cannot come?

37   Now on the last day, the great *day* of the feast, Jesus stood and cried,
38 saying, If any man thirst, let him come unto me, and drink. He that
believeth on me, as the scripture hath said, out of his belly shall flow
39 rivers of living water. But this spake he of the Spirit, which they that
believed on him were to receive: ⁴for the Spirit was not yet *given*;

---

¹ *Gr.* demon.
² *Or* marvel because of this. Moses hath given you circumcision
³ *Gr.* of.
⁴ *Some ancient authorities read* for the Holy Spirit was not yet given.

40 because Jesus was not yet glorified. *Some* of the multitude therefore,
41 when they heard these words, said, This is of a truth the prophet. Others
said, This is the Christ. But some said, What, doth the Christ come out
42 of Galilee? Hath not the scripture said that the Christ cometh of the
43 seed of David, and from Bethlehem, the village where David was? So
44 there arose a division in the multitude because of him. And some of
45 them would have taken him; but no man laid hands on him. The officers
therefore came to the chief priests and Pharisees; and they said unto
46 them, Why did ye not bring him? The officers answered, Never man so
47 spake. The Pharisees therefore answered them, Are ye also led astray?
48 Hath any of the rulers believed on him, or of the Pharisees? But this
49 multitude which knoweth not the law are accursed. Nicodemus saith
50
51 unto them (he that came to him before, being one of them), Doth our
law judge a man, except it first hear from himself and know what he
52 doeth? They answered and said unto him, Art thou also of Galilee?
Search, and ²see that out of Galilee ariseth no prophet.

EXPOSITION OF SECTION 4. 7¹⁻⁵²

If the chronology of this gospel, according to the scheme set out on
pp. 148 f., has been correctly stated, the Lord remains in Galilee
[7¹] during the six months between the second passover of His
ministry [6⁴] and the autumn festival of the feast of tabernacles
[7²]. At this vintage feast, which lasted for a week and formed the
chief holiday season in the Jewish year, Jerusalem was filled with
pilgrims, for whom temporary booths or huts were erected all over
the city (cf. Neh. 8¹⁴⁻¹⁸). The Lord's brethren therefore, who are
aware of His claims and powers (cf. Mk. 6¹⁻⁶), and also, we may
believe, of His teaching that these are one day to be made manifest
[Lk. 8¹⁷, 12²], urge Him to go into Judaea and to use this opportunity to acquire fame and following, no longer in the isolation and
obscurity of the provinces, but on the high stage of the crowded
capital.² No doubt they know that 'many of His disciples' in
Galilee now 'walked no more with Him' [6⁶⁶]; these will presumably go to the feast and may be won back, if the Lord will do as
they suggest. St. John's readers, it is assumed [7⁵], will perceive
that the Lord's brethren, in giving this advice, reveal both their
disbelief in Him and their failure to understand His mission. They

---

¹ *Or*, see: for out of Galilee &c.
² Their advice in 7³, ⁴ strongly recalls the temptation put to the Lord in
Mt. 4⁵⁻⁷ = Lk. 4⁹⁻¹².

are 'of the world', and therefore assume that He too will use the methods of the world. But the Lord does not seek His own glory [5^{41}, 7^{18}, 8^{50}]; His purpose is solely to carry out His Father's will [6^{38}], and so to glorify the Father [17^4]. Hence there will be no compelling manifestation to the world, such as they suggest; for because of its wickedness the Lord in its midst encounters not popularity, but hatred; and therefore when His time or occasion does arrive and He is manifested to the world, it will be in His elevation on the cross; but that time or hour is not yet.

The Greek word, here translated 'time', occurs in John only in this paragraph, at $7^{6, 8}$, and seems to mean the suitable or right occasion. The fact that in the Lord's ministry, being that of the Word become flesh, heaven, as we may say, has come down to earth, and eternity is made manifest in time, by no means implies that there are not, in that ministry, particular moments of crisis, or that an action of His at one time would be equally in place at another.[1] The right occasion for the Lord is thus essentially different from that for His brethren, who are not seeking the glory of the Father, but are of the world, which loves its own [15^{19}]. For them, therefore, one occasion or moment is as good and appropriate as another.

In 7^8, if we read 'not yet', there is no difficulty; and this reading accords well with the reason given, viz. that the appropriate moment for the Lord to go up to Jerusalem has not yet come. But not only is it unlikely that the Lord's 'time' is to be regarded as 'fulfilled' a few days later, but also of two variant readings the more difficult is likely to be the original; hence an attempt must be made to account for the reading of the R.V. mg, which omits 'yet'. In the first place, the Lord should be understood as refusing in this verse to go up to the feast in deference to and as a result of His brethren's suggestion. In going up later, when, we may assume, it has become His Father's will that He should do so, He acts exactly as He does in 2^{3-8} and 11^{3-7}. Secondly, the verb 'to go up' is used by St. John not only of the Lord's visits to Jerusalem, but also, at 3^{13}, 6^{62}, 20^{17}, of His ascent or return to the Father, which in this gospel is vitally connected with His 'elevation' on the cross (cf.

---

[1] Some words of Isaac Pennington may be quoted here. 'All truth is shadow except the last. But every truth is substance in its own place, though it be but a shadow in another place. And the shadow is a true shadow, as the substance is a true substance.'

3^{14}, 8^{28}, $12^{32, 34}$). Possibly therefore, although using the word in this passage in its natural sense so far as the Lord at $7^{10, 14}$ and His brethren at $7^{8, 10}$ are concerned, at 7^8 St. John uses it, in reference to the Lord, of His ascent to the Father through the cross: 'I go not up at this feast.' However strange this meaning of the word in the present context may seem to us, it is probably not impossible for a writer like St. John.

In the earlier gospels the Lord only goes up from Galilee to Jerusalem once; and great emphasis is laid upon the step which He thus takes—in secrecy [Mk. 9^{30}, as here [7^{10}],—as forming the prelude to His passion and resurrection. Important references to this journey occur in Mt. 16^{21}, 20^{18}, Mk. 10^{32-34}, Lk. 9^{51}, 18^{31-33}; and the same view of the Lord's ministry is probably implied in Acts $10^{37, 39}$, 13^{31}. It is usual to regard this journey as having had, for its immediate object, the Lord's attendance at the feast of the passover; but there is nothing in the earlier gospels which requires this view; not only does Mk. 10^1 suggest a ministry, of undefined duration, in Transjordan; but the passover, at which the Lord died, is not mentioned until Mk. 14^1. But for our present purpose, we need only recall that in the earlier gospels the Lord's single visit to Jerusalem during the ministry ends with the passover, that at which He died.

In the course of St. John's gospel, however, not only are three passovers mentioned; but some of the events associated in the earlier gospels with the Lord's one visit to Jerusalem during the ministry are, in John, ascribed to previous visits; and, above all, reference in one way or another is continually made, throughout this gospel, to His death and resurrection, a reference which in the earlier gospels is not explicitly made until either Galilee has been left or at least preparations are being made to leave it. Thus in John the Lord has already, at 2^{13-22}, attended 'the passover of the Jews', and has cleansed the temple, an action in which the reader is taught to see the Lord's death and resurrection in a figure. At 5^1 He attends another festival in Jerusalem, and at it, as a result of His good work on an impotent man on a sabbath, the Jews oppose Him and, by reason of the justification which he makes of His action, 'seek to kill' Him [5^{16-18}]; and the Lord replies by teaching that by the Father's gift He, the Son, has 'life in Himself' [5^{26}].

Each of these earlier visits to Jerusalem was preceded by a work of the Lord, leading to the happiest results [2¹⁰, ¹¹, 4⁵³] in Galilee; but at the next festival mentioned, 'the passover, the feast of the Jews' [6⁴], there is indeed no visit to Jerusalem, but a change in the Galilean atmosphere becomes noticeable. The Galileans, represented in this chapter first by 'the multitude' [6², ²²] and later by 'the Jews' [6⁴¹, ⁵²], not only misunderstand [6¹⁴, ¹⁵] the significance of the Lord's action in 6¹⁻¹³, His third work in Galilee (just as His earlier actions in Jerusalem, although not previously those in Galilee, have been misunderstood), but next day, when the Lord explains its meaning, and teaches that His gift to them implies His own death [6⁵¹⁻⁵⁸], and that He, the life-giving bread, lives because of the Father [6⁵⁷], they murmur [6⁴¹] and engage in controversy among themselves [6⁵²]. Indeed, before the chapter ends, many of the Lord's disciples leave Him; and at its close [6⁶⁴, ⁷¹] there is an explicit reference to the coming action of a disciple which is in fact to be the first link in the final chain of events leading to the Lord's death. Galilee, therefore, is shown in the end to prove itself no more receptive than Jerusalem; and in ch. 6 the Lord's death, resurrection, and return to the Father are adumbrated only less clearly than they have been and will be in the events recorded in chs. 1 to 12 as occurring in Jerusalem.

The Lord in this gospel is now leaving Galilee for the last time, in order to attend the feast of tabernacles [7², ¹⁰, ¹⁴]; and He will henceforth be found in or near Jerusalem until 10⁴⁰, when he goes away to Transjordan. In the fact that in 7¹⁴⁻⁵² (as also, later, in 10²²⁻³⁹) there is debate about the Lord's Messiahship, we may find an explanation why He does not go up to the feast of tabernacles as a pilgrim, like His brethren [7¹⁰]. For the Messiah's arrival at the temple was to be unexpected and sudden, according to Mal. 3¹ᵇ (also with the words 'whom ye seek' in this verse cf. Jn. 7¹¹); and Jn. 7¹⁰, ¹⁴ is evidence that these conditions were fulfilled.

In 7¹⁰ to 8⁵⁹ the disciples, as such, do not appear. In ch. 7 the Lord is in contact both with the Jews and with the multitude. The latter, mentioned eight times in ch. 7, forms conflicting opinions [7¹², ⁴⁰⁻⁴³], and is essentially unstable. In ch. 8 the multitude does not appear, but only the Jews, and the breach between them and the Lord is found to be irreparable.

Both to the Jews and to the multitude the Lord's presence or absence at the feast is of interest [7¹¹, ¹²; cf. 11⁵⁶]; but the reader is aware that the Lord, when He comes to Jerusalem, will not and cannot be truly known except by those, whether of the Jews [8³⁰] or of the multitude [7³¹] who 'believe on' Him, in other words who are reborn [3³] and 'abide in His word' [8³¹], being drawn by the Father to Him [6⁴⁴]. Hence an ethical opinion, such as is expressed in 7¹², or even a theological inference, such as is mentioned in 7⁴⁰⁻⁴², is of no real value.

The paragraph 7¹⁵⁻²⁴ has certainly some connexion with ch. 5, and possibly at one time, before being used by St. John, may have continued the Lord's address in 5¹⁹⁻⁴⁷. Thus His teaching in 7¹⁶ recalls that of 5³⁰, and in 7¹⁸ that of 5⁴¹, ⁴⁴; 7¹⁹ᵇ seems to refer to 5¹⁸ (but note also 7¹), and 7²¹, ²³ to 5⁹. And in the R.V. the same Greek word is translated 'writings' in 5⁴⁷ and 'letters' in 7¹⁵. On account of this last similarity it has been suggested that in the Jews' question at 7¹⁵ there is an implicit reference to the Lord's knowledge of the Mosaic law. But 7¹⁵ is best understood, in its present context, as simply expressive of the Jews' surprise that one who had not had a rabbinical education was, none the less, able to teach, as the Lord was now teaching. The Lord replies that His teaching is not His, but that of God who sent Him. He adds that it is open to anyone, who wishes to do God's will (i.e. to believe on Him whom God has sent), to assure himself whether the teaching is from God, or whether the Speaker is speaking (only) from Himself. In the latter case such a speaker would be seeking his own honour; but in the case of the Lord it is not so; He who seeks the honour of Him that sent Him, is worthy of credence and of trust.

To the Jew readiness to do God's will would imply fulfilment of the law of Moses, and the Lord now turns upon His hearers and charges them, one and all, with disobedience to it. Their desire to kill the Lord, of whom Moses wrote [5⁴⁶], is evidence of this. (Or, perhaps less probably, the accusation of breaking the law may refer to circumcision on a sabbath; see below.) Disregarding the protest of the multitude, which has no knowledge of the Jews' intention, the Lord recalls the work wrought by Him in 5¹⁻⁹, a work which aroused their wonder. If the argument here is to be understood, some explanation is needed.

The law forbade any form of work on the sabbath [Ex. 31¹⁵, 35²]. On the other hand it also prescribed circumcision on the eighth day after birth [Lev. 12³]; and this precept, if the day in question was a sabbath, was regarded as overruling the former precept.

If we follow the R.V. mg at $7^{21, 22}$, the Lord's argument is that, if the ordinance of circumcision on the eighth day, an action regarded by the Jew as of supreme importance, justifies the breach of another ordinance of the law, that which forbids any kind of work on the sabbath, then His action in giving perfect health on the sabbath [5^{1-9}] is even more justifiable, and should not arouse angry indignation. Those who thus condemn His action show how superficial their verdicts are [7^{24}]; had they placed the ordinance of circumcision alongside the (apparently contradictory), ordinance of sabbath observance, they might have learned what was Moses' purpose, and their judgement would have been just, not superficial.

If, however, we follow the R.V. text at $7^{21, 22}$, as we probably should, the argument is that Moses gave the enactment of circumcision on the eighth day, an enactment which in certain cases overruled the law of the sabbath rest, expressly in order to point forward to the perfect work and wholeness to be achieved in later days, also on a sabbath, by the Lord Himself, He being the fulfilment of the hope of Israel. This interpretation would perhaps be in line with the Lord's words at 5^{46} that Moses wrote of Him, and with the thought of Heb. $7^{18, 19}$. (For the bracket in 7^{22} see Gen. $17^{10, 12}$; the form of words here is characteristic of St. John; cf. $6^{45, 46}$.)

It will be remembered that according to the earlier gospels messianic expectations seem to have been strongly aroused when the Lord entered Jerusalem shortly before the passion (Mk. 11^{1-10} and parallels), and also that He openly acknowledged His Messiahship only at the very end, in the course of His examination by the Sanhedrin. If we read the rest of Jn. 7 and also 10^{22-39} with these thoughts in our minds, and in the light of what we already know of St. John's methods, we may find it probable that he desires to deal in these chapters with the question of the Lord's Messiahship, including that of His origin, nature, and destiny, instead of reserving it, and his exposition of its character, until the final scenes. Thus in 7^{25-31} this question is directly raised, and 'some of them of Jerusalem' for a moment entertain the thought that, since the Lord is speaking openly and is unmolested, the rulers have recognized His office. But the thought is at once dismissed as impossible, on the ground that, whereas the origin of the Messiah is to be a secret, the Lord's origin is known (cf. 6^{42}).

The belief that the origin of the Messiah must be a secret is correctly stated (cf. Justin, *Dial.* 8. 4); but the nature of the secret is misunderstood. To admit the truth of the doctrine of the secret origin of the Messiah is, or should be, equivalent to the admission that all human judgement about it is, and is bound to be, inadequate; and this admission the Lord's opponents are not prepared to make.

The first sentence of the Lord's reply in 7²⁸ need not be ironical, or a question; it may express agreement with 7²⁷ᵃ; His hearers may be regarded as knowing His origin 'after the flesh'. If so, the 'and' in 'and I am not come of myself' will imply 'and yet', as often in John, e.g. 7³⁰. But the latter part of His reply shows that His hearers do not know the Father, who has sent Him; and therefore they do not truly know the Speaker, nor His origin (cf. 8¹⁴). Those only can know Him and His origin, who acknowledge His authority and hear His word, and see in Him not only, or not primarily, a man speaking to men, but the Representation of the Father Himself (cf. 8¹⁹, 14⁷). He (the Father) is 'true', and the Speaker knows Him.

At 7³⁰, as also at 7³², ⁴⁴, 8⁵⁹, 10³¹, ³⁹, the Lord's opponents are unable to achieve their purpose, because 'His hour', which from another point of view, very different from that of St. John, may be regarded as 'their hour' [Lk. 22⁵³], has not yet come. Throughout the passion narrative, as recorded in John, the reader should bear in mind that no one is taking the Lord's life from Him against His will [10¹⁸]; He is laying it down of Himself, in obedience to the Father; and therefore, and therefore only, do His opponents at length achieve their purpose (cf. 18³⁻⁹). Rightly regarded, the Lord's death will be found to be, in this gospel, the hour of His exaltation and glorification, and the power of light, rather than the power of darkness [Lk. 22⁵³].

The reason given in 7³¹ for belief on the Lord may be interpreted as being typically inadequate. It is true that in John the Lord's signs or works are regarded as witnessing to His divine origin (cf. 5³⁶, 10²⁵, ³⁸, 14¹¹, 15²⁴), and in certain cases leading to belief on His name [2²³], although this kind of belief is not that which He most desires (cf. 14¹, ¹¹ᵃ); but belief on the ground of the number of His signs is especially imperfect.

The attempt by the authorities to arrest the Lord [7³²], although at present fruitless, will before long succeed; and the Lord calls attention to the great importance, for His hearers, of the intervening period. When He returns to the Father—the thought that this will come to pass through their action does not enter into the picture (contrast Lk. 22⁵³)—they will, by their rejection of Him, have condemned themselves; and where He is, they cannot come. (Although the emphasis here is on the brief presence of the incarnate Lord among men, the thought is common to it and to the rest of the N.T. that the present moment, in so far as it is to any man the means of revelation and also gives him the opportunity to embrace it, has vital and eternal significance for him; cf. 2 Cor. 6², Heb. 3¹³.)

The words 'where I am' are found on the Lord's lips in John not only at 7³⁴, ³⁶ but also at 12²⁶, 14³, 17²⁴. The same truth is expressed in another form by His words 'whither I go' at 8¹⁴, ²¹, 13³³, and the present tense in the words 'where I am' may perhaps be used loosely for the future. But it seems more probable that a spiritual truth is being expressed both in terms of motion ('whither I go') and in terms of rest ('where I am'). Even now, when the Lord is standing before His opponents, they cannot come where He is, because they do not share His mind. For, in spite of what He has just said in 7³³, it is also true that separation from Him is caused not by distance in space, but by unlikeness of heart and mind and spirit. (It has indeed been suggested that with a different accentuation the Greek word for 'am' could mean 'will go'; but in that case would there not be a change in the word for 'where', which would become the word for 'whither'?)

In 7³⁵, ³⁶ the Jews, bewildered by the Lord's words in 7³⁴, which, as always, they understand in a literal, superficial sense, suggest that, in order to escape from them, He will leave Judaea and go to other countries and inaugurate a mission among the Gentiles. The passage is a striking example of St. John's irony. Like Caiaphas at 11⁵¹, ⁵², the Jews unconsciously and involuntarily prophesy truly. For the Lord's word will indeed evangelize the Gentiles, not, however, because He has fled from Jewish hostility in Palestine, but because in obedience to His Father He voluntarily accepts death as a result of that hostility, and will thus draw or attract *all* men to Himself [12³²]. But the Jews, the chosen race, will have lost their opportunity (cf. Mt. 21⁴³, Acts 28²⁵⁻²⁸).

If the significance of the Lord's declaration about Himself in 7³⁷, ³⁸, 8¹², 9⁵ is to be grasped, some account must be given of the autumn feast of tabernacles, which in this gospel forms the occasion for His utterance of these declarations. The festival was regarded as a foreshadowing of the day of the Lord, or the messianic age, since popular sentiment connected it not only with the harvest and vintage now completed, but with a future, very different harvest, that of the final ingathering or harvest of the nations in the days of the Messiah. It was believed that in face of a combined and final onslaught of the nations of the world upon Jerusalem Yahweh would at length Himself intervene on behalf of His people and usher in that perfect era to which all Jews looked forward. On its arrival the majority in all nations would undergo terrible penalties, but a remnant would become faithful to Judaism and would join at Jerusalem in the celebration of the festival.

The last few lines are almost a brief summary of Zech. 14, which, as a prophecy of this coming day of the Lord, formed a special or proper lesson read at the feast of tabernacles. This chapter of Zechariah also contains reference to two features of the messianic age, continuous daylight combined with an absence of winter, and an unfailing supply of water, this last having been always a major problem and anxiety for dwellers in Jerusalem. There is Rabbinic evidence that at this festival two ceremonies, closely connected with the features just mentioned, were regarded as of great significance, first, the ritual drawing of water each day by daylight, and secondly, the all-night illumination of one of the temple courts on the first night of the festival and possibly on others also, an illumination so brilliant that every court in Jerusalem was said to be lit up by it.

In the former ceremony a golden pitcher filled with water from the pool of Siloam was carried up to the temple in procession, with the singing of Is. 12³, 'With joy shall ye draw water out of the wells of salvation'; and at the temple the contents were solemnly poured into two pipes, whence they passed underground into the Kidron valley. This ceremony was regarded as prophetic of the time when Jerusalem's great problem of water-scarcity would be overcome, and an unfailing stream would issue from beneath the temple, making glad the city of God. Of the latter ceremony it might almost be said that its purpose was to turn night into day; and it ended just before dawn with a procession of priests and a blare of trumpets, introducing a final vow of fidelity to Yahweh and to Him only.¹

---

¹ The Lord several times in ch. 8 (verses 24, 28, 58) uses the words 'I am

Cardinal features in the teaching of St. John's gospel are that (*a*) the Lord Jesus is set forth as the full and perfect realization of the aspirations and anticipations of Judaism, and (*b*) His life and death bring the New Age. It is therefore both appropriate and by no means accidental that at the culminating point of the feast of tabernacles [7³⁷⁻³⁹] He should invite those who thirst for life-giving water to resort to Him, and at 8¹² and 9⁵ should describe Himself as the light of the world.

To introduce the great declaration in 7³⁷, ³⁸, the strong word 'cried' (cf. 7²⁸) is supplemented by the word 'stood'. If, as has been suggested, the daily ritual of water-drawing during this festival has influenced the form of the Lord's words at this point, 'the last day, the great day', here mentioned, is probably the seventh day, called the Great Hosanna, after which this ritual ended. An eighth day, to close the festival, was indeed added; but the ceremonies on this day were different (cf. Lev. 23³⁶, Num. 29³⁵).

With a different punctuation, it is possible to read, 'If any man thirst, let him come unto me [cf. 6³⁵], and let him that believeth on me drink [cf. 4¹⁰].' (The remainder of 7³⁸ will then refer to the Lord Himself.) A parallelism in the Lord's words is thus gained, but it is imperfect; for whereas to come to the Lord and to drink of Him are no doubt synonymous, the believer on Him is by no means in the same case as he who thirsts; and probably the rendering of the R.V. should be accepted. If so, 7³⁸ may be illustrated by 4¹⁴; from within the believer will flow forth springs of living water.

The quotation in 7³⁸ cannot be precisely identified in the O.T., and although St. John speaks here of 'the scripture', not 'the scriptures', it is possible that he is 'collecting the sense' of various O.T. passages, such as Num. 20¹¹, Is. 43²⁰, 55¹, rather than quoting any one of them. If, however, a particular passage is to be sought, the words in 7³⁸ may perhaps be regarded as a paraphrase of Zech. 14⁸, 'living waters shall go out from Jerusalem' (cf. also Ezek.

[He]', an expression which recalls the divine utterance in such passages as Is. 41⁴, 43¹⁰, 48¹². Further, the priests are said to have acclaimed Yahweh at this festival in the words 'I and He', possibly a variation of the divine utterance, and designed to emphasize the union between Yahweh and Israel. Since in John the Lord both represents and achieves the true union of God and man, attention may be called also to such verses as 8¹⁶, ¹⁸, ²⁹. If this is correct, there are three self-declarations by the Lord in chs. 7–9: 7³⁷,³⁸, 8¹² (= 9⁵), and 8²⁴, ²⁸, ⁵⁸ (to which expression is given in a different way in 8¹⁶, ¹⁸, ²⁹); and these three declarations, connected, it seems, with the events of the festival, are also related to three statements in the prologue: 1⁴ᵃ, ⁴ᵇ, ².

47¹⁻¹¹). It seems that readers in the synagogues sometimes sub-
stituted for the word Jerusalem the pseudonym by which it was
popularly known, 'the navel', Jerusalem being thought to be at the
centre of the earth (where in fact it is placed in some medieval
maps). It would perhaps be in accordance with the teaching of this
gospel, if there is a transference of thought here from the city,
which was the capital and heart's home of Judaism, to the believer
(cf. 14²³), who draws his fresh springs of life from the Lord [4¹⁴;
cf. Ps. 87⁷ᵇ].

In the editorial note of 7³⁹ St. John explains that the reference
in the Lord's words to 'rivers of living water' was to the Spirit, the
new endowment to be granted to believers; an endowment, however, which could and would only be operative after the Lord was
glorified, in other words, when His work was completed. The
words 'Spirit was not yet', which is certainly the right reading,
would bear no such meaning for St. John's readers as they might
carry in hellenistic or patristic thought. St. John, whose conception
of revelation is fundamentally Hebraic and therefore dynamic
rather than static, has already said that, before the Lord's ministry
began, the Spirit descended and abode upon Him [1³³]; and he is
here [7³⁹] concerned with the 'new creation' [2 Cor. 5¹⁷] of which
believers first became aware, as a result of the Lord's life and
death on their behalf (cf. 20²²). For them, during the ministry, the
dispensation of the Spirit 'was not yet'.

The reason why an explicit reference is made here to the Spirit
may be that, according to a passage in the Talmud, the Jews themselves regarded the libation of water at the feast of tabernacles as a
symbol of the future outpouring of God's Spirit, in connexion
with the messianic age (cf. Joel 2²⁸); and note also that in Jn. 7⁴⁰, ⁴¹,
while some of the multitude, after hearing the Lord's words in
7³⁷, ³⁸, assert that He is the prophet, others see in Him the Messiah.

As a result of the renewed debate and vacillation on the part of
the multitude we hear at 7⁴³ for the first time of a schism or
division on account of Him (cf. 9¹⁶, 10¹⁹, Lk. 12⁵¹⁻⁵³). St. John's
readers were no doubt well aware of the traditions that the Lord
was of the seed of David, and was born at Bethlehem. In accordance, therefore, with St. John's method (cf. 6⁴²) the objections
raised in 7⁴² can be mentioned, but left unrefuted. If, however,
we recall such a passage as 7²⁸⁻³⁰, it seems possible that the
evangelist may wish to impress upon his readers that the real

question requiring decision, and the only one which need truly
cause division, is that of the relation of the Lord to Him who sent
Him, that is, to the Father.

Surprise is sometimes expressed that the officers, sent at 7^{32}
to arrest the Lord, apparently do not return until the next day.
It may be replied with confidence that St. John would not have
appreciated the difficulty, if such it is; his interest is in the theological development of the narrative rather than in its complete
historical consistency.

The reason given by the officers for their failure to bring the
Lord should be compared with the prostration of the soldiers and
officers sent to arrest the Lord in the garden [18^{1-9}], when they find
themselves faced with 'Jesus of Nazareth'. On that occasion the
soldiers and officers, with His permission, in the end have their
way, because His hour is come; but at present this is not so [7^{30}],
and the officers, having heard His words, are powerless in His
presence.

In 7^{47} the word 'also' in the Pharisees' taunt of the officers seems
to refer back to 7^{31}, where we read that 'of the multitude many
believed on Him' (cf. also $7^{40, \ 41a}$). It is assumed that the Lord's
purpose is to 'lead astray' (cf. the rueful remark, again of the
Pharisees, at 12^{19}), whereas in fact the Lord, seeking the glory of
Him who sent Him, 'is true, and no unrighteousness is in Him'
[7^{18}]. In 7^{48} 'the rulers' are no doubt the members of the Sanhedrin, while 'the Pharisees', on religious grounds, were held in
chief esteem by the people; hence it is implied that although some
of the multitude, through ignorance of the law, have been led
astray and have believed on the Lord, the combined forces of
order and religion have remained unmoved, and their rejection
of Him, based on their knowledge of the law, should be sufficient
evidence against him. The contemptuous condemnation of 'the
people of the land', as they were often called, by their better
educated leaders strengthens the view that in St. John's frequent
references to 'the Jews' as the Lord's principal opponents he is
thinking especially of 'the chief priests and the Pharisees'.

One voice, however, at the highest level attempts to raise a
protest. Nicodemus points out that the Pharisees, who claim
knowledge of the law, are ignoring implications of that law (cf.
Ex. 23^1, Deut. 1^{16}). Nicodemus bases his contention on the Jewish
law; but the reader is aware that, while 'the law was given by

Moses, grace and truth came by Jesus Christ' [1¹⁷]; but of this
Nicodemus shows no appreciation. Hence the reader will not be
surprised that Nicodemus is, it seems, easily silenced and that
at the next, crucial meeting of the Sanhedrin [11⁴⁷⁻⁵³] he will be
silent; and when at length we hear of him again [19³⁹] his inter-
vention comes too late.

NOTES TO SECTION 4. 7¹⁻⁵²

7³, ⁵, ¹⁰. The Lord's 'brethren', in the sense of His physical relatives, are
only mentioned in this gospel here and at 2¹². Whenever reference is made
to them in the N.T., this term is used and the natural inference is that
they also were children of Mary (cf. Mk. 6³). The Church, however, later
inclined strongly to the belief that the Lord must have been her only
child, and the term 'brethren', as applied in the N.T. to His physical
relatives, was therefore usually explained in one of two ways: either as
meaning cousins, or as referring to children of Joseph by a former wife.

7²⁸. 'cried'. This word, used in 1¹⁵ of the Baptist, and here and 7³⁷ and
12⁴⁴ of the Lord, often in the N.T. introduces utterances made either
under inspiration or under strong spiritual compulsion.

'in the temple'. The temple is mentioned ten times in John; and five
of these are in 7¹ to 10³⁹, that part of this gospel which deals particularly
with the Lord's Messiahship: 7¹⁴ at the outset, 7²⁸, 8²⁰, ⁵⁹, and 10²³ at the
close.

7³³. 'Yet a little while': cf. p. 84.

7³⁵. 'the Dispersion', a term used in the LXX for the Jews resident in
other lands than Palestine, came to be used also, as here (cf. Judith 5¹⁹),
for the countries in which these dispersed Jews lived; and such territories
were regarded as those 'of [R.V. mg] the Greeks', or Gentiles.

7⁴². The contention raised here does not necessarily conflict with the
doctrine of the hidden origin of the Messiah [7²⁷]; or it may be St. John's
purpose to illustrate the great variety and uncertainty in messianic expectations at this time.

7⁵²ᵃ. The sneer is presumably not to be taken seriously; it serves only
to couple the Lord and Nicodemus in a single appellation. As regards
7⁵²ᵇ, according to rabbinic tradition a prophet had arisen out of every tribe
of Israel; and in 2 Kings 14²⁵ it is said that the prophet Jonah, son of
Amittai, was of Gath-Hepher in Galilee.

SECTION 4 (contd.) 8¹²⁻⁵⁹. *The Lord as the Light of the World.*

12 Again therefore Jesus spake unto them, saying, I am the light of the
world: he that followeth me shall not walk in the darkness, but shall

13 have the light of life. The Pharisees therefore said unto him, Thou
14 bearest witness of thyself; thy witness is not true. Jesus answered and
said unto them, Even if I bear witness of myself, my witness is true; for
I know whence I came, and whither I go; but ye know not whence I
15 come, or whither I go. Ye judge after the flesh; I judge no man. Yea
16 and if I judge, my judgement is true; for I am not alone, but I and the
17 Father that sent me. Yea and in your law it is written, that the witness
18 of two men is true. I am he that beareth witness of myself, and the
19 Father that sent me beareth witness of me. They said therefore unto
him, Where is thy Father? Jesus answered, Ye know neither me, nor my
20 Father: if ye knew me, ye would know my Father also. These words
spake he in the treasury, as he taught in the temple: and no man took
him; because his hour was not yet come.

21   He said therefore again unto them, I go away, and ye shall seek me,
22 and shall die in your sin: whither I go, ye cannot come. The Jews
therefore said, Will he kill himself, that he saith, Whither I go, ye cannot
23 come? And he said unto them, Ye are from beneath; I am from above:
24 ye are of this world; I am not of this world. I said therefore unto you,
that ye shall die in your sins: for except ye believe that ¹I am *he*, ye shall
25 die in your sins. They said therefore unto him, Who art thou? Jesus
said unto them, ²Even that which I have also spoken unto you from the
26 beginning. I have many things to speak and to judge concerning you:
howbeit he that sent me is true; and the things which I heard from him,
27 these speak I ³unto the world. They perceived not that he spake to them
28 of the Father. Jesus therefore said, When ye have lifted up the Son of
man, then shall ye know that ⁴I am *he*, and *that* I do nothing of myself,
29 but as the Father taught me, I speak these things. And he that sent me is
with me; he hath not left me alone; for I do always the things that are
30 pleasing to him. As he spake these things, many believed on him.

31   Jesus therefore said to those Jews which had believed him, If ye abide
32 in my word, *then* are ye truly my disciples; and ye shall know the truth,
33 and the truth shall make you free. They answered unto him, We be
Abraham's seed, and have never yet been in bondage to any man: how
34 sayest thou, Ye shall be made free? Jesus answered them, Verily, verily,
I say unto you, Every one that committeth sin is the bondservant of sin.
35 And the bondservant abideth not in the house for ever: the son abideth
36 for ever. If therefore the Son shall make you free, ye shall be free indeed.
37 I know that ye are Abraham's seed; yet ye seek to kill me, because my
38 word ⁵hath not free course in you. I speak the things which I have seen
with ⁶*my* Father: and ye also do the things which ye heard from *your*

---

¹ *Or* I am   ² *Or How is it* that I even speak to you at all?   ³ *Gr.*
into.   ⁴ *Or* I am *Or* I am *he*: and I do   ⁵ *Or* hath no place in you
⁶ *Or* the Father: do ye also therefore the things which ye heard from the
Father.

39 father. They answered and said unto him, Our father is Abraham. Jesus
saith unto them, If ye ¹were Abraham's children, ²ye would do the
40 works of Abraham. But now ye seek to kill me, a man that hath told you
41 the truth, which I heard from God: this did not Abraham. Ye do the
works of your father. They said unto him, We were not born of fornica-
42 tion; we have one Father, *even* God. Jesus said unto them, If God were
your Father, ye would love me: for I came forth and am come from God;
43 for neither have I come of myself, but he sent me. Why do ye not
44 ³understand my speech? *Even* because ye cannot hear my word. Ye are
of *your* father the devil, and the lusts of your father it is your will to do.
He was a murderer from the beginning, and ⁴stood not in the truth,
because there is no truth in him. ⁵When he speaketh a lie, he speaketh
45 of his own: for he is a liar, and the father thereof. But because I say the
46 truth, ye believe me not. Which of you convicteth me of sin? If I say
47 truth, why do ye not believe me? He that is of God heareth the words of
48 God: for this cause ye hear *them* not, because ye are not of God. The
Jews answered and said unto him, Say we not well that thou art a
49 Samaritan, and hast a ⁶devil? Jesus answered, I have not a ⁶devil; but
50 I honour my Father, and ye dishonour me. But I seek not mine own
51 glory: there is one that seeketh and judgeth. Verily, verily, I say unto
52 you, If a man keep my word, he shall never see death. The Jews said·
unto him, Now we know that thou hast a ⁶devil. Abraham is dead, and
the prophets; and thou sayest, If a man keep my word, he shall never
53 taste of death. Art thou greater than our father Abraham, which is dead?
54 and the prophets are dead: whom makest thou thyself? Jesus answered,
If I glorify myself, my glory is nothing: it is my Father that glorifieth
55 me; of whom ye say, that he is your God; and ye have not known him:
but I know him; and if I should say, I know him not, I shall be like unto
56 you, a liar: but I know him, and keep his word. Your father Abraham
57 rejoiced ⁷to see my day; and he saw it, and was glad. The Jews therefore
said unto him, Thou art not yet fifty years old, and hast thou seen
58 Abraham? Jesus said unto them, Verily, verily, I say unto you, Before
59 Abraham ⁸was, I am. They took up stones therefore to cast at him: but
Jesus ⁹hid himself, and went out of the temple.¹⁰

---

¹ *Gr.* are.   ² *Some ancient authorities read* ye do the works of Abraham.
³ *Or* know   ⁴ *Some ancient authorities read* standeth.   ⁵ *Or* When
one speaketh a lie, he speaketh of his own: for his father also is a liar.
⁶ *Gr.* demon.   ⁷ *Or* that he should see   ⁸ *Gr.* was born.
⁹ *Or* was hidden, and went &c.   ¹⁰ *Many ancient authorities add* and
going through the midst of them went his way and so passed by.

EXPOSITION OF 8¹²⁻⁵⁹

The contents of 8¹²⁻⁵⁹ are even more polemical than those of ch. 7, and lead up to a dramatic close. The question of the Lord's Messiahship is not raised again in this chapter; the controversy deals with the still more fundamental issues of the Lord's origin and nature, His relationship to the Father, and the inevitable condemnation of those who do not recognize Him.

At 8¹² the Lord makes the second of His self-declarations in this gospel. Quite apart from the special suitability of the theme of light at the feast of tabernacles, its use in religious metaphor is already frequent in the O.T. (e.g. Ps. 27¹, 36⁹, Is. 60²⁰), and also in pagan literature. The Lord is the world's light, not in the sense that He shows to men the means to discover things which they may wish to find, but that He, and He only, irradiates human existence with the knowledge of its nature, meaning, and purpose. 'The light of the world' bestows 'the light of life' (cf. 1⁴, ⁵); and in having this light, the disciple, follower, or believer—the words may be used interchangeably—has the Speaker, the Lord Himself. But he has Him, or it, not as an acquisition or a quality which, when once it has been acquired or received, is henceforth independent of the Giver; 'the light, which the believer *has*, is always the light, which Jesus *is*'; and in this sense the recipient must never regard it as his own. Indeed, he and his fellow disciples can themselves be called 'the light of the world' [Mt. 5¹⁴], only in so far as they abide in their Lord, and He in them [15⁴]. The theme of light, however, is not developed here, being reserved for ch. 9; and the rest of ch. 8 is devoted, in the face of strong and even violent opposition, to the exposition of truths about the Lord's Person.

The Pharisees, seizing upon the Lord's declaration in 8¹², object that a man's evidence on his own behalf is bound to be suspect. The Lord's reply is twofold. First, He alone knows both His origin and His destiny; His hearers do not, and therefore are not in a position to form a judgement in the matter. And secondly, the Lord is not alone in the witness which He gives; the Father, who sent Him, also bears witness of Him; and thus the requirement of the Jewish law is met. On both counts, therefore, His witness should be accepted. The argument, however, as so often in this gospel (e.g. 7³⁴, 8²³), has been taken into a region where the hearers are not at home, and the latter are now shown, as at 5³⁷, ³⁸, to have no (true) knowledge of either Him or His Father. Their question in 8¹⁹ should be compared with that of Pilate in 18³⁸, 'What is truth?' Just as, when Pilate asked his question, the truth, incarnate in the Lord [14⁶], was before him, so here the only visible embodiment of the Father [14⁹] is standing before His questioners, and to seek for the invisible God elsewhere is a fruitless quest. Only through the Word become flesh can men receive knowledge of the Father [1¹⁸]; but the Lord's hearers cannot abandon their preconceptions, in order to dispose themselves to receive this knowledge from Him; and thus He inevitably, and as it were in spite of Himself, becomes their Judge.

In 5¹⁹⁻³² the Lord had taught that the Father had given Him authority to judge, and also that if He bore witness of Himself, His witness would not be true. In apparent contradiction He here says that, even if He bears witness of Himself, His witness is true; and also that He judges no man. In each case the reverse truth of the statements in ch. 5 finds expression in 8¹⁴⁻¹⁸; and the solution of the contradiction in each case is to be found in the doctrine of the mutual indwelling of the Father and the Son. Thus the Lord does not bear witness of Himself, as one concerned with his own 'glory' or reputation [5⁴¹, ⁴⁴]. On the other hand He who, and who only, is 'from above', bears and must bear witness of Himself in His self-revelation; and His witness is true, because it is also that of the Father who sent Him [8¹⁸]. The truth that His witness is also that of the Father can equally well be expressed in His words 'I know whence I came, and whither I go' [8¹⁴ᵇ]; and so long as His hearers do not know His origin and destiny, they will also be at a loss, although they do not know it, concerning their own origin and destiny.

Similarly the Lord does not of Himself pass judgement in independence of the Father. Such a judgement would be, like that of His hearers [8¹⁵], an outward judgement, 'according to appearance' [7²⁴], and would be in accordance with the standards of the world, be these never so good or enlightened. None the less, because of His union with the Father, He cannot but judge [9³⁹], and with an absolute, unerring judgement [8¹⁶].

It should be noticed that in 8²¹⁻⁵⁹, as the controversy proceeds to its climax, the reader is not only taught truths of the Lord's origin, destiny, and Person, and of His relationship to the Father, but is also shown, in the characterization of the Jews, the precise opposite of all that is ascribed to the Lord. They cannot come, whither He is going [8²¹]; they are from below [8²³]; they are no true seed of Abraham [8³⁷, ³⁹], but of the devil, and are therefore murderers [8⁴⁴] and liars [8⁵⁵].

Just as at 7³³⁻³⁶ the Jews interpreted a deeply spiritual saying of the Lord by the suggestion that He might be planning to escape from them by means of a mission among the Gentiles, so at 8²², with a similar misinterpretation of His reference in 8²¹ to His coming death, they ask whether, since He says that He is going away beyond their reach, He intends to kill Himself. The truth is rather that the Lord's death, by which He departs 'out of this world unto the Father' [13¹], whither the Jews cannot come [8²¹], far from having any suicidal character, is brought about by the Jews themselves, and on His part is a voluntary and sacrificial act for the sake of the world [1²⁹, 3¹⁷, 4⁴², 10¹¹, ¹⁵, 12⁴⁷]. Indeed, one purpose of the Lord's coming was to open a way 'from beneath', from 'this world' [8²³], into the region to which He Himself by right belongs [3¹³]; but this purpose can only be accomplished in believers [8²⁴]; and this belief the Jews refuse. In this verse [8²⁴] the R.V. mg should probably be followed; the Lord's words imply, at any rate to the reader, His claim to divinity.

With the Jews' question [8²⁵], evoked by the Lord's words in 8²⁴, the significance of which they appear to fail to understand at present (contrast 8⁵⁸), we may compare 1¹⁹, 8¹⁹, 19⁹. Although the translation of 8²⁵ in R.V. mg is a possible rendering of the Greek, in the light of the contents of 8²⁶ it seems unsuitable. If, then, the translation in R.V. text is followed, the meaning will be that the Lord has from the first told the Jews the truth about His Person. The Greek, however, can also be construed, 'From the beginning I am that which I am also telling you'; and this not only agrees well with the Lord's words in 8²⁴, but recalls the basic teaching of this gospel that the Speaker is the Word, who 'was in the beginning with God' [1²].

The interpretation of 8²⁶⁻²⁸ is difficult. We are perhaps to understand the Lord's words as meaning that He will continue His witness and judgement concerning His hearers to the end, thus carrying out the task laid upon Him by the Father; but they will only realize the truth about Him, when it is too late. When they have exalted the Son of man upon the cross, they will learn (we are not told how, or when) the truth of His Person, and of His obedience to the Father, who is always with Him.

It can hardly be doubted that St. John wishes the reader to draw a distinction between those who in 8³⁰ are described as 'believing on' the Lord, and those who in 8³¹ are declared to have 'believed' Him, that is, it seems, to have given Him only credence, a belief short of complete allegiance. It should, however, be remembered that even belief on Him, or on His name, may be in certain respects defective, as is made clear at 2²³ and 7³¹; and we read in 12⁴² that 'even of the rulers many believed on' Him, but owing to motives of self-interest did not acknowledge Him. Again, those who in 8³¹ are said to have 'believed' the Lord, none the less are said at 8³⁷ to be seeking to kill Him. St. John perhaps wishes to suggest that all the kinds of belief mentioned in chs. 7 and 8 are defective.

To those Jews who had believed Him the Lord in 8³¹, ³² gives a conditional promise of knowledge of the truth, and therewith of future freedom; His hearers reply that owing to their relationship to Abraham they are already free. Rightly understood, there is no reference here, on either side, to political freedom or bondage, but only to a freedom dependent on man's relation to God. The Lord, however, proceeds to give a solemn reminder that no sinner is free. Previous to this chapter sin has been mentioned in this gospel only in the Baptist's reference at 1²⁹ to the Lord as 'the Lamb of God, who takes away the sin of the world'; but at 8²¹, ²⁴ the Jews were warned that rejection of the Lord's manifestation will involve their death in sin; and it is now shown that sin is a form of slavery. Anyone who makes himself an instrument, not, as at 3²¹, of the truth, but of sin, is in a state of slavery, and can only be set free by the gift and act of Another, the Lord Himself, He being the Son who has a rightful and permanent place in His Father's house. The Jews' reliance on the past, that is, on their physical descent from Abraham, would be in place, if it led them not to regard themselves as being already in possession of freedom, but to look to the future for the fulfilment of God's promises to them through Abraham, in fact to the Lord, who now, as the fulfilment of the hope of Israel [Acts 28²⁰], offers them the freedom which they mistakenly think is, by reason of their lineage, already theirs. For indeed, as sinners, they are slaves; and the slave has no security of tenure. But the Lord, the Son [8³⁵], has this security, and is prepared also to grant it to those [8³⁶] who in and through Him (cf. Gal. 4⁴⁻⁷) become the sons of God; and since this is the only path to freedom, the latter, freed by the Son, will be really free. As things are, however, the Jews' desire to kill the Lord shows clearly what their position actually is, and therefore also how false is their claim to be true descendants of Abraham, 'the friend of God' [James 2²³], whereas the true seed of Abraham 'abides in the house for ever' [8³⁵; cf. 14²]. The two parts of 8³⁸ are antithetical, and the R.V. text therefore certainly gives the correct sense, the Jews' father being, as will soon be explicitly stated, the devil. The Jews perceive that the Lord is in some sense denying their descent from Abraham, and accordingly at 8³⁹ they repeat their claim already made in 8³³. This claim the Lord now denies, on the ground that no true child of Abraham would seek to kill Him, 'a man who had told' them 'the truth', heard by Him from God, and who thereby had been to them the Revealer of God, He in fact to whom Abraham looked forward. There is thus no contradiction here with 8³⁷ᵃ, since the descent in view is no longer physical, but moral and spiritual.

At 8⁴¹ the Jews are once more said to show by their actions who their father is; and clearly the reference is neither to Abraham nor to God. Perceiving this, they reiterate the purity of their descent; as children of Abraham, they are children of God, and of Him only. The claim, however, is rejected, in view of their present attitude to Him whom God has sent; He is not acting on His own initiative; and failure to understand the meaning of His speech is due solely to inability to hear His word, which indeed is not His, but that of the Father who sent Him [14²⁴]. And at this point the statement, implied in 8³⁸, ⁴¹, is openly made; the Jews' father is the devil, and they reveal their father's qualities, murder, falsehood [8⁴⁴], and failure to love Him who is the life and the truth. Thus the precise nature of the 'unrighteousness', ascribed by implication to the Jews at 7¹⁸, is here made clear; it is falsehood, leading to desire to murder (cf. 7¹⁹).

The Jews, who claim descent from Abraham, have been shown rather to be, as a result of their slavery to sin, children of the devil. The remainder of the chapter sets forth the truth about the Lord, and His relation to Abraham. It is precisely because He gives expression to the truth, that the Jews, being the children of falsehood, disbelieve Him. And yet, admittedly, no suggestion of sin has been alleged against Him; 'Christian piety at no point founders on the rock of its origin in the life of Jesus'. The Jews could not

but respond to Him if, as they claim, they had God for their
Father. At 8⁴¹ the Jews, asserting their own purity of birth, had
perhaps hinted (see note on that verse) that the Lord's birth was
otherwise. The charge in 8⁴⁸, that He was a Samaritan, may be
similar, since the Samaritans were a mixed race, descended from
both the original inhabitants and the Gentile immigrants who were
brought in, when the northern kingdom was removed into captivity
[2 Kings 17²⁴]. Or it may be simply a term of abuse, similar to the
charge of possession with which it is coupled. It is in favour of
this view that the double charge only receives a single reply. The
Lord, in denying the charge, refers, as before, to His relations with
His Father. He Himself is unmoved by the Jews' verdicts on Him;
He knows that He is seeking His Father's honour. If it be asked how
the Son honours the Father, the answer is, by His love and
obedience in proclaiming the Father's word and in doing the
Father's works [10³⁷]. At 8⁴⁹, instead of the words 'ye dishonour
Me', we might have expected, 'ye dishonour Him' (the Father);
but the form of words used recalls 5²³, where honour or dishonour
to the Son is shown to be honour or dishonour to the Father. The
Lord does not 'seek' His own glory or repute; the Father is 'seeking'
it, in the mission and work of the Son. The further reference in
8⁵⁰ to the Father's work in judgement recalls the teaching of 5²⁴
that the true disciple does not come into judgement, but has passed
out of death into life; and in 8⁵¹ the Lord promises freedom from
death to those of His hearers who in 8³¹⁻³⁶, if prepared to 'abide in
His word', were promised freedom from sin. He, who keeps His
Father's word [8⁵⁵], gives a solemn assurance that the disciple, who
keeps His (the Lord's) word, shall never see death. The Jews, being
'from beneath' and 'of this world' [8²³], understand the words
solely in a literal sense, and are confirmed in their conviction of the
derangement of the Lord. (Their 'now we know' may be compared
and contrasted with the disciples' 'we have believed and know'
at 6⁶⁹.) If, though this is uncertain, a distinction is to be made
between 'see death' in 8⁵¹ and 'taste of death' in 8⁵², the Lord in
8⁵¹ may mean, as in 11²⁵, that he who keeps His word and believes
on Him, 'though he die, yet shall he live', whereas the Jews in 8⁵²
typically assume Him to claim that such an one will never experience
dissolution. Is, then, the Lord, the Jews ask, greater than their
father Abraham (cf. 4¹²) and the prophets, who all have passed
away? Does He rank Himself above them? The Lord replies that

He does not assign any rank to Himself; His rank is assigned to Him by His Father, whom He knows and obeys, whereas the Jews, although they say, untruly, that the Father is their God, do not know Him. In 8⁵⁶, where R.V. text should be followed, it is shown how grievously in error is the Jews' suggestion of a comparison in greatness between the Lord, the incarnate Word of God, and the chief religious figures of O.T. history. There may be here a reference to a rabbinic interpretation of Gen. 24¹, where the words 'well stricken in age' represent an original 'far gone into the days', and were understood as signifying that Abraham was in some way allowed to see the days of the Messiah, here interpreted as the Lord's 'day' or ministry. The Jews once more understand the Lord's words only in the literal sense, and therefore express incredulity, whereupon the Lord answers with a solemn assertion of His eternal or divine existence. Whereas Abraham (like the Baptist; cf. 1⁶) 'came into existence' at a definite moment, He, the Lord, the Word of God, is above and beyond time. The Jews regard the claim as blasphemous, and seek to inflict the appropriate punishment [Lev. 24¹⁶]; but the manifestation, which they have rejected, is withdrawn, and the light of the world [8¹²] leaves the temple.

The intensely controversial character of large parts of chs. 7 and 8 is perhaps explained if we recall that, long before, Amos had asked [5²⁰] whether the day of the Lord would not be 'darkness, and not light, even very dark, and no brightness in it'. For in these chapters the light is represented as made manifest, with the inevitable result, already set forth in 3¹⁶⁻²¹, that the general surrounding darkness, on the part of all that does not or cannot associate itself with the light, is emphasized, as never before. To St. John it had become clear that the Jews, in rejecting their Messiah and bringing Him to the cross, had in fact chosen darkness and not light, and further that, so far from the day of the Lord bringing condemnation and judgement to the nations, and deliverance and exaltation to the Jews, the reverse was nearer to the truth. Accordingly the picture of the day of the Lord, as painted in such passages as Zech. 14, a chapter closely connected, as we have seen, with the festival of tabernacles, now makes way for the reality; and in this section the judgement or discrimination, caused by the very fact of the Lord's presence, is shown both in its work of testing and sifting individuals and parties, and in its results, the chief of which is the increased and reiterated determination of the Jews to achieve the Lord's destruction. For, although it is no doubt true that, in the attempt to understand the teaching of this gospel, we should regard the moment of the Lord's death as, above all, the moment of the judgement and condemnation of the world, yet chs. 7 and 8, which describe His manifestation, describe also His rejection, and show that this rejection, which will have the cross as its result, is also the judgement and condemnation of those who in these chapters reject the Lord. The chapters thus occur suitably near the centre of the record and, more definitely than the earlier chapters, prepare the reader for the final issue of events.

NOTES TO 8^{12-59}

$8^{17, 18}$. The Lord, as at 5^{31}, refers to and accepts a provision of the Jewish law. His own witness and that of His Father, in the light of Their complete union [10^{30}], combine to fulfil the requirement of Num. 35^{30}, Deut. 17^6, 19^{15}. But the way in which, here and elsewhere in this gospel [$7^{19, 22}$, 10^{34}, 15^{25}], He refers to the law, marks the width of the gulf between Him and His hearers. Though born, indeed, under the law [Gal. 4^4], He is set forth in John as also above and beyond it.

8^{20}. 'in the treasury'. The reference is possibly to that part of 'the Court of the Women' where, it seems, chests were set for the receipt of offerings. In this court, which adjoined the meeting-place of the Sanhedrin, the illumination took place at the feast of tabernacles. The introduction of ocasional notes of time and place, as here (cf. 6^{59}, $10^{22, 23}$), helps to re- mind the reader of the historical and geographical setting, in which the various themes treated in this gospel are placed.

8^{21}. Here, as at 1^{29}, 9^{41}, 15^{22} the sin of many is regarded as forming a single entity. The crucifixion, for example, was an act of co-operative guilt; it was not, and could not have been, achieved by any one person acting alone. At 8^{24}, as at 9^{34}, 20^{23}, in the plural 'sins' the thought is of individual acts of sin.

8^{37}. The rendering of both R.V. text and R.V. mg is possible.

8^{41}. It is possible that the Jews here make an indirect attack upon the manner of the Lord's birth, as recorded by St. Matthew and St. Luke. See note on 1^{45}.

8^{43}. The Lord's 'speech' is His audible utterance, whereas His 'word', at the end of this verse, is its content and import, to which the Jews cannot hearken, because His word has no place, or free course, in them [8^{37}]. In this and similar contexts it should be kept in mind that the Lord's word is, in the last resort, the Lord Himself.

8⁴⁴. 'from the beginning'. The reference is probably to man's loss of immortality by the Fall (cf. Wisd. 2²³, ²⁴, Ecclus. 25²⁴, Rom. 5¹²), rather than to the murder of Abel by Cain [Gen. 4⁸].

'stood not in the truth'. R.V. text is more likely to be correct than R.V. mg. The meaning of the whole sentence will then be that the devil is, and always has been, essentially opposed to the truth.

'When he speaketh a lie . . .'. R.V. text should be followed; it is the devil's nature to propagate falsehood.

8⁵⁶. There is other evidence of a Jewish belief that Abraham rejoiced in a foresight of the messianic age.

8⁵⁷. 'fifty years', which was regarded as the normal period of a man's working life [Num. 4³, ³⁹, 8²⁴, ²⁵], is contrasted with the centuries which had intervened between the Lord and Abraham.

'hast thou seen Abraham?' After the previous verse we might have expected, 'has Abraham seen thee?' as indeed is read in some MSS. But the text of the R.V. is certainly right. The Jews do not accept the doctrine of the Lord's Messiahship, implied in 8⁵⁶, and ask incredulously how one of His age can have come in contact with Abraham.

SECTION 4 (contd.) 9¹⁻⁴¹. *The Lord as the Light of the World.*

9 And as he passed by, he saw a man blind from his birth. And his
2 disciples asked him, saying, Rabbi, who did sin, this man, or his parents,
3 that he should be born blind? Jesus answered, Neither did this man sin,
nor his parents: but that the works of God should be made manifest in
4 him. We must work the works of him that sent me, while it is day: the
5 night cometh, when no man can work. When I am in the world, I am
6 the light of the world. When he had thus spoken, he spat on the ground,
7 and made clay of the spittle, ¹and anointed his eyes with the clay, And
said unto him, Go, wash in the pool of Siloam (which is by interpretation,
8 Sent). He went away therefore, and washed, and came seeing. The
neighbours therefore, and they which saw him aforetime, that he was a
9 beggar, said, Is not this he that sat and begged? Others said, It is he:
10 others said, No, but he is like him. He said, I am *he.* They said therefore
11 unto him, How then were thine eyes opened? He answered, The man
that is called Jesus made clay, and anointed mine eyes, and said unto
me, Go to Siloam, and wash: so I went away and washed, and I received
12 sight. And they said unto him, Where is he? He saith, I know not.
13 They bring to the Pharisees him that aforetime was blind. Now it was
14 the sabbath on the day when Jesus made the clay, and opened his eyes.
15 Again therefore the Pharisees also asked him how he received his sight.
And he said unto them, He put clay upon mine eyes, and I washed, and

¹ *Or* and with the clay thereof anointed *his* eyes

16 do see. Some therefore of the Pharisees said, This man is not from God, because he keepeth not the sabbath. But others said, How can a man that is a sinner do such signs? And there was a division among them.
17 They say therefore unto the blind man again, What sayest thou of him,
18 in that he opened thine eyes? And he said, He is a prophet. The Jews therefore did not believe concerning him, that he had been blind, and had received his sight, until they called the parents of him that had
19 received his sight, and asked them, saying, Is this your son, who ye say
20 was born blind? how then doth he now see? His parents answered and said, We know that this is our son, and that he was born blind: but how he now seeth, we know not; or who opened his eyes, we know not: ask
22 him; he is of age; he shall speak for himself. These things said his parents, because they feared the Jews: for the Jews had agreed already, that if any man should confess him *to be* Christ, he should be put out of
23 the synagogue. Therefore said his parents, He is of age; ask him. So they
24 called a second time the man that was blind, and said unto him, Give
25 glory to God: we know that this man is a sinner. He therefore answered, Whether he be a sinner, I know not: one thing I know, that, whereas I
26 was blind, now I see. They said therefore unto him, What did he to
27 thee? how opened he thine eyes? He answered them, I told you even now, and ye did not hear: wherefore would ye hear it again? would ye
28 also become his disciples? And they reviled him, and said, Thou art his
29 disciple; but we are disciples of Moses. We know that God hath spoken
30 unto Moses: but as for this man, we know not whence he is. The man answered and said unto them, Why, herein is the marvel, that ye know
31 not whence he is, and *yet* he opened mine eyes. We know that God heareth not sinners: but if any man be a worshipper of God, and do his
32 will, him he heareth. Since the world began it was never heard that any
33 one opened the eyes of a man born blind. If this man were not from
34 God, he could do nothing. They answered and said unto him, Thou wast altogether born in sins, and dost thou teach us? And they cast him out.
35   Jesus heard that they had cast him out; and finding him, he said,
36 Dost thou believe on [1]the Son of God? He answered and said, And who
37 is he, Lord, that I may believe on him? Jesus said unto him, Thou
38 hast both seen him, and he it is that speaketh with thee. And he said,
39 Lord, I believe. And he worshipped him. And Jesus said, For judgement came I into this world, that they which see not may see; and that they
40 which see may become blind. Those of the Pharisees which were with
41 him heard these things, and said unto him, Are we also blind? Jesus said unto them, If ye were blind, ye would have no sin: but now ye say, We see: your sin remaineth.

[1] *Many ancient authorities read* the Son of man.

EXPOSITION OF 9¹⁻⁴¹

There appears to be no real break between ch. 8 and ch. 9, for the reader will be ill advised if he raises the question how it comes about that the Lord can move freely in ch. 9, in spite of the attempt on His life at 8⁵⁹. It would be equally unwise to ask whether 9³⁹⁻⁴¹ is to be regarded as following at once on 9³⁵⁻³⁸, so that the Pharisees of 9⁴⁰ are present during the Lord's conversation with the beggar in 9³⁵⁻³⁸. St. John is not concerned to answer questions of this sort.

In the prologue life and light are closely associated as primary attributes of the Logos. The theme of life is prominent in the first six chapters, but that of light less so; and although in 8¹² the Lord declares Himself to be the light of the world, the development of this theme is reserved for ch. 9. We have seen that chs. 7 and 8 are more continuously occupied with controversy than any others in John; and at their close light and darkness, good and evil, Jesus the Son of God [8³⁸] and the Jews the children of the devil [8⁴⁴], are left diametrically opposed; the incarnate Logos has come to His own, but His own people as a whole have given Him no welcome [1¹¹]. In accordance with the teaching of 3¹⁸, ¹⁹, ch. 9 will now show what the result is, both for the disciple of the Light, who does welcome Him [1¹²], and for the children of darkness.

According to O.T. prophecy, the giving of sight to the blind would be a feature of the messianic age; and no doubt St. John has this in mind, especially if, as seems to be the case, the scene in ch. 9 is still laid at the feast of tabernacles. But since here alone in the gospels a person is described as 'born blind', the evangelist probably wishes to emphasize, even more strongly, that the record in this chapter of the blind man's experience, thanks to the love of God made effectual in the Lord, represents the transition of man, perhaps we should say of fallen man (cf. 9³⁴), out of darkness into full enlightenment. It is particularly noticeable how the passage of the beggar [9⁸] from religious ignorance [9¹²] to complete illumination [9³⁸, ³⁹ᵃ] is counterbalanced by the progressive darkening of the Pharisees, his judges.

Thus, if we start at 9¹², the beggar, although now possessing physical sight [9⁷, ¹¹], has at present never seen Jesus (cf. 9³⁶, ³⁷, and note also 14⁹) and therefore cannot know where He is (cf. 14³ ᵉⁿᵈ); he can only speak of 'the man that is called Jesus' [9¹¹]. Later, in the course of his enlightenment, he recognizes Him as a prophet (cf. 4¹⁹), on the ground that through the Lord's action he himself now possesses physical sight. Later still, and now knowing the risk that he runs [9²²], he is none the less prepared to ally himself with his Benefactor in face of the aspersions of the authorities against Him, and avows, on the ground of the unparalleled work [9³²; cf. 15²⁴] wrought by Jesus on him, that Jesus must be from God. And finally, having been cast out by his judges [9³⁴] as a result of his loyalty to the Lord, he is sought and found by Jesus, sees Him, learns who He is, and worships Him.

Conversely, the neighbours of the blind man, who hitherto believed themselves to have full knowledge of his state and case, are now thrown into perplexity about him [9⁸,⁹]; they, as little as he at present, know where the Lord is [9¹²]; and being at a loss to understand what has happened to him as a result of the Lord's work (cf. 3³⁻⁸), they bring him to the Pharisees, as being authorities competent to give a ruling in the matter. (The reader perceives that this step will lead to trouble, since the Lord's divine action will now be subjected to human scrutiny and judgement.) Like the beggar's neighbours, the Pharisees begin by an inquiry into the circumstances of the case; and the fact, which now emerges, that the work was wrought on a sabbath, for some at once brands the Lord's origin as godless, while others (of whom we hear no more) are more strongly influenced by the astounding nature of His act; and a schism or cleavage (cf. 7⁴³, 10¹⁹) arises forthwith among the judges. Next, when the beggar's own opinion is asked and he declares that Jesus is a prophet, the Jews respond, first by disbelieving his story and seeking to disprove it [9¹⁷⁻²³], and next by trying to make him disown it, on the ground that they know the Lord to be a sinner [9²⁴]. (Both by thus appealing for an explanation, first to the beggar [9¹⁷], and then to his parents [9¹⁹], who are not prepared to become involved in the issue, and finally by calling him for a second hearing [9²⁴] in which they seek to go over the case again [9²⁶], the judges reveal the embarrassment and difficulty in which they find themselves, although in fact their minds are already made up against the Lord [9²⁴].) When the beggar shows that he cannot be shaken in his adherence to his story [9²⁵⁻²⁷], the Jews turn to bluster, and taunt him with discipleship of a man of unknown origin,[1] whereas they themselves are disciples of Moses, to whom admittedly God spoke. To this the beggar replies that,

[1] At 6⁴², however, the Jews object to the Lord's teaching in 6³²⁻⁴⁰, on the

the good work wrought on him being unparalleled, its author cannot but be from God (and therefore, so far from being in opposition to Moses, must be in agreement with him); and the Jews, finding it now desirable to admit the beggar's former blindness [9³⁴], which previously they had questioned [9¹⁸], use it as a means to dismiss his right to differ from them in their understanding of the matter, and expel him from their company. Finally, when the Lord enuntiates the cardinal truth that His Gospel involves a discrimination which confounds all the judgements and standards accepted by the world, the Pharisees, who perceive that His words involve the challenge whether they themselves are in the light or in darkness, learn, on putting the question to the Lord, that their claim to sight, their belief that they see, is in fact their condemnation.

The connexion with chs. 7 and 8 thus seems to be maintained. For in 8²¹ the Jews were told that they are in sin, and will die in it, and at 8³⁴ it was implied that, owing to their sin, they are slaves. At 9³⁴ the beggar is declared by his judges to have been born in sins, since he has been blind from birth; but the Lord, the light of the world [8¹², 9⁵], Himself without sin (contrast 9²⁴ with 9³¹, and cf. 8⁴⁶), gives him sight and thus frees him from darkness, that is, from sin and its slavery. The beggar's judges, on the contrary, remain in sin; for, the Lord having come, only those who believe on Him [8²⁴] have sight [12⁴⁶] and themselves become 'sons of light' [12³⁵, ³⁶]; any other claim to sight no longer implies merely, as before the Lord's coming, a darkness which in time may be changed into light, but a darkness which, in the belief that it sees, has lost this possibility. It thus 'comes into judgement' [3¹⁸, 5²⁴], and its sin 'remains' or 'abides', just as the wrath of God 'abides' on him who does not obey the Son [3³⁶].

NOTES TO 9¹⁻⁴¹

9¹. Certain features of ch. 9, one of the most vivid narratives in this gospel, closely resemble those of 5¹⁻¹⁵; these resemblances were considered on pp. 16 and 138. A slight resemblance may perhaps also be traced between ch. 9 and 4⁴⁶⁻⁵³, in so far as there is development and progress both in the

ground that they believe themselves to know His origin. To understand St. John's method and purpose in this matter, consult also 3⁸⁻¹⁰, 7²⁷, ²⁸, 8¹⁴, ¹⁹.

nature or quality of the father's belief in 4⁴⁶⁻⁵³ and in that of the beggar's belief in ch. 9.

9². 'his disciples'. These have not been explicitly mentioned since the Lord's departure from Galilee at 7¹⁰; but their attendance on the Lord seems to be assumed; cf. 11⁷, where they are next mentioned.

'born blind'. Jewish thought, regarding even congenital defect as a divine punishment for sin, was inclined in such a case to explain the sin as having been committed in the womb, or in a previous existence, or by the parents.

9³. The Lord dismisses the speculations thus raised, and looking, not to the origin, but to the purpose, of the defect, sees it only as a signal and destined occasion for a manifestation of the divine action (cf. 11⁴). We may compare also St. Paul's ready acceptance of his weaknesses as giving opportunity for the revelation of the divine strength [2 Cor. 12⁹, ¹⁰].

9⁴. In using the plural 'we' rather than the singular 'I' (which is read in some texts here), the Lord associates His disciples, who are to be, in St. Paul's words in 1 Cor. 12²⁷, the members of His body, with Himself; similarly 3¹¹, and cf. Mt. 5¹³, ¹⁴.

9⁵. Whereas the Lord's declaration in 8¹² is as wide and all-embracing in its scope as the teaching in the prologue [1⁴, ⁹] about the light, here (to judge from certain features of the Greek original, and from the preceding verse) His declaration seems to refer only to the period of His incarnate life; it recalls the reference in 7³³ to the brief period of His sojourn among men. Thus regarded, 9⁴ is in agreement with 19³⁰, 'It [the Lord's work] has been completed'.

9⁶. Since the day is a sabbath [9¹⁴], on which day both the actions now performed by the Lord were forbidden, we are presumably to see here a further illustration of the doctrine of 5¹⁷, that the Lord, like His Father, never ceases, even on the sabbath, from His work of giving life. Jewish traditional observance is set aside in favour of the salvation of men.

Irenaeus, *adv. haer.* 5.15.2, and other early writers see a connexion between this verse and Gen. 2⁷, where man is formed from the dust of the ground. If they are right—and there is much in the context to support their view—the thought here is either of re-creation or of complete creation.

Saliva has been often and widely believed to possess curative power. 'The transfer of saliva', says one writer, 'is more than a gift of a portion of the spitter's life. It is a gift of a portion of himself, which is thus put into the power of the recipient as a pledge of goodwill'.[1]

9⁷. The word 'Siloam', which is connected with a Hebrew verb meaning 'to send', was the name of a pool at Jerusalem, so called because water was either brought to it or discharged from it by a conduit (cf. 2 Kings 20²⁰). As has been already stated, two Greek verbs, both meaning 'to send', are together used more than forty times in this gospel of the Father sending the Son (into the world), and the Greek participle here used as an explanation of the word Siloam means strictly 'he who has been sent'.

---

[1] E. S. Hartland, *Legend of Perseus*, ii. 260.

We are therefore to understand that in and by the water of the pool the blind man is granted sight, because the pool represents Him who has been sent. Part of the purpose of the Lord's coming, we have already learned, was to give living water; and just as the theme of water in John has already been frequently associated with the gift of life (e.g. $4^{10, 14}$, 5^{7-9}, 6^{35}, 7^{38}), so now it is connected also with that of light [$9^{7, 11, 15}$].

$9^{8, 9}$. Underlying these two verses is the question whether a man after baptism and rebirth is the same person as before, or not. It should be noticed also that the beggar's reply, which simply establishes his identity, is identical with the expression used more than once by the Lord in this gospel to describe His divine nature. The significance of the expression, therefore, must in each case be decided by the context.

9^{13}. It is not clear what court 'the Pharisees' here mentioned represent; and at $9^{18, 22}$ they are described by the more general term 'the Jews', just as in ch. 6 'the multitude' of verses 2, 5, 22, 24 seems to become 'the Jews' in verses 41, 52.

9^{22}. The word here used, which implies, if not complete excommunication, at any rate some form of exclusion, temporary or otherwise, from the commonwealth of Israel, occurs again in 12^{42}, 16^2, but not elsewhere in the Greek Bible.

9^{24}: 'Give glory to God' was a common Jewish adjuration to a person, in a law-court or elsewhere, to speak the truth; thus Joshua addresses Achan in this way, when urging him to make confession of his theft (Josh. 7^{19}). Here therefore the Jews invite the beggar to admit that in some way he has been deceiving them, though St. John may wish his readers to have in mind also the less technical and more obvious meaning of the words.

9^{35}. 'finding him' (as also at 5^{14}). In 4^{23} the Father was said to be seeking true worshippers; and here, through the Son's work in fulfilment of His Father's will [$9^{3, 4}$], one such true worshipper is found [9^{38}].

'the Son of man', R.V. mg. This reading should be followed. Not only does the textual evidence appear to favour it, but the context also strongly suggests its correctness. For in 9^{39} we come upon the note of judgement, and this function was closely connected in Jewish thought with the office and coming of the Son of man. But the truth is at once emphasized, that the beggar is not to look for a future Judge; his Judge is before him, and speaking to him, but indeed no longer as Judge, for by his confession of the Lord the beggar now 'does not come into judgement, but has passed out of death into life' [5^{24}].

9^{39}. The Greek word translated 'judgement' only occurs here in this gospel, but it is closely connected with the word generally used by the evangelist to express this conception. If the two words are to be distinguished, the word here used emphasizes the result, the decision, reached after the process of judging.

SECTION 4 (contd.) 10¹⁻³⁹. *The Lord as the Door and the Good Shepherd.*

10 Verily, verily, I say unto you, He that entereth not by the door into the fold of the sheep, but climbeth up some other way, the same is a 2 thief and a robber. But he that entereth in by the door is ¹the shepherd 3 of the sheep. To him the porter openeth; and the sheep hear his voice: 4 and he calleth his own sheep by name, and leadeth them out. When he hath put forth all his own, he goeth before them, and the sheep follow 5 him: for they know his voice. And a stranger will they not follow, but 6 will flee from him: for they know not the voice of strangers. This ²parable spake Jesus unto them: but they understood not what things they were which he spake unto them.

7 Jesus therefore said unto them again, Verily, verily, I say unto you, 8 I am the door of the sheep. All that came before me are thieves and 9 robbers: but the sheep did not hear them. I am the door: by me if any man enter in, he shall be saved, and shall go in and go out, and shall find 10 pasture. The thief cometh not, but that he may steal, and kill, and destroy: I came that they may have life, and may ³have *it* abundantly. 11 I am the good shepherd: the good shepherd layeth down his life for the 12 sheep. He that is a hireling, and not a shepherd, whose own the sheep are not, beholdeth the wolf coming, and leaveth the sheep, and fleeth, 13 and the wolf snatcheth them, and scattereth *them*: *he fleeth* because he 14 is a hireling, and careth not for the sheep. I am the good shepherd; and 15 I know mine own, and mine own know me, even as the Father knoweth 16 me, and I know the Father; and I lay down my life for the sheep. And other sheep I have, which are not of this fold: them also I must ⁴bring, and they shall hear my voice; and ⁵they shall become one flock, one 17 shepherd. Therefore doth the Father love me, because I lay down my life, 18 that I may take it again. No one ⁶taketh it away from me, but I lay it down of myself. I have ⁷power to lay it down, and I have ⁷power to take it again. This commandment received I from my Father.

19 There arose a division again among the Jews because of these words. 20 And many of them said, He hath a ⁸devil, and is mad; why hear ye him? 21 Others said, These are not the sayings of one possessed with a ⁸devil. Can a ⁸devil open the eyes of the blind?

22 ⁹And it was the feast of the dedication at Jerusalem: it was winter; 23 And Jesus was walking in the temple in Solomon's porch. The Jews 24 therefore came round about him, and said unto him, How long dost 25 thou hold us in suspense? If thou art the Christ, tell us plainly. Jesus

---

¹ *Or* a shepherd   ² *Or* proverb   ³ *Or* have abundance   ⁴ *Or* lead   ⁵ *Or* there shall be one flock   ⁶ *Some ancient authorities read* took it away.   ⁷ *Or* right   ⁸ *Gr.* demon.   ⁹ *Some ancient authorities read* At that time was the feast.

answered them, I told you, and ye believe not: the works that I do in
26 my Father's name, these bear witness of me. But ye believe not, because
27 ye are not of my sheep. My sheep hear my voice, and I know them, and
28 they follow me: and I give unto them eternal life; and they shall never
29 perish, and no one shall snatch them out of my hand. ¹My Father, which
30 hath given *them* unto me, is greater than all; and no one is able to snatch
31 ²*them* out of the Father's hand. I and the Father are one. The Jews took
32 up stones again to stone him. Jesus answered them, Many good works
have I shewed you from the Father; for which of those works do ye
33 stone me? The Jews answered him, For a good work we stone thee not,
but for blasphemy; and because that thou, being a man, makest thyself
34 God. Jesus answered them, Is it not written in your law, I said, Ye are
35 gods? If he called them gods, unto whom the word of God came (and
36 the scripture cannot be broken), say ye of him, whom the Father
³sanctified and sent into the world, Thou blasphemest; because I said,
37 I am *the* Son of God? If I do not the works of my Father, believe me not.
38 But if I do them, though ye believe not me, believe the works: that ye
may know and understand that the Father is in me, and I in the Father.
39 They sought again to take him: and he went forth out of their hand.

¹ *Some ancient authorities read* That which my Father hath given unto me.
² *Or aught*   ³ *Or* consecrated

EXPOSITION OF 10¹⁻³⁹

Just as it proved possible to find a connexion between ch. 9 and
chs. 7 and 8, so 10¹⁻²¹ seems to be closely connected with ch. 9.
This connexion may become clear, if we recall some of the uses for
religious purposes in the O.T. (as was natural for a pastoral and
God-fearing people like the Hebrews—cf. Gen. 47³—) of the
imagery of a shepherd and his sheep. In the Psalms Yahweh is
often portrayed as the Shepherd of Israel, His flock, e.g. Ps. 80¹;
and Ezek. 34 is important for an understanding of Jn. 10. In that
chapter Yahweh strongly condemns the rulers of Israel as tyran-
nous and negligent shepherds who have grossly abused their office,
feeding themselves instead of the sheep, so that the latter have
become scattered upon all the face of the earth and a general prey.
Now, however, the hour of righteous judgement has come, and
Yahweh Himself intervenes. The unworthy shepherds will be
dispossessed, and He will Himself become responsible for the
cause of the sheep. He will bring them into their own land and
secure their well-being; and He will appoint His servant David
(that is, the Messiah) as their shepherd.

Apart from such brief references as 7¹³, ⁴⁷⁻⁴⁹, we have heard little, in chs. 1 to 8, of the relations of the Jewish authorities with their people; when the religious leaders are introduced, they are usually engaged in controversy with the Lord. Ch. 9, however, is largely concerned with the Pharisees' examination and expulsion of the beggar, the Lord not being present between 9⁸ and 9³⁴. In the light of Ezek. 34, which it can hardly be doubted was in St. John's mind as he wrote 10¹⁻²¹, it seems probable that the beggar of ch. 9 is represented in ch. 10 in the guise of the faithful sheep, who recognize and know their shepherd [10³, ⁴, ¹⁶], while the Pharisees of ch. 9 reappear in ch. 10 either as thieves who only come in order to steal and destroy the sheep, or as hirelings who, just because they are hirelings and nothing more, readily abandon the sheep on the approach of danger [10¹², ¹³].

This interpretation of the passage might well be thought doubtful if the latter ended at 10⁵, since thus far there has been no reference to the immediate situation; but in 10⁷⁻¹⁶ the parabolic form wears thin, for the Lord now reveals His own part in the picture, and defines His relationship to the sheep, contrasting it with that of thieves [10⁸, ¹⁰] and hirelings [10¹², ¹³]. It also becomes clear that some of the functions here ascribed to the shepherd are thus ascribed because they are especially applicable to the Lord Himself, regarded as shepherd of the sheep. For it is not the duty of every shepherd to give his life on behalf of his charge [10¹¹], or to bring into the fold other sheep, at present not belonging to it [10¹⁶]. This also explains why the same person can fill the role of shepherd [10¹¹, ¹⁴] and also of the gate giving access to the courtyard which is the home of the sheep [10⁷, ⁹]; for the Lord not only gives life [10¹⁰], but is Himself the way, or means of entrance, into life [14⁶, Heb. 10²⁰].

A distinctive feature of this section is, however, to be noticed. In such passages of the earlier gospels as Mt. 9³⁶, 10⁶, 15²⁴, Mk. 6³⁴, as in such passages of the O.T. as Num. 27¹⁶, ¹⁷, the sheep represent 'the house of Israel'. But in Jn. 10¹⁻¹⁸, although the fold is still Israel (cf. 10¹⁶), there is a difference; for now, to judge from 10³, where the shepherd calls 'his own sheep' by name, not all the sheep in the fold belong to him; and in 10¹⁶ it is expressly said that the Lord, now openly identified with the good shepherd, has other sheep, which do not belong to the fold of Israel, and that these also He must bring, and they (unlike those in the Jewish fold who did not understand His words; cf. 8⁴³, 10⁶) shall hear His voice, and that together with His original sheep in 10³ they shall become one flock, one shepherd. The Jewish believers are to be joined by Gentile believers in the one flock of the new Israel, under the one Shepherd, Jesus Christ. Indeed, in several passages of ch. 10 we are on the verge of the teaching of chs. 14 to 16 (cf., e.g. 10¹¹ with 15¹³, 10¹⁴ with 14²⁰, 10¹⁷, ¹⁸ with 15¹⁰), the chief difference being that in this chapter the Lord's relationship to 'His own' is described, as it were, from outside, whereas in chs. 14 to 16, when He is addressing His disciples directly, it is seen from within; thus in 10¹⁴ the Lord says, 'I am the good shepherd, and know mine own, and my own know me'; in 15⁵ He says, 'I am the vine, ye are the branches.' Since, therefore, this chapter contains the last addresses delivered by the Lord in public, they may be regarded as a final revelation of the gift which He offers, so far as this revelation can be made from outside, i.e. to those who do not believe [10²⁶], and therewith as a final appeal to His hearers [10³⁸].

In chs. 7 and 8 there was frequent reference to the intention of the Jews [7¹, ¹⁹, ²⁵, 8³⁷], and even to attempts on their part [7³⁰, ⁴⁴, 8⁵⁹], to arrest and kill the Lord. At the moment these intentions and attempts were frustrate, since the Lord's 'time' or 'hour' had not come; but the reader might, however erroneously, have gained an impression that at the final crisis, when the Lord's hour does arrive, the Jews will indeed have Him in their power and, having wreaked their will on Him, will emerge triumphant. In 10¹⁻¹⁸ therefore the Lord repeatedly [10¹¹, ¹⁵, ¹⁷, ¹⁸] makes clear that this will not be so. Already at 6⁵¹ He had said that He would give His flesh for the life of the world, and now more explicitly He reveals Himself as the good shepherd, voluntarily and deliberately laying down His life, in order that His sheep may themselves through Him have that fulness of life [10¹⁰] which He came to give to them. This act on His part, which is His right and is in no way forced upon Him [10¹⁸], more than any other action of His renders Him the object of His Father's love. For not only is it the Father's commandment that He should so act and thereby resume that life which is His by right [10¹⁷], but only so can the other sheep, at present not of the fold, be brought into it, and thus the purpose of His coming be achieved [10¹⁶]. It is indeed a leading thought of this gospel that Judaism, the religion of the chosen people, is to be universalized, and thus to become available for all men, as a result and by means of the Lord's coming and death [11⁵², 12³²; cf. 3¹⁶, ¹⁷]. And the flock thus formed will become one, because it will have one Guardian and Leader, the Lord. As He loves and obeys His Father and thus abides in perfect union with Him, so the sheep will love and obey Him and thus abide in perfect union with Him, and therefore also, through Him, with the Father.

The Jews 'encircle' the Lord [10²⁴], as the end draws nearer. As regards their question and demand, it is true that the Lord has never in this gospel, any more than during the ministry in the other gospels, told them that He is the Messiah; the term was, in their hearing, although not, it seems, in the hearing of the Samaritan woman [4²⁶], too susceptible of misunderstanding. He has, however, repeatedly made clear that, if the word is rightly understood, He is that, and also much more, as His works bear witness. The true reason for His hearers' difficulty lies, as He proceeds to show, elsewhere; it is that they do not belong to Him, they are not of His sheep; they have not been drawn to Him by the Father [6⁴⁴]. As regards the Lord's reference in this section [10²⁵, ³², ³⁷, ³⁸] to His works, He clearly and frequently implies in this gospel that those who truly and progressively learn to know and obey Him in personal love and trust will increasingly be able to free their devotion to Him from such adventitious aid as is furnished by His works; they will 'have the witness' in themselves [1 Jn. 5¹⁰]; and He would prefer this method of approach to Himself [14¹¹]. But He is also willing that His hearers should take their first steps [10³⁸] towards belief in Him and recognition of His Person by a consideration of the works which He does in virtue of the knowledge and love existing between Him and the Father [5¹⁹, ²⁰, 10²⁵, 14¹⁰]. If the Jews will sincerely consider these, all of which have the same quality [10³²], they will be led to the only possible conclusion about Him. Unhappily they cannot approach without hostile presuppositions the evidences thus offered. They admit, it seems, that His works may be good [10³³]; but His claim to complete union with the Father [10³⁰] is blasphemy; accordingly they seek to stone Him [10³¹].

The teaching of the prologue throws light on the meaning of the Lord's words in 10³⁴⁻³⁷. There we learned that the Word, the Instrument in creation and the Upholder of all that is, came to that which was His own as its life and light, but those who were His own did not receive Him; and the reference is no doubt in particular to the great majority in that nation of which Yahweh had said in Ex. 4²², 'Israel is my son, my firstborn'. Those few, however, who received the Word, were given the right, in virtue of a divine birth, 'to become children of God' [1¹²]. Similarly in these verses [10³⁴⁻³⁷] the Lord, pointing out to the Jews that their own scriptures contain examples of men called by 'the word of God' to carry out divine functions for Him, quotes the words, 'I said, Ye are gods', addressed by Yahweh to the judges in Israel, a passage which at once continues, 'And ye are all sons of the Most High' [Ps. 82⁶]. If, then, according to the scriptures divinity in some sense may be or has been ascribed to recipients of 'the word of God', who, however, showed themselves unworthy of the trust reposed in them, what justification have the Jews for bringing the charge of blasphemy against Him who has been hallowed or consecrated, and sent into the world, by the Father, and, Himself the Word become flesh, is now doing the works of His Father?

It seems likely that to a certain extent the passage 10²²⁻³⁹ plays the same part in this gospel as the section Mk. 14⁵⁵⁻⁶⁴ in Mark, the section which describes the examination of the Lord by the Sanhedrin after His arrest. For at Mk. 14⁶¹ the high priest puts to the Lord the question of His Messiahship, as the Jews do here [10²⁴]; and His answer to the high priest's further question whether He is the Son of the Blessed One, i.e. of God [Mk. 14⁶¹], appears to have a counterpart in His words at 10³⁶. And finally the ground of the condemnation of the Lord in Mk. 14⁶⁴ is an allegation of blasphemy; and this is also the final reason given by the Jews in 10²²⁻³⁹ for their opposition to the Lord (cf. 5¹⁸, 8⁵⁸, ⁵⁹, 19⁷).

This suggestion seems the more probable, in view of the fact that in this gospel the examination of the Lord before Annas is extremely brief [18¹³, ¹⁹⁻²³], and nothing seems to turn upon it, and no account at all is given of the examination before Caiaphas [18²⁴, ²⁸].

NOTES TO 10¹⁻³⁹

10¹. The belief that 10¹⁻²¹ is connected closely with ch. 9 is strengthened, if it be the fact that the expression 'Amen, amen I say to you (or, to thee)', a duplication occurring twenty-five times in John and nowhere else in the N.T., 'always has reference to something that has been said already, which is [now] expanded or set in a new light' (J. H. Bernard, *I.C.C.*,

St. John, p. 348), and is never used to introduce an entirely fresh topic or to begin a new discourse.

10¹⁻⁶. 10¹⁻⁵, described in 10⁶ as a *paroimia*, is the only, or at any rate the nearest, approach in John to the familiar parable (*parabolē*) in the earlier gospels. Since in the latter strong emphasis is laid on the inability of the hearers, apart from the disciples [Mt. 13¹¹], to understand the import of the parables,[1] it is noteworthy that this *paroimia* in Jn. 10¹⁻⁵ is also said in 10⁶ to have been unintelligible to those who heard it, namely the Pharisees addressed by the Lord at the end of ch. 9. Again, in the earlier gospels the inability of the hearers to understand is said to have been due to blindness, e.g. Mt. 13¹³⁻¹⁶; and we notice that in John, at the close of ch. 9, these same Pharisees inquire incredulously [9⁴⁰] whether they are blind.

The word *paroimia*, translated 'parable' or 'proverb' in the R.V., only occurs five times in the N.T.—Jn. 10⁶, 16²⁵ (twice)· ²⁹, 2 Pet. 2²²—and in Jn. 10⁶ means a figurative or symbolical word-picture. The word *parabolē*, always used in the other gospels for parable—elsewhere in the N.T. only at Heb. 9⁹, 11¹⁹—means similarly something placed beside another in illustration, comparison, or analogy. Both Greek words are suitable translations of a Hebrew word meaning a saying or story which needs explanation, if it is to be understood.

The sheepfold pictured here is a courtyard, enclosed but uncovered, where the sheep were folded at night; and the chief point made is that of the trust and close relationship between the shepherd and his sheep. The shepherd approaches the fold openly and naturally, not stealthily and deviously; his own sheep are individually known to him, and they know him and his voice; he directs them out, and then precedes them to their pasture. No stranger can gain the confidence of the sheep in this way.

10⁸. It is a basic tenet of this gospel that the true leaders of Israel, from Abraham and Moses to John the Baptist, looked forward to the coming of the Lord and bore witness to Him; hence there is obviously no reference in this verse to them, or indeed to any forerunner of the 'Lord who could be said to have partaken, in any way, of the divine Logos. It is probably an error to seek for historical characters, in order to explain the reference in this verse. Rather, the verse is a very strong expression, in negative form, of the fact that all truth is now present in the incarnate Lord; and just as now those who are truly His sheep hear and know His voice, so all those who at any time have truly belonged to Him have as it were instinctively turned away from those who did not truly point the way to Him.

10⁹. In 10⁷ the words 'I am the door of the sheep' seem, in the light of 10⁸, to mean 'I am the door, by which the true shepherd gains entrance into the fold'; but in 10⁹ the words 'I am the door' seem, in the light of the rest of this verse, to mean rather, 'I am the door, by which the sheep gain entrance into the fold'.

10¹¹ᵇ. A new thought is introduced here. The thief's purpose is to

---

[1] And not only the parables (cf. Mt. 11²⁵).

kill [10¹⁰]; the good shepherd, on the contrary, offers his own life as a sacrifice for the sheep.

As before, at 7⁴³ and 9¹⁶, so now at 10¹⁹⁻²¹ we read of 'schism' or division among the Lord's hearers, and the passage ends with an expression of varying judgements. Many would forthwith dismiss Him from consideration, as being mentally deranged (cf. Mk. 3²¹) through demoniacal possession, a charge already made at 7²⁰, 8⁴⁸, ⁵²; but others are impressed, both by His teaching, and by His act or sign in ch. 9. Thus it is indirectly but clearly emphasized that the Lord's words and acts together make up His one work.

In 10²²⁻³⁹ we read of the last direct encounter of the Lord with the Jews during the ministry. The verses deal with the question of the Lord's Messiahship, an essentially Jewish problem; and His replies to the Jews include an argument in 10³⁴⁻³⁶, based, in very Jewish fashion, on a passage of scripture. The doctrine of the Lord's oneness with the Father [10³⁰] was also likely to cause especial difficulty to the Jews, whose religion was so strongly monotheistic. Hence, just as at the outset, before the ministry opens with the Lord's presence at a wedding in Cana of Galilee at 2¹⁻¹², the tone and atmosphere of the introductory passage 1¹⁹⁻⁵¹, in which traditional Jewish messianic titles are given to the Lord, are more markedly Jewish than those of the following sections, so now in this final controversial passage the Jewish atmosphere is once more prominent.

Although we pass here to a new festival, that of the encaenia or dedication [10²²], the narrative is closely linked with the events of the preceding feast of tabernacles [7¹⁰ to 10²¹], and the teaching given in 10¹⁻²¹ is taken up afresh and developed. For the Jews now once more attempt to arrest [10³⁹] and to kill [10³¹] the Lord, as they did at 7²⁵, ³⁰, ³², 8⁵⁹; and the imagery in 10¹¹⁻¹⁵ of the sheep and of their relation to the Lord, their good Shepherd, is resumed in 10²⁷, ²⁸.

But 10²²⁻³⁹ also looks forward, and here too in respect not only of events but also of teaching; for, as regards the event, the Jews, in the passion, will soon achieve their purpose; while, as regards the teaching, the words of 10²⁷, ²⁸, 'My sheep hear my voice . . . and I give unto them . . . life, and they shall never perish', are about to be fulfilled in the Lord's gift of life to and on behalf of Lazarus, in a work independent of the plotting and achievement of the Jews.

On the surface the purpose of 10²², ²³ is to acquaint the reader with the occasion, the season, and the locality of the Lord's final controversy with the Jews, which follows. The feast of the dedication was celebrated in December, and commemorated the most recent Jewish national deliverance, which had culminated in the rededication of the temple by Judas Maccabaeus in 165 B.C., three years after its desecration by the Seleucid conqueror, Antiochus Epiphanes. And on the present occasion the Lord, owing to the severity of the weather, is found in the covered cloister of one of the oldest and most historic parts of the temple. But it would be entirely in accord with the evangelist's method, if these simple details of the external circumstances are found, on deeper consideration, to provide also a reference to the spiritual crisis now at hand. We have already learned at 2¹⁹⁻²¹ that the Jewish temple is to be destroyed and will be replaced, after and as a result of the Lord's death and resurrection, by the temple of His body; and immediately before He Himself is delivered up at His arrest, He speaks [17¹⁹] of consecrating or dedicating Himself for the sake of His disciples; and in the present section we read at 10³⁶ that the Father has consecrated or dedicated Him and sent Him into the world. Accordingly, just as in chs. 7 and 8 at the feast of tabernacles, with its ritual of the drawing of water and the kindling of lights, the Lord offers life-giving water and proclaims that He Himself is the light of the world, so here the Lord's ministry, which will reach its climax in the passion, is set forth as the true dedication, which is to supersede and replace the Jewish festival.

But the events are full of tragic paradox. For Jesus is the Messiah of the Jews; He has been sent to realize, at their capital Jerusalem, the age-long hopes of the people of Israel, which would appropriately be much in mind at a festival commemorating a heroic national deliverance. And yet His own nation, as represented by its leaders, has already rejected and is now about to do away with Him, and in so doing will effect its own destruction. It is indeed winter, the season of death, without and within.

10¹⁴, ¹⁵. It is a feature of the teaching of this gospel, already apparent in 6⁵⁷ but more strongly emphasized in the later chapters (e.g. 14²⁰, 17¹⁸, 20²¹), that the relationship between the Lord and His disciples is to reproduce the perfect, permanent relationship between the Father and Himself.

10¹⁷, ¹⁸. In the N.T. the Lord's resurrection is usually regarded as the act of His Father, who raises Him from the dead (e.g. Gal. 1¹); but in Mark (with one exception, at 14²⁸), as here, the Lord speaks of the 'rising again' as His own act (cf. Lk. 18³³, 24⁷, ⁴⁶).

10¹⁸. The R.V. mg 'took it away' may be correct. If so, the Lord speaks here, as He speaks also throughout chs. 14 to 17 (e.g. 16³³, 'I have overcome the world'), as though His death were already an accomplished fact.

10²². The variant reading of R.V. mg may be correct; for although the Greek word translated here 'at that time' only occurs in John some ten times, its use perhaps marks the contexts in which it appears, as having special significance. If so, the word is used here to introduce the account of the Lord's last controversy with the Jews.

10²³. If St. John was acquainted with Mark, it may be no accident that he here mentions that the Lord 'was walking in the temple'. For in Mark these same words occur at Mk. 11²⁷, immediately before the religious leaders come to Him and raise the question of His authority, a section followed at once by the Lord's parable of the only son and the wicked husbandmen [Mk. 12¹⁻¹²], in which He shows that in killing the only son the husbandmen will themselves perish and will lose their vineyard. And, as we have seen, it is the question of the Lord's Messiahship and therefore of His authority which lies behind Jn. 10²⁴⁻³⁸ also; and in these verses He shows further that, whereas His sheep will never perish [10²⁸], the Jews, because they do not believe [10²⁶], are not of and do not belong to His sheep.

Similarly we may compare the mention of 'the treasury' at 8²⁰, in the middle of a controversial section, with the mention of it in Mk. 12⁴¹, at the close of the questions put to or by the Lord in 12¹³⁻³⁷, and His warning uttered against the scribes in 12³⁸⁻⁴⁰.

10²⁴. The R.V. rendering of the Jews' question is perhaps correct, although the Greek words would more naturally and also more literally be translated, 'How long dost thou excite (or, uplift, stimulate) our soul?', an impossible rendering in this context. Hence it should be considered whether there is not here a signal example of St. John's subtlety. For the Greek noun means 'life' as well as 'soul', and the Greek verb means 'to take away' (as at 1²⁹) as well as 'to uplift', and it is these two same words which the Lord has used just before in the preceding verses, when He says at 10¹⁸, 'No one taketh (or, took) it [my life] away from me, but I lay it down of myself'. If, then, the Jews' question in 10²⁴ is translated in the same way, it must mean, 'How long dost thou take away our life?' i.e. destroy us. At 11⁴⁸ the high priest Caiaphas will be found arguing that, if the Lord is left any longer at liberty, all men will believe on Him, and the Romans will intervene and take away (the same Greek verb) the Jews' place and their nation. It is therefore agreed [11⁵³] that the Lord must be put to death. But in chs. 7 and 8 the Lord had twice warned the Jews that, unless they accepted His claims, they would die in their sin, which at 9⁴¹ is said to remain (or abide, continue); and at 10¹⁶ He has spoken of other sheep which He must add to those of the original fold; and of this united flock He will be the one Shepherd. The Jews therefore realize that, if He is the Messiah, with, so to speak, a universal programme, there can be no future for a Jewry which rejects Him; the historic, exclusive Judaism which they value and to which they cling is being undermined and its life sapped. Everything therefore turns on the question, which they proceed to raise, of the Lord's messianic office and authority.

10²⁵. In this gospel, although the Lord is described by Andrew in the introductory section 1¹⁹⁻⁵¹ as the Messiah or Christ [1⁴¹], and although in the following chapters (consistently with the fact that in John there is no secrecy about His Person) He has used of Himself many expressions clearly implying divinity, e.g. 5¹⁷, ¹⁸, 8⁵⁶⁻⁵⁸, He has not yet, in conversation with the Jews, explicitly called Himself by the title of Messiah. The necessity for this reserve was probably due, not so much to the contemporary vagueness about the Messiah's office and functions, as to some of the implications about its nature which were entertained by the Jews at the time and were altogether at variance with the mind and work of the Lord. St. John prefers, it seems, to emphasize again and again that the Lord has been sent from and by the Father, who knows Him, and whom He knows; in this mission of His and its fulfilment he finds the true work of the Lord's messianic office; and therefore, in spite of the first sentence of this note, no difficulty should be found in the Lord's reply [10²⁵].

Again, many of the readers of this book would be Gentile Christians, ignorant of the traditional Jewish hope of the Messiah, a term which therefore held little of religious meaning for them. Accordingly, although the evangelist expressly says at 20³¹ that part of his purpose in writing the book has been to convince his readers that Jesus is the Messiah, yet he prefers on the whole to present the Lord as the unique Son, e.g. 3³⁵, 5¹⁹⁻²¹, the one and only Mediator [3¹³] between heaven and earth, who both brings the Father's life and gifts to men and also presents men, in and through Himself, to the Father.

10²⁷⁻³⁰. The union of the Father and the Son is such that the Lord's words and works are indeed the words and works of God. For the same reason it can be said with equal truth that the Lord's sheep cannot be torn from His keeping, and that they cannot be torn from the keeping of the Father.

10²⁹. The readings in this verse are uncertain; the R.V. text may be accepted as probably correct.

The Lord as the Resurrection and the Life

40 And he went away again beyond Jordan into the place where John was
41 at the first baptizing; and there he abode. And many came unto him;
and they said, John indeed did no sign: but all things whatsoever John
42 spake of this man were true. And many believed on him there.

11 Now a certain man was sick, Lazarus of Bethany, of the village of
2 Mary and her sister Martha. And it was that Mary which anointed the
Lord with ointment, and wiped his feet with her hair, whose brother
3 Lazarus was sick. The sisters therefore sent unto him, saying, Lord,
4 behold, he whom thou lovest is sick. But when Jesus heard it, he said,
This sickness is not unto death, but for the glory of God, that the Son
5 of God may be glorified thereby. Now Jesus loved Martha, and her
6 sister, and Lazarus. When therefore he heard that he was sick, he abode
7 at that time two days in the place where he was. Then after this he saith
8 to the disciples, Let us go into Judaea again. The disciples say unto him,
Rabbi, the Jews were but now seeking to stone thee; and goest thou
9 thither again? Jesus answered, Are there not twelve hours in the day?
If a man walk in the day, he stumbleth not, because he seeth the light
10 of this world. But if a man walk in the night, he stumbleth, because the
11 light is not in him. These things spake he: and after this he saith unto
them, Our friend Lazarus is fallen asleep; but I go, that I may awake
12 him out of sleep. The disciples therefore said unto him, Lord, if he is
13 fallen asleep, he will ¹recover. Now Jesus had spoken of his death: but
14 they thought that he spake of taking rest in sleep. Then Jesus therefore
15 said unto them plainly, Lazarus is dead. And I am glad for your sakes
that I was not there, to the intent ye may believe; nevertheless let us go
16 unto him. Thomas therefore, who is called ²Didymus, said unto his
fellow-disciples, Let us also go, that we may die with him.

17   So when Jesus came, he found that he had been in the tomb four days
18 already. Now Bethany was nigh unto Jerusalem, about fifteen furlongs
19 off; and many of the Jews had come to Martha and Mary, to console
20 them concerning their brother. Martha therefore, when she heard that
Jesus was coming, went and met him: but Mary still sat in the house.
21 Martha therefore said unto Jesus, Lord, if thou hadst been here, my
22 brother had not died. And even now I know that, whatsoever thou shalt
23 ask of God, God will give thee. Jesus saith unto her, Thy brother shall
24 rise again. Martha saith unto him, I know that he shall rise again in the
25 resurrection at the last day. Jesus said unto her, I am the resurrection,

---

¹ *Gr.* be saved.   ² *That is* Twin.

and the life: he that believeth on me, though he die, yet shall he live:
26 And whosoever liveth and believeth on me shall never die. Believest
27 thou this? She saith unto him, Yea, Lord: I have believed that thou
28 art the Christ, the Son of God, *even* he that cometh into the world. And
when she had said this, she went away, and called Mary [1]her sister
29 secretly, saying, The [2]Master is here, and calleth thee. And she, when
30 she heard it, arose quickly, and went unto him. (Now Jesus was not yet
come into the village, but was still in the place where Martha met him.)
31 The Jews then which were with her in the house, and were comforting
her, when they saw Mary, that she rose up quickly and went out,
followed her, supposing that she was going unto the tomb to [3]weep
32 there. Mary therefore, when she came where Jesus was, and saw him,
fell down at his feet, saying unto him, Lord, if thou hadst been here, my
33 brother had not died. When Jesus therefore saw her [4]weeping, and the
Jews *also* [4]weeping which came with her, he [5]groaned in the spirit, and
34 [6]was troubled, and said, Where have ye laid him? They say unto him,
35 Lord, come and see. Jesus wept. The Jews therefore said, Behold how
36
37 he loved him! But some of them said, Could not this man, which opened
the eyes of him that was blind, have caused that this man also should not
38 die? Jesus therefore again [7]groaning in himself cometh to the tomb. Now
39 it was a cave, and a stone lay [8]against it. Jesus saith, Take ye away the
stone. Martha, the sister of him that was dead, saith unto him, Lord, by
40 this time he stinketh: for he hath been *dead* four days. Jesus saith unto
her, Said I not unto thee, that, if thou believedst, thou shouldest see the
41 glory of God? So they took away the stone. And Jesus lifted up his eyes,
42 and said, Father, I thank thee that thou heardest me. And I knew that
thou hearest me always: but because of the multitude which standeth
43 around I said it, that they may believe that thou didst send me. And
when he had thus spoken, he cried with a loud voice, Lazarus, come forth.
44 He that was dead came forth, bound hand and foot with [9]grave-clothes;
and his face was bound about with a napkin. Jesus saith unto them,
Loose him, and let him go.

45   Many therefore of the Jews, which came to Mary and beheld [10]that
46 which he did, believed on him. But some of them went away to the
Pharisees, and told them the things which Jesus had done.

47   The chief priests therefore and the Pharisees gathered a council, and
48 said, What do we? for this man doeth many signs. If we let him thus
alone, all men will believe on him: and the Romans will come and take
49 away both our place and our nation. But a certain one of them, Caiaphas,

---

[1] *Or* her sister, saying secretly   [2] *Or* Teacher   [3] *Gr.* wail.
[4] *Gr.* wailing.   [5] *Or* was moved with indignation in the spirit
[6] *Gr.* troubled himself.   [7] *Or* being moved with indignation in himself
[8] *Or* upon   [9] *Or* grave-bands   [10] *Many ancient authorities read* the
things which he did.

50 being high priest that year, said unto them, Ye know nothing at all, nor
do ye take account that it is expedient for you that one man should die
51 for the people, and that the whole nation perish not. Now this he said
not of himself: but being high priest that year, he prophesied that Jesus
52 should die for the nation; and not for the nation only, but that he might
also gather together into one the children of God that are scattered
53 abroad. So from that day forth they took counsel that they might put
him to death.

EXPOSITION OF SECTION 5.   10⁴⁰–11⁵³

The Lord's word and work again combined:
  1. Work. The illness and death of Lazarus at Bethany, 11¹⁻¹⁶; the Lord's
     journey there, 11¹⁷⁻¹⁷; His restoration of Lazarus to life, 11⁴³⁻⁴⁴.
  2. Word. The Lord teaches Martha that He is the resurrection and
     the life, 11²⁰⁻²⁷.

This section ends with the formal condemnation of the Lord to death by
the Sanhedrin, 11⁴⁵⁻⁵³.

Except for the Lord's final entry into Jerusalem and the events
which follow it, His work in the capital, and in particular His
mission to the leaders of His nation, is now over; and we hear of
Him residing for a time east of Jordan, a residence which may be
identical with that mentioned in Mk. 10¹, probably at the first
scene of John's preaching and baptism (1²⁸ as opposed to 3²³),
which seem to be recalled here with a special purpose. For 'the
things spoken by John' about the Lord in the earlier chapters
consisted chiefly in his witness to the Lord as (1) the Lamb of God
lifting, removing the sin of the world [1²⁹], and (2) the Son of God
[1³⁴], infinitely greater than himself [1¹⁵, ²⁷], who would increase in
proportion as he, John himself, decreased [3²⁷⁻³⁰], and whose
baptism would be in Holy Spirit [1³³]. In the present context,
however, which contains the last reference to John in this gospel,
it is even more important to recall 1³¹, where the Baptist says that
he came, baptizing in water, in order that the Greater than he
'might be made manifest to Israel'. This manifestation has just
been completed, and, since official Judaism has rejected the Lord,
it might perhaps seem that the Baptist's testimony had proved
false, or that the Lord had failed to carry out John's expectation
of Him. This passage, on the contrary, emphasizes that John's
every word was true; the Lord was manifested to Israel; unlike

the Baptist himself, who did no sign, the Lord has done works which carried their inward significance with them, and His witness therefore has been greater [5³⁶] than that of John; but yet Israel did not respond and believe. Many, however, who now resort to the Lord, are enabled to realize the truth of the Baptist's witness to Him and accordingly 'believed on Him there'. Thus this introduction to ch. 11, with which its epilogue 11⁵⁴⁻⁵⁷ should be compared, serves two purposes. First, it separates off the supreme event of 11¹⁻⁴⁴, together with the meeting of the Sanhedrin which is called in consequence of that event, from the immediately preceding context, and thus gives it a certain independence, and even isolation; and secondly, it reminds the reader that the chief priests and Pharisees are not the only people in the story. Beyond Jordan, at any rate, were many holy and humble men of heart, for whom the Lord's work had not proved vain; and therewith we pass to ch. 11.

Advice, direct or indirect, is given to the Lord in this gospel at 2³, when His mother, during the wedding feast at Cana, tells her Son of the failure of the wine, in the words 'They have no wine'; at 7³, when His brethren urge the Lord to leave Galilee and to manifest Himself openly in Judaea; and here [11³], where the form of the message sent by the two sisters, especially if considered in the light of 11²¹, ³², reveals their belief that the news of their brother's illness will at once, and in time, bring the Lord to the help of His sick friend and therefore of themselves. In each of the three cases the Lord in the end acts as it is suggested that He should; but, again in each case, He does not do so forthwith. We are thus reminded of the constant teaching of this gospel that He does not do His own will, but the will of Him who sent Him; thus in the present case He does not act on human instigation, but does, as always, the things that are pleasing to His Father [8²⁹] and the issue of events will show that in the present case the will of the Father is delay.

On hearing of the illness the Lord pronounces that it is not fatal, but has as its purpose the glory of God, a glory in which the Son of God is also to share. The Lord, we read at 8⁵⁰, does not seek His own glory, but the glory of Him that sent Him, that is, the Father [7¹⁸]; but since the glory of the Father and that of the Son form a unity, the Lord, in glorifying the Father, is also glorified Himself [12²⁸, 13³¹, ³²]. It is natural to think that the reference in 11⁴ is to the event of 11³⁹⁻⁴⁴, and no doubt a reference to it is included, especially when we recall the Lord's words to Martha in 11⁴⁰; but we are to learn, explicitly, in the later chapters, that the Father is glorified in the death, the self-offering, of His Son, who in thus revealing the glory of God is Himself glorified; and, as will be shown, later in this chapter, at 11⁴⁷⁻⁵³, it is after and because of the events of 11¹⁻⁴⁶, that the Jewish council resolves upon the Lord's death. Thus the deeper meaning of the Lord's words in 11⁴ becomes clear; the Lord's revelation of Himself, not in an act of healing, as suggested and desired by the sisters, but as Himself the resurrection and the life, and shown to be such through the restoration of their brother, will be the immediate cause of the Lord's death upon the cross, and therefore of the glory of God, and therewith of the glorification of the Son of God.

An interval therefore of two days, a period no doubt of vital importance if the Lord's purpose had been to prevent Lazarus from dying,¹ is allowed to pass, in spite, it might seem, of the Lord's affection for the sisters and their brother.

I turn aside for a moment to consider Dr. Bernard's criticism (*I.C.C.*, St. John, p. 375) of the view here taken. It is, he thinks, unlikely to be correct, since it implies that the Lord 'was content to leave the sisters in the agony of grief for three or four days, in order that "the glory of God" might be more signally vindicated in the end'. I would submit that this contention fails to perceive the direction or the depth of St. John's thought. If Lazarus had not died, his sisters would not have witnessed the Lord's conquest of death, the last enemy [1 Cor. 15²⁶], and therefore they would not have experienced the final and fullest revelation of God, a conquest requiring and indeed only achieved by the death of His Son; for it should always be kept in mind that in this gospel the Lord's death is presented as due, above all else, to His gift of life to Lazarus.

---

¹ The Lord's cure of the nobleman's son from a distance [4⁴⁶⁻⁵⁴] shows that Lazarus' health could have been restored, had such been the divine will, as soon as the news of his illness reached the Lord. For it does not seem probable that, as has been suggested on the ground of the notes of time in this chapter [11⁶, ¹⁷, ³⁹], Lazarus was already dead when the news of his illness first reached the Lord, and that the Lord was at that time aware of his death. The Lord is aware of it by 11¹¹; but it appears that He only learns when it occurred, on His arrival at Bethany [11¹⁷]. The question whether the Lord had Himself to be present at Bethany for the raising of Lazarus need not and should not be raised. St. John's purpose is to show that His voluntary return to Judaea, a place of danger [11⁸, ¹⁶], for the restoration of Lazarus to life, becomes the immediate cause of His own death.

Because Lazarus lives, He died. Hence the Lord by His action, or rather inaction, showed the deepest and truest love for His friends, a deeper and truer love than would have been manifested if He had only cured Lazarus of a temporary illness; and perhaps this is silently emphasized by St. John when he writes of the Lord's affection for the sisters and their brother immediately before his mention of the Lord's apparently strange delay in 11⁶. Only through this delay can they and the disciples be brought to belief [11¹⁵].

When at 11⁷ the Lord proposes a return into Judaea, the disciples think at once of the danger to their Master's safety. He, however, as is implied in verses 9 and 10, is thinking, not of Himself, but of His work in obedience to the Father's will. And His knowledge of the reason for the illness of Lazarus shows Him the Father's will that He and His disciples should now so return. In thus obeying the Father, He cannot but be walking in the light [11⁹, ¹⁰], even if it leads Him, as it will, into the night, when His work in the salvation of men will have been accomplished [9⁴, ⁵]; and the same law will hold good also of those who accompany or follow Him; for since He is Himself 'the light of the world', those who follow Him 'shall not walk in the darkness, but shall have the light of life' [8¹²]. The unexpected 'in him' at the end of verse 10 warns the reader that the purpose of the apparently simple words in verses 9 and 10 is to teach spiritual truth; and even in verses 11 to 16, when we are brought back to what we may call the surface record of events, certain expressions will convey more than their surface implications to the attentive reader. Thus the Lord's words 'I go' in verse 11 are of great importance; for He is going (*a*) to enter the domain of death, in order to recover Lazarus therefrom, and (*b*) in consequence of this act, Himself to die. Next, in verse 12 the disciples suggest that a refreshing sleep will of itself effect the cure; but unconsciously they state the truth that men must fall asleep, that is, die, in order to be saved —note the R.V. margin. Again, in verse 15 the disciples learn that, as a consequence of the Lord's absence when His friend died, they are to be led to belief; and we recall the Lord's assurance at 6⁴⁷, 'He that believeth hath eternal life'. And finally the remark of Thomas in verse 16 is probably to be understood, in accordance with the portrayal of his temperament elsewhere in this gospel, as despairingly yet doggedly faithful; but the reader will understand it also in the light of 12²⁴⁻²⁶, or of Rom. 6⁸, 'If we died with Christ,

we believe that we shall also live with him'. As it happens, this is
the first occasion in this book, when the truth is brought to light,
that disciples must be prepared to share their Master's fate (cf.
Mk. 8³⁴⁻³⁷).

At 11¹⁹ we read of Jews who had anticipated the Lord in coming
out from Jerusalem, about two miles off, to offer consolation to
Martha and Mary; and when the paragraph 11¹⁷⁻⁴⁴ opens, they are
in the house with the sisters [11¹⁹, ²⁰, ³¹], but the Lord is still at a
distance [11³⁰]. On receiving news of the Lord's approach, Martha,
true to her temperament, if we may judge from 12² and Lk. 10⁴⁰,
is at once up and doing; but the doing consists in meeting the
Lord, first (as it seems probable that her words should be understood) with an indirect reproach for His delay in coming and His
consequent failure to save her brother's life, and secondly with a
half request, which again she does not dare to put directly. So
great, she is convinced, is His power with God, that even now, at
His request, the delay may be made good. It should be particularly
noticed that Martha speaks of a boon to be obtained from God,
and dispensed by the Lord, the Lord Himself being, as it were,
no more than an intermediary in the matter. In reply the Lord
appears only to offer comfort by reminding Martha of the Jewish
hope of resurrection, a comfort which had no doubt been already
offered by her other friends [11¹⁹]. Martha acknowledges her
acceptance of the doctrine, but implies also that it does not restore
her brother or assuage her present grief; the last day is a long way
off. Hereupon the Lord, in correction of her thought, offers her
Himself; He is the resurrection and the life; let her concentrate
her thought on Him. She had spoken of a boon to be obtained by
Him from God; He replies that the boon is a personal communication of the Lord Himself, who has taken human nature upon Him,
precisely in order to be able to impart this gift. Accordingly for
those who believe in Him, that is, who see in Him the divine Word
become flesh on their behalf, death has lost its sting; so far from
having power to destroy, it has become the gate of life. The fact,
however, that the Lord speaks of Himself here primarily as the
resurrection, and not only as the life, emphasizes the truth that the
life which comes through Him is only attainable through death;
the believer, if he is to receive or gain all, must be prepared also to
sacrifice all. There is no depreciation of life as we already know it;
all life forms a part of that which is here in view; the same word

'life' is applied to existence as we know it, and to that which is here offered by the Lord; but he who is born anew will never look to any form of life, which he at present knows, as able to give him a full or final satisfaction. Not only, therefore, is nothing too good to be true; but equally nothing which at present forms part of his experience is good enough to be altogether or finally true. *Nescio, nescio quae iubilatio* must always be the last human word on these mysteries.

To the Lord's question 'Believest thou this?' Martha responds with a formal confession of faith, showing that she sees the author of salvation in the Lord. But although her confession is largely formulated in the same words as those which form the conclusion of the book, it is noticeable that in her response there is no reference, as there is at 20³¹, to the receiving of life by the believer from the Lord, and further, that her addition of the words 'he that cometh into the world' is part of the imperfect confession of the multitude at 6¹⁴. When we also consider that her words are accompanied by no act of worship, as at 9³⁸, or of prostration, as at 11³², and when we recall the protest which she will make at 11³⁹, on the Lord's command to take away the stone from the grave, it becomes probable that the reader should regard her formal confession as less perfect than the simpler but whole-hearted 'I believe' of 9³⁸.

The Lord's revelation has now been made, in word; but it remains to be carried out, in action; for, as will be suggested later, St. John seems to wish to emphasize that no degree of belief, except perhaps that of Mary, is able to dispense with outward evidence. As the Lord Himself says, earlier in this gospel, 'Except ye see signs and wonders, ye will in no wise believe' [4⁴⁸].

Martha now returns to her sister, whom she informs privately of the Teacher's arrival, and of His wish to see her. Possibly, just as the disciples at 11⁸, and elsewhere in this gospel, address the Lord as 'Rabbi', a word which means 'teacher', so here John, by Martha, applies the simple word 'teacher' to the Lord, in spite of the stupendous self-revelation which He has just made, in order that the reader may keep steadily in view the human nature of the Lord, especially in this chapter, and thereby the cost to Him of performing this, His greatest work.

On receiving the Lord's summons, Mary, who had hitherto remained with the Jews in the house, at once sets out to go to Him; and the Jews from Jerusalem, mistaking her purpose, accompany her, as they suppose, towards the grave and are thus brought, unexpectedly and involuntarily, into the presence of the Lord, who, as the reader knows, has just revealed Himself to the believer as the conqueror of death. On coming into His presence and seeing Him, Mary prostrates herself and repeats the words already uttered by her sister; no doubt they had been often on the lips of the sisters in the last four days, and possibly they still contain an indirect reproach; but in the light of her prostration at His feet and of the facts that the words are used by Mary, whose temperament, as we know, is different from that of Martha, and that, unlike Martha, she does not follow them up by any request but leaves the issue wholly to the Lord, the reader is perhaps meant to think now chiefly of their deeper implication, namely, that death and the presence of the Lord are incompatible. At present, however, Mary, no less than the Jews who accompany her, is blind to this truth, as is shown by their and her lamentation; and the Lord, in the face of the distress around Him, now takes their distress upon Himself. We should notice particularly the R.V. margin as regards the last words of verse 33. He Himself, in His first words recorded in this gospel, at 1^{35-42}, had invited two of John's disciples, who were following Him, to 'come and see' where He abode; and this had resulted in their own discipleship and that of others; in other words, by following Him, they had themselves received 'the light of life' [8^{12}]. But now He is Himself invited by the mourners round Him to leave the place and the light which are His by nature and by right, and to 'come and see' [11^{34}]—and so, if the analogy with $1^{38, 39}$ may be pressed, to become associated with—darkness and death, since those around Him regard darkness and death as being in control of the situation; and the strain upon Him finds expression in an outburst of tears. The Jews [11^{36}] interpret the Lord's emotion as revealing His sense of the greatness of His loss in the death of His friend; but the reader perceives that they are giving unconscious testimony to a far greater proof of the Lord's affection, which is about to be shown in His bestowal on Lazarus of life; the Lord is laying down His life for His friend, and there can be no greater love than this [15^{13}]. Others among the Jews, also assuming that the Lord's grief shows Him to have reached the limit of His powers, express surprise that He who had given sight where no sight was, could not also have saved Lazarus from dying. In this way the coming sign, the Lord's crowning act of His ministry, is linked closely with the work which immediately preceded it; and all the Lord's signs are shown to be parts of His one great work (cf. 11⁴⁷; for it is no accident that, although this final meeting of the Sanhedrin is called as a result of this, the Lord's, last work, the proceedings open with the words, 'This man doeth many signs').

The grave itself seems to have been of the same kind as that of the Lord. In His case, no human agency was required, to move the stone [20¹; cf. 10¹⁸]; but in the present case the Lord has to order its removal. Martha's protest [11³⁹] reveals that she, no less than her sister and the Jews, and in spite of the revelation made to her in 11²⁵, ²⁶, is unable to believe, unless the miracle takes place. She should have known that, where the Lord is, there cannot be corruption; and the glory of God is shown in that He, the Lord, by taking death, for man's sake, into and upon Himself, is and is about to show Himself to be the resurrection and the life. But His reply to her [11⁴⁰] also reminds the reader that only a believer can or will see the glory of God. On the present occasion not only Martha and Mary, but the Jews [11¹⁹, ³¹⁻³⁴], the disciples [11¹⁵], and the multitude [11⁴²] are present, and all, as is emphasized later [12⁹, ¹⁷, ¹⁸], witness with their physical sight that which now takes place; but only believers are enabled to see or penetrate its significance, namely, the conquest of death by the Lord, and therefore the depth of His love for man. Some of the Jews indeed only become confirmed in their hostility (cf. Lk. 16³¹), and add to their hostility to the Lord hostility also to the recipient of His gift [12¹⁰].

We now reach the latter part of 11⁴¹. The Lord twice raises His eyes to His Father in this gospel, here and at 17¹; but the words are not exactly the same in the two places. Here the Lord is found at the lowest depth of His condescension for our sake, and the Greek words here express this: 'He raised His eyes upward.' And yet, even at this moment, since He knows the Father and the Father knows Him [10¹⁵] and the Father's will is His will also [4³⁴, 5³⁰, 6³⁶, 8²⁹], He knows that His wish (a wish which in the case of the Lord is, as always, a prayer) that He may save men to the uttermost is in complete accordance with the Father's wish; and therefore He can now, *before* uttering the words of power, thank the Father that His request has already been heard, and will now be granted. Cause will thus be given both to His disciples [11¹⁵] and to the multitude present [11⁴²] to believe that the Father did send Him (cf. 17²³, ²⁵), and thereby to know the truth and to be free [8³²].

In passing to 11⁴³, it is important to bear in mind that in all the earlier gospels the Lord is recorded as having uttered a loud voice or cry, immediately before His death.[1] This is not so in St. John's record of the crucifixion; in his gospel the loud voice or cry is uttered now; and further, the use of a comparatively rare Greek verb here for 'cried' is remarkable, especially as it is applied to the Lord; for it will be used four times, in the last scenes in this gospel, of those who cry out for the Lord's death. It seems, therefore, that in more ways than one St. John closely links the Lord's bestowal of life upon Lazarus with the traditional accounts of the Lord's last moments, when according to our first two gospels,[2] quoting the first words of Ps. 22, He found or believed Himself deserted by His Father; and a careful study of all the facts, of which only two are mentioned here, may convince the reader that according to St. John in this moment, at the grave of Lazarus, at least as truly as in that of 19³⁰, the moment of the Lord's death, is to be found the lowest depth of the Lord's devotion and self-abasement for man's sake. And once more we find a contrast to the story of the Lord's resurrection in ch. 20. We have already noticed, in connexion with 11³⁸, ³⁹, that at the Lord's resurrection the stone was found removed; and we should now notice also that the linen-cloths, and the napkin which was upon His head, were left behind Him in the grave. Again, the Lord had said to the Jews, 'Destroy this shrine, and in three days I will raise it up' [2¹⁹], and 'Therefore doth the Father love me, because I lay down my life, that I may take it again. No one taketh it away from me, but I lay it down of myself. I have the right to lay it down, and I have the right to take it again. This commandment I received from my Father' [10¹⁷, ¹⁸]. Hence, in the case of the Lord's resurrection, human help and action do not come into the matter at all. But in the case of Lazarus, just as the stone had to be moved [11³⁹] before the action of the Lord, so Lazarus now comes forth indeed, but he is still helpless, tied and bound with the shackles of the grave. He cannot free

[1] The student, who wishes to grasp all the important issues in this matter, should consult a valuable article by the Rev. E. K. Lee, M.A., in *The Expository Times* for February 1950.

[2] It will be found profitable in this connexion to compare carefully St. Luke's record, including his use of words, with that of (*a*) St. Matthew and St. Mark, (*b*) St. John.

himself of his impediments without the help of friends; but, this being given at the bidding of the Lord, he can go upon his way.

On pp. 144–5, in connexion with the Lord's address to the Jews in 5¹⁹⁻⁴⁷ on His work as life-giver and as judge, it was pointed out that, whereas in 5²⁴, ²⁵ the emphasis, with regard to the Lord's gift of life, is primarily in respect of the present (we may compare 6⁴⁷, 'he that believeth hath eternal life'), in 5²⁸, ²⁹ the reference is solely to the future; 'all that are in the tombs' are to 'hear His voice' and to 'come forth to a resurrection', in some cases to 'a resurrection of life', in others to 'a resurrection of judgement'. The fulfilment of 5²⁴, ²⁵, in other words the Lord's gift of life as a present fact, has received frequent illustration, both by His works and by His words, in John; but only in ch. 11, first in the Lord's words to Martha at 11²⁵, and then in His work at 11⁴³, ⁴⁴, do we find a fulfilment of 5²⁸, ²⁹; and the feature already noticed, that in 11²⁵ the primary reference is to resurrection, invites us to connect 11¹⁻⁴⁴ very closely with 5²⁸, ²⁹. In ch. 11, therefore, the future is, in a single case, brought into the present; the resurrection 'at the last day', a doctrine which Martha accepted, but in which she had not found the comfort that she hoped, becomes a present fact; for a single human being that hour, which is to come for every man, now is. The inference is clear; He who thus speaks and acts is the Lord not only of life but also of death; and the difference between the life now offered by the Lord to the believer and that which he will receive from Him hereafter is a difference of degree only, not of kind. But the reader will be careful to remember the place which ch. 11¹⁻⁴⁴ holds in St. John's record; as a result of this final revelation by the Lord in word and deed, He Himself will die; He is made known as the conqueror of death, only because for man's sake He willingly subjects Himself to it [10¹¹, ¹⁵, ¹⁷, ¹⁸, 11⁷⁻¹⁰]. And here we may notice a final difference between the Lord's resurrection and that of Lazarus. The Lord, being raised from the dead, dieth no more [Rom. 6⁹]; but Lazarus, although his present individual resurrection is set forth in Jn. 11 as a sign of the future universal resurrection, was not thereby freed from future dissolution in the course of time.

Throughout the Lord's ministry His works or signs have had different effects upon those who witnessed or experienced them, the chief of these effects being the two extremes of attraction and repulsion, belief and disbelief; contrast, for example, 2¹¹, ²³, 4⁵³, ⁵⁴ with

5¹⁶, ³⁶⁻³⁸, 7³⁻⁵; and the same results have followed from His word (or words) and teaching; contrast, for example, 2²², 4⁴¹, ⁵⁰, ⁵³, 8³⁰ with 3¹², 5⁴⁷, 8⁴⁵. It is therefore to be expected that the Lord's last and greatest revelation during the ministry, a revelation, as we have seen, both in word [11²⁵, ²⁶] and in deed [11⁴²⁻⁴⁴], will produce the two contrasted states in the highest degree; and this we now find in 11⁴⁵, ⁴⁶ to be the case. Whereas many of the Jews, who on account of their affection for Mary [11⁴⁵] were present and had shared her grief [11³³], believed on Him, others of them went away and reported the Lord's latest activities to the Pharisees, thereby forging the first link in the final chain of events which ended in His death upon the cross.

The evangelist first deals with the negative result, disbelief and hatred. The Pharisees, who in this as in the earlier gospels seem to be the greatest opponents of the Lord and have already once combined with the chief priests against Him [7³², ⁴⁵], now do so again [11⁴⁶, ⁴⁷]. At the meeting it seems to be admitted, by the use of the word 'signs', that the Lord's works carry a certain significance with them; but no attempt is made to estimate what this significance may be, and even Nicodemus, who at a previous meeting had put forward a plea for elementary justice [7⁵⁰], is now silent; and there is general agreement that immediate action is necessary. Otherwise, if the policy is continued of allowing the Lord to work His will unhindered, 'all men will believe on Him', that is, will accept His Messiahship as they understand it (cf. 6¹⁴, ¹⁵), and the occupying power will deprive the Jews of both their temple-worship and their national existence.

No decision, however, is reached until the high priest himself intervenes, and after a rebuke to his colleagues for their lack of resource and of perception of their interests recommends that a single life should be sacrificed on behalf of God's people rather than that the safety of the whole nation should be imperilled. In an editorial note it is pointed out that Caiaphas, the member of the council who thus speaks, was giving no merely personal advice, but was saying, with the full authority of his office, much more than he himself could know. He himself believed, no doubt, that he was pointing out the desirability, for the council, of the Lord's death, if the chosen people was to survive as the Jewish nation; but in fact, as a result of that death, the chosen people is to become the universal Church, and the whole nation is to become one with mankind; and it is for these, the Church and the world, that the Lord dies. Again, it was a distinctive function of the Jewish high priest to enter alone, once each year, into the Holy of holies, and there to offer blood, not his own, both for himself and for the ignorances of his people. Accordingly, in thus unconsciously prophesying that the Lord was about to die not only for the Jewish nation but also for 'the scattered children of God', two unities thereby to be brought together [10¹⁶] into one (although up to now the second could hardly be called a unity, except in respect of its members' common Fatherhood), Caiaphas was speaking in the only year of Jewish history when the man who held his office could so speak; for it was 'from that day', St. John continues, that the council concentrated its deliberations on the Lord's death.

NOTES TO SECTION 5.   10⁴⁰–11⁵³

11¹, ². Possibly we have here an involved form of introduction, similar to those at 4¹⁻³, 6²²⁻²⁴. On the other hand it will be suggested later that Mary's act, as described in 12¹⁻⁸ and here mentioned in anticipation, is very closely connected with the Lord's work in this chapter; and some may think this a better explanation of the forward reference in 11² to her act.

In Lk. 10³⁸⁻⁴² the name of the village where Martha and Mary lived is not given; but we now learn that it is Bethany, and that they have a brother, Lazarus. The name is the same as Eleazar, and means 'he whose help is God'. The only other person of this name in the gospels is the beggar, the counterpart of the rich man, in the parable of Lk. 16¹⁹⁻³¹.

11³. The word 'Lord' when addressed to Jesus in the vocative in John, sometimes is simply a word of respectful address, as at 4¹¹, ¹⁵, like our 'Sir'; but sometimes it implies discipleship and devotion, as at 6⁶⁸, 14²², and here.

11⁵. In 11¹ Mary is mentioned before Martha, and at 11⁴⁵ Mary alone is mentioned (contrast 11⁵, ¹⁹), although Martha was clearly the hostess (cf. Lk. 10³⁸) and therefore probably the elder. If, therefore, the order in 11¹ has any significance, it may be due to the part to be played by Mary in 11¹⁻⁴⁴ and 12¹⁻⁸, which will reveal her greater devotion to, and understanding of, the Lord.

11¹⁵. 'to the intent ye may believe'. The Lord's words, rightly understood, do not contradict what was said of the disciples, for example, at 2¹¹. Belief is a faculty which grows and develops; and the disciples' belief, although imperfect to the end [16³⁰⁻³²], will be deeper after the Lord's work, which they are now to witness, than it was before.

11¹⁶. A Hebrew word, here transliterated into 'Thomas', means 'twin'.

Thomas is mentioned in this gospel here and at 14⁵, 20²⁴⁻²⁹, 21²; and his matter-of-fact and unmystical but loyal and courageous character is clearly defined.

11¹⁸. 'fifteen furlongs' are rather less than two miles.

11³³, ³⁸. The word translated 'groaned' ('in the spirit') 11³³, 'groaning' ('in himself') 11³⁸, is used also at Mt. 9³⁰, Mk. 1⁴³, 14⁵, and seems to express resentful indignation. And just as the Lord experienced this emotion after cleansing the leper [Mk. 1⁴³], a signal example of human misery entreating His help, so here [11³³], when He is about to give life to the dead and to restore the brother to his sisters, He undergoes the same emotion at the sight of a wailing of Mary and the Jews which is due solely to their want of knowledge of His Father and of Him [17³], and of belief in His ability to help.

'troubled himself', R.V. mg. The same verb is used of the Lord in the passive voice at 12²⁷, 'Now is my soul troubled', His hour having come, and at 13²¹, He 'was troubled in spirit', just before His announcement of the disloyalty of one of the disciples; and at 14¹, ²⁷, after Judas has left [13³⁰], they are bidden, because of their belief in their Lord and in His victory, not to let their heart be overcome by this emotion. But only here do we meet the active form, He 'troubled himself'; and we recall the teaching of 5¹⁹ that the Son's actions are based upon and reproduce those of the Father. Hence what is said of the love of God at 3¹⁶, ¹⁷ is now seen working itself out in the love of the Son for the world. Just as at 10¹⁷, ¹⁸ the Lord says that He lays down His life of Himself and thereby has the Father's love, so the expression used here implies that He now voluntarily and deliberately accepts and makes His own the emotion and the experience from which it is His purpose to deliver men.

11³⁵. Juvenal, *Sat.* 15. 133 speaks of sorrow, shown by tears, as 'the noblest part of our emotions'. Other references to the Lord as weeping are found in the N.T. at Lk. 19⁴¹, Heb. 5⁷. We do not read that He also laughed, although no doubt He did so; the gospels were written for edification.

11³⁸. The stone would be extremely heavy, in order to keep beasts of prey out of the tomb.

11³⁹. The following quotation from O. C. Quick's *Christianity and Justice*, p. 39, may be apposite here. 'All men, whether in Christ or not, must be numbered with the transgressors. The death-penalty is never abolished; but to accept it in willing love as a penalty to be shared with all sinners is to change it from a penalty into a sacrifice. This metamorphosis of death is the most essential and enduring miracle of Christ. Perhaps a symbol of it in the New Testament is the fact that Christ's mortal body "saw no corruption". No sacrifice given to God could be allowed to decay. The fact that Christ's body did not decay is the proof that God accepted as a sacrifice a death which Jesus accepted as vicariously penal. That is why juridical and sacrificial language must always be used together in the theology of the Atonement, although the thoughts of a sacrificial and of a penal death are in logic mutually exclusive.'

11⁴³. 'he cried'. The Greek verb thus translated is used elsewhere in this gospel five times, always of a crowd or number of people under the influence of strong emotion: once, at 12¹³, of the great multitude shouting a welcome to the Lord on His approach to Jerusalem (it will be sought, later, to show that in thus welcoming Him, the multitude completely misunderstands the significance of His entry), and four times of the Jews [18⁴⁰, 19¹², ¹⁵] or of the chief priests and the officers [19⁶] crying for His death. See p. 250.

11⁴⁷⁻⁵⁰. In these verses the order of the Greek words more than once emphasizes the self-regarding interests of the council, as here displayed (cf. 5⁴⁴, 12⁴³).

11⁴⁸. The term 'the Romans' occurs only here in the gospels. The word 'place' may refer to Jerusalem, but more probably in particular to the temple there (cf. 4²⁰); and 'nation' will imply a community organized for social life. The Greek word thus translated occurs four times in this paragraph, and again at 18³⁵, and always in the singular. The two words 'place' and 'nation', here combined, certainly justify the view that some reference to national territory is included.

11⁴⁹. Caiaphas was high priest from A.D. 18 to A.D. 36.

'that year' (so also 11⁵¹, 18¹³), i.e. that memorable year, the year being that of the salvation of the world, and also, and therewith, of the birth of the universal religion.

11⁵⁰. On Caiaphas' lips the expressions 'the people' and 'the whole nation' will have carried the same meaning. But in the light of 11⁵¹, ⁵² the reader is meant to perceive that, while the reference in 'the people' is to the chosen people, the Jews, 'the whole nation' signifies, ultimately, all men. The human race is to become one family as a result of the Lord's death (cf. Gal. 3²⁸).

11⁵². 'the children of God that are scattered abroad', an expression normally used of the Jewish dispersion outside Palestine (cf. 7³⁵), is here applied to the Gentiles, i.e. the members of all non-Jewish nations, throughout the world. Only by the Shepherd's death can the scattered sheep be gathered into 'one flock' [10¹⁶]. In 12¹⁹, ²⁰, ²⁴, ³² St. John will emphasize strongly, though indirectly, that the Lord's death is necessary, in order to universalize the result of His mission (cf. 3¹³⁻¹⁷).

The Lord as the Messianic King through death

54 Jesus therefore walked no more openly among the Jews, but departed thence into the country near to the wilderness, into a city called Ephraim;
55 and there he tarried with the disciples. Now the passover of the Jews was at hand: and many went up to Jerusalem out of the country before
56 the passover, to purify themselves. They sought therefore for Jesus, and spake one with another, as they stood in the temple, What think ye?
57 That he will not come to the feast? Now the chief priests and the Pharisees had given commandment, that, if any man knew where he was, he should shew it, that they might take him.

12 Jesus therefore six days before the passover came to Bethany, where
2 Lazarus was, whom Jesus raised from the dead. So they made him a supper there: and Martha served; but Lazarus was one of them that sat
3 at meat with him. Mary therefore took a pound of ointment of ¹spikenard, very precious, and anointed the feet of Jesus, and wiped his feet with her hair: and the house was filled with the odour of the ointment.
4 But Judas Iscariot, one of his disciples, which should betray him, saith,
5 Why was not this ointment sold for three hundred ²pence, and given to
6 the poor? Now this he said, not because he cared for the poor; but because he was a thief, and having the ³bag ⁴took away what was put
7 therein. Jesus therefore said, ⁵Suffer her to keep it against the day of
8 my burying. For the poor ye have always with you; but me ye have not always.

9 The common people therefore of the Jews learned that he was there: and they came, not for Jesus' sake only, but that they might see Lazarus
10 also, whom he had raised from the dead. But the chief priests took
11 counsel that they might put Lazarus also to death; Because that by reason of him many of the Jews went away, and believed on Jesus.

12 On the morrow ⁶a great multitude that had come to the feast, when
13 they heard that Jesus was coming to Jerusalem, took the branches of the palm trees, and went forth to meet him, and cried out, Hosanna: Blessed *is* he that cometh in the name of the Lord, even the King of
14 Israel. And Jesus, having found a young ass, sat thereon; as it is written,
15 Fear not, daughter of Zion: behold, thy King cometh, sitting on an
16 ass's colt. These things understood not his disciples at the first: but

---

¹ *See marginal note on* Mark 14. 3.   ² *See marginal note on* Mat. 18. 28.
³ *Or* box   ⁴ *Or* carried what was put therein   ⁵ *Or* Let her alone:
it was that she might keep it   ⁶ *Some ancient authorities read* the common people.

when Jesus was glorified, then remembered they that these things were
17 written of him, and that they had done these things unto him. The
multitude therefore that was with him when he called Lazarus out of the
18 tomb, and raised him from the dead, bare witness. For this cause also
the multitude went and met him, for that they heard that he had done
19 this sign. The Pharisees therefore said among themselves, ¹Behold how
ye prevail nothing: lo, the world is gone after him.
20   Now there were certain Greeks among those that went up to worship
21 at the feast: these therefore came to Philip, which was of Bethsaida of
22 Galilee, and asked him, saying, Sir, we would see Jesus. Philip cometh
and telleth Andrew: Andrew cometh, and Philip, and they tell Jesus.
23 And Jesus answereth them, saying, The hour is come, that the Son of
24 man should be glorified. Verily, verily, I say unto you, Except a grain
of wheat fall into the earth and die, it abideth by itself alone; but if it
25 die, it beareth much fruit. He that loveth his ²life loseth it; and he that
26 hateth his ²life in this world shall keep it unto life eternal. If any man
serve me, let him follow me; and where I am, there shall also my servant
27 be: if any man serve me, him will the Father honour. Now is my soul
troubled; and what shall I say? Father, save me from this ³hour. But
28 for this cause came I unto this hour. Father, glorify thy name. There
came therefore a voice out of heaven, *saying*, I have both glorified it, and
29 will glorify it again. The multitude therefore that stood by, and heard it,
said that it had thundered: others said, An angel hath spoken to him.
30 Jesus answered and said, This voice hath not come for my sake, but for
31 your sakes. Now is ⁴the judgement of this world: now shall the prince
32 of this world be cast out. And I, if I be lifted up ⁵from the earth, will
33 draw all men unto myself. But this he said, signifying by what manner of
34 death he should die. The multitude therefore answered him, We have
heard out of the law that the Christ abideth for ever: and how sayest
35 thou, The Son of man must be lifted up? who is this Son of man? Jesus
therefore said unto them, Yet a little while is the light ⁶among you.
Walk while ye have the light, that darkness overtake you not: and he
36 that walketh in the darkness knoweth not whither he goeth. While ye
have the light, believe on the light, that ye may become sons of light.
    These things spake Jesus, and he departed and ⁷hid himself from them.
37 But though he had done so many signs before them, yet they believed
38 not on him: that the word of Isaiah the prophet might be fulfilled,
which he spake, Lord, who hath believed our report? And to whom
39 hath the arm of the Lord been revealed? For this cause they could not
40 believe, for that Isaiah said again, He hath blinded their eyes, and he
hardened their heart; lest they should see with their eyes, and perceive

¹ *Or* Ye behold   ² *Or* soul   ³ *Or* hour?   ⁴ *Or* a judgement
⁵ *Or* out of   ⁶ *Or* in   ⁷ *Or* was hidden from them

41 with their heart, and should turn, and I should heal them. These things
42 said Isaiah, because he saw his glory; and he spake of him. Nevertheless
even of the rulers many believed on him; but because of the Pharisees
they did not confess ¹*it*, lest they should be put out of the synagogue:
43 for they loved the glory of men more than the glory of God.
44 And Jesus cried and said, He that believeth on me, believeth not on
45 me, but on him that sent me. And he that beholdeth me beholdeth him
46 that sent me. I am come a light into the world, that whosoever believeth
47 on me may not abide in the darkness. And if any man hear my sayings,
and keep them not, I judge him not: for I came not to judge the world,
48 but to save the world. He that rejecteth me, and receiveth not my sayings,
hath one that judgeth him: the word that I spake, the same shall judge
49 him in the last day. For I spake not from myself; but the Father which
sent me, he hath given me a commandment, what I should say, and what
50 I should speak. And I know that his commandment is life eternal: the
things therefore which I speak, even as the Father hath said unto me,
so I speak.

¹ *Or him*

EXPOSITION OF SECTION 6. 11⁵⁴–12⁵⁰

1. The Lord's work. Having been anointed by Mary at Bethany for
   burial [12¹⁻¹¹], next day He enters Jerusalem as King of Israel, 12¹²⁻¹⁹.
2. The Lord's word. Hearing of the desire of the Greeks to see Him,
   He unfolds the truth of life through death, and dedicates Himself
   for the passion, 12²⁰⁻³⁶.

At 12³⁶ the ministry is ended.

In an appendix, (*a*) scripture is quoted, showing that the rejection of
the Lord fulfils prophecy, 12³⁷⁻⁴³; and (*b*) the Lord gives a brief summary
of His teaching, 12⁴⁴⁻⁵⁰.

This section includes three episodes, each carrying great significance (12¹⁻⁸ the anointing of the Lord, 12¹²⁻¹⁹ His entry into
Jerusalem, 12²⁰, ²¹ the arrival of the Greeks), and words of the
Lord, some addressed to disciples 12²³⁻²⁸, and some to the multitude 12³⁰⁻³⁶, words which in both cases have reference to the Lord's
passion, now imminent, and its results. Accordingly, just as in the
previous sections the Lord's words revealed the significance of His
actions (e.g. in ch. 6 His teaching on the bread of life showed the
meaning of His feeding of the multitude), so here His words in
12²³⁻³⁶ throw light on the way in which the reader is to understand
the three incidents related in 12¹⁻²¹, and especially the contrast

between the apparent and the true significance of the Lord's
messianic coming to Jerusalem.

The Lord, whose 'hour', although close at hand, has not quite
arrived, now [11⁵⁴] withdraws even more completely than He did
in 10⁴⁰⁻⁴², after His last altercation with the Jews, just before the
illness of Lazarus; for He goes to the neighbourhood of 'the
Wilderness' (the site of the 'city called Ephraim' is uncertain); nor
do we hear, as on the previous occasion, of many going to Him,
and believing on Him there; now, only His disciples are with Him.

This 'transitional section' 11⁵⁴⁻⁵⁷, as it may be called, is an
excellent example both of the extreme care with which this gospel
must have been composed, and also of the evangelist's method in
conveying, to those who look for it, a deeper significance than is
apparent on the surface of the record. We notice first that, although
references to feasts of the Jews are not infrequent in this gospel,
the only other passage where we find the exact words used here,
'the passover of the Jews was at hand', is 2¹³, at the outset of the
ministry, when the Lord seems to have gone up to Jerusalem along
with others in the normal way. But now the Lord, whose disciples
remain with Him, does not go up with the 'many' who 'went up to
Jerusalem out of the country before the passover, to purify themselves'. Their purpose was to cleanse or purify themselves, according to the levitical rites, in preparation for the (Jewish) passover;
whereas the Lord's disciples 'before the feast of the passover' [13¹]
will be made clean in another way [13¹⁻¹¹; and cf. also 15³]. The
cleavage between the Jews, on the one hand, and the Lord and His
disciples, on the other, is now absolute. Next, the search for the
Lord (as at 7¹¹), and the questioning in the temple whether He is
likely to come to the festival or not, and finally the desire of the
chief priests and Pharisees for information of His whereabouts,
which might lead to His arrest, all help to remind the reader that,
if the Lord had not come to the feast and had not been apprehended
at it, there would have been no 'feast of the passover' in the sense
to which St. John is leading; in the sense, namely, that the Lord
Himself is the passover feast, and the temple is the shrine of His
body.

'Six days before the passover' the Lord, of His own will and act,
returns to Bethany, a place of danger [11⁸]. The machinations of
the Jews thus proceed alongside and together with the deliberate

actions and self-dedication of the Lord [12¹]. The references to Lazarus in 12¹, ² remind the reader that in and for him the Lord has conquered death, and he is one of those who now, together with the Lord, share in the meal. Martha, true to her calling, is waitress; but the incident to which our attention is especially directed is the action of Mary, followed by the objection raised to it by Judas and the Lord's defence of Mary.

There is widespread agreement that, even if St. John did not know the stories of the anointing of the Lord as described in the earlier gospels, he knew a tradition, or the traditions, which lie behind them at this point;¹ and it may become less difficult to understand his record here, if we remark three notable differences between it and St. Mark's account. In Mk. 14³⁻⁹ the meal at which the anointing occurs is placed *after* the Lord's triumphal entry into Jerusalem, and *an unnamed woman* anoints His *head*. In Jn. 12¹⁻⁸, however, the supper takes place the day *before* the Lord's triumphal journey to the capital; and *Mary*, the sister of Martha and Lazarus, anoints the Lord's *feet*, almost at once removing the spikenard, and wiping His feet dry with the tresses of her hair.

The position of the section in Mark, placed as it is between 14¹, ² and 14¹⁰, ¹¹, encourages the belief that the following interpretation of his version of the anointing, and therefore indeed also of his understanding of the incident, may be justified. In the midst of the darkness gathering round the Lord an unnamed woman, by an act of costly devotion, shows her recognition of Him as being, none the less, the King-Messiah. Hence she anoints His head. When her lavish action is criticized by some of those who witness it, the Lord defends her, on the ground that the occasion of the action is exceptional; and He accepts her offering as an anticipatory preparation of His body for burial. There seems no reason to think that the unnamed woman, when she anointed the Lord's head, regarded her action as connected with His coming burial. In St. Mark's version of the anointing, it is the Lord who, by His words in 14⁸, first brings them into connexion.²

---

¹ The argument in the text presumes the belief that there was probably only one anointing of the Lord during His ministry, and that the story embodying it took various forms, according to the different aspects of religious truth for which different churches or individuals valued it (see further, pp. 247-9).

² It may be, of course, that St. Mark regarded the woman, when she anointed the Lord as Messiah, as already conscious of the significance of her action in connexion with His coming burial, and therefore as bringing His Messiahship

The fact that in St. John's gospel the anointing is the act of Mary leads us to consider what we learn about her elsewhere. In a little section of St. Luke's gospel [10³⁸⁻⁴²] she is described as sitting at the Lord's feet, and hearing His word; and the Lord declares her to have chosen the good part, of which she shall not be deprived. In Jn. 11, the chapter which immediately precedes the story of the anointing, we are told [11⁵] that the Lord was deeply attached to the family at Bethany, consisting of Martha, Mary, and Lazarus; and the story in Luke perhaps justifies us in believing that it was Mary who best understood the Lord and responded to the affection felt by Him for them. On the Lord's arrival at Bethany [11¹⁷], Mary remains at home, until He summons her; she then at once obeys. The only words ascribed to her in ch. 11 are those which had already been uttered by her sister [11²¹, ³²]; but it seems to be the sight of her wailing, and of the wailing of those who accompany her, which first arouses the Lord's distress and leads Him to ask to be conducted to the grave of Lazarus. Possibly one small further point may have significance. Whereas we read in 11¹⁹ that 'many from among the Jews had come to Martha and Mary', to offer their condolences, at the close of the section it is said, in 11⁴⁵, that 'many of the Jews, those who had come to Mary and beheld that which He did, believed on Him'. It was not, it seems, from among their number, from those who had been especially associated with Mary, that 'some of the Jews went away to the Pharisees, and told them the things which Jesus had done'.

In all four stories of the anointing it is made clear that the action of her who anointed the Lord was a supreme expression of devotion. If, confining ourselves henceforward to St. John's version of the incident, and putting all thought of the other versions away, we ask why in his gospel Mary anoints the Lord's feet, possibly an answer may be found in the story of the washing of the disciples' feet in 13²⁻¹². There, as here [12⁷], we encounter a verse [13¹⁰] presenting difficulties of text and interpretation; but the Lord's words to Simon Peter in 12⁶⁻¹⁰ seem to imply that His action, although confined to the disciples' feet, is equivalent to a complete washing; and possibly the same principle may hold good here. If so, the reader is invited to see in Mary's action a symbolical embalming of His body for burial, as though He were already dead.

into close connexion with His coming death. If so, St. John only makes the meaning of her action more clear and definite than it is in Mark.

Originally, it may be, the spikenard had been designed by Mary, aware of the Lord's approaching death, to embalm His whole body (St. John alone records the weight of the ointment), and in a permanent embalming, after His death; and its entire consumption at the present moment on His feet (for this certainly seems to be implied in 12³), increases the impression of Mary's absolute devotion. Not only the dining-room, but the whole house, is filled with fragrance. Forthwith, however, according to St. John, she at once removes the spikenard; and this may suggest that, in the light of all she has learned as a result of the Lord's visit to Bethany in the previous chapter, she has realized the inability of the grave to hold Him; and she shows a further proof of her devotion in using, in order to complete her action, not a towel, but the tresses of her hair, described by St. Paul as the glory of a woman [1 Cor. 11¹⁵].

Reasons are given in the notes for thinking that, instead of following the R.V. in 12⁹ ('the common people') or in 12¹² ('a great multitude'), we should in each case read 'the great multitude' and trace a connexion between the 'great multitude' of 6², ⁵ and that of this chapter. If so, then those who in ch. 6 were following the Lord because of His signs upon the sick are now eager to see not only the Lord Himself but His last and greatest sign, Lazarus recalled to life. In consequence the chief priests take the same decision about Lazarus that they have already taken in the case of the Lord, since it was because of Lazarus that many of the Jews were tending to be drawn away and to believe on Jesus [12¹¹]. It is thus shown that those who decided, shortly before, on the ground of expediency to sacrifice one man on behalf of the people [11⁵⁰] find themselves before long on a slippery slope, and resort to, or are forced into, further resolutions of injustice. And the reader is taught that, the Lord having shown Himself, in the case of Lazarus, to be the Conqueror of death, the Jews by finally deciding for this very reason against Him have allied themselves, as the forces of death, not only against Him but against all to whom He grants His gift of life.

The reader, before passing to St. John's account of the journey, next day, to Jerusalem, should remind himself that (*a*) the Lord has given life to Lazarus, and has thereby shown Himself to be the Conqueror of death; (*b*) in consequence He has Himself been condemned to death by the chief Jewish tribunal; and (*c*) He has been symbolically buried, although Mary's action in at once removing the spikenard emphasizes the grave's impotence to have a lasting hold upon Him. This then is He, the Conqueror of death and Lord of life, who now enters His capital in triumph as the King of Israel.

It will be remembered that those, who composed the 'great multitude' in ch. 6, if they could have had their way, would as a consequence of the sign of the loaves and fishes have made the Lord king by force [6¹⁵], and were only prevented from doing so by His withdrawal. Having come up for the feast [12¹²], they now hear [12¹⁸] that, after His last and even more wonderful sign, so far from withdrawing, He is making a public entry into the city; and therefore, confident that now at any rate His hour has come, they go out, taking palm branches with them, to meet and greet Him as the King of Israel. In Lev. 23⁴⁰ the festal use of palm branches is prescribed for the feast of tabernacles; but it is clear from 1 Macc. 13⁵⁰⁻⁵² and 2 Macc. 10¹⁻⁹ that their use was also associated with the annual commemoration of the Maccabaean triumphs in the second century B.C., which gave the Jews political freedom for sixty-five years, from 129 to 64 B.C. Again, Jewish coins inscribed with a palm-tree or palm branch are common between 140 B.C. and A.D. 70, and some carry a palm-tree with 'the redemption of Zion' in Hebrew characters. Hence St. John, the only evangelist who mentions palm branches in connexion with the entry, may wish to imply that the great crowd saw in the Lord's arrival the coming of one who, like the high priest in the great age of the Maccabees, would unite in his person both spiritual and temporal power, dispensing these from his seat of office in the temple; and thus the Jews would be once more free, delivered from the hated sovereignty of Rome.

In St. John's gospel it is only after the Lord has been thus met and greeted by the multitude—and not from the beginning of His journey, as in the earlier gospels—that He utters a silent protest against its almost complete misunderstanding of His royal mission. He procures a young ass and advances seated on it, in fulfilment, St. John points out, of the prophecy [Zech. 9⁹] that Zion's King would come, not on a war horse, suggestive of destruction, but on a colt, the beast of peace.

At 12¹⁶ St. John inserts one of his editorial comments, pointing out that for some time afterwards the disciples failed to realize the significance of this entry of the Lord. Just as he notes at 2²², in connexion with the Lord's cleansing of the temple, that not until His resurrection did the disciples remember His words, 'Destroy this temple, and in three days I will raise it up', and grasp that they referred to the destruction and resurrection of 'the temple of His body', so that in this saying of His was to be found the significance of His cleansing of the Jewish temple, so here at 12¹⁶. Only when the Lord was glorified (that is, in His death and resurrection), as a result of which they themselves received the life-giving outflow of the Spirit [7³⁹], did they discern the meaning of the prophecy in Zech. 9⁹ and its fulfilment in the entry.

By his reference in the two following verses [12¹⁷, ¹⁸] to the multitude's enthusiasm as a result of the sign of the resurrection of Lazarus, St. John reminds the reader in what aspect of the Lord's Person and work (cf. 11²⁵) is to be found His true triumph, and finally in 12¹⁹ he makes use of a distressful utterance of the Pharisees in order to emphasize His universal kingship. For whereas the Pharisees are represented as complaining to one another that their plans have all miscarried and the Lord has defeated them by winning the allegiance of the masses, the instructed reader realizes that in truth they are proclaiming, on the one hand, their utter impotence and, on the other, the destined allegiance of the world to its Saviour (cf. 4⁴²).

St. John's interest in the procession seems to die away as soon as he has set forth those features of it which his readers, for their own sakes and as a lesson and warning to themselves, should bear in mind; the same phenomenon is found elsewhere, e.g. in 2¹³⁻²⁰ at the cleansing of the temple, and at 3¹⁻¹⁴ in the conversation with Nicodemus. There can be little doubt that the procession, taking place in an eastern country, must have ended at the temple, as it does in the other gospels; but St. John has already recorded the Lord's action in the temple, the action which follows in those gospels, at 2¹³⁻²⁰. It was there shown at the outset of the ministry that, since the Lord, whose body is the shrine of God, has come, the temple of stone is 'nigh unto vanishing away' [Heb. 8¹³]; and it is therefore appropriate that here, at the climax of the ministry, the passage which in St. John's gospel follows the story of the procession should strike the reverse or positive note, by showing the real significance of the words, 'the world is gone after Him', which ended the previous paragraph. For the Redeemer has come to Zion (cf. Is. 59²⁰), and what is the immediate result? The arrival on the scene of certain Greeks, who for the evangelist and his readers will have represented those of his own time in the Gentile world who were seeking, like these Greeks, to come into contact with the Lord. These latter may thus be regarded as the 'promise' or 'earnest', from among the Gentiles, of the catholic or universal Church, which was to be one chief result of the Lord's completed work. This living body, the Church, is indeed built on the foundation of Judaism, and it should be noticed that these men, although non-Jews, had come up to Jerusalem 'to worship at the [Jewish] festival'; but none the less the new body is to take the place of the Jewish Church, represented by the Jewish temple, the building of stone.

These Greeks, then, desiring to 'see Jesus' (cf. 14⁹), request the help of Philip, one of the two members of the twelve, the other being Andrew, who bear Greek names; and these two apostles report the matter to the Lord. In the request of these Gentiles the Lord sees the coming of that 'hour', which had not yet arrived—at any rate as it has now arrived (for we must not forget such a passage as 2¹¹)—at 2⁴ or 7³⁰ or 7³⁹ or 8²⁰, the hour of the glorification of the Son of man, when His work and His Gospel are to become available for all men [12²⁵]; and it is at once made clear in what events His glorification is to consist; the events are what we may call the complex of the passion.

First, in solemn assurance He points out to the two disciples that a seed only becomes fruitful if it is first buried in the earth in death. The seed dies, as we say; it does not perish entirely, or its usefulness here as an analogy would fail; but it must die as a single seed; only so can it bring forth abundance of new life.

Next, in 12²⁵ expression is given to a doctrine central also in the other gospels; and this law of life through death, it is made clear, is incumbent not only on the Lord Himself but on His servant also. But for the disciple too the requirement is also a promise; by obedience to it, or rather to the Lord, he too, the Lord's servant or minister—the Greek word here means minister, not slave—will find himself in the Lord's presence, and will be held in honour by the Father. And just as, at the grave of Lazarus, the Lord, before He could dispel the grief of Mary and her friends, 'troubled Himself', if the Greek is literally translated, so here, immediately after His reference to the universal law of service and self-sacrifice, His soul is troubled. In order that those who follow Him may not be vainly troubled [14¹, ²⁷], but in the midst of trouble [16³³] may possess His parting gift of peace [14²⁷], He Himself now undergoes distress. He thus shows that He can understand the prayer, 'Father, save me from this hour', even if He does not use it for Himself. This He cannot do, because both in thought and action He must experience 'this hour'; in it He sees the very purpose and climax of His mission. For Him the only possible prayer is 'Father, glorify thy name'; and the Lord's utterance of this prayer is followed by a voice out of heaven, which declares that the Father has glorified His name in the past, and will glorify it in the future. The Father, in and through the work of the Son, has glorified His name, and thereby has been glorified Himself. In the death of the Son, which is to complete the sacrifice made by the Son throughout His earthly life, the Father will again glorify His name, and thereby will Himself be glorified. The life and the death of the Son are (together) the revelation and the work of the Father; and the glory of the Father is revealed, and made actual, in the life and the death of the Son.

Thirdly, just as at the grave of Lazarus the Lord expressed aloud His thanksgiving to the Father for granting Him the life of Lazarus, in order that those present might believe in Him and in His mission from the Father, so here we read that the voice, which followed on His prayer, 'Father, glorify thy name', the voice out of heaven, 'I have both glorified it and will glorify it again', was uttered, not for His sake, but for the sake of the multitude which was standing by and heard it. Unhappily the multitude, owing to the half-light in which it lives, cannot discern or appreciate the import of the utterance from heaven. To some the sound, which they hear, resembles a natural phenomenon, a clap of thunder; they are the indifferent, who fail to realize that any event, in nature or otherwise, may contain a religious message for mankind. Others are prepared to attest a message from the unseen world, but are unaware that it could be for their sakes; doubtless, they think, it was a message from above to the mysterious Personage before them. The Lord Himself, in His unbroken union with the Father, needed no assurance that His prayer had been and would be granted; but for those around Him the voice, if they could not only hear but also understand it, was of the highest import. Not only did the prayer of Jesus, 'Father, glorify thy name', and the voice which followed it, reveal the law and pattern for all the intercourse of God and man, and thus show men individually how to face the hours of distress and suffering and death; but in the fact that the Lord at this moment (the repetition of the word 'now' in verses 27 and 31 is significant), when His soul is troubled, none the less wills the glory of the Father and that only, and will upon the cross carry out this obedience in action to the end, they may learn that the judgement of this world takes place, and that its ruler, the devil, will be so no longer.

As regards the judgement, it has already been made clear in such passages as 3$^{17-21}$, 5$^{22-30}$ that in the presence of the incarnate Jesus men *ipso facto* pass judgement on themselves by their attitude to Him, and are thus revealed for what they truly are. This truth, we now learn, is to be manifested supremely in the passion, which will once for all condemn the world. As regards the sense in which we are to understand the imminent expulsion of the devil, it may be of help to recall the scene in ch. 9. There the beggar, who has remained loyal to his Benefactor, is found and received by Him; although cast out by the Pharisees his judges, who have thus passed judgement on themselves and remain in condemnation, the beggar does not come into judgement; thanks to his Lord, he is freed from the power of the enemy; and the same is henceforth to be true, as the early church soon found (e.g. Col. 1^{13}, 1 Thess. 2^{12}), of all those who will allow themselves to be drawn to the exalted and crucified Lord [12^{32}]. It is noticeable that at this moment, when in the face of His distress of soul (the equivalent, in this gospel, of the Lord's struggle, in the other gospels, in the garden of Gethsemane) the Lord has finally reaffirmed His absolute obedience to the Father, all the questions connected with His functions and office, and the expression of His relation to the Father, are allowed to fall away; and He says simply, 'I, if I be lifted up from the earth, will draw all men to myself.' At 3^{14} Nicodemus in his perplexity was told that 'as Moses lifted up the serpent in the wilderness, so must the Son of man be lifted up; that whosoever believeth may, in Him, have eternal life'. Again, at 8^{28}, when the Lord has told the Jews, 'Except ye believe that I am, ye shall die in your sins', and they reply, 'Who art thou?' and show themselves unable to understand what He tells them of the Father, the Lord says, 'When ye have lifted up the Son of man, then shall ye know that I am, and that I do nothing of myself, but as the Father taught me, I speak these things. And he that hath sent me is with me; he hath not left me alone; for I do always the things that are pleasing to him.' But now to the multitude the Lord says simply, 'I if I be lifted up from the earth, will draw all men to myself.' He and the Father are one.

The lifting up must of course be understood in its twofold meaning, each side being rigorously maintained. On the one hand, the Lord will be lifted up from the earth upon the cross; and St. John adds an editorial note in 12³³—'this he said, signifying'—showing by means of a sign or symbol—'by what manner of death he should die'—in order to ensure that the plain and primary reference to the Lord's death by crucifixion should be kept steadily in mind. We are told, indeed, that the Aramaic equivalent for the Greek words here used can also mean 'I, if I be removed from the land'; and this interpretation of the words may well have been included in the thought of the evangelist, although it must not be allowed to displace their primary meaning. But, on the other hand, this lifting up is to be also the exaltation, the glorification, of the Lord; and this exaltation, this glorification, has its central feature in His death. Thereby, we read, the Lord will draw all men to Himself; that is, He will attract everyone to Him, although the possibility will of course only become actuality among those who are His servants [12²⁶], those who have been drawn [6⁴⁴] and given [17⁹] to Him by the Father. Thus the Lord's death, and its manner, will universalize His work. The day of a national religion, of a select or chosen people, is now over; the Lord will draw all men to Himself. And He will draw them by His submission to and conquest of death on their behalf, thus giving them part in the glory which He shares with the Father, in eternal life. But since His exaltation is found in and is conditioned by His death upon the cross, the share of His disciples in His glory will depend on their ability to withstand the world, as He did [15¹⁸⁻²¹, 16¹⁻³, 17¹⁴]. Unlike Him, they are to remain in the world; but the life which they will draw from their share in the eternal life bestowed by Him will or should show them that 'they are not of the world' [17¹⁶]. Thus the invitation to share the Lord's glory is essentially also an invitation to share the sufferings which were brought upon Him by the world.

We had already learned, before the Lord uttered the words in 12³⁰⁻³², that the multitude or crowd, living in the half-light of uncertainty and doubt, had failed to understand the import of the utterance from heaven. It is now mentioned for the last time in this gospel, asking in its perplexity some final questions, which remain unanswered. As at Mk. 8²⁹⁻³¹, the two titles 'the Messiah' and 'the Son of man' are here found very close together. On that occasion the Lord, in reply to St. Peter's ascription to Him of Messiahship, proceeded at once to teach His disciples of the coming rejection of the Son of man, a term which henceforth in Mark becomes more frequent on His lips, especially in connexion with a destined future suffering, death and resurrection. Similarly here the multitude, or its leaders, introduce the thought of the Messiah. Not only do they recall the promises in the O.T. of an unending golden age under the rule of the Messiah [12³⁴], but their minds, we may believe, are also full of the immediately preceding event of the entry in 12¹²⁻¹⁵. Of the Messiah's office and function, as also of his identity with the Lord, they therefore believe themselves to have full knowledge. Following the same train of thought, they may have noticed that the Lord has just spoken of His exaltation [12³²], and His words may have carried their thoughts back to 8²⁸, when He had said that later on the Jews would 'lift up' or 'exalt' the Son of man. They see, therefore, that there must be a connexion between the two titles; but since they perceive also that the Lord has just spoken of His being 'lifted up' in a sense which, as they instinctively feel, so far from implying an everlasting dominion, is connected rather with death, they inquire what He means and to whom He refers, when He speaks of the 'lifting up' or 'exaltation' of the Son of man.

The Lord has indeed just made the matter clear by His use of the first person singular at 12³²; but the multitude is blind, and cannot understand His doctrine of Himself any more than the Jews could understand His doctrine of the Father at 8²⁷; and it therefore passes from the scene, asking a question[1] about the lifting up of the Son of man, and His identity, or, as we might express the matter in more familiar language, about the meaning of the cross of Christ.

The Lord, before giving sight to one who previously had never seen, had said, 'We must work the works of him who sent me, while it is day; the night cometh, when no man can work' [9⁴]. And applying this maxim more directly to Himself, He continued, 'When I am in the world, I am the light of the world' [9⁵]. Again,

---

[1] Just as Pilate at 18³⁸, when confronted with the Truth [14⁶] bearing witness to Himself, will ask 'What is truth?' In both cases the questioners, through lack of faith, are unable to discern the glory of the Word made flesh in Jesus.

when He declared His intention to return into Judaea, and the disciples protested, since He would thus be endangering His life [11⁷, ⁸], His answer showed that obedience to the will of God is equivalent to 'walking in the day'; and he who does so does not stumble. This will only happen if a man walks in the night, and is thus without light to guide him [11⁹, ¹⁰]. In the even more critical context of the present chapter, the Lord's final warning to the multitude is that the light is both among and in them, only for a little while. Let them turn from wishful thoughts about the (messianic) future to live and act in the present, while the light is still at their disposal, and can show them whence they come and whither they go. If, while the light is with them, they will yield themselves up to it, darkness, when it comes, as it will, should cause no difficulty or fear; for by that time they will have had opportunity to become, themselves, the 'sons of light' [12³⁶].

Reaching 12³⁶ᵇ, we remember that on a previous occasion, when the Jews 'took up stones to cast at Him' [8⁵⁹], the Lord 'was hidden' (R.V. mg), and left the temple. At that time His hour had not yet come [8²⁰], and at 10²³, therefore, He is found there again. But now the hour of His glorification has arrived [12²³]; the Jews are carrying out their decision to destroy Him; the temple of stone is about to be replaced by the shrine of His body; and accordingly He is now finally hidden, as regards the significance of His Person and the meaning of His work, from the sight of the multitude; His ministry, and their opportunity, are over. (The reader will recall that in all the gospels the Person and the fact of the risen Lord are made known to His friends, and to His friends only.) But, before passing to the Lord's words to be spoken in chs. 13 to 17 to, or in the presence of, His new shrine, i.e. His disciples representing the Church, St. John points out that full and ample opportunity for belief, with most compelling evidence, has been offered to the Jews. For that which throughout their history had always appealed and brought conviction to them as the most sure and certain evidence of the divine presence and activity was signs, wonders, and mighty works (cf. Ex. 4¹⁻⁷, 34¹⁰, Judges 6³⁶⁻⁴⁰, 1 Cor. 1²²); and these, St. John says, had been performed in full measure by the Lord before them, but had not produced belief. The Lord's ministry had thus been a demonstration, *in petto*, of the universal truth that the Logos 'was in the world, . . . and the world knew him not'; that 'he came unto his own, and they that were his own received him not'. For indeed, as St. John proceeds to show, the rejection by the Jews, as a nation, of the manifestation of the Lord in the flesh, and therewith of His glory, had been long ago foreseen in prophecy and was, as the fulfilment of prophecy, inevitable. And he concludes by drawing attention to one great cause of unbelief, already emphasized by the Lord at 5⁴⁴. Although the implication of the Pharisees' taunt in 7⁴⁸ is now shown in 12⁴² to be false, since (in addition to the many of less exalted station, to whose belief on the Lord St. John has frequently referred [2²³, 7³¹, 8³⁰, 10⁴², 11⁴⁵, 12¹¹]) many also of the rulers did indeed adhere to Him, yet these were deterred from admitting their belief, because it might involve the loss of their membership in the commonwealth of Israel, and therewith of the public honour and respect accorded to them; accordingly they came under judgement. With the words 'the glory of God' in 12⁴³ we may compare the last words of 12²⁶.

The strong Greek verb translated 'cried' [12⁴⁴], which introduces the concluding verses [12⁴⁴⁻⁵⁰] of the first half of the book, has been used of the Lord twice previously in this gospel, on both occasions at His manifestation of Himself at the festival of tabernacles: first, at 7²⁸ during the festival, in the temple, and secondly, at 7³⁷ in a final invitation on its last and great day. (It is used elsewhere in John only at 1¹⁵, of the Baptist's witness to the Lord.) It is now used of Him for the last time, and introduces a summary, assigned to no especial place or season, of the principal themes treated during the ministry in this gospel.

The Son is the revelation of the Father. He has come to bring out of darkness into light all who believe on Him. And since the purpose of His coming was the salvation not the judgement, of the world, He does not Himself, or forthwith, condemn those who hear but do not keep His teaching. And yet, since the verdict of God is also the verdict of the Lord, it is true that the Lord's word, which He has spoken, will be the standard of final judgement. For, from first to last, the Lord has spoken nothing from Himself. It is the Father who sent Him and told Him what He was to say and speak. And the commandment which the Father thus gave Him is eternal life; and to that commandment, even if or when its proclamation results or has resulted in the choice of darkness by those who reject the commandment, the Lord is and has been true.

Almost all the contents of this summary have explicit or implicit parallels in the earlier chapters; but in a few cases these are best sought in chs. 13 to 17; with 12^{45}, for example, cf. 14^9; and with 12^{50} cf. 14^{31}. We are thus reminded that the last word of the Lord's mission is yet to be spoken; for the purpose of that mission was and is the salvation, not the judgement, of men; and not all men have rejected Him; and therewith we prepare to pass from the sombre atmosphere of the closing chapters of the ministry to the revelation about to be given in chs. 13 to 17, and 20, to those who did receive Him.

NOTES TO SECTION 6. 11^{54}–12^{50}

12$^{1-8}$. In any consideration of St. John's account of the anointing of the Lord the following points must be borne in mind:

1. In Mk. 14$^{3-9}$ the anointing is placed some time *after* the Lord's triumphal entry into Jerusalem, and in close connexion with the beginning of St. Mark's passion narrative. The incident occurs during a meal at Bethany in the house of Simon the leper; the woman who anoints Him is unnamed; and she breaks an alabaster flask of precious ointment of spikenard and pours the contents on the Lord's head. Some of those present express resentment among themselves, saying that the ointment might have been sold for a high price (they name a specific sum) and have benefited the poor; and they make no secret of their indignation. The Lord, however, defends the woman's action, describing it as a good work done to Him. The poor, He adds, with a possible reference to Deut. 15^{11}, are always available and can be helped at any time; but it is not so with Him. The woman has done her utmost; she has anointed His body in anticipation of His burial; and wherever in the future the Gospel is proclaimed, the story of this deed, He assures His hearers, will be told with it, to her memory.

2. The account in Mt. 26$^{6-13}$ follows closely that of Mark. For our present purpose only the following differences from Mark in Matthew need be noticed. It is the disciples who express resentment; a precise value for the ointment is not named; and the Lord's words about helping the poor are omitted, His words in Matthew being only, 'For the poor ye have always with you, but me ye have not always.'

There can be little doubt that the purpose with which this form of the story is narrated in both Matthew and Mark is to show, at the outset of the chain of events [Mt. 26$^{1-5,\ 14-16}$, Mk. 14$^{1,\ 2,\ 10,\ 11}$] which end in the crucifixion of the Lord, that the passion narrative more than any other part of the record reveals His royalty as messianic king; and this purpose is achieved, both by the place which this story holds in the narrative, and by the anointing of the Lord's head.

But in John the Lord is recognized as Messiah even before the ministry opens [1^{41}]; and although it is true that in John the passion is the occasion of His 'hour' [12^{23}], when His exaltation takes place [8^{28}, 12^{32}, 19^{15}] and

His glorification is completed [13³¹, ³²; cf. 7³⁹], yet His works throughout reveal His glory [2¹¹, 8⁵⁴, 17⁴]; 'Jesus of Nazareth' (words which are included in the title on the cross in 19¹⁹) is, from first to last, 'the King of the Jews'. Hence in John an anointing of the Lord's head at this moment could not carry the same significance as the form which the story has in Matthew and Mark.

3. St. Luke's story of the anointing [7³⁶⁻⁵⁰] differs markedly from that in Matthew and Mark. It has no connexion with the events immediately preceding the passion narrative, but occurs during the ministry in Galilee. The Lord has accepted an invitation to a meal from a Pharisee, named Simon, and is found reclining at the meal in Simon's house. On learning of this, an unnamed woman, of ill repute locally, brings an alabaster flask of ointment and takes her station behind, at the Lord's feet, in tears. With these she moistens the Lord's feet and, after wiping them dry with her hair, kisses them devotedly and anoints them with the ointment.

Simon reflects that the Lord, if truly 'a prophet', would have known the character of the woman who thus touches Him. Hereupon the Lord, after showing by the parable of the two aebtors that He had followed the train of Simon's thought, contrasts the treatment which He has received from His host with the devotion accorded to Him by the woman, and, addressing Himself to her, assures her that owing to her love and faith she has obtained forgiveness of her sins.

4. The story as given in John has distinctive points both of agreement and of disagreement with each of the other three versions. In John the story is closely connected with the passion, as in Matthew and Mark, but it is now found before the triumphal entry. It is placed at Bethany; there is, however, no mention of the house of Simon the leper, and we naturally assume the house to be that of Lazarus and his sisters, since Lazarus is at table with the Lord, Martha serves, and Mary anoints. Mary's gift is described as a pound of costly ointment of spikenard, and it is emphasized, by repetition of the term (cf. also 11²), that it is the Lord's feet which she anoints and then dries with her hair, the house as a result being filled with the fragrance of the ointment. Objection to her act is raised, not by the disciples generally, as in Matthew, but by one of them, Judas Iscariot, the future traitor, who values the ointment at the same sum, probably, as that in the original text of Mark, since the latter may not have included the word 'above'.[1] An editorial note by St. John explains the real motive of Judas' resentment, it being shown thereby that the self-seeking attitude of Judas is the reverse of that of Mary. The story ends with a rebuke to Judas by the Lord, consisting in a defence of Mary's action, and a reference to the poor in the same form of words as is found in Matthew.

An examination of the Greek of all four versions makes it probable that all four stories are different versions of a single event, and that St. John was aware of the earlier traditions of the story (whether or not through knowledge, on his part, of the other gospels), and that his devia-

---

[1] See a note by Dr. G. D. Kilpatrick in *J.T.S.* xlii. 181.

tions from them are deliberate. This has been kept in mind in the exposition of St. John's version above.

12^4. The reader has already encountered Judas at 6^{71}, when, after St. Peter's expression of the devoted loyalty of the twelve, the Lord utters the warning that even among them, the objects of His choice, 'one is a devil'. In the present passage [12$^{1-8}$], Judas now for the first time reveals something of his character; and his resentment at Mary's deed shows him, and now openly, in even stronger contrast to her than he was previously shown to be, privately, to St. Peter and the rest.

12^6. 'the money-box' (cf. R.V. mg) would be the common property of the party, to receive the small coins offered to the Lord and His company by passers-by.

12^7. Since the ointment has all been poured out, it is unlikely that the translation of R. V. text is right, although it is the most natural rendering of the Greek here; the R. V. mg possibly points to a satisfactory understanding of the Lord's words. In reply to Judas' charge of waste, He says that Mary is to be unmolested; her purpose was (or perhaps rather, had been, until quite recently) to keep the ointment for the day of His actual burial. The reason for her lavish expenditure of it now, upon His feet, is not given; that is known only to the Lord and to herself; it is enough that her action is one of personal devotion to Him.

12^9. The order of the Greek for the first three words of the English R.V. here is unusual, and the R.V. has sought to express this by its translation here; but there is reason for thinking that the Greek in 12^{12} is probably the same, and that in spite of the strange order of the Greek words we should translate, in each case, 'the great multitude'. Is it possible that St. John uses this strange order to identify the 'great multitude' last mentioned in 6$^{2, 5}$, and composed of men who were following the Lord in Galilee because they saw the signs which He was doing on the sick, with the 'great multitude' here, whether that 'of the Jews' in 12^9, or that which 'had come to the feast' in 12^{12}?

12$^{12-19}$. If St. John's method and meaning in this section are to be understood, the other accounts of the entry must be kept in mind.

1. In Mark the Lord sends two of His disciples for a colt; garments are placed upon it, the Lord takes His seat, and a triumphal procession is formed, with garments and foliage strewn upon the road. The procession seems to be made up of the pilgrims accompanying the Lord to the city, and shouts of welcome are raised both in front and behind. The content of the shouts as recorded in Mark raises some problems; and we need only notice now that they include a reference to the approach of the messianic kingdom.

2. St. Matthew's account is similar to that in Mark, and only two points call for comment. First, apparently through a misunderstanding of the Hebrew idiom in Zech. 9^9, a verse which is quoted at Mt. 21^5, a second beast is introduced; and secondly, the content of the acclamations, as given in Matthew, emphasizes the personal welcome to the messianic Lord.

3. St. Luke also follows Mark closely up to the latter part of the procession. He relates, however, that, when the Lord was nearing the city, the

whole multitude of the disciples in their joy burst out in a loud shout of praise to God for all the mighty works which they had witnessed; and the version of the acclamations in this gospel, besides containing the words 'the king' in reference to the approaching Lord, suggests also that the occasion reflects or has as its result the peace and radiance of heaven. Finally, when some of the Pharisees in the crowd protest that the Lord should rebuke and restrain His disciples, He replies that, if His disciples were silent, the very stones would be constrained to shout. On the other hand, St. Luke adds that, when now in clear view of the city, the Lord shed tears of sorrow over it, bewailing its blindness to the conditions of its peace with God, and foretelling as a consequence its future complete military destruction by its enemies, because it had not been alive to the season when the divine visitation came upon it.

12¹³. St. John alone of the evangelists mentions that the branches were of palm, and the Greek perhaps suggests that these had not been cut in passing (as seems to have been the case with the boughs and foliage mentioned in Matthew and Mark), but had been previously prepared. To carry palms was a mark of triumphant homage to a victor or a king (cf. Rev. 7⁹).

'cried out'. See pp. 229–30. The Greek word used here occurs only once in the LXX, at Ezra 3¹³ (of the shouting of the people when the foundation of the temple was laid, after the return from the exile), and either eight or nine times in the N.T. (the reading in Lk. 4⁴¹ being doubtful), six of which are in John. It carries an unfavourable sense in the N.T., as is clear from its use at Mt. 12¹⁹, Acts 22²³, but an especially sinister sense in this gospel, where it is used four times [18⁴⁰, 19⁶, ¹², ¹⁵] of those who cried out for the Lord's death. This is probably sufficient evidence that the cries of the crowd are to be understood here also as having an unfavourable— perhaps we may say, fanatical—character. But, most remarkable of all, St. John uses it at 11⁴³ of the Lord's loud cry, commanding Lazarus to leave his grave. St. John's purpose in using this verb at 11⁴³ is perhaps best understood in the light of such a doctrine as that in 2 Cor. 5²¹.

'Hosanna' is a Jewish shout of joy, like the German 'Heil!' It is rendered in the LXX by Greek words meaning 'save now'. The first part of the shout here is a quotation from Ps. 118²⁵, a psalm sung in procession at the Feast of Tabernacles. When this verse was reached, palm branches were waved, and thus themselves came to be called 'hosannas'.

'Blessed in the name of the Lord (i.e. Yahweh) is the coming one.' The divine blessing thus invoked by the crowd could be and was applied by the priests to any pilgrim coming up to Jerusalem to worship, but the words 'even the king of Israel' which follow here, define and limit clearly enough their present application.

12¹⁹. 'the world is gone after him'. Confining ourselves at present to St. John's record in 1¹⁹ to 12⁵⁰, we find that the expression 'the world' carries at first little unfavourable meaning and is presented, rather, as the object of God's love. Thus the Lamb of God takes away its sin [1²⁹], God loves it [3¹⁶], and sent His son to save it [3¹⁷]. Light has come into the world [3¹⁹] in the Person of the Lord [12⁴⁶], who is indeed its light [8¹², 9⁵] and Saviour [4⁴²]. On the other hand, from ch. 6 onwards, a shadow begins to fall upon the scene. At 6⁵¹ the Lord says that He will give His flesh for the life of the world; at 7⁷ that the world hates Him; at 8²³ that the Jews are 'of this world', whereas He is 'not of this world'; and at 9³⁹ that He came into this world for judgement. And later in the present chapter we shall read that a judgement of this world is taking place and its prince will be expelled [12³¹].

It seems likely therefore that St. John wishes the reader to understand the Pharisees' words here in two different ways: first, as understood by themselves, their words imply that the Lord has the crowd on His side; but the reader will soon learn that, even if this is so, many in the same crowd will within a few days be shouting for His death, the same verb being used for the shouting then as for the shouts of welcome now; and secondly, the reader must not forget that the crowd is unconsciously welcoming Him who has conquered death at the graveside of Lazarus, His friend, and who has thereby made the results of His work available for all men [3¹⁶, 10¹⁴⁻¹⁶, 11⁵⁰⁻⁵³]. It should not, therefore, surprise him that in the verses which immediately follow he reads of some Gentiles, i.e. non-Jews, who have come up to worship at the passover and desire to come into the presence of the Lord. In this sense all the peoples of the world, and not the Jewish nation only, have found their Messiah and more than their Messiah and king in Jesus.

12²⁰. In Solomon's prayer at the dedication of the first temple provision is explicitly made for non-Jews who wish to come and adore there the God of Israel [1 Kings 8⁴¹⁻⁴³; cf. Acts 8²⁷].

12²¹. The emphasis laid at this point on the fact that Philip was a native of Bethsaida of Galilee demands attention. In the introductory section 1¹⁹⁻⁵¹ the Lord, after being associated with the Baptist and his work in the south, and having been joined by Andrew and his brother Simon, leaves for Galilee, and for this purpose finds and takes with Him Philip; and the evangelist notes that 'Philip was from Bethsaida, of the city of Andrew and Peter'. Here in 12²¹, on the arrival of the Greeks or Gentiles who desire to see the Lord and for this purpose approach Philip, St. John repeats that Philip was 'of (from) Bethsaida of Galilee'. It seems possible that the evangelist may have in mind Is. 9¹⁻⁷. Whereas in Is. 8¹⁷ it is said that Yahweh 'hideth his face from the house of Jacob', in ch. 9 'Galilee of the nations' or Gentiles is named as the land where light will dawn. Possibly therefore as early as 1⁴⁴, and still more in the opening scene of the ministry laid at Cana of Galilee in 2¹, St. John suggests indirectly the future, universal scope of the Gospel, and mentions in this connexion the native place of three of the early disciples who were or may have been especially prominent in this development. Of St. Peter we have evidence that this is true [Acts 10¹ to 11¹⁸, 15⁷]; and as regards St. Andrew and St. Philip, they are the only two who bear Greek names among the twelve.

12²³. 'them' is Andrew and Philip. St. John, no doubt purposely, says no more about the Greeks; and we shall be well advised not to ask whether they were forthwith admitted to the presence of the Lord, or not. If we insist on putting the question, probably the answer is, Not yet, but soon

[12³²], although this will not be in the way that they now expect. The important point is that they have arrived and desire to see the Lord, with all that this implies [1³⁹ᵃ, 14⁹].

12²⁴. This analogy from the natural order is also used by St. Paul in 1 Cor. 15³⁶, but appears only here in the gospels.

12²⁵. St. John's expression of this law, which is near the heart of the Lord's teaching, is even more strongly worded here than it usually is in the earlier gospels; but we find the verb 'to hate' in this connexion also at Lk. 14²⁶; cf. Mt. 6²⁴ = Lk. 16¹³. The reason may perhaps be that 12²⁶, especially as spoken in this context, certainly includes the possibility of martyrdom as one result of following the Lord.

12²⁶. It is a valuable exercise to trace in the gospels the development of the meaning of the verb 'to follow', when used of following the Lord, from the literal, outward sense of 'following about' (e.g. Mk. 2¹⁵ 'they (disciples) were beginning to follow Him about'), to the sense of religious discipleship, as here.

'Where I am'. The Lord is, permanently, one with the Father, wherever He may be, whatever He is doing; and thanks to Him His servant may also share this presence, though never as of right.

12²⁷. The sentence beginning 'Father' may be either a prayer, as R.V. text, or, more probably, a question (as R.V. mg), '(Am I to say), Father, save me from this hour?'

12²⁸. This prayer by the Lord may be compared with the first petition in the prayer given by Him to disciples as a pattern prayer, 'May thy name be hallowed' [Mt. 6⁹]; but here there is greater or more obvious emphasis than in the pattern prayer that it is the part of the Father Himself to glorify His name.

At 1⁵¹ the Lord promised disciples that in the ministry and work of the Son of man they would see heaven unveiled, and perfect intercourse between heaven and earth. The divine voice here expresses these same truths in another form. To the end the angels of God will ascend and descend upon the Son of man.

12³². The Greek verb for 'to lift up' means also 'to exalt', and is used in Acts 2³³, 5³¹ of the Lord's 'exaltation' to the Father's side. Since the Lord's first words in this important passage state that 'the hour is come, that the Son of man should be glorified' [12²³], and here at its close [12³²] He refers to His 'exaltation' from the earth, an exaltation explained by the evangelist in 12³³ to be a reference to the manner of His death upon the cross, it is noteworthy that in the LXX of Is. 52¹³ the two Greek verbs for 'to be exalted' and 'to be glorified' are used, side by side, of the servant of the Lord (Yahweh).

The Greek verb used here for 'to draw' is used in the LXX at Jer. 31³ of Yahweh's constraint (whether gentle or otherwise), arising from His great love for Israel.

12³⁴. The two titles, 'the Messiah' and 'the Son of man', are found close together, as here, not only (as is pointed out in the exposition) at Mk. 8²⁹⁻³¹, but also at Mk. 14⁶¹, ⁶², in the high priest's question and the Lord's reply. But whereas at Mk. 8³¹ the Lord, speaking to disciples, forthwith re-interprets the doctrine of the Son of man in terms of suffering, death, and resurrection, at Mk. 14⁶² in His reply to the Jewish tribunal He retains the traditional language about the destiny of the Son of man. Thus both replies, markedly different as they are, prove to be entirely free from any trace of the revolutionary, political ambitions, which in many quarters at this time may have been an especially valued feature of the Jewish doctrine of the Messiah.

12³⁷. 'So many signs'. Although St. John makes clear that the Lord's restoration of life to Lazarus was the act on His part which led forthwith to the fatal decision of the Jews [11⁵³], yet both here and at 11⁴⁷ he is careful to co-ordinate this, the Lord's chief sign in John, with others. He thus implies that they form a single and united whole or series, and must be considered and treated as such. At 7³¹ the reason given by many of the multitude for their belief on the Lord was the number of His signs, and since in such remarks of the Jews or of the multitude, as found in John, there usually lurks something unsatisfactory or at least inadequate, the reader was perhaps being reminded that, rightly understood, all the Lord's works are but parts of His one great work [4³⁴, 17⁴], being indeed the expression of Himself and therefore of His Father [5¹⁷, 10³²⁻³⁸]. Here in 12³⁷ therefore, both in respect of the quantity of the evidence and of its quality (as signs), St. John is deliberately accommodating himself to the position and outlook of the Jews, which is not his (cf. 4⁴⁸, 14¹¹, 20²⁹).

12³⁸⁻⁴¹. Two passages are cited from the book of Isaiah, in order to show (1) that the scriptural prediction of the Jews' disbelief in their Messiah has now been fulfilled, and (2) that this disbelief was certain and inevitable.

The first quotation, that in 12³⁸, is from Is. 53¹ (cited here, as also at Rom. 10¹⁶, in exact agreement with the LXX), and forms part of the last and greatest of the sections in that book which deal with the servant of Yahweh. As understood here, the first sentence in the quotation refers to the Lord's words or teaching; the second to His signs or mighty works (cf. Is. 51⁹). The way in which in ch. 11 the Lord revealed Himself both in word [11²⁵, ²⁶] and in action [11³⁹⁻⁴⁴] is probably designed to show that both His words and His works convey the same message and are acts of God.

The second quotation, that in 12⁴⁰, is from Is. 6¹⁰, and is quoted, or at least recalled, in at least four other passages of the N.T. [Mt. 13¹⁴, ¹⁵, Mk. 4¹², Lk. 8¹⁰, Acts 28²⁶, ²⁷]. In the first and last of these it is quoted textually in agreement with the LXX; but here, in Jn. 12⁴⁰, the citation suggests familiarity with both the Hebrew and the LXX, although it agrees textually with neither. If the deviations are his own, St. John's purpose seems to be to emphasize the divine action in producing the disbelief of the Jews, and his quotation is therefore in form the sternest of them all. He wishes the reader to discern the divine activity not only in the belief of disciples [6⁴⁴], but also in the disbelief of the Jews.

12³⁹. 'For this cause' refers to the coming, second prophecy.

12⁴⁰. 'hardened', better, 'dulled'.

12⁴¹. Just as at 8⁵⁶ Abraham is said to have seen the day of Jesus, so here Isaiah is said to have seen His glory, and to have spoken of Him. And it was precisely because Isaiah saw the Lord's glory that he became conscious also of the inevitable condemnation of Israel; indeed the sentence of condemnation on Israel forms the conclusion of Isaiah's vision and call in Is. 6$^{1-13}$. Similarly in John the rejection of the Lord by the Jews does not diminish His glory; rather, because of their rejection of Him His glory is revealed in the cross to the fullest extent.

12^{42}. The Pharisees here, as elsewhere in John (e.g. 4^1, 7^{32}, 9^{13}, 11^{46}), appear as the bitterest opponents of the Lord and His cause.

12^{44}. This verse should be compared not only with Jn. 13^{20}, but with Mt. 10^{40}, Mk. 9^{37}, Lk. 9^{48}, 10^{16}.

12$^{44, 45}$. Although it is true that the Lord's words in 14^{6b}, 'No one cometh unto the Father, but through me', can also be expressed in the form 'No one can come unto me, except the Father which sent me draw him' [6^{44}], yet the goal of the life of faith is the Father, to whom the Lord is the way [14^{6a}], since He has been sent by the Father to guide men to their goal. In this sense, although the Son and the Father are one [10^{30}], and in beholding the Son men behold the Father [12^{45}, 14^9], yet the Father is the greater [14^{28}].

III

The passion and exaltation of the Lord

SECTION 7. 13¹–20³¹

The Self-oblation of the Lord

The Lord's words. At the last supper, after His washing of the disciples' feet [13¹⁻²⁰] and the departure of Judas [13²¹⁻³⁰], the Lord reveals the necessity, meaning, and results of His passion.

(a) First instruction, 13³¹ to 14³¹: the Lord's departure and return.

(b) Second instruction, 15¹ to 16³³: the Lord and his disciples, 15¹⁻¹⁷; the disciples in the world, 15¹⁸ to 16¹⁵; return to the theme of the first instruction 16¹⁷⁻²⁸; the Lord alone victorious, 16²⁹⁻³³.

(c) The prayer of the Lord, 17¹⁻²⁶.

The Lord's works.

(a) The arrest and binding of the Lord in the garden, and the freedom of the disciples, 18¹⁻¹².

(b) The Lord before the Jewish tribunals; Peter's denials, 18¹³⁻²⁷.

(c) The Lord before the Roman tribunal; His kingship and its nature, 18²⁸ to 19¹⁵.

(d) The crucifixion: the Lord's kingship realized in His 'exaltation' from the earth and the title on the cross, 19¹⁶⁻²²; the soldiers, 19²³, ²⁴; the Lord's mother and the beloved disciple, 19²⁵⁻²⁷; the death and burial, 19²⁸⁻⁴².

(e) The resurrection: the empty tomb, 20¹⁻¹⁰; the risen Lord revealed to Mary Magdalene, 20¹¹⁻¹⁸; and to the disciples, 20¹⁹, ²⁰; their commission, and the bestowal of the Holy Spirit, 20²¹⁻²³.

(f) The doubt of Thomas, 20²⁴, ²⁵; a week later, his confession; the last beatitude, 20²⁶⁻²⁹.

Conclusion. The evangelist's purpose in writing the book, 20³⁰, ³¹.

SECTION 7a. 13¹–14³¹. *The Lord and His own. The first instruction.*

13 Now before the feast of the passover, Jesus knowing that his hour was come that he should depart out of this world unto the Father, having loved his own which were in the world, he loved them ¹unto the 2 end. And during supper, the devil having already put into the heart of 3 Judas Iscariot, Simon's *son*, to betray him, *Jesus*, knowing that the Father had given all things into his hands, and that he came forth from 4 God, and goeth unto God, riseth from supper, and layeth aside his 5 garments; and he took a towel, and girded himself. Then he poureth water into the bason, and began to wash the disciples' feet, and to wipe

---

¹ *Or* to the uttermost

6 them with the towel wherewith he was girded. So he cometh to Simon
7 Peter. He saith unto him, Lord, dost thou wash my feet? Jesus answered
and said unto him, What I do thou knowest not now; but thou shalt
8 understand hereafter. Peter saith unto him, Thou shalt never wash my
feet. Jesus answered him, If I wash thee not, thou hast no part with me.
9 Simon Peter saith unto him, Lord, not my feet only, but also my hands
10 and my head. Jesus saith to him, He that is bathed needeth not ¹save to
11 wash his feet, but is clean every whit: and ye are clean, but not all. For he
knew him that should betray him; therefore said he, Ye are not all clean.
12 So when he had washed their feet, and taken his garments, and ²sat
13 down again, he said unto them, Know ye what I have done to you? Ye
14 call me, ³Master, and, Lord: and ye say well; for so I am. If I then, the
Lord and the ³Master, have washed your feet, ye also ought to wash one
15 another's feet. For I have given you an example, that ye also should do
16 as I have done to you. Verily, verily, I say unto you, A ⁴servant is not
greater than his lord; neither ⁵one that is sent greater than he that sent
17 him. If ye know these things, blessed are ye if ye do them. I speak not of
18 you all: I know whom I ⁶have chosen: but that the scripture may be
19 fulfilled, He that eateth ⁷my bread lifted up his heel against me. From
henceforth I tell you before it come to pass, that, when it is come to
20 pass, ye may believe that ⁸I am *he*. Verily, verily, I say unto you, He that
receiveth whomsoever I send receiveth me; and he that receiveth me
receiveth him that sent me.
21 When Jesus had thus said, he was troubled in the spirit, and testified,
and said, Verily, verily, I say unto you, that one of you shall betray me.
22 The disciples looked one on another, doubting of whom he spake. There
23 was at the table reclining in Jesus' bosom one of his disciples, whom
24 Jesus loved. Simon Peter therefore beckoneth to him, and saith unto
25 him, Tell *us* who it is of whom he speaketh. He leaning back, as he was,
26 on Jesus' breast saith unto him, Lord, who is it? Jesus therefore answereth, He it is, for whom I shall dip the sop, and give it him. So when he
had dipped the sop, he taketh and giveth it to Judas, *the son* of Simon
27 Iscariot. And after the sop, then entered Satan into him. Jesus therefore
28 saith unto him, That thou doest, do quickly. Now no man at the table
29 knew for what intent he spake this unto him. For some thought, because
Judas had the ⁹bag, that Jesus said unto him, Buy what things we have
30 need of for the feast; or, that he should give something to the poor. He
then having received the sop went out straightway: and it was night.
31 When therefore he was gone out, Jesus saith, Now ¹⁰is the Son of man
32 glorified, and God ¹⁰is glorified in him; And God shall glorify him in

---

¹ *Some ancient authorities omit* save, *and* his feet.   ² *Gr.* reclined.   ³ *Or*
Teacher   ⁴ *Gr.* bondservant.   ⁵ *Gr.* an apostle.   ⁶ *Or* chose
⁷ *Many ancient authorities read* his bread with me.   ⁸ *Or* I am   ⁹ *Or* box
¹⁰ *Or* was

33 himself, and straightway shall he glorify him. Little children, yet a little
while I am with you. Ye shall seek me: and as I said unto the Jews,
34 Whither I go, ye cannot come; so now I say unto you. A new commandment I give unto you, that ye love one another; ¹even as I have loved
35 you, that ye also love one another. By this shall all men know that ye
are my disciples, if ye have love one to another.

36 Simon Peter saith unto him, Lord, whither goest thou? Jesus answered,
Whither I go, thou canst not follow me now; but thou shalt follow
37 afterwards. Peter saith unto him, Lord, why cannot I follow thee even
38 now? I will lay down my life for thee. Jesus answereth, Wilt thou lay
down thy life for me? Verily, verily, I say unto thee, The cock shall not
crow, till thou hast denied me thrice.

14 Let not your heart be troubled: ²ye believe in God, believe also
2 in me. In my Father's house are many ³mansions; if it were not so, I
3 would have told you; for I go to prepare a place for you. And if I go
and prepare a place for you, I come again, and will receive you unto
4 myself; that where I am, *there* ye may be also. ⁴And whither I go, ye
5 know the way. Thomas saith unto him, Lord, we know not whither thou
6 goest; how know we the way? Jesus saith unto him, I am the way, and
7 the truth, and the life: no one cometh unto the Father, but ⁵by me. If ye
had known me, ye would have known my Father also: from henceforth
8 ye know him, and have seen him. Philip saith unto him, Lord, shew us
9 the Father, and it sufficeth us. Jesus saith unto him, Have I been so
long time with you, and dost thou not know me, Philip? he that hath
seen me hath seen the Father: how sayest thou, Shew us the Father?
10 Believest thou not that I am in the Father, and the Father in me? the
words that I say unto you I speak not from myself: but the Father
11 abiding in me doeth his works. Believe me that I am in the Father, and
12 the Father in me: or else believe me for the very works' sake. Verily,
verily, I say unto you, He that believeth on me, the works that I do shall
he do also; and greater *works* than these shall he do; because I go unto
13 the Father. And whatsoever ye shall ask in my name, that will I do, that
14 the Father may be glorified in the Son. If ye shall ask ⁶me anything in
15 my name, that will I do. If ye love me, ye will keep my commandments.
16 And I will ⁷pray the Father, and he shall give you another ⁸Comforter,
17 that he may be with you for ever, *even* the Spirit of truth: whom the
world cannot receive; for it beholdeth him not, neither knoweth him: ye
18 know him; for he abideth with you, and shall be in you. I will not leave
19 you ⁹desolate: I come unto you. Yet a little while, and the world behold-

---

¹ *Or* even as I loved you, that ye also may love one another   ² *Or* believe
in God   ³ *Or* abiding-places   ⁴ *Many ancient authorities read* And
whither I go ye know, and the way ye know.   ⁵ *Or* through   ⁶ *Many
ancient authorities omit* me.   ⁷ *Gr.* make request of.   ⁸ *Or* Advocate
Or Helper *Gr.* Paraclete.   ⁹ *Or* orphans

eth me no more; but ye behold me: because I live, ¹ye shall live also.
20 In that day ye shall know that I am in my Father, and ye in me, and
21 I in you. He that hath my commandments, and keepeth them, he it is
that loveth me: and he that loveth me shall be loved of my Father, and I
22 will love him, and will manifest myself unto him. Judas (not Iscariot)
saith unto him, Lord, what is come to pass that thou wilt manifest
23 thyself unto us, and not unto the world? Jesus answered and said unto
him, If a man love me, he will keep my word: and my Father will love
24 him, and we will come unto him, and make our abode with him. He that
loveth me not keepeth not my words: and the word which ye hear is not
mine, but the Father's who sent me.
25　These things have I spoken unto you, while *yet* abiding with you.
26 But the ²Comforter, *even* the Holy Spirit, whom the Father will send in
my name, he shall teach you all things, and bring to your remembrance
27 all that I said unto you. Peace I leave with you; my peace I give unto
you: not as the world giveth, give I unto you. Let not your heart be
28 troubled, neither let it be fearful. Ye heard how I said to you, I go away,
and I come unto you. If ye loved me, ye would have rejoiced, because I
29 go unto the Father: for the Father is greater than I. And now I have
told you before it come to pass, that, when it is come to pass, ye may
30 believe. I will no more speak much with you, for the prince of the world
31 cometh: and he hath nothing in me; but that the world may know that
I love the Father, and as the Father gave me commandment, even so
I do. Arise, let us go hence.

¹ *Or* and ye shall live　　　² *Or* Advocate *Or* Helper　*Gr.* Paraclete.

EXPOSITION OF SECTION 7a. 13¹–14³¹

As we have seen, it is a feature of this gospel that a work or
action of the Lord is usually accompanied by teaching designed to
show the significance or meaning of the work or action. In ch. 6, for
example, the Lord's feeding of the multitude is explained by His
teaching on the bread of life, next day, in the synagogue at Capernaum. Chs. 13 to 20 only differ from this earlier example, in that
now the teaching (in chs. 13 to 17) *precedes* the action (in chs.
18 to 20).

In St. John's prologue [1¹⁻¹⁸] it is not stated until 1¹⁴ that the
Word became flesh; but it was pointed out that the greater part of
verses 10 to 13 would form a faithful description, not only of the
activity of the Logos in the world throughout the world's history,
but also of the Lord's ministry, as this is set before us by St. John.
In 1⁹, ¹⁰, ¹¹ we read that 'the true light was in the world, . . . and

the world knew him not. He came to that which was his own, and
they who were his own did not receive him'. These verses are
illustrated in the record of chs. 2 to 12, which describes the Lord's
ministry in both word and deed. The motive for this ministry, we
read in 3¹⁶, was God's love for the world; out of His great love God
sent, indeed gave,¹ His only Son. And in chs. 2 to 12 it is shown
how and why, when this love was manifested in a human life, it
became a stumbling-block to the world, and therefore a judgement
of the world. So far as the world is concerned, the Lord's ministry
is now over [12³¹ᵃ]; the world, as such, has rejected Him and dis-
believed in Him. Outside, therefore, it is night [13³⁰]. But chs.
13 to 20, to which we now come, illustrate verses 12 and 13 of the
prologue; for happily there were exceptions to the general rejection.
'But as many as received him, to them, those who believe on his
name, he gave the right to become children of God'; they received
a divine, as opposed to a merely human, birth.

If it be asked why verses 12 and 13 of the prologue are said to
illustrate not only chs. 13 to 17, in which the Lord is alone with the
disciples, but also chs. 18 to 20, which narrate the subsequent
events, the answer is that, although the events of chs. 18 to 20,
St. John's account of the Lord's passion and resurrection, are
not mentioned as such (see p. 266) in chs. 13 to 17, yet these
chapters are the explanation in word, to the disciples, of the meaning of the events which will be narrated in chs. 18 to 20. And it is
for disciples that the events of chs. 18 to 20 have their importance.
To others they are not likely to be more than the record of a
shocking miscarriage of justice, carried out with violence; to
disciples they are the record of events to which they owe their life.
And it can hardly be emphasized too strongly that to disciples, and
to disciples only, was the meaning of the crucifixion revealed, first
in word, in the teaching of chs. 13 to 17, and later in deed, in the
fact of their reunion with their risen Lord (cf. 14¹⁹). For the exaltation of the Lord upon the cross, the final and crowning sign of
God's love [3¹⁶] and therefore of the Lord's work, although in one
way it will part Him from the disciples, in another way will enable
Him for the first time to be fully theirs. Just as the Spirit descended
and abode upon Him in full measure during His ministry [1³³, 3³⁴],

---

¹ Although the compound verb, used by St. Paul in Rom. 8³², is not used in
Jn. 3¹⁶, yet in the light of the context [Jn. 3¹⁴, ¹⁵, ¹⁷] we are not likely to be wrong,
if we have the thought of sacrifice also in our minds.

so as a result of His exaltation He, in the Person of the Spirit, will descend and abide on them [7³⁹]. Hence the first verse of ch. 13 may be regarded as a kind of headline for the remainder of this gospel. The Lord, knowing before the feast of the passover that His hour has come to transfer from this world to the Father, now concentrates on those who peculiarly belong to Him and in a special degree form the object of His love; for, after He has gone, they are to remain in the world [17¹¹].

A brief account of the relations of the disciples with the Lord, as these relations are set forth in this gospel, is given on pp. 68–73 and attention is there drawn to the emphasis laid by the evangelist on their faithfulness, but also on their imperfect understanding of their Master. It will suffice here to consider the problems put to the Lord in ch. 14 by one disciple or another; and it may also be found instructive to reflect whether these are not also the questions which in every generation of believers it is desired to put. 'Lord, we know not whither thou goest; how know we the way?' [14⁵.] 'Lord, show us the Father; this is all we ask' [14⁸]. 'Lord, what is come to pass, that thou wilt manifest thyself to us, and not to the world?' [14²².] In ch. 16 we find the disciples seeking help from one another, because they are unable to penetrate their Master's meaning [16¹⁷, ¹⁸]; and when finally they say, 'Lo, now speakest thou plainly, and speakest no riddle. Now we know that thou knowest all things, and needest not that any man should ask thee; by this we believe that thou camest forth from God' [16²⁹, ³⁰], the Lord's answer is, 'Do ye now believe? Behold, the hour cometh, yea, is come, that ye shall be scattered, every man to his own way, and shall leave me alone' [16³¹, ³²]. Thus, in respect of the Lord's actions, His words at 13⁷ to St. Peter are doubtless true also of the rest, 'What I do, thou knowest not now; but thou shalt understand hereafter'; and in respect of His words, we recall 16¹², 'I have many things to say to you, but ye cannot bear them now'. Finally, in the events of ch. 18, Simon Peter in the garden, out of loyalty to his Master, attempts for a moment to use the methods of the world with regard to Malchus; but his action is discountenanced by the Lord. And soon afterwards the same disciple, as a result of his introduction into a place of danger by a friend, also a disciple [18¹⁵, ¹⁶], the position of danger being the courtyard of the house of the high priest, finds himself constrained to disown his Lord three times.

Such, according to these chapters, is the thought and action of these men; and yet, again according to these chapters, they have kept the Father's word, [17⁶]. They are indeed the gift of the Father to the Son [17⁹], and are therefore the Son's 'own' [13¹], in a sense in which the world is not, or at least has proved itself unable to become. And the Lord, who during the ministry has kept and guarded them [17¹²], so that with one inevitable exception they have come safely through the judgement which His ministry caused, now, on the eve of His departure from them, 'loves them to the end', that is, not to the moment only of His leaving them, but 'to the uttermost' (R.V. mg), both in time and in eternity.

It should be particularly noticed that in this gospel no locality is mentioned as the scene of the meal which is found in progress at 13², and therefore of the washing, by the Lord, of the disciples' feet, or of His teaching, His words which follow this His work. When these are ended, the Lord will take the disciples with Him into the presence of the Father [17¹], and only at 18¹, when He goes forth with them across the Kidron to a garden, are we brought once more into contact with the world, and with its 'prince' or 'ruler', now about to come upon the scene [14³⁰]. Between 13³¹ and 17²⁶, although outside it is 'night' [13³⁰], 'the prince of the world' is excluded from the intercourse of the Lord with His disciples. St. John was no doubt well aware of the tradition of the 'upper room'; but it seems that with the exception of the words 'before the feast of the passover' in 13¹, words perhaps carrying a double meaning (see pp. 234, 353–4) and of the allusion to the supper in 13², he avoids mention of any particular place or time in connexion with the events and instruction of chs. 13 to 17, until 18¹ is reached. It seems that both in the record of the cleansing effected by the Lord's washing of the disciples' feet, a cleansing bound to recall the Church's rite of baptism by water, and of His instruction to them which follows—itself another form of the cleansing which He offers [15³]—an instruction revealing the results for them of His death and resurrection, St. John wishes the reader to have in mind not only the original disciples, but all the future members of the Lord's body. May it be partly for this reason that these chapters contain no direct parallel to the narrative of Mk. 14²²⁻²⁵ and its parallels, a narrative describing a unique event, but everywhere reveal the permanent meaning and significance of those verses? We notice the same phenomenon in the evangelist's attitude to the Church's rite of baptism. The religious importance and significance attached to water could hardly be more strongly stressed than it is in this gospel; but so far as the Church's rite is concerned, the teaching is indirect, rather than direct.[1]

But we have not yet considered a feature of St. John's narrative, which is very prominent in 13¹⁻³⁰. Its importance is shown in that it is the first matter which he mentions in 13², in his account of the supper. As we have seen, 13¹ may be regarded as a kind of headline for the remaining chapters of this gospel; but 13², after opening with the words, 'And during supper', continues, 'the devil having already put into the heart of Judas Iscariot, Simon's son, to deliver him up' (that is, the Lord). Later, in the course of the narrative, the Lord Himself twice makes an exception, first when, during His washing of the disciples' feet, He tells them that they 'are clean, but not all'; and secondly when, after the feet-washing, He says that His action is to be an example to them as His servants and emissaries, and that, if they know these things and act accordingly, they are blessed, but then adds 'I speak not of you all.' And finally a whole section of ten verses [13²¹⁻³⁰] is devoted to the events which immediately precede the exit of Judas, and his identification of himself with darkness.

In order to understand the significance of St. John's narrative here, it is necessary to go back to ch. 6. That chapter opens with a picture of the Lord seated on a mountain top with His disciples, and a great multitude coming to Him; but as it draws to a close, if we may use here the language, not of St. John, but of St. Paul in Gal. 5¹¹, His teaching on 'the offence of the cross' not only arouses opposition but causes many of His disciples to leave Him. When the Lord turns to the twelve, asking whether they also desire to go away, St. Peter, as their spokesman, replies in words of devoted loyalty. The Lord, answering them as a body, reveals that, although they are indeed the object of His choice, none the less even among them is an evil heart of unbelief. The evangelist's editorial note in 6⁷¹ is apt to obscure the important fact that neither then nor indeed at any time before the Lord's arrest at 18¹⁻¹¹ are the disciples as a whole aware to which of their number the Lord has thus referred; and there for the present the matter is left.

[1] The problem set by St. John's method here is more usually explained by his unwillingness to disclose to non-Christian readers of his book the origin and ground of the two chief Christian sacraments.

Let us now return to ch. 13, bearing in mind what ch. 6 has taught us. Evil is present in the inmost circle of the twelve, and therefore has now penetrated even into the sanctity of the Lord's last meal with His disciples. And yet, although these as a body have been presumably made aware of its presence in their midst by the Lord's words in 6⁷⁰, it is still unidentified. It should once more be emphasized that from 13² to the end of ch. 17 the Lord is alone with His disciples, who still form a unit, and that throughout these chapters the world is rigidly excluded, except that at an early stage in the proceedings one of those present quits the Lord's presence and rejoins the world (cf. 15¹⁹).

And this absence of the world is not due to accident or chance; all takes place with the Lord's full knowledge and consent; Judas himself goes out at the Lord's bidding. This knowledge is emphasized by the participle 'knowing', with reference to the Lord, in 13¹, repeated in 13³; we shall meet this participle again, with reference to Him, in 18⁴, when at the betrayal the world once more appears upon the scene; and for the fourth and last time at 19²⁸, a few moments before His death upon the cross. Here, in 13³, the emphasis is on the Lord's knowledge of His complete and absolute authority as the representative of God, from whom He came, to whom He goes. This authority He now proceeds to manifest in a remarkable way. He leaves His place at the table, and undertakes, in the disciples' service, the status and task of a slave. For the last time in this gospel we now read of water (except when we learn at 19³⁴ that after the Lord's death 'blood and water' issued from His side). With this water, which He has poured into the bason, the Lord proceeds to wash the feet of the disciples, one by one, and then to wipe them dry, or clean, with the towel which He wore. Those who receive this treatment apparently receive it in silence, until the Lord comes to Simon Peter. He, conscious of the strangeness of this action by the Lord, his Master, questions it. The Lord's reply, the importance of which is emphasized by the words 'answered and said', is that the disciple cannot at present know what the Lord's action is or means; but an assurance is given that later he shall come to know. (No doubt the primary reference here is to the understanding to be brought to the believer through the death and resurrection of the Lord and the coming of the Holy Spirit; but a universal law of the religious life—cf. 1 Cor. 13¹²—is also to be kept in view.) For St. Peter, however, as for little children, the present is of much more interest and importance than the future; and he now protests strongly that his Master shall never perform this menial service on him. The Lord answers that a share in the Lord's life and work is only possible to one whom He has cleansed. Only if Peter is prepared to dismiss his pride, and to allow the Lord to do this work upon and for him, can he hope to be where Jesus is. Simon Peter's consent is now at once forthcoming; but his words show also how little as yet he understands, since he now goes to the opposite extreme, and thinks that he can prescribe a larger measure of the gift than the Lord Himself has offered. On the contrary, as the Lord's reply shows (the reading of the R.V. margin is being followed here), he who has received the washing offered by the Lord is wholly clean. In the words 'Ye are clean, but not all', it is made clear, in the first place, that the Lord has been addressing St. Peter as the representative disciple. For every disciple, therefore, who receives the cleansing offered by the Lord, the words hold good, 'What I do, thou knowest not now; but thou shalt come to know hereafter.' But in the second place the words 'And ye are clean, but not all' contain a warning. We may remind ourselves that the disciples as yet have no knowledge, nor will have it to the end, who among them is to fall away; the reader knows, but not the actors in the scene themselves. By an editorial note at 13¹¹, as at 6⁷¹, the evangelist once more makes clear for the reader to whom the Lord refers; but for the disciples the Lord's words remain a mystery. They learn that as a body they are clean; but not all. Although they have been chosen by the Lord, and indeed just cleansed by Him, yet evil is still present.

The Lord has now completed His work, and has resumed His garments and His rightful place at the meal; something has been done, and has become possible, for disciples, which, at any rate at present, has not been done, and has not become possible, for others; and the disciples must now learn what it is. They call Him 'Teacher' or Rabbi, and 'Lord' or Mari; and they are right. If then He, 'the Lord and the Teacher', has washed their feet, they also have now a corresponding task and office to perform for one another. This disclosure does not contradict what was said a moment ago to Simon Peter, that only later would he understand his Lord's act upon him. For the behaviour and conduct which are now enjoined upon disciples are to be the result of His work upon them, the outcome of His love; the conduct at issue here is not that which is the outcome of a kindly temperament or of good nature; the disciples are to love one another, 'according as their Lord has loved them' [13³⁴]; and they have now received the means to do this; let them then fulfil it, and so follow the example of their Lord.

But, once more, this is not all. In fact the disciples are not, in this respect, as yet a unity. One whom the Lord Himself chose and sought to cleanse, one who has assimilated His bread, is even now about to turn against Him and to compass His undoing. St. Peter had said, 'Lord, to whom shall we go? Thou hast words which confer eternal life' [6⁶⁸]; but according to Mk. 14¹⁰, ¹¹ one of themselves has previously gone away to the chief priests, who have undertaken to confer upon him money; and the Lord now prepares the disciples for the discovery, which within a few hours they will have to face, of the meaning of His warnings. That He now lets them know what is to happen, before the event itself takes place, will or should steady them, when it does happen, and should strengthen their belief in Him. And they must remember their mission, and the height of their calling; as their Master represents the Father who sent Him, so they represent their Master.

At the close of these prescriptions and warnings, and before finally revealing, in solemn assurance, that one of their own body, one of themselves, is about to hand Him over, the Lord, we read, was troubled in His spirit. This is the last time that we read, in this gospel, of distress on His part. Before asking to be taken to the grave of Lazarus, He 'troubled Himself'; again, when He told Philip and Andrew that the hour was come 'that the Son of man should be glorified', and what this would involve for those who wished to serve and follow Him, His soul was troubled; now, for the last time, when His disciple is about to leave Him, He is troubled in the spirit. As a result of the Lord's warnings just given, or should we rather say of the Lord's work upon them in the cleansing, the disciples appear to have begun to lose the wrong kind of self-confidence, and they now look one upon another in perplexity. No one, however, dares to speak, until Simon Peter beckons to the disciple nearest to the Lord—'the beloved disciple' whom we now meet for the first time in this gospel—and seeks from and through him a solution of the riddle. The disciple does as Peter asks, and the Lord in a single sentence, followed forthwith by an action, makes the desired disclosure; after which, we read, Satan took possession of Judas. It seems to be implied that no one except the disciple nearest to the Lord, and possibly but improbably St. Peter, heard the Lord's words to the disciple and therefore understood the significance of the act which followed. The first words to be heard by all present are the Lord's instructions to Judas to carry out his action with speed, and it is expressly stated that no one at the table understood their import. The thought of the disciples instinctively connected Judas with finance and economics; it was he who had assessed the financial worth of Mary's gift and had suggested, for his own purposes, that it might more profitably have been given to the poor; and so they now assume that he is told to make some purchase or to give an alms; they do not realize that he will not return. But in fact Judas goes out, to identify himself with darkness; and only when evil, in his person, has been banished, does the full revelation contained in 13^{31} to 17^{26} become possible.

The events narrated by St. John as occurring at the supper, namely the washing of the disciples' feet and the departure of Judas, have now been set forth; and the rest of the narrative in chs. 13 to 17 is confined to instruction, although the bearing of this instruction on action is by no means forgotten (cf. 14^{31}). The instruction falls into three parts, 13^{31} to 14^{31}, 15^{1} to 16^{33}, 17^{1-26}, which must be treated separately; but first, two features of the way in which the complex of the events of the passion is treated throughout the instruction must be mentioned.

1. The events are never described by the usual terms, crucifixion, death, resurrection, ascension. The terms used, which none the less clearly refer to the events just named, are those of the Lord's departure and return.

2. The events themselves, although they still lie in the future and will be narrated in chs. 18 to 20, are treated in the instruction as already happening [14^{31}, 16^{5}], indeed sometimes as having already happened; thus the Lord has conquered the world [16^{33}]; He has accomplished the work given Him to do [17^{4}]; He speaks as One who has already passed through death.

We now pass to consider the three parts of the instruction separately.

(a) 13^{1} to 14^{31}. The Lord and His own. First Instruction. This part consists of preliminary instruction, and deals chiefly with the themes of the Lord's departure in 'a little while' [13^{33}], and His return to His disciples [14^{18}]. Subjects such as the coming of the

Paraclete [14¹⁶, ¹⁷, ²⁶] and the future relation of the disciples, through the Lord, to the Father [14²⁰, ²¹, ²³] are only mentioned briefly, being reserved for fuller treatment in the second part of the instruction. A further difference between these two parts is that in this first part individual disciples from time to time interject queries and difficulties [13³⁶, ³⁷, 14⁵, ⁸, ²²], whereas in chs. 15 and 16 they are completely silent, except at 16¹⁷, ¹⁸ when they question among themselves about the meaning of the Lord's words, and in the conclusion, at 16²⁹, ³⁰, when they collectively address the Lord. The chief purpose, then, of this first part is to provide what St. John believes to be the true explanation of the Lord's crucifixion, death, resurrection, and ascension.

It is clear that now, after the departure of Judas, the Lord's glory is revealed more fully and completely than it was revealed, for example, at 2¹¹, in His first sign at Cana of Galilee. Not only was it bluntly stated in 7³⁹ that 'Jesus was not yet glorified', but in 11⁴ we learned that the purpose of Lazarus' illness was the glory of God and of His Son; and by showing that the result of the Lord's work on Lazarus was the resolution of the authorities to compass His death [11⁴⁶⁻⁵³], St. John teaches that His glory is to be fully and finally revealed in the complex of the events of the passion. This is confirmed by the Lord's words in 12²³, that the hour of the glorification of the Son of man has arrived, and by the following verses which deal with His coming death, accepted by Him to the glory of the Father's name [12²⁷, ²⁸]; and we now read [13³¹] that, Judas having departed, the Son of man has been glorified, and God has been glorified in Him, the verbs in the Greek signifying that the glory is an accomplished fact. The Lord has borne His witness or testimony; this has resulted in a testing or judgement, in which men have ranged themselves for or against Him, the final example of the latter attitude being Judas, and of the former attitude the disciples who remain. Therein the revelation of the glory of the Lord is made. There is, however, a further stage to be completed very shortly (with the 'straightway' of 13³² cf. 13³³ᵃ), when God will glorify the Son of man in Himself (that is, in God); in other words, this last stage will be the glorification of Him who is not only the Son of man (cf. 5²⁷), but also, and by right, the Son of God (cf. 11⁴, 14¹³, 17¹, 19⁷). This last stage, the meaning of which is now to be revealed in the instruction, is to be effected in the events of chs. 18 to 20; it consists in the raising of the disciples by the Lord into fellowship, through Him, with the Father; and doubtless for this reason the word 'Father', which in ch. 13 only occurs twice (at 13¹, ³, in reference to the unique Sonship of the Lord Himself), will recur more than forty times in the Lord's words to the disciples in chs. 14 to 16, whereas the word 'God', used here [13³¹, ³²], will occur on the Lord's lips only thrice.

At present, however, the disciples do not know the Father (cf. 14⁷); and the Lord therefore addresses them as (His own) children (14³³), who can receive but little of all that He desires, and has, to give to them (cf. 16¹²); they must be fed with milk. As long as they remain in this state, they will inevitably seek Him; for, like the Jews [8²¹], they cannot come where He is going, that is, to the bosom of the Father's love [1¹⁸, 17²⁴ᵉⁿᵈ]. The reason for this is that they do not love one another with the infinite love with which He has loved them; and He now gives them a new commandment, that their love together should be as His for them. His love, reproduced in their love for one another, is to be the sign to all men, that is, to the world (cf. 17²¹ᵉⁿᵈ), of their discipleship.

It is now shown how far the disciples are at present from ability to follow their Lord, loyal though they desire to be; and also how much they still have to learn. Simon Peter by his question at 13³⁶ reveals his present ignorance of the implications of discipleship; and although he receives a promise that later he shall follow, he shows himself to be the little child which he has just been called, by unwillingness to wait until the proper time; and when he asserts that he is ready to do for his Master what that Master, as the good Shepherd, is about to do for His sheep [10¹¹, ¹⁵], he has to learn how great and imminent a fall, on the contrary, awaits him.

For the Lord has just bidden the disciples to love one another, as He has loved them. This, however, they cannot do of themselves, but only when, after His glorification, they have received His Spirit. They are to be enabled to carry out His new commandment in the future, only as a result of His work or action in the past. Hence, until that work or action is complete, they cannot come whither He goes [13³³; cf. 13⁷]; He must first tread the way alone; no one, however strong, can follow, until the Lord becomes 'the way' for him [14⁶]. So far from Peter being able at the moment to help the Lord by giving his life for Him, the Lord must first give His life for the disciple; the latter, if he relies on his own strength or loyalty, will fail [13³⁸]. When the Lord's victory is won, He will draw the disciple to Him, in order that, where He is, there His disciple may be also [12²⁶]; thus will the disciple glorify God (cf. 21¹⁹).

The use of the plural in 14¹ shows that St. Peter is again regarded as the disciples' representative; they must one and all go through distress and sorrow, as the result of their own failure, before they can attain to the joy of their Lord (cf. 15¹¹, 16²⁰⁻²²). None the less, the Lord knows that He has whereon to build, and the disciples are not to be discouraged by temporary failure. They have been brought up in the Jewish faith, and already they believe in God; let them now learn to believe also in their Master [14¹]; and therewith the unique Son of the Father proceeds to reveal to them what that Fatherhood implies and is.

In His Father's house there is room enough and to spare; let them rest assured of it; for the very purpose of their Master's journey (i.e. His death, resurrection, and ascension) is to prepare a place there for them. But this action of His implies also His return, when He will receive them to Himself, His purpose being that where He is they may be also. Of and by themselves they could not make the journey, any more than the Jews [7³⁴⁻³⁶]; but their Master, who has descended from heaven to impart knowledge of the Father and is now returning thither [16²⁸; cf. 3¹⁴], has by His life and death shown the way (in 14⁴ the R.V. text should be followed).

But Thomas, not yet knowing the goal, that is, the Father, wonders how the disciples can be said to know the way thither; upon which the Lord refers them to Himself; He, their Master, is the only way, and not only the way; He is also the truth, which sets free [8³²] and the life which enables action [3²¹]. Hitherto they have not known Him, and therefore have not known the Father; but from this moment they, unlike the Jews whether during the ministry [5³⁷, 8¹⁹, ⁵⁵] or in the future [16³], know the Father and have seen Him. (We may contrast the converse truth in 1¹⁸ and find the explication of the contradiction in 6⁴⁶.)

The assurance which Philip now offers to the Lord, that the disciples' difficulties would be at an end, if the Lord would grant them this sight of which He speaks, recalls the words of Martha at 11²². She also had put forward a request, which implied a separation, as it were, between the Lord and His Father; and now again, as there, the Lord shows that such a request implies inadequate,

imperfect understanding of Himself. For there is no such separation between the Father and Himself; and only the language
of mutual indwelling, a language inapplicable to the facts of the
physical world but readily understood in the religious life, can
set forth the completeness of the union. Whether the question be
of the Lord's words or of the Father's works, they both are one
and proceed from the same source. If the disciples cannot accept
the Lord's assurance of the mutual indwelling, let them, as a second
best, believe Him on the evidence of the Father's works as done by
Him. For indeed the disciple himself is deeply concerned in the
matter. Since the Lord, in His death, is going to the Father, the
believer on the Lord must be prepared to do not only works like
His, but works on a greater, wider scale. This is a promise, and
in so far as the disciples depend on their Lord [14¹³, ¹⁴], there is
no limit to its extent, with a view to the glory of the Father in the
Son. But they must show their love for their Lord by keeping His
commandments [14¹⁵]; and at His request the Father will give them
another Advocate or Helper, the Spirit of truth, who will be to
them no less an Advocate or Helper than their Lord has been.
The ministry of this other Advocate or Helper will be marked by
two characteristics: first, its permanence (contrast 8³³⁻³⁵, 13³³), and
secondly, the failure of the world to see or know His ministry, and
therefore inability to receive its working. The disciples, however,
have knowledge of the Spirit. Before they came in contact with
their Master, the Spirit in full measure [3³⁴] descended and abode
upon Him [1³², ³⁴]. This Spirit of truth, or reality, ever since has
dwelt with them in the Lord, and now, owing to the Lord's
departure, will be in them. They shall not be left fatherless; their
Lord Himself is coming to them. Yet a few hours, and He will be
seen no longer by the world; but the disciples will continue to see
Him in the life (the risen life), which it is His purpose to impart to
them; and 'in that day' they will share, through Him, in His life
with the Father. The love of the disciple for his Lord is conditional
on knowledge of and obedience to his Lord's commandments, and
will win for him the love of the Father and also the love and self-
revelation of the Lord. A question from Judas, not Iscariot, about
the change in the manner of this self-revelation of the Lord shows
how little the disciples can still grasp of the nature of the manifestation promised to them of their Master, or of its condition (His
death). The question, as such, receives no direct answer; but a

renewed assurance is given, subject, as always, to the essential condition of love and consequent faithfulness to the Lord's word. The assurance is that both the Father and the Son will come and abide with the faithful disciple. The use of the plural ('we'), and the fact that the coming results in an 'abiding', both suggest that the reference here is not so much to the coming of the risen Lord, as at 14¹⁸, or to the last day, as perhaps at 14³, but to the permanent abiding of the divine Persons with the individual member of the Church. On the other hand, absence of the condition of love must inevitably show itself in disobedience to the Lord's precepts (and therefore to the Father's word); and this, it is implied, precludes the possibility of the 'abiding' promised to obedience.

We now reach the concluding paragraph of this first part of the instruction; and we might well think that its contents represent the Lord's final words to His disciples, did we not know that chs. 15 and 16 are yet to follow. It is clear that some other explanation of its character must be found; and the difficulty may be lessened, if we reflect that in this gospel the Lord's 'hour' is a process, made up of stages which lead up to the climax of His death. These stages consist, on one side, of the external events of the passion, and, on the other, of internal resolution and self-dedication by the Lord, as He increasingly imparts Himself to His disciples. This paragraph will then represent the close of one such stage, on the internal side; and it is noteworthy that, whereas at its close, in His devotion and obedience to the Father, He invites the disciples to arise and act along with Him, the first person plural being used, at the close of the next instruction He is the only Agent in the conquest of the world [16³³]; the first person singular alone is used. On this view the final paragraph of this first instruction does represent the end of a stage, on the internal side, of the Lord's 'hour', a stage which will in due course have its counterpart on the external side (with 14³¹ᵉⁿᵈ cf. the same words in Mk. 14⁴²); but at present there is no change of scene and, after this break, the instruction will proceed.

In these concluding words [14²⁵⁻³¹] the Lord contrasts the revelation which, as the incarnate Lord, He has made to the disciples with that which awaits them in the future. Accordingly a final reference to the Paraclete or Holy Spirit, who is to take His place among them, is appropriate. He Himself is leaving them; but in uttering the word *Shalôm* or peace (the customary word

both of greeting and of farewell in eastern countries) He is using
no conventional expression. They have seen His peace, and know
on· what it rests; and this peace He now leaves with them as a
parting gift. The word which, uttered in the world's daily intercourse, is little more than an expression of good wishes or goodwill,
is in this case a gift indeed. Hence, as they were told already at the
outset [14¹], although their leader Simon Peter had then just
learned of his imminent fall [13³⁸], there is no need, and should be
no room, for distress or cowardice on their part. As He has said,
He is now leaving them, but is to return to them in a new way.
Were their love as His, they would have rejoiced for His sake,
because His 'descent' [3¹³] is now all but over, and He is about to
'ascend' to the Father. And finally, nothing that is about to
happen should take them by surprise; the fact that He has given
them warning should strengthen their belief (cf. 13¹⁹). His words
with them are almost ended; the power which *de facto*, although
not *de iure*, rules the world, is on its way to meet Him. Since the
Lord is not 'of the world' [8²³, 17¹⁴· ¹⁶], and is Himself without sin
[Heb. 4¹⁵], this power has no part in or hold on Him. None the less,
He is on His way to face this power, which will to all appearance
wreak its will on Him. And the reason for His action is that the
world may know the reality and depth of His love for and obedience
to the Father. These are the motives, leading Him to action: let
them join Him in it.

NOTES TO SECTION 7a. 13¹–14³¹

13¹. It is no doubt possible to understand the words 'unto the end'
as referring only to the close of the Lord's life on earth, 'his hour' already
mentioned in this verse; but the Greek words here can also mean 'to the
utmost bound or limit' (cf. R.V. mg); and the Lord is about to show that
any limit to His love can only be caused by inability or unwillingness in
His disciples to receive it.

13². The word 'Iscariot' probably means man of Kerioth, a place the
site of which is uncertain. Judas is twice mentioned in John during the
ministry; according to the most probable readings, at 6⁷¹ he is called
'Judas, son of Simon of Kerioth', and at 12⁴ 'Judas, he of Kerioth', the
reference to his father being now omitted. In chs. 13 to 20, at 13² he
appears as 'Judas, a man of Kerioth, son of Simon'; at 13²⁶ (as at 6⁷¹)
'Judas, son of Simon of Kerioth'; at 14²² (as at 12⁴) 'he of Kerioth'; but in
13²⁹, 18²⁻⁵ as 'Judas' only. It seems unlikely that the variations are acci-

dental; if St. John usually has a spiritual as well as an historical purpose in view, is it possible that he wishes to imply that father and son were of similar character? Dr. C. C. Torrey,¹ however, is confident that the word Iscariot has nothing to do with any place-name, and finds in it an Aramaic epithet *šqaryā*, meaning 'false' or 'hypocrite'. He regards the application of the word in Jn. 6⁷¹, 13²⁶ to Simon, Judas' father, as due to an error in translation from Semitic into Greek.

13³. The feet-washing of the disciples, with all that it implies, is prefaced by a description of the Lord's authority, origin, and goal, a description no doubt designed to emphasize the significance of the lowly task which He forthwith undertakes. In the feet-washing is shown, in brief, the meaning both of the Lord's life, His coming in the flesh, and of His death.

13⁵. Strangely enough, the Greek word for 'began', common in the other gospels in the sense of 'proceeded to', occurs in John only here.

13⁶. The position of the words for 'thou' and 'my' in the Greek shows that they are very emphatic; and similarly 'I' and the first 'thou' in 13⁷.

13⁷. 'hereafter': literally, 'after these things'. The reference is to the Lord's departure (in death) and the coming of the Holy Spirit (cf. 12¹⁶).

13⁹, ¹⁰. The Lord's reply to St. Peter's impulsive request, in the text followed in R.V. mg, 'he that is bathed does not need to wash, but is wholly clean', suggests that the washing of the disciples' feet by the Lord is equivalent to a complete cleansing, as well as providing an example in humility. This is probably the right reading; and, if so, the matter is parallel to the anointing of the Lord's feet by Mary in 12³; her action in embalming His feet was sufficient as a symbolical embalming of His body. The addition of the words in R.V. text, although strongly supported in the MSS., reduces the Lord's action in washing the disciples' feet to a lesson in humility and service only; and although this was one of its objects [13¹⁴, ¹⁵], the action also implied much more, as is shown by the Lord's words in 13⁸. For if chs. 13 to 17 are rightly said to be parallel to chs. 18 to 20, the feet-washing is the counterpart to the Lord's death and resurrection; and therefore, although the subsequent addition of the words as found in R.V. text can well be understood, the feet-washing is probably best interpreted as having the same significance and efficacy as the Lord's death.

13¹²⁻²⁰. St. Peter was warned in 13⁷ that the Lord's action in washing the disciples' feet is at present beyond his understanding; and in 13¹²⁻²⁰ it seems to be interpreted at present only as an example to the disciples of humility, to be expressed in mutual service.

13¹³. 'Master', or 'Teacher', is said at 1³⁸ to be a translation of Rabbi, and at 20¹⁶ of Rabboni. The titles 'Teacher' and 'Lord', applied to Jesus and here accepted by Him, represent His twofold office of teaching the truth and of revealing it.

13¹⁶. Cf. Mt. 10²⁴, Lk. 6⁴⁰.

13¹⁷. Religious knowledge, if it is to remain and to increase, must also express itself in action.

¹ *H.T.R.*, Jan. 1943.

13$^{18, 19}$. If these verses are considered along with 2$^{24, 25}$, 6$^{64, 70}$, St. John's teaching seems clear that, when Judas was chosen as one of the twelve, the Lord was aware what the result would be. He now reveals that the reason for His choice was the fulfilment of scripture; in other words Judas' act is to be regarded as only the supreme instance of the activity of evil throughout the ages, and the Lord's choice of him shows that evil is always subject to divine knowledge and permission, however terrible the problem may be which is thus raised. And this fact of the Lord's foreknowledge, which He now discloses, so far from weakening the disciples' faith in Him, should strengthen it.

The word here translated 'eateth' is an unusual verb, not found in the LXX translation of Ps. 41^9, which is here quoted, but occurring four times in Jn. 6$^{54-58}$; the connexion between 6$^{51-71}$ and 13$^{2-30}$ is perhaps thus emphasized.

'lifted up his heel against me'. The original Hebrew of Ps. 41^9 is literally 'made great his heel against me'.

13^{19}. Cf. 14^{29}, 16^4.

13^{20}. The thought returns for a moment to those who, in contrast to Judas, have responded to the Lord's cleansing [13$^{2-17}$]. For this important feature of His teaching cf. Mt. 10^{40} and also Mk. 9^{37}, Lk. 9^{48}. It expresses the reverse side of the truth set forth in 13^{16}. In 13^{19} the Lord has just uttered the divine claim 'I am', implying His union with the Father; and in 13^{20} He proceeds to emphasize, in solemn assurance, His own union with him whom He sends. Those therefore who welcome His emissary are welcoming both Him and His Father. This teaching receives its final expression in 20$^{21-23}$.

13^{23}. Those present at the meal would be reclining sideways, their feet stretched out behind (cf. Lk. 7^{38}). The host, or chief person present, would be in the centre. Thus, when St. Peter appeals to the beloved disciple for information, the latter, reclining on the immediate right of the Lord and therefore with his head slightly below that of his Master [12$^{23, 25}$, 21^{20}], learns that a coming gesture by the Lord will give the information sought. It is said to be a mark of especial civility in the East, if the host, after dipping a piece of food in the common bowl of sauce, gravy, or the like, placed in the centre of the table, gives it to a guest.

It is probably no accident that the word 'bosom' occurs elsewhere in John only at 1^{18}, where the Lord is said to be 'in the bosom of the Father'. In a similar relationship the disciple, here mentioned for the first time, for whom the Lord had a special affection, is now reclining on his Master's bosom. In this respect (as indeed always when this disciple is mentioned in John) he has precedence of St. Peter, since 13^{24} shows clearly that the latter was farther away from the Lord.

13^{27}. If the Lord's action in 13^{26} is to be understood as a final appeal to Judas and an assurance of the Lord's goodwill towards him, then with its rejection Judas became the servant of Satan. None the less, the Lord is still completely master of the situation; and it is at His bidding that Judas goes forth upon his task.

'quickly': lit. 'more quickly'. The Lord's words in Lk. 12^{50}, where He is referring indirectly to His coming death, perhaps throw light on His words in this verse.

13³⁰. In the last four words of this verse St. John's habit of seeing the inward in the outward receives its most signal expression (cf. 11¹⁰, 12³⁵).

13³¹. In 12²⁰⁻³⁶, the last occasion, previous to this verse, in which the term 'the Son of man' was used, occurring there three times, the Lord, His soul troubled by the arrival of 'the hour' [12²³]—since He would wish, if it were possible, to be saved from it and yet knows that only so can His mission be fulfilled [12²⁷]—prays in 12²⁸, 'Father, glorify thy name'; and a voice is heard, 'I have both glorified it, and will glorify it again'. It is clear from the position of 13³¹ (placed immediately after the Lord, again 'troubled in spirit' [13²¹], has allowed Judas to depart on his fatal purpose) that the Lord has thus glorified God, and has Himself been glorified as the Son of man, since the glory of the Son of man consists in obedience and the surrender of His will.

13³². If the explanation of this verse in the exposition is accepted, the Lord's imminent complete offering of Himself in death will be God's glorification of Him, not only as the Son of man, but as the Son of God. The divine life itself is to be imparted to believers. Verses 33 to 35, which follow, show that the reference is to the Lord's coming death and to the life which is to be imparted by His death to the disciples. This life His disciples may receive, but cannot of themselves impart, although they may imitate His self-sacrifice. Their task is to show their discipleship by the depth of the love which binds them together.

14¹. Both R.V. text and R.V. mg are possible translations; but since a chief purpose of the teaching in chs. 14 to 16 is to strengthen and deepen the disciples' confidence in their Master (e.g. 14⁶, ⁷, 16³³), the R.V. text is preferable. It is no doubt also true that, since His purpose is to bring them to the Father, their increased knowledge of Him will also increase their belief in God.

14². The word translated 'mansions' only occurs in John here and 14²³, and is rare in Greek. It is connected with the verb 'to abide' (which is used thrice in ch. 14 and eleven times in 15¹⁻¹⁶); cf. R.V. mg here. It can mean a temporary halting-place, where the traveller can rest in the course of his journey, like the dak-bungalows in eastern countries; and it is true that St. John is careful to portray the religious life of the believer as one of steady growth and progress. Thus, as we have seen (p. 25), he never uses the substantives 'belief' and 'knowledge', but uses the verbs 'to believe', 'to come to know', constantly. None the less, since at 14²³ the word is used in the singular and certainly cannot there emphasize or perhaps even suggest this meaning, we are probably to understand that the Lord refers here to the many diverse chambers or habitations in His Father's one great house.

14³. It is often thought that this is the one passage in John in which we hear of a final return of the Lord, a 'parousia' similar to that described in the other gospels. No doubt it is true that St. John speaks of 'the last day' (cf. pp. 49, 167–8); but this expression does not occur here; and it also seems unlikely that, if he desired the Lord's words here to be understood in this way, the reference, in the case of a belief held so strongly in the early Church, would be so brief. On the other hand, the Lord's 'coming again', as mentioned here, is perhaps unlikely to be the same as His 'coming' within a little while, which is promised in 14¹⁸, ¹⁹, as also in 16¹⁶⁻²². The 'coming' in 14¹⁸, ¹⁹ and 16¹⁶⁻²² is undoubtedly a coming of the Lord to His disciples while they are still active in the world, whereas the coming in 14³ seems to refer to the final reception of the disciples by their Master in His Father's house. Hence His words here are perhaps best understood in the light of 17²⁴, which speaks of a vision, one day to be granted to disciples (but not, it seems, while they live in the world), of the unveiled glory of the Lord, a glory granted to Him by the Father's love. Then indeed He will receive them to Himself; but at present He concentrates their thoughts rather upon the way to that of which He speaks; for the goal is only to be reached by the right treading of the way.

14¹⁰, ¹¹. At 5³⁶, 10²⁵ the Lord appealed to the evidence of His works as a ground for belief in His mission from the Father; and at 10³⁸ the Jews were told that through belief in His works they could come to know that the Father was in Him and He in the Father. Here, if the disciples cannot believe in consequence of their Master's words and teaching (cf. 7¹⁷), the same evidence—that of His works—is offered with a view to the same result; but whereas at 10³⁸ the Jew's disbelief brought the conversation to an end, here the disciples' belief, whether it rests on the Lord's words or on His works, is to result not only in the works described in 14¹², but in a still deeper belief which can also be called knowledge [14²⁰].

14¹², 4³⁵⁻³⁸, 10¹⁶, ¹⁷, 11⁵², 12²⁰, ²¹ suggest the nature of the 'greater works' to be done by the disciples. These works, however, are only made possible by the Lord's work, His surrender of Himself in death.

14¹³⁻¹⁵. See the last part of the note on 15¹⁶.

14¹⁶⁻²⁰. The prayer of the Lord, in answer to which the Father will give the disciples another Advocate or Helper, is, like His teaching, the internal or invisible counterpart of His external or visible deed in giving Himself up to die, since only as a result of His death will the dispensation of the Spirit become possible [7³⁷⁻³⁹]. The Spirit is said to be 'another' Advocate, not because He differs in essence from the Lord, who is also and will remain an Advocate of the disciples [1 Jn. 2¹], but because there are differences between His activity and that of the Lord. The Lord's work in the days of His flesh, for example, was visible and for a time only; the Spirit's work is invisible and permanent. Here, 15²⁶ and 16¹³, He is called 'the Spirit of truth', because He both knows (and indeed is) all truth and also imparts truth to believers.

14¹⁹. The R.V. mg is probably to be preferred. Unlike the world, the disciples will behold their risen Lord, and will live in Him, through His gift of the Spirit.

14²⁰. 'In that day'. This expression, used here and 16²³, ²⁶, is found constantly in the O.T. in reference to the future 'day of the Lord'; and its use here is no doubt meant to recall its surpassing implications there. Here, however, its meaning is not only temporal, but describes, under the form of a temporal expression, that participation in the divine life which must always be regarded as future, when contemplated by those who are still 'in the flesh'. The Lord, far from leaving the disciples bereft, comes to them after the 'little while' of the passion, since then they will live in His new life; and through Him share in His union with the Father.

14²⁴. The repeated emphasis that true love and belief will and must show themselves in obedience to the Lord's commandments should be noticed [14¹⁵, ²¹, ²³, ²⁴, 15¹⁰]; cf. the same stress in 1 Jn. 1⁶, 2³⁻⁶, 3⁷, ¹⁷, ¹⁸, ²⁴, 4²⁰. True spiritual union with the Lord must be preceded and accompanied by a truly moral union.

14²⁶. This, the fullest description of the Holy Spirit in John, should be compared with 15²⁶, ²⁷, 16¹³⁻¹⁵. It thus becomes clear that, just as the Lord has full knowledge of the Father, so the Spirit has full knowledge of the Son, and will impart this knowledge to believers, as they are able to receive it. But the work of the Spirit will and must consist solely in 'bringing to remembrance' the Lord's teaching; the Lord being one with the Father, and the disciples being admitted to the presence of the Father only in and through the Son, no advance beyond the Lord in His historical manifestation is or ever will be possible.

14²⁷. 'neither let it be fearful'. The Greek verb here has the same root as the adjective, meaning 'cowardly', in Mt. 8²⁶, Mk. 4⁴⁰, Rev. 21⁸, and the substantive in 2 Tim. 1⁷.

14²⁸. 'the Father is greater than I'. This truth is to be held along with its converse 'I and the Father are one' in 10³⁰. It may indeed seem possible in certain respects to exchange, as it were, the functions of the Father with those of the Son; thus 'no one cometh unto the Father but through me' in 14⁶ must express the same truth as 'no one can come unto me, except the Father, who sent me, draw him' in 6⁴⁴; and it is also true that the Son by His life and death has revealed the Father [1¹⁸, 14⁹]. None the less, 'one that is sent' is inevitably less than 'he that sent him' [13¹⁶]; and the fact that the Son at the bidding of the Father took upon Him our flesh and for the sake of men suffered death upon the cross is sufficient to explain the words of this verse.

14²⁹. The same note is struck as in 13¹⁹, 16⁴.

14³¹. It has been pointed out in the exposition that the instruction in chs. 13 to 17 is the internal counterpart to the external action in chs. 18 to 20. The result of that action was the complete revelation of the Father; and this result is also the aim of the instruction in these chapters, in which step by step the disciples are led forward by their Master into the knowledge of the true God, which is eternal life [17³]. A careful study will show that the instruction in chs. 15 and 16 is no mere repetition of that given in this chapter; see, for example, the notes on 15¹⁶, ²⁶.

It is also no accident, probably, that the last words of this verse recall the Lord's same words in Mk. 14⁴², uttered immediately before Judas' arrival in Gethsemane, and the consequent arrest. St. John seems to wish his readers to perceive that the revelation becomes clearer and deeper, as we go forward by degrees towards the passion. Although, in spite of the last words of 14³¹, there is to be no change of scene at present, the advance in the instruction and the advance in the action are shown to be parallel throughout.

The translation of this verse in R.V. receives support from similar passages in this gospel; but it is also possible, and here probably preferable, to render the verse, 'but, in order that the world may know that I love the Father and am thus acting, even as the Father commanded me, arise, let us go hence'.

SECTION 7b. 15¹–16³³. *The Lord and His own. The second instruction.*

15 I am the true vine, and my Father is the husbandman. Every branch
2 in me that beareth not fruit, he taketh it away: and every *branch* that
3 beareth fruit, he cleanseth it, that it may bear more fruit. Already ye are
4 clean because of the word which I have spoken unto you. Abide in me, and I in you. As the branch cannot bear fruit of itself, except it abide
5 in the vine; so neither can ye, except ye abide in me. I am the vine, ye are the branches: He that abideth in me, and I in him, the same beareth
6 much fruit: for apart from me ye can do nothing. If a man abide not in me, he is cast forth as a branch, and is withered; and they gather them,
7 and cast them into the fire, and they are burned. If ye abide in me, and my words abide in you, ask whatsoever ye will, and it shall be done
8 unto you. Herein ¹is my Father glorified, ²that ye bear much fruit; and
9 *so* shall ye be my disciples. Even as the Father hath loved me, I also
10 have loved you: abide ye in my love. If ye keep my commandments, ye shall abide in my love; even as I have kept my Father's commandments,
11 and abide in his love. These things have I spoken unto you, that my joy
12 may be in you, and *that* your joy may be fulfilled. This is my command-
13 ment, that ye love one another, even as I have loved you. Greater love hath no man than this, that a man lay down his life for his friends.
14 Ye are my friends, if ye do the things which I command you. No longer
15 do I call you servants; for the ⁴servant knoweth not what his lord doeth: but I have called you friends; for all things that I heard from my Father
16 I have made known unto you. Ye did not choose me, but I chose you, and appointed you, that ye should go and bear fruit, and *that* your fruit should abide: that whatsoever ye shall ask of the Father in my name,
17 he may give it you. These things I command you, that ye may love one
18 another. If the world hateth you, ⁵ye know that it hath hated me before
19 *it hated* you. If ye were of the world, the world would love its own: but because ye are not of the world, but I chose you out of the world,
20 therefore the world hateth you. Remember the word that I said unto

---

¹ *Or* was   ² *Many ancient authorities read* that ye bear much fruit, and
be my disciples.   ³ *Gr.* bondservants.   ⁴ *Gr.* bondservant.   ⁵ *Or*
know ye

you, A ¹servant is not greater than his lord. If they persecuted me, they
will also persecute you; if they kept my word, they will keep yours also.
21 But all these things will they do unto you for my name's sake, because
22 they know not him that sent me. If I had not come and spoken unto
23 them, they had not had sin: but now they have no excuse for their sin.
He that hateth me hateth my Father also. If I had not done among them
24 the works which none other did, they had not had sin: but now have
25 they both seen and hated both me and my Father. But *this cometh to pass*,
that the word may be fulfilled that is written in their law, They hated
26 me without a cause. But when the ²Comforter is come, whom I will
send unto you from the Father, *even* the Spirit of truth, which ³proceed-
27 eth from the Father, he shall bear witness of me: ⁴And ye also bear witness, because ye have been with me from the beginning.

16 These things have I spoken unto you, that ye should not be made to
2 stumble. They shall put you out of the synagogues: yea, the hour cometh,
that whosoever killeth you shall think that he offereth service unto God.
3 And these things will they do, because they have not known the Father,
4 nor me. But these things have I spoken unto you, that when their hour
is come, ye may remember them, how that I told you. And these things
5 I said not unto you from the beginning, because I was with you. But
now I go unto him that sent me; and none of you asketh me, Whither
6 goest thou? But because I have spoken these things unto you, sorrow
7 hath filled your heart. Nevertheless I tell you the truth; It is expedient
for you that I go away: for if I go not away, the ²Comforter will not come
8 unto you; but if I go, I will send him unto you. And he, when he is
come, will convict the world in respect of sin, and of righteousness, and
9 of judgement: of sin, because they believe not on me; of righteousness,
10 because I go to the Father, and ye behold me no more; of judgement,
11 because the prince of this world hath been judged. I have yet many
12 things to say unto you, but ye cannot bear them now. Howbeit when he,
13 the Spirit of truth, is come, he shall guide you into all the truth: for he
shall not speak from himself; but what things soever he shall hear, *these*
shall he speak: and he shall declare unto you the things that are to come.
14 He shall glorify me: for he shall take of mine, and shall declare *it* unto
15 you. All things whatsoever the Father hath are mine: therefore said I,
16 that he taketh of mine, and shall declare *it* unto you. A little while, and
ye behold me no more; and again a little while, and ye shall see me.
17 *Some* of his disciples therefore said one to another, What is this that he
saith unto us, A little while, and ye behold me not; and again a little
18 while, and ye shall see me: and, Because I go to the Father? They said
therefore, What is this that he saith, A little while? We know not what

---

¹ *Gr.* bondservant   ² *Or* Advocate *Or* Helper   *Gr.* Paraclete.
³ *Or* goeth forth from   ⁴ *Or* And bear ye also witness

19 he saith. Jesus perceived that they were desirous to ask him, and he said unto them, Do ye inquire among yourselves concerning this, that I said, A little while, and ye behold me not, and again a little while, and
20 ye shall see me? Verily, verily, I say unto you, that ye shall weep and lament, but the world shall rejoice: ye shall be sorrowful, but your sorrow
21 shall be turned into joy. A woman when she is in travail hath sorrow, because her hour is come: but when she is delivered of the child, she remembereth no more the anguish, for the joy that a man is born into
22 the world. And ye therefore now have sorrow: but I will see you again, and your heart shall rejoice, and your joy no one taketh away from you.
23 And in that day ye shall [1]ask me nothing. Verily, verily, I say unto you, If ye shall ask anything of the Father, he will give it you in my name.
24 Hitherto have ye asked nothing in my name: ask, and ye shall receive, that your joy may be fulfilled.
25 These things have I spoken unto you in [2]proverbs: the hour cometh, when I shall no more speak unto you in [2]proverbs, but shall tell you
26 plainly of the Father. In that day ye shall ask in my name: and I say not
27 unto you, that I will [3]pray the Father for you; for the Father himself loveth you, because ye have loved me, and have believed that I came
28 forth from the Father. I came out from the Father, and am come into
29 the world: again, I leave the world, and go unto the Father. His disciples
30 say, Lo, now speakest thou plainly, and speakest no [4]proverb. Now know we that thou knowest all things, and needest not that any man should ask thee: by this we believe that thou camest forth from God.
31 Jesus answered them, Do ye now believe? Behold, the hour cometh,
32 yea, is come, that ye shall be scattered, every man to his own, and shall leave me alone: and *yet* I am not alone, because the Father is with me.
33 These things have I spoken unto you, that in me ye may have peace. In the world ye have tribulation: but be of good cheer; I have overcome the world.

---

[1] *Or* ask me no question   [2] *Or* parables   [3] *Gr.* make request of.
[4] *Or* parable.

EXPOSITION OF SECTION 7b. 15¹⁻16³³

In this second part the instruction given deals more fully with certain subjects briefly treated in the first part, especially the relation of the disciples to the Lord after His return to them, and, through Him, to the Father [15¹⁻⁷; cf. 14¹⁸⁻²¹], and the work of the Holy Spirit [15²⁶, ²⁷, 16⁵⁻¹⁵; cf. 14¹⁶, ¹⁷, ²⁶]. It also looks, more definitely than the first part, into the future, dealing with the internal life of the Church [15⁸⁻¹⁷], the treatment which the Church is to expect at the hands of the world [15¹⁸ to 16⁴], and the Church's permanent dependence on the Lord's historic revelation, which will be interpreted by 'the Spirit of truth' [16¹²⁻¹⁵]. At 16¹⁶ we return to the thought, already encountered at 14¹⁹, of the 'little while' of the Lord's separation from the disciples, in other words the brief interval between all that is implied in His arrest and death and all that is implied in His resurrection, ascension, and the coming of the Holy Spirit. This 'little while' is now explained by the Lord in the metaphor of the sorrow of a woman in travail, a sorrow to be followed by a joy which could not have been hers without the sorrow which preceded it. This explanation, however, as the Lord Himself says, is given in figurative language only; and finally He sums up, in a single simple sentence [16²⁸], the facts of His coming forth from the Father into the world, and His return from the world to the Father. This declaration the disciples welcome for its clearness, and respond with a confession of faith. In spite of it, however, they are warned that the hour of their desertion of their Lord is imminent, indeed has come; but since their peace is to be rooted in Him and His words, not in themselves, they may be of good courage; He has conquered the world.

We now return to 15¹. At the end of the lament in Isaiah 5¹⁻⁷ over the vineyard, which has proved unfruitful, in spite of all the care bestowed upon it by the Lord of hosts, its owner, the reader is definitely told that the reference is to Israel; and the picture of the chosen nation as a vine planted by Yahweh is found also in Jer. 2²¹, 12¹⁰, Ezek. 15²⁻⁸, 19¹⁰⁻¹⁴, Hosea 10¹. In all these passages, in which Israel is thus represented, the vine has become 'a degenerate plant' [Jer. 2²¹], which has brought its sufferings upon itself (cf. Mk. 12¹⁻⁹). Ps. 80⁸⁻¹⁷, however, in which the history of Israel is set forth under the figure of a vine, seems to be exceptional (though cf. also 2 Esdras 5²³⁻³⁰), in that the poet here attributes the sad plight of the nation, when he wrote, not to its own failure, but to injuries and spoliation inflicted upon it by others; and he appeals to Yahweh, the owner and husbandman, to visit and revive the vine of His own planting, that is, Israel, 'the man of' His 'right hand', 'the son of man whom' formerly He made 'strong for' Himself.

In St. John's use, in ch. 15, of the metaphor of the vine, we hear no more of Israel as the vine of God's tending; but the Lord, in whom we have already learned to see the true or real 'Son of man', now in 15¹, in the last of His seven self-declarations in this gospel, declares Himself to be 'the true (or, real) vine', tended by His Father; and we pass at once to the thought of the vine's relationship to the branches which belong to it and form the care of the husbandman, that is, to the thought of the Lord's relationship to His disciples, under the guiding care of the Father. This personal relationship is expressed in the language of mutual indwelling. The words used to denote it, 'to remain (or, abide) in', have hitherto been used only once in this book, of the reciprocal indwelling of the Lord and the individual disciple, namely at 6⁵⁶, where he who eats the Lord's flesh and drinks His blood is said to abide in the Lord, and the Lord in him. But in 15¹⁻⁷ the expression occurs repeatedly, and (except in part of 15⁵) only with reference to the disciples as a body. Since true discipleship is bound to show itself in fruit-bearing [15⁸], any unfruitful branch is removed (in 15², ⁶ there is perhaps an indirect reference to the defection of Judas, as being typical of all faithless discipleship), and fruitful branches are pruned, to increase their capacity to bear fruit. Further, in ch. 6 the Lord revealed Himself as the bread which sustains life; but now, by comparing Himself to a vine and His disciples to its tendrils, He makes Himself known as not only the sustainer but also the origin and source of true or real life, a life, however, only to be had by the disciples from and in union with Him. In the prologue [1³] we learned that the Logos was and is the sole originator of all life, and that man therefore owes his being to God; and now we learn how this dependence of man upon God is to be realized, and what, owing to the Lord's work, is to be the true and final relationship of men to their Creator.

In 15³ we are reminded of the feet-washing in 13²⁻¹¹, for this is the only other passage in John where the word for 'clean' is used; and if it was correct to see in the Lord's action there a symbol of His incarnation and death, it is easy to see in this verse, as well as in 15², a wider than the immediate reference to the eleven disciples. The Word has cleansed His Church and has implanted His word in it, and the task of its members, as 'true men in love', is 'to grow up in all things into him' [Eph. 4¹⁵]. But there is an absolute condition; they must abide in Him, as He abides and will, subject to their co-operation, continue to abide in them [15⁴, ⁵], that so they may bear fruit.

At 15⁷, as at 17⁸, the Greek for 'my words' (a different substantive from that used in 15³, but identical with that in 6⁶³, ⁶⁸) emphasizes the actual words uttered by the Lord in the days of His flesh; these are the truth itself (cf. 18³⁷), and if they abide in His disciples, they will be interpreted ever afresh by the Paràclete, Himself 'the Spirit of truth' [16¹³⁻¹⁵], and will be a life-giving power [6⁶³] and a source of growth, to which no limit is set, in disciples.

In 14¹³ the disciples were told that the Lord would grant the disciples' prayers made in His name, in order that the Father might be glorified in the Son. But now in 15⁸ He Himself as it were stands aside; by their bearing much fruit the Father is directly glorified by the disciples, although the Lord's work for them and their relationship to Him are not, if we may so speak, for a moment forgotten; and the truth is for the first time set before them that (*a*) the measure of the Father's love for the Son (cf. 3³⁵, 5²⁰) is the measure of their Lord's love for them, and (*b*) His obedience to His Father's commandments must be the measure of their obedience to His, their Master's, commandments [15⁹, ¹⁰]. His purpose in revealing this truth to them is that they may share His joy (cf. Heb. 12²), a fullness of joy [15¹¹, 17¹³], and capable, unlike that of the Baptist [3²⁹], of limitless increase.

At 13³⁴ the Lord had given His disciples a new commandment, in charging them that their love for one another should be according to the measure of His love for them. To this charge He returns at 15¹², but now reveals, indirectly but unmistakably, that there can be no greater love than His, since a man can show no greater love for his friends than when he gives his life for them; and the disciples, if they keep their Lord's commandments, are His friends. His purpose in dying is that they may live. He has now made known to them the content and meaning of His knowledge of and obedience to the Father; they can now see in His (the Son's) death the nature and depth of God's love (cf. 3¹⁶); henceforth, since they too now have this knowledge, He can call them not bondservants, as previously, but friends. And nothing of all this has or could have happened as the result of initiative on their part; He chose them, not they Him, His object being that, as men whom He appointed, they should go their way and bear lasting fruit, in order that, as the Father always hears the prayers of the Son [11⁴²], so He (the Father) may hear and grant every prayer of theirs made in accordance with their Lord's character and will [15¹⁶].

This command of mutual love, which is to weld them together, and the nature and depth of which has been now made clear to them, is now uttered for the last time [15¹⁷]; for indeed they will need this bond. The treatment which they are likely to receive at the hands of the world will not be different from that which, as they know, their Lord received. At 14²², ²³ Judas, not Iscariot, had wondered what had happened that the Lord was now speaking of a manifestation of Himself to the disciples, but not to the world; and his question had received no direct reply. But now the difficulty is solved. By the Lord's death and resurrection, here regarded as events already in the past, the disciples, as the vessels of His choice, have been raised out of the world; they, like their Lord [8²³], are now 'not of the world' [15¹⁹; cf. 17¹⁴, ¹⁶], and therefore form the object, as He did, of the world's hatred—in so far, we ought no doubt at once to add, as they indeed belong to Him (cf. 'for my name's sake' 15²¹). On the one hand, therefore, the promises made to believers in the earlier chapters are now realized in them; they see the kingdom of God [3³]; they are not judged [3¹⁸]; they come to the light [3²¹]; they have within them a well of water springing up unto eternal life [4¹⁴]; they have passed out of death into life [5²⁴]. On the other hand the treatment accorded to them by the world will be no different from that accorded to their Lord, the reason for this being the world's failure to know Him who sent their Lord. Their Lord in word and in work has uniquely revealed His Father, and the response which He has received is hatred, a sinful and unjustified hatred, but no cause for surprise, nor unforeseen; witness the evidence of the Jews' scripture itself. And this hatred for their Lord implies also hatred of His Father (cf. 1 Jn. 2²³), and is without excuse.

There seems to be a certain similarity between ch. 9 and the passage 15¹⁸ to 16¹¹. In the action in ch. 9 the three chief 'parties' are the Pharisees, the enlightened beggar, and the Lord; and in the instruction in 15¹⁸ to 16¹¹ they are the world, the disciples, and the Paraclete. It may also be no accident that the word sin, which in John, as in the other gospels, is rare, occurred last in 9⁴¹ where, in language very like that here [15²²], the Lord tells the Pharisees that, if they were blind, they would not have sin; precisely because they claimed to see, their sin remained. Again, in 9³², ³³ the once blind but now enlightened beggar protests to the Pharisees, his judges, that the action wrought upon him by the Lord is unparalleled; and his words are very similar to the Lord's claim in 15²⁴ that His works had been such as 'none other did'. And finally, the last words of the beggar in ch. 9, when he has been found by the Lord, are a confession of faith, 'Lord, I believe' [9³⁸]. This is also, in spite of temporary failure [16³¹, ³²], supremely true of the disciples [6⁶⁹, 16³⁰, 17⁸]. It seems, then, that we may be justified in tracing a parallel between the beggar and the Pharisees in ch. 9, and the disciples and their opponents, representing the world, here. Just as the beggar at the Lord's bidding washed and was enlightened, and in consequence, after being harried by the authorities, was expelled from the synagogue [9²², ³⁴], so here the disciples, who have been cleansed by the Lord [13³⁻¹⁰, 15³], are warned of the reception which awaits them 'for His name's sake' [15²¹; cf. 16³] from the representatives of 'the world' [15¹⁹, ²⁰, 16²]. We saw also, when we considered ch. 9, that although the Lord was not present while the beggar was being tried before the Pharisees yet it was He, as much as the beggar, who formed the object of their condemnation; and that, when in 9³⁵⁻⁴¹ He once more comes upon the scene and exercises a discrimination which He here says was one of the purposes of His coming into the world, not only is the clearest enlightenment granted to the beggar, himself now a full disciple, but those who have tried him are themselves put on trial before a Tribunal incapable of error, and fail to pass it.

It is therefore noteworthy that, although according to the Lord's warning in 15¹⁸⁻²¹, 16¹⁻⁴ the disciples, like the beggar, will have to bear witness [15²⁷] in the absence of their Master to an unbelieving world, yet in doing so they, like the beggar, will not be without invisible support and help. An unseen, unerring Judge, the Paraclete, will do for them what the Lord in ch. 9, whether absent, as in 9¹³⁻³⁴, or present, as in 9³⁵⁻³⁸, did for the beggar; and the verdict of the Paraclete upon the world [16⁸⁻¹¹] will be the same as the verdict of the Lord upon the Pharisees in 9³⁹⁻⁴¹. First, the Pharisees did not believe on the Lord [9²², ²⁴, ²⁹], nor does the world; herein lies its sin [16⁹]. Secondly, the Lord was not visibly present, when the beggar was tried and condemned [9¹³⁻³⁴]; even so now He, 'the Lord our righteousness' [Jer. 23⁶], is on His way to the Father, and will be visibly seen by the disciples no more [16¹⁰]; a standard of righteousness has been set up, which no tribunal in this world can reach. To this standard the Paraclete bears witness, and thus condemns the world. And thirdly, the Lord in ch. 9, when exercising a discrimination which alone is perfect and unerring, had passed judgement on the Pharisees [9³⁹⁻⁴¹]. So now in the light of the true and perfect judgement of the Paraclete the ruler of this world, a murderer from the beginning and the father of lies [8⁴⁴], stands condemned [16¹¹]; he has no part [12³¹] in the life and truth which are granted to those who hear the Lord's voice [5²⁴, 18³⁷].

At 16⁴ᵇ the Lord had explained to the disciples why He had not told them previously of the difficulties which would confront them as His followers. The reason was that He Himself was still with them, and so could train them gradually, feeding them with milk rather than with meat. But now His departure is imminent, and therewith the subject of His destination is taken up afresh [16⁵]. To understand the train of thought here, it is necessary to return to 13³³, when the Lord first tells the disciples that He is about to leave them, and that they cannot come where He is going. (It is noticeable that at this moment they receive the new commandment that their love for one another should be according to the measure of His love for them; such a love on their part is to be the evidence to all men of their allegiance to Him [13³⁴, ³⁵].) At 13³⁶ Simon Peter asks the Lord where He is going, and receives the reply that he cannot follow Him at present, but that later he shall do so. In 14¹⁻³ the Lord, directing the disciples' thoughts towards Himself, explains that He is going away to make ready a place for them in His Father's house. Clearly therefore this is the place to which they cannot go at present; He must first (by His death) prepare it for them (we could say equally well, prepare them for it). But in 14⁴ He tells them that, although as yet where He is going they do not know and cannot go, they know the way to it (the reading of R.V. text is certainly correct). When Thomas objects that, since they do not know where their Master is going, they can hardly know the way to it, the Lord answers that He Himself is the way to it, reminding them at the same time that He is truth (cf. 1¹⁴, ¹⁷) and life (cf. 11²⁵). He adds that He is the only way to the Father. Philip's interjection [14⁸] shows that he thinks a sight of the Father would dispel all their difficulties. But this is not so; Philip, like Peter [13³⁷], is in too great a hurry; he is asking for that which as yet he has not earned. The disciples cannot reach the goal (very near although in fact it is to them in and through the presence of their Master), unless they first tread the way to it, that is, come to love one another as their Master has loved them [13³⁴]; this is the way by which He Himself is going to the Father [14¹²]; and there is no other way [14⁶].

At 16⁵, since the disciples now know the Lord's destination, namely, the Father [14¹², ²⁸], they no longer ask where He is going; but they are distressed to realize that no sooner do they lose Him, than all the troubles, of which He has been speaking in 15¹⁸⁻²¹ and 16¹⁻⁴, will fall upon them. Instead of rejoicing [14²⁸] for His sake that His journey is all but ended, because His union with the Father is about to be sealed in His self-oblation on the cross, they cannot as yet forget themselves, or believe that they will not be left orphans [14¹⁸]; whereas in fact it is only by going away (i.e. dying the death of the divine love), that in the Person and power of the Paraclete He can come to them, and be to them both truth and life, and so bring them to the Father [14³].

In 16¹³⁻¹⁵ the Lord's work, as the complete revelation of the Father [16¹⁵], a work now regarded as all but lying in the past [16⁴, ⁵], is brought into closest connexion with the work of the Spirit of truth in the future. The idea of progressive revelation could hardly find clearer expression than it now receives. Just as in 8²⁶, ²⁷ the Lord tells the Jews that, as a result of His knowledge of the Father, He has many things to say, in judgement, concerning them, so here He tells the disciples that He has many things to say to them—may we add, to their growing enlightenment?—which at present are beyond their grasp. But again, just as their Lord did not speak or teach from Himself [7¹⁶, 8²⁸, 12⁴⁹], so the Spirit of truth will not speak from Himself, but only all things that He 'hears'; and this will include explanation and interpretation of the events now imminent (cf. 2²², 12¹⁶). For that which He 'hears' and will make plain will be the things of their Master, to whom belong all things that the Father has. Accordingly, just as the Lord in His ministry glorified the Father [17⁴], by revealing in word and work the nature, depth, and meaning of the Father's love, so the Spirit of truth will glorify the Son [16¹⁴], by revealing the nature, depth, and meaning of the Son's love. The disciples will thus be guided into all the truth [16¹³]. But it is their Master's truth into which they will be thus guided; and since their Master is Himself the truth [14⁶] and is one with the Father [10³⁰], no limit can be set to their advance in knowledge of the truth. On the other hand this advance will only be in the increasing understanding and assimi-
.ation of their Lord's revelation already made in His historic

ministry; any such advance, therefore, can and will only result in an increased knowledge of the historic Lord. Beyond or outside Him no advance is possible.

It is unfortunate that the R.V. does not start a new paragraph at 16¹⁶, for by 16¹⁵ the Lord has dealt with all the subjects which He wished to lay before the disciples. He now sees, however, that it is necessary, in conclusion, to revert to one of them, the 'little while' when He will be invisible to them, a subject already treated briefly in 14¹⁸⁻²⁰. Between 13³¹ and 14³¹ the Lord's words were interrupted from time to time by questions or remarks on the part of one or another among the disciples; but, ever since at 14³¹ they were bidden to rise and go out with Him to action, they have been listening in silence, nor do they now address Him directly; only, on His reverting to the subject of the 'little while' when He will be invisible to them, some of them express, one to another, their inability to understand His meaning in this matter, bringing it into connexion also with the difficulty of His words in 16¹⁰ about His journey to the Father. The further fact that in 16¹⁶⁻¹⁹ the words 'a little while' occur no less than seven times may increase the probability that on no point did the evangelist think his contemporaries more likely to find difficulty, and therefore to need instruction, than on this; and also that on none was it more important, in his view, for them to understand and to be able to assimilate the teaching given.

Seeing their perplexity, the Lord solemnly assures them that in the 'little while', when they will not see Him, lies the deepest secret of their future faith.[1] That is at hand, which will bring satisfaction, indeed joy, to the world, and to them deep sorrow. But only through this sorrow on their part is the joy to be won which was set before Himself [Heb. 12²], which is His [15¹¹], and which He gives [17¹³]. For like His peace, which is given not after the manner of the easy, casual greetings of the world [14²⁷], it is the joy of fulfilling to the utmost the work which they, like their Master, have been sent into the world to do; and in their case, unlike that of the world, the motive of this work is service, self-sacrifice, and love. This joy, therefore, is different indeed from the joy natural to the world; and yet it is also the outcome of a universal law, known to every young mother, when her child is born.

---

[1] It is believed that, apart from other considerations, the language of 16²²⁻²⁴ justifies these words.

In the case of the disciples, as they followed their Lord during His ministry, they had had to give up, one by one (although in every case for something purer and better), the hopes with which they had started, as regards the nature, work, and future of the Jewish Messiah [1⁴¹, ⁴⁹]. And no sooner have they perhaps made some progress towards the light and truth in this respect, than they learn that they must lose the visible presence of Him who first showed these deeper truths of life to them. For the moment therefore their sorrow is inevitable; but only through such a sorrow as theirs will be can they learn the lesson of the cross, that loss is gain. Only through their sorrow can they learn to see Him when He comes to them again, to know Him as their life (cf. 14¹⁹), and therefore in and through Him to have immediate access to the Father. In that day they will no longer, as in ch. 14 it was suggested that they would, put requests or questions to the Lord [14¹³, ¹⁴]. In their union with Him they will pray directly to the Father, and the Father will forthwith grant their prayer, whatever it may be. From henceforth, with the completion of their Lord's work on their behalf, let them ask in His name (that is, in His power and with His character and purpose), and they shall receive, in order that their joy, as keepers and doers of His commandments [15¹⁰⁻¹²], may also be complete.

Just as the Lord's works have been frequently described in John as signs, expressive of a truth or reality beyond themselves, so now, in respect of His words, we read [16²⁵] that He has spoken in symbols or parables to His disciples, but that they may look forward to a time when symbol and figure will have done their work, and He will tell them, in unveiled language, of the Father. Then they will ask in His name and, their prayers being now in full accord with those of their Lord, He will no longer have to refashion their requests in order to present these to the Father; for the Father Himself loves them, because they, being in the world, none the less have loved their Master and have believed in His mission from the Father's side. That mission into the world had its starting-place from the Father and has run its course; and to the Father He who has fulfilled it now goes, and leaves the world.

For the first time in chs. 15 and 16 (and for the only time, in 13³¹ to 16³³, as a body) the disciples now address the Lord directly. In order to understand their words in 16²⁹, ³⁰ and the Lord's reply, it may be of help to compare this passage with 6⁶⁷⁻⁷¹. There, at the end of the teaching in ch. 6, Simon Peter, in the name of the twelve, makes a confession of faith in the Lord, not entirely unlike that found here; thus the confession there, as here, is an expression of both knowledge and belief; and there, as here, the confession is followed by a reply of the Lord calculated to dispel any self-confidence in those who have just confessed their faith. If then this comparison of the two passages holds, the disciples, it seems, imagine in 16$^{29, 30}$ that now they have the promised unveiled teaching, free of any symbol or figure. Since at 16$^{17, 18}$ the disciples found themselves perplexed by the Lord's words and now, on the contrary, declare [16^{29}] that He speaks in unveiled language, they probably refer to His teaching from 16^{25} onwards, and say that it is clear to them. They appear to fail to realize that in 16$^{25, 26}$ the Lord had been speaking not of the present as well as of the future as at 4^{23} and 5^{25}, but of the future only ('an hour cometh'), and had implied [16^{25}] that as yet, even in these His last words to them, He could not tell them in unveiled language of the Father. Hence their words, although 16^{30} is a true confession of their Master, reveal, if considered in the light of His reply, that those who have made it are not yet capable of absolute devotion. The disciples say that they rest their belief in His divine mission on the certainty which they now have of His full knowledge, a knowledge which renders question and prayer to Him unnecessary. They are no doubt right in their belief about their Master's knowledge (cf. 2^{25}, 5^{42}, 6$^{61, 64}$, 13$^{1, 3}$, 19^{28}); but a belief resting on the ground of His knowledge was found at the outset in Nathanael [1$^{47-50}$] and in the Samaritan woman [4^{29}]; and a faith which has now seen greater things than these [1^{50}] should have a deeper basis. Again, they are right in their belief in their Lord's divine mission; and yet, in speaking of it, in spite of the Lord's revelation of the Father in these three chapters, in which the word 'Father' has already fallen from His lips more than forty times, they do not, in these their last words to Him before the passion, use this word, but the word 'God'. (The only other verse in which this word certainly occurs in chs. 15 and 16 is 16^2, and there its use is altogether natural; but not so here.) The Lord therefore exposes the inadequacy of their belief by facing them abruptly with the coming crisis, which indeed is now in process. Their company is to be scattered, and He is to be left alone—but not so, because the Father is with Him. Such has ever been His teaching [8$^{16, 29}$], and its purpose has been to give them peace and confidence in Him, not in themselves. In their intercourse with the world their lot, if and in so far as they are faithful to Him, involves opposition; but let them have courage; He, their Master, has overcome the world.

NOTES TO SECTION 7b. 15¹–16³³

15¹⁻⁸. Christian readers of this gospel would need no reminder that the sacramental means by which they shared in their Lord's sacrificial death and received a pledge of reunion with Him were a loaf and 'the fruit of the vine'. The former element was chiefly emphasized (as contrasted with the latter) in ch. 6; the latter alone is emphasized here. In both passages the sacramental reference, as always in John, is indirect, but none the less unmistakable. And whereas in the earlier gospels there is a strong emphasis upon the future (e.g. Mk. 14²⁵), in both Jn. 6 and Jn. 15 (although the repeated reference to 'the last day' in ch. 6 should not be overlooked) the emphasis is on a present union with the Lord by mutual indwelling.

15². Readers of the original Greek will notice a word-play in the two main verbs of this verse, *airei* and *kathairei*.

15³. Both the work of the Lord [13¹⁰] and His word or message [15³] are needed for men's cleansing. Cf. also p. 163.

15⁴. In contrast with the language, now used, of mutual indwelling, it is of interest to compare the prepositions used to describe the Lord's intercourse with disciples during the ministry. At 1³⁹ the two disciples remain with (lit. at the side of) Him for a day; and the same preposition is used when the Samaritans ask Him to remain with them [4⁴⁰]. Similarly at 14¹⁷ it is said of the Paraclete that He (now, in the Lord) 'abides with' the disciples, and (later) 'shall be in' them. At 11⁵⁴, 13³³, 16⁴ yet a third preposition is used, meaning 'together with'. It is also used, at 7³³, of the Lord being with the Jews 'yet a little while'.

Now, however, in 15⁴, ⁵, ⁷ language is used of the relations about to be established between the Lord and His disciples, which is used in 14¹⁰ of the permanent relations between the Father and the Lord. The mutual indwelling of the Lord and the disciples, through the Spirit, is to resemble the relationship which eternally exists between the Father and the Son.

15⁵. Just as the Son can do nothing of Himself [5³⁰], His will being always one with that of the Father [4³⁴, 5¹⁹], so the disciples can do nothing apart from their Lord. The converse truth is expressed, in reference to the individual disciple's union with his Lord, in Phil. 4¹³, 'I can do all things in him that strengtheneth me'.

15⁸. 'Herein' refers to the condition laid down in 15⁷. In 15⁸ the R.V. text should be followed throughout. As regards the first alternative in R.V. mg, although a past tense is used in the Greek here, there is no reference to any particular time.

15¹⁵. In 13¹⁶ the Lord had implied that the disciples were His bondservants, and it is explicitly stated at 13^7 that His action in washing their feet was not understood at the time. And although the relationship implied in the word 'bondservant' still holds [15^{20}], yet the Lord, having shared with them His knowledge of the Father, is now able to call them His friends.

15^{16}. The verb here translated 'appointed' is the same as that used in 15^{13} (and 10$^{11-18}$) of the laying down of life. If this is no accident, it emphasizes, indirectly, that it is the Lord's redemptive death which enables and empowers the disciples to undertake their work in His name. They are being taught to understand the meaning of the divine love, and the pledge of this love, namely the Lord's death; and this understanding is to issue in their bearing fruit which will 'abide'.

In respect of the last part of this verse, as elsewhere in chs. 15 and 16, we become conscious of certain contrasts between the instruction given to the disciples in 13^{31} to 14^{31}, and that in chs. 15 and 16. Possibly the explanation of the contrasts may be found in the Lord's call in the last words of 14^{31} to action on the part of the disciples; for after this point there seems to be a definite advance in His instruction to them. If this is so, although no actual movement takes place before the instruction of chs. 15 and 16 is given, the last words of 14^{31} may be intended to suggest to the reader not only that the instruction of the disciples is to have its counterpart in action by them, but also that there is to be, after this point, an advance and progress in their thought and understanding of their Master, as well as (later) in their action and conduct. An example of the contrasts between the instruction in 13^{31} to 14^{31} and that in chs. 15 and 16 may be given.

In 14$^{13-15}$, according to the best-attested reading, the disciples, who have just shown how little, as yet, they know the Father [14$^{8, 9}$], are encouraged to direct their prayers to the Lord; and provided that these are 'in His name', i.e. in accordance with His character and will, and that they in their love for Him keep His commandments, He, their Lord, promises that He will answer those prayers, that the Father may be glorified in the Son. But in 15^{16} one purpose of the Lord's choice of the disciples is said to have been that they may receive (directly) from the Father whatever they ask in their Lord's name; and in 16^{23} the Lord solemnly assures them that 'in that day' the Father will give them in His (the Lord's) name anything that they ask; they will not ask their Lord Himself for anything; nor will He pray the Father for them, because their prayers will be in their Lord's name, and also the Father Himself loves them, on account of their love for and belief in the Lord. For another contrast between the teaching of 13^{31} to 14^{31}, on the one hand, and that of chs. 15 and 16, on the other, see the note on 15^{26}.

15^{20}. The response of the world to the disciples will be identical with its response to the Lord. The world has persecuted Him, it will also persecute His disciples; some, however, have kept His word, and some will keep the disciples' word.

15^{21}. 'for my name's sake'. The same expression occurs in the similar context Mk. 13^{13} and its parallels.

15²⁵. Since the reference must be either to Ps. 35¹⁹ or to Ps. 69⁴, the 'law' is here regarded as extending to the whole of the O.T. scriptures; and the words 'their law', with which we may compare 'your law' in 8¹⁷ and 10³⁴, are a reminder that the scriptures, on which the Jews rely [5³⁹], themselves testify to the rejection of God's servant by those to whom he is sent.

15²⁶. 'whom I will send unto you from the Father'. In 14¹⁶ the Lord promises to pray the Father, who at His request will give the Paraclete to the disciples; and similarly in 14²⁶ the Father will send the Paraclete in the Lord's name. But, in the advance in the instruction which is noticeable after 14³¹, the Lord in 15²⁶ and 16⁷ promises that, after He has 'gone away', i.e. after His exaltation, He Himself will send the Paraclete to the disciples from the Father.

15²⁶, ²⁷. Just as the presence, work, and teaching of the Lord during His ministry were a visible witness to the truth [8¹⁴], a witness concentrated at that time in His single Person, so the presence, work, and teaching of the Paraclete, the Spirit of truth (coming forth from the Father and to be sent by the Lord to the disciples from the Father as a result of the Lord's completed work), will bear an invisible, universalized witness to Him; and this witness of the Paraclete will have its visible counterpart in the presence, work, and teaching of the disciples, who shared the companionship of their Lord throughout His ministry (cf. 2¹¹, 14⁹, and the 'we' in 3¹¹).

16². Expulsion from the synagogue is mentioned also at 9²², 12⁴². A warning of exclusion is found also in Lk. 6²², and of martyrdom, among other passages, in Mt. 10²¹, Mk. 13¹², Lk. 12⁴, together with an accompanying reference in these three passages, as here, to the Holy Spirit [Mt. 10²⁰, Mk. 13¹¹, Lk. 12¹¹, ¹²]. In this context in John, however, the warnings are especially appropriate; for such has been the experience of the disciples' Lord (cf. 11⁵⁰), and in these chapters He seeks to impart Himself and His Spirit (cf. Acts 16⁷) to those who follow Him.

16⁸, ¹⁰. The word 'righteousness' occurs in John here only.

16¹⁰. The Greek verb here translated 'behold' (as also in 12⁴⁵, 14¹⁷, ¹⁹, 16¹⁶⁻¹⁹) may be used of either physical or mental apprehension. At 14¹⁹ it is used of spiritual vision; here [16¹⁰] of physical vision.

16¹⁶. 'A little while'. At 7³³, ³⁴ the Lord had told the Jews that He would only be with them for 'yet a little time', and that they would seek Him, but would not find Him; and at 8²¹ He added that they could not come where He was going. Similarly in His last words at the end of His public ministry [12³⁵, ³⁶] the multitude was warned that the light was among them for 'yet a little time'. It is noticeable, however, that in the Lord's instruction to the disciples in 13³¹ to 16³³, where the words 'yet a little while' occur at 13³³, 14¹⁹, 16¹⁶⁻¹⁹, the Greek substantive for 'time', used in 7³³ and 12³⁵ and there unfortunately translated 'while' in R.V., is omitted. This perhaps strengthens the argument in the exposition on pp. 286 ff. that in these references to time and place we are to think not only of the external events of the passion, but of the internal results which these are to have on the disciples in respect of their moral and spiritual growth towards union with their Lord.

16²¹. In the O.T. the metaphor of the pains of childbirth, followed by a joyful delivery, is sometimes used in connexion with the woes which, it was believed, must precede the arrival of the messianic age; and St. John may well have had in mind such passages as Is. 26¹⁶⁻¹⁹, 66⁷⁻¹⁴. But the present sorrow of the disciples is to be followed by a joy greater far than the expected joy of the Jewish messianic age; theirs is to be a joy of which they cannot be deprived.

16²⁵. 'in proverbs'. See p. 210.

16²⁷. If the argument in the exposition (p. 290) is accepted, the variant reading here, 'from God' instead of 'from the Father', is unlikely to be correct. But, even if correct, it is at once replaced in the next verse by the words 'from the Father', and the evidence as a whole would still justify the argument.

16³². 'the hour cometh, yea, is come': in contrast to 16²⁵, which spoke of an hour still wholly future, a point which at the moment the disciples failed to grasp.

'ye shall be scattered'. The Greek word here is almost identical with that in the Lord's last words to the disciples, on the way to Gethsemane, in Mk. 14²⁷, ²⁸, when He quotes Zech. 13⁷. Cf. also 16¹ with the R.V. mg of Mk. 14²⁷, ²⁹. 'The truth is that the discourse always tends to return to its origin in the earlier tradition, and any new material that is incorporated also rests upon the sayings of Jesus preserved in the synoptic record' (*The Fourth Gospel*, Hoskyns and Davey, 2nd ed., p. 492).

16³³. 'These things have I spoken unto you.' These words occur seven times in the instruction between 13³¹ and 16³³.

'I have overcome the world.' Although the world is the object of God's love [3¹⁶], it remains to the end, and must remain, a battlefield. In this battlefield, however, victory already lies with the Lord (cf. 12³¹, 16¹¹), and is therefore guaranteed also to His followers.

SECTION 7c. 17¹⁻²⁶. *The prayer of the Lord.*

17 These things spake Jesus; and lifting up his eyes to heaven, he said, Father, the hour is come; glorify thy Son, that the Son may glorify 2 thee: Even as thou gavest him authority over all flesh, that whatsoever 3 thou hast given him, to them he should give eternal life. And this is life eternal, that they should know thee the only true God, and him 4 whom thou didst send, *even* Jesus Christ. I glorified thee on the earth, 5 having accomplished the work which thou hast given me to do. And now, O Father, glorify thou me with thine own self with the glory 6 which I had with thee before the world was. I manifested thy name unto the men whom thou gavest me out of the world: thine they were, and 7 thou gavest them to me; and they have kept thy word. Now they know

8 that all things whatsoever thou hast given me are from thee: for the
words which thou gavest me I have given unto them; and they received
them, and knew of a truth that I came forth from thee, and they believed
9 that thou didst send me. I ¹pray for them: I ¹pray not for the world, but
10 for those whom thou hast given me; for they are thine: and all things
that are mine are thine, and thine are mine: and I am glorified in them.
11 And I am no more in the world, and these are in the world, and I come
to thee. Holy Father, keep them in thy name which thou hast given me,
12 that they may be one, even as we *are*. While I was with them, I kept
them in thy name which thou hast given me: and I guarded them, and
not one of them perished, but the son of perdition; that the scripture
13 might be fulfilled. But now I come to thee; and these things I speak in
14 the world, that they may have my joy fulfilled in themselves. I have
given them thy word; and the world hated them, because they are not of
15 the world, even as I am not of the world. I ¹pray not that thou shouldest
take them ²from the world, but that thou shouldest keep them ²from ³the
16 evil *one*. They are not of the world, even as I am not of the world.
17 ⁴Sanctify them in the truth: thy word is truth. As thou didst send me
18 into the world, even so sent I them into the world. And for their sakes I
19 ⁵sanctify myself, that they themselves also may be sanctified in truth.
20 Neither for these only do I ¹pray, but for them also that believe on me
21 through their word; that they may all be one; even as thou, Father, *art*
in me, and I in thee, that they also may be in us: that the world may
22 believe that thou didst send me. And the glory which thou hast given me
23 I have given unto them; that they may be one, even as we *are* one; I in
them, and thou in me, that they may be perfected into one; that the
world may know that thou didst send me, and lovedst them, even as
24 thou lovedst me. Father, ⁶that which thou hast given me, I will that,
where I am, they also may be with me; that they may behold my glory,
which thou hast given me: for thou lovedst me before the foundation of
25 the world. O righteous Father, the world knew thee not, but I knew
26 thee; and these knew that thou didst send me; and I made known unto
them thy name, and will make it known; that the love wherewith thou
lovedst me may be in them, and I in them.

¹ *Gr.* make request.   ² *Gr.* out of.   ³ *Or* evil   ⁴ *Or* Consecrate
⁵ *Or* consecrate   ⁶ *Many ancient authorities read* those whom.

EXPOSITION OF SECTION 7c. 17¹⁻²⁶

In the final words of the Lord's instruction to the disciples
[16³³] He had proclaimed His victory, a victory still to be won on

the field of history in the events of chs. 18 to 20, but already achieved in the sphere of the will and the spirit. In this victory the disciples are to share; indeed, it has been won primarily for their sake, in order that by abiding in Him, as He abides in them, they may have their part in His perfect union with the Father. By virtue of this union He is always in the presence of the Father [8¹⁶, ²⁹, 16³²], and in the prayer of ch. 17, to which we now come, the disciples are allowed to see this union, as it were, in operation. Their Lord has now taken His journey [17¹¹], and has made ready a place for them [14²]; hence at 17¹ they are enabled to go with Him into the presence of the Father, and to hear His prayer that they too, while remaining in the world, may share in this union [17¹¹, ²¹], since the continuance and progress of their Master's work is now to fall to them [17¹¹, ²⁰]. He Himself is no longer in the world; but the disciples are in the world, and for their sakes He is now speaking these things in their hearing, in order that His joy, the joy of a commission and a task perfectly and completely carried out, may also become, in full measure, theirs [17¹³].

Three times St. John records that the Lord 'lifted His eyes'. At 6⁵ He lifts up His eyes and sees that a great multitude is coming to Him; the Greek words are the same as those used of Him in Lk. 6²⁰ and of the disciples in Jn. 4³⁵. At 11⁴¹, by the grave of Lazarus, at a moment when, more than at any other in this gospel, the Lord, it seems, is weighed down by the sight of human physical and spiritual infirmity, the Greek is slightly different. The Lord, we read, 'raised His eyes upwards', before uttering His thanksgiving to the Father for having heard His prayer. Finally here, at 17¹, we return to the words of 6⁵, with the significant addition, if the Greek may be pressed, 'into the heaven'; and presumably the disciples also share His vision, since they hear the prayer which follows.

The Lord's prayer in this chapter deals with three subjects:

(i) 17¹⁻⁸, His own commission, and fulfilment of it;

(ii) 17⁹⁻¹⁹, the community of the disciples, which is to represent Him in the world;

(iii) 17²⁰⁻²⁶ those in the future who receive their faith through the disciples' teaching. The Lord prays that through their union in love, both with one another and with the Father and the Son, the world may come to believe in the mission of the Son, and also, through the perfected union of believers, to know not only the mission of the Son, but the

Father's love for believers, a love no less than His love for the Lord.

(i) 17¹⁻⁸. At this hour, which is to see the climax and completion of His work, the Lord in 17¹⁻³ prays the Father to grant Him the glory which will enable Him to glorify the Father. He, the Son, was given by the Father a position of authority and trust over all creation; and the glory, for which He now prays, will be shown in the gift of eternal life to everyone given to Him by the Father. This eternal life is defined as a growing knowledge of the Father, the only true God, and of His emissary, Jesus Christ. The Lord during His ministry has glorified the Father; He has carried out, completely and perfectly, the task entrusted to Him. He now prays that in this the final hour He may be glorified at the Father's side with the glory which was His at the Father's side before the world existed. He proceeds to render to the Father an account, as it were, of His stewardship, as thus far accomplished (cf. 12²⁸). The stewardship has consisted in making known to the men, entrusted to Him by the Father, whose they were, the Father's 'name', His nature, character, and purpose; and they have been obedient and responsive to the Father's word. Now they have come to know that all that their Master has received from the Father does indeed proceed from the Father; for the teaching which the Son received from the Father (cf. 7¹⁶, 8²⁸) He has imparted to them, and they received it. They now know it to be true that their Lord came forth from the Father; they believe that the Father sent Him. They thus know whence their Master came, and believe in His mission and its origin.

(ii) 17⁹⁻¹⁹. In the review [17⁴⁻⁸] of His work during the ministry among and for the men given to Him by the Father out of the world, the Lord has shown that the task laid upon Him by the Father has been carried out; the Father has been glorified in the Son. But that ministry is now over, and He is no longer in the world [17¹¹], to which indeed He never belonged [8²³]. As a result of His work, the men for whom He prays in this section of the prayer are now also, like their Master, not of the world [17¹⁴, ¹⁶]; but, unlike Him, they remain in it and, since He is leaving them [17¹¹], they now form the subject of His prayer. For the world He does not make request [17⁹]. The world is indeed the object of God's love [3¹⁶], and the Son gives His human or incarnate life for its life [6⁵¹]; and in a few moments the Lord will pray that the life of believers may be such that the world may be led to believe in their Master's mission from the Father [17²¹], and to know that the Father's love for the Son is the measure of His (the Father's), love for believers. But these truths can only be perceived, as it were, from within; the world as such cannot see or enter the kingdom of God [3³, ⁵]; it does not believe; and since to see and enter the kingdom of God is of necessity to be called and admitted to redemptive work, the world as such, unlike believers, cannot represent the Son, or become the Father's instrument for bringing His creatures within the compass and knowledge of the divine love.

Hence, although the Lord's desire that the world may believe will, before the end of the prayer, be strongly emphasized, and although the bringing of the world to believe on and to know both the mission of the Son and also the life of the divine unity, will be stressed as forming the very purpose of the perfected union, in life and love, of believers [17²¹⁻²³], yet the extent and nature of the world's response are left in doubt, and the Lord here does not pray for it or look to it to carry on His work. Those for whom He prays are the men given to Him by the Father, whose they are; indeed all that belongs to the Son belongs also to the Father, and all that belongs to the Father belongs also to the Son; and as the Father has been glorified in the Son [17⁴], so the Son has been glorified [17¹⁰] in the men who, although their Master, being on His way to the Father, is no longer in the world, are in the world.

The Lord has just referred to the world, for which He does not pray. The world, as such, is not conscious of the holiness of God (the root idea of holiness [17¹¹] is separation). To this holiness, which forms part of the 'name' of the Father, given by Him to the Son, the Lord in the days of His flesh has been and remains faithful; Father and Son have been and remain in perfect unity and union; and the Lord now prays that the Father will keep the disciples in His (the Father's) 'name', given by Him to the Son, in order that their unity and union may be like that of the Father and the Son. While He (the Son) was with them, He had kept them in this 'name', the Father's gift to Him, and under His guardianship none of them was lost but one, for whom this lot was cast as a result both of his inborn nature and of the sacred purpose.

The Son's perfect work on earth, therefore, was not achieved without the presence and activity and, to a certain extent, the potency of evil; and while still on His way to the Father He gives utterance in the world to these truths about His work in order that, in spite of the presence and malignity of evil in the world, the joy, which is and has been His, may be shared also by the disciples, who remain in the world and are to work in it, and shared in fullest measure. To them He gave the Father's word, thus raising them out of the world to His own stature, which is not that of the world; and this earned for them the hatred of the world. None the less He does not make request that the Father would remove them out of the world, but that He would keep them, who, like their Master, are not of the world, from the grasp of evil. Let the Father keep them, although in the world, separate and consecrate from it, and also in the truth, that truth or reality which is the Father's word. As the Father sent the Son into the world, so the Son sent them into the world, and for their sakes He separates and consecrates Himself, in order that they too may be separate and consecrate in truth.

(iii) 17²⁰⁻²⁶. In this third and final section of the prayer the Lord includes those who come to faith in Him through the word of the original disciples, and prays that they all may be a unity, a unity and union which will not only resemble but also share in the unity and union of the Father and the Son. As the Father is in Him and He in the Father, so may believers also be in Them, in order that the world may believe that the Father sent the Son. To these believers the Lord has given the glory which was the Father's gift to Him. This is the glory mentioned in 17¹,⁴, the glory of the Lord's incarnate life and work [1¹⁴, 2¹¹]; and His prayer is that, as a result of this gift, believers may be one, even as the Father and the Son are one: He (the Son) in them, and the Father in Him, that they (believers) may be made perfectly one, the purpose being that the world may come to know that the Father sent the Lord and, further, that He loved believers according to the measure of His love for the Lord.

Thus far the Lord has addressed the Father in prayer; He has put a series of requests. Now in the concluding sentences He expresses a desire or wish of His own. It is His will that those who formed the Father's gift to Him may also be with Him, where He is; and He desires that they may behold His glory. This glory was also the Father's gift to Him; but it is not the glory which was manifested in the Lord's incarnate life, nor the love which was revealed in His ministry; it is the love of the Father for the Son before the foundation of the world. This glory, already mentioned in 17⁵, it is the Lord's will that the disciples, His Father's gift to Him, may behold; but mention has just been made of the world, and therewith a barrier has come into existence, which must first be overcome, a barrier which might be thought insuperable. For in 17¹¹ the Lord had referred to the holiness of the Father, a holiness which separates Him from the world; and now in 17²⁵ He recalls the Father's righteousness, a righteousness which will not allow His countenance to look on that which falls short of perfect righteousness, on that which is other than Himself. And it is true that the world has failed to acknowledge the Father, and for it, as we have seen, the Lord does not make request [17⁹]; but He Himself is able to say to the Father that He, being in the world, has acknowledged Him, and to add that the men, now standing with Him in the Father's presence, have acknowledged His mission from the Father. And to them He has made known and will make known the Father's 'name', that the love which the Father has ever had and has for Him may be in them, and He (the Son) in them.

NOTES TO SECTION 7c. 17¹⁻²⁶

17¹. In the two previous passages where 'the hour' is said to have arrived, it was added, at 12²³, on the occasion of the arrival of the Greeks (cf. also 'all men' in 12³²), 'that the Son of man should be glorified'; and, at 13¹, when the Lord is about to concentrate His love on the disciples, 'that he [the Lord] should depart out of the world to the Father'. Here, where the arrival of the hour is mentioned for the last time, it has no further definition. The Lord, with His disciples, stands in the presence of the Father.

17². 'authority'. For this gift of authority by the Father to the Son cf. 5²⁷; and for the communication of the gift of authority by the Logos to those who received Him cf. 1¹², where the word, here rendered 'authority', is translated in the R.V. 'the right'.

'all flesh' is a Hebrew expression, meaning mankind in its weakness and transitoriness, as contrasted with the majesty of God.

17², ³. The expression 'eternal life' is frequent in chs. 3 to 12, but is never defined there. In chs. 13 to 20 it only occurs here, and 17³ may be regarded as a sentence in brackets, defining the eternal life mentioned for the last time in 17².

On the words 'Jesus Christ' see note on 1¹⁷, the only other place in John where the term occurs.

17⁵. The glory for which the Lord, His work on earth completed, prays here, and to which He refers in 17²⁴, is the glory of the eternal Word, the glory which is His by nature and right; the glory for which He prayed in 17¹ is the glory of self-sacrificing love, as manifested by Him throughout His ministry and, supremely, in His death.

17⁸. St. John does not contrast faith (or belief) and knowledge, or rather (since he avoids these substantives, using only the verbs) the processes which these words represent. If faith in the Lord's mission from the Father and adherence, in conduct, to the Lord's teaching are steadily held and pursued, the result is an increasing knowledge of God and of Jesus Christ, the knowledge defined in 17³ as eternal life.

17¹². Readers of Greek will notice the connexion between the words translated 'perished' and 'perdition'.

'the son of perdition'. The common oriental expression 'son of . . .' has such implications as 'belonging to' (e.g. 'the sons of flame' Job 5⁷ R.V. mg, 'a son of peace' Lk. 10⁶), 'destined for' (e.g. 2 Sam. 12⁵ R.V. mg, Mt. 23¹⁵ 'a son of Gehenna' R.V. mg), 'concerned with' (e.g. 'the sons of the citadel' 1 Macc. 4² Gk., 'the sons of the bridechamber' Mt. 9¹⁵).

In 2 Thess. 2³ St. Paul teaches that, before the day of the Lord can arrive, apostasy must first come and 'the son of perdition' be revealed. Since, however, in this gospel the day of the Lord is regarded as realized in the life, the work, and, above all, the death of Jesus Christ, St. John invites those who welcome his interpretation of the Gospel to see in Judas 'the man of sin, the son of perdition'.[1]

'that the scripture might be fulfilled'. If it is correct to think that a particular passage of the O.T. is in mind here, reference may be made to Ps. 41⁹, already cited at 13¹⁸, or to Ps. 109⁸, cited, with reference to Judas, at Acts 1²⁰.

17¹⁷, ¹⁸. Cf. 10³⁶, where we read that the Father rendered the Son separate or consecrate, and sent Him into the world.

17²⁰. The prayer passes to the thought of the 'much fruit' [15⁵, ⁸] to be borne by the original disciples, fruit by which they glorify the Father.

17²⁴. The R.V. text should be followed. The relative clause in the singular refers to the 'they' (i.e. believers) mentioned later in the verse, and thus emphasizes the union and unity which the Lord desires for them. It should be noticed that this prayer is, throughout, a prayer for disciples and believers as a single body; the only individual mentioned is the disciple who has left the body. The same is broadly true of the Lord's promises in chs. 14 to 16; promises are made, exceptionally, to the individual member of the body at 14¹², ²¹, ²³, 15⁵.

SECTION 7 d. 18¹–19⁴². *The crucifixion of the Lord.*

18 When Jesus had spoken these words, he went forth with his disciples over the ¹brook ²Kidron, where was a garden, into the which he entered,

---

[1] I owe this valuable suggestion to the Rev. R. W. H. Phillips.

[1] *Or* ravine   *Gr.* winter-torrent.   [2] *Or* of the Cedars

2 himself and his disciples. Now Judas also, which betrayed him, knew
3 the place: for Jesus oft-times resorted thither with his disciples. Judas
then, having received the ¹band *of soldiers*, and officers from the chief
priests and the Pharisees, cometh thither with lanterns and torches and
4 weapons. Jesus therefore, knowing all the things that were coming upon
5 him, went forth, and saith unto them, Whom seek ye? They answered
him, Jesus of Nazareth. Jesus saith unto them, I am *he*. And Judas also,
6 which betrayed him, was standing with them. When therefore he said
7 unto them, I am *he*, they went backward, and fell to the ground. Again
therefore he asked them, Whom seek ye? And they said, Jesus of
8 Nazareth. Jesus answered, I told you that I am *he*: if therefore ye seek
9 me, let these go their way: that the word might be fulfilled which he
10 spake, Of those whom thou hast given me I lost not one. Simon Peter
therefore having a sword drew it, and struck the high priest's ²servant,
11 and cut off his right ear. Now the ²servant's name was Malchus. Jesus
therefore said unto Peter, Put up the sword into the sheath: the cup
which the Father hath given me, shall I not drink it?
12   So the ¹band and the ³chief captain, and the officers of the Jews,
13 seized Jesus and bound him, and led him to Annas first; for he was
14 father in law to Caiaphas, which was high priest that year. Now Caiaphas
was he which gave counsel to the Jews, that it was expedient that one
man should die for the people.
15   And Simon Peter followed Jesus, and *so did* another disciple. Now that
disciple was known unto the high priest, and entered in with Jesus into
16 the court of the high priest; but Peter was standing at the door without.
So the other disciple, which was known unto the high priest, went out
17 and spake unto her that kept the door, and brought in Peter. The maid
therefore that kept the door saith unto Peter, Art thou also *one* of this
18 man's disciples? He saith, I am not. Now the ⁴servants and the officers
were standing *there*, having made ⁵a fire of coals; for it was cold; and
they were warming themselves: and Peter also was with them, standing
and warming himself.
19   The high priest therefore asked Jesus of his disciples, and of his
20 teaching. Jesus answered him, I have spoken openly to the world;
I ever taught in ⁶synagogues, and in the temple, where all the Jews come
21 together; and in secret spake I nothing. Why askest thou me? ask them
that have heard *me*, what I spake unto them: behold, these know the
22 things which I said. And when he had said this, one of the officers
standing by struck Jesus ⁷with his hand, saying, Answerest thou the
23 high priest so? Jesus answered him, If I have spoken evil, bear witness

---

¹ *Or* cohort   ² *Gr.* bondservant.   ³ *Or* military tribune   *Gr.*
chiliarch.   ⁴ *Gr.* bondservants.   ⁵ *Gr.* a fire of charcoal.   ⁶ *Gr.*
synagogue.   ⁷ *Or* with a rod

24 of the evil: but if well, why smitest thou me? Annas therefore sent him bound unto Caiaphas the high priest.

25 Now Simon Peter was standing and warming himself. They said therefore unto him, Art thou also *one* of his disciples? He denied, and 26 said, I am not. One of the ¹servants of the high priest, being a kinsman of him whose ear Peter cut off, saith, Did not I see thee in the garden with 27 him? Peter therefore denied again: and straightway the cock crew.

28 They lead Jesus therefore from Caiaphas into the ²palace: and it was early; and they themselves entered not into the ²palace, that they might 29 not be defiled, but might eat the passover. Pilate therefore went out 30 unto them, and saith, What accusation bring ye against this man? They answered and said unto him, If this man were not an evil-doer, we 31 should not have delivered him up unto thee. Pilate therefore said unto them, Take him yourselves, and judge him according to your law. The 32 Jews said unto him, It is not lawful for us to put any man to death: that the word of Jesus might be fulfilled, which he spake, signifying by what manner of death he should die.

33 Pilate therefore entered again into the ²palace, and called Jesus, and 34 said unto him, Art thou the King of the Jews? Jesus answered, Sayest 35 thou this of thyself, or did others tell it thee concerning me? Pilate answered, Am I a Jew? Thine own nation and the chief priests delivered 36 thee unto me: what hast thou done? Jesus answered, My kingdom is not of this world: if my kingdom were of this world, then would my ³servants fight, that I should not be delivered to the Jews: but now is 37 my kingdom not from hence. Pilate therefore said unto him, Art thou a king then? Jesus answered, ⁴Thou sayest that I am a king. To this end have I been born, and to this end am I come into the world, that I should bear witness unto the truth. Every one that is of the truth heareth my 38 voice. Pilate saith unto him, What is truth?

And when he had said this, he went out again unto the Jews, and saith unto them, I find no crime in him.

39 But ye have a custom, that I should release unto you one at the pass-over: will ye therefore that I release unto you the King of the Jews? 40 They cried out therefore again, saying, Not this man, but Barabbas. Now Barabbas was a robber.

19 Then Pilate therefore took Jesus, and scourged him. And the soldiers 2 plaited a crown of thorns, and put it on his head, and arrayed him in a 3 purple garment; and they came unto him, and said, Hail, King of the 4 Jews! and they struck him ⁵with their hands. And Pilate went out again, and saith unto them, Behold, I bring him out to you, that ye may know 5 that I find no crime in him. Jesus therefore came out, wearing the crown

---

¹ *Gr.* bondservants.   ² *Gr.* Praetorium.   ³ *Or* officers: *as in* ver. 3, 12, 18, 22.   ⁴ *Or* Thou sayest *it*, because I am a king.   ⁵ *Or* with rods

of thorns and the purple garment. And *Pilate* saith unto them, Behold,
6 the man! When therefore the chief priests and the officers saw him, they
cried out, saying, Crucify *him*, crucify *him*. Pilate saith unto them, Take
7 him yourselves, and crucify him: for I find no crime in him. The Jews
answered him, We have a law, and by that law he ought to die, because
8 he made himself the Son of God. When Pilate therefore heard this saying,
9 he was the more afraid; and he entered into the ¹palace again, and saith
10 unto Jesus, Whence art thou? But Jesus gave him no answer. Pilate
therefore saith unto him, Speakest thou not unto me? knowest thou not
that I have ²power to release thee, and have ²power to crucify thee?
11 Jesus answered him, Thou wouldest have no ²power against me, except
it were given thee from above: therefore he that delivered me unto thee
12 hath greater sin. Upon this Pilate sought to release him: but the Jews
cried out, saying, If thou release this man, thou art not Cæsar's friend:
13 every one that maketh himself a king ³speaketh against Cæsar. When
Pilate therefore heard these words, he brought Jesus out, and sat down
on the judgement-seat at a place called The Pavement, but in Hebrew,
14 Gabbatha. Now it was the Preparation of the passover: it was about the
15 sixth hour. And he saith unto the Jews, Behold, your King! They therefore cried out, Away with *him*, away with *him*, crucify him. Pilate saith
unto them, Shall I crucify your King? The chief priests answered, We
16 have no king but Cæsar. Then therefore he delivered him unto them to
be crucified.

17   They took Jesus therefore: and he went out, bearing the cross for
himself, unto the place called The place of a skull, which is called in
18 Hebrew Golgotha: where they crucified him, and with him two others,
19 on either side one, and Jesus in the midst. And Pilate wrote a title also,
and put it on the cross. And there was written, JESUS OF NAZARETH, THE
20 KING OF THE JEWS. This title therefore read many of the Jews: ⁴for the
place where Jesus was crucified was nigh to the city: and it was written
21 in Hebrew, *and* in Latin, *and* in Greek. The chief priests of the Jews
therefore said to Pilate, Write not, The King of the Jews; but, that he
22 said, I am King of the Jews. Pilate answered, What I have written I have
written.

23   The soldiers therefore, when they had crucified Jesus, took his
garments, and made four parts, to every soldier a part; and also the
⁵coat: now the ⁵coat was without seam, woven from the top throughout.
24 They said therefore one to another, Let us not rend it, but cast lots for
it, whose it shall be: that the scripture might be fulfilled, which saith,
They parted my garments among them, And upon my vesture did they
25 cast lots. These things therefore the soldiers did. But there were stand-

---

¹ *Gr.* Prætorium.   ² *Or* authority   ³ *Or* opposeth Cæsar   ⁴ *Or*
for the place of the city where Jesus was crucified was nigh at hand   ⁵ *Or*
tunic

ing by the cross of Jesus his mother, and his mother's sister, Mary the
26 *wife* of Clopas, and Mary Magdalene. When Jesus therefore saw his
mother, and the disciple standing by, whom he loved, he saith unto his
27 mother, Woman, behold, thy son! Then saith he to the disciple,
Behold, thy mother! And from that hour the disciple took her unto his
own *home*.

28 After this Jesus, knowing that all things are now finished, that the
29 scripture might be accomplished, saith, I thirst. There was set there a
vessel full of vinegar: so they put a sponge full of the vinegar upon
30 hyssop, and brought it to his mouth. When Jesus therefore had received
the vinegar, he said, It is finished: and he bowed his head, and gave up
his spirit.

31 The Jews therefore, because it was the Preparation, that the bodies
should not remain on the cross upon the sabbath (for the day of that
sabbath was a high *day*), asked of Pilate that their legs might be broken,
32 and *that* they might be taken away. The soldiers therefore came, and
brake the legs of the first, and of the other which was crucified with him:
33 but when they came to Jesus, and saw that he was dead already, they
34 brake not his legs: howbeit one of the soldiers with a spear pierced his
35 side, and straightway there came out blood and water. And he that hath
seen hath borne witness, and his witness is true: and he knoweth that
36 he saith true, that ye also may believe. For these things came to pass,
that the scripture might be fulfilled, A bone of him shall not be ¹broken.
37 And again another scripture saith, They shall look on him whom they
pierced.

38 And after these things Joseph of Arimathaea, being a disciple of Jesus,
but secretly for fear of the Jews, asked of Pilate that he might take away
the body of Jesus: and Pilate gave *him* leave. He came therefore, and
39 took away his body. And there came also Nicodemus, he who at the
first came to him by night, bringing a ²mixture of myrrh and aloes, about
40 a hundred pound *weight*. So they took the body of Jesus, and bound it in
41 linen cloths with the spices, as the custom of the Jews is to bury. Now
in the place where he was crucified there was a garden; and in the garden
42 a new tomb wherein was never man yet laid. There then because of the
Jews' Preparation (for the tomb was nigh at hand) they laid Jesus.

¹ *Or* crushed   ² *Some ancient authorities read* roll.

EXPOSITION OF SECTION 7 d. 18¹–19⁴²

The Lord's teaching on His work in the passion is now ended, and
we pass to St. John's record of the action itself.

It was pointed out in the exposition of chs. 2 to 12 that the connexion between the Lord's works and His words or teaching is very close, the teaching usually following, and showing the deeper or ultimate meaning of, the work. In ch. 11 work and word are inextricably interwoven, the teaching being given in the middle of the action.

It was also mentioned (pp. 20, 258), that the passion narrative in chs. 13 to 20 is no exception to the general rule; but in this case the Lord's teaching, given to the disciples in 13^{31} to 17^{26}, precedes His work in chs. 18 to 20, and explains the significance, necessity, and efficacy of the latter.

The reader is thus enabled to approach St. John's narrative of the events of the passion in the spirit of a worshipper, knowing that the Lord thereby, on the one hand, overcomes the world $[16^{33}]$ and goes to the Father $[14^{12, 28}, 16^{28}]$, and, on the other hand, bestows the Paraclete, the Spirit which descended and remained on Him from the first $[1^{33}]$, upon the disciples, and raises them with Him into the presence of the Father $[17^{1, 25}]$. The reader should therefore try to see in each successive incident an example, when rightly understood, of the victory and triumph of the Lord and of the divine righteousness on the one hand, and of the defeat and expulsion, on the other hand, of the *de facto* prince or ruler of the world, and therefore also of the condemnation of the world, in so far as it submits to its *de facto* ruler; and from time to time St. John gives the reader a pointer, as it were, to assist him in this task. In the first paragraph of ch. 18 $[18^{1-11}]$, which tells of the arrest, this is especially clear.

The Lord's death was only brought about by the co-operation of several very different parties, and we learn from 19^{11} that varying degrees of guilt attached to them. The chief priests, we there read,[1] were more guilty than Pilate; and Judas, we may believe, was more guilty than the Jews. In this gospel all these three parties or their representatives, the agents of the prince or ruler of the world, who has no part in or hold upon the Lord, come to take part in the arrest. All, however, retreat before Him and become forthwith prostrate and helpless, when He goes out to meet them; nor are they able to take any action, until He has laid down the

---

[1] 'he that delivered me unto thee'. Just as we speak of 'the party' which did this or that, using the singular, whether the reference is to an individual or to a group of persons regarded as a unity, so here; the reference seems to be primarily to the action of those who deliver the Lord to Pilate in 18^{28-30}.

condition on which He gives Himself into their hands, namely, the freedom of those who are with Him.

Simon Peter's hasty and ill-considered act of violence [18¹⁰] is parallel to the same disciple's impetuous and ill-considered words in 13⁸, ⁹, ³⁷ and, like the latter, is not countenanced. Similarly his disavowals in 18¹⁵⁻¹⁸, ²⁵⁻²⁷ of any connexion with his Master show that at present He truly knows neither his Master, as we saw at 13⁷, nor where his Master is going, as we saw at 13³⁶.

St. Matthew and St. Mark do not mention the binding of the Lord [18¹²] until, after condemnation by the Sanhedrin, He is handed over to Pilate. (St. Luke nowhere mentions the binding.) St. John, however, who has just mentioned the freedom of the disciples at the Lord's request [18⁸, ⁹], forthwith mentions the binding of the Lord, and again at 18²⁴.

A table of the variations in the four gospels as regards those who drew attention to Simon Peter before his successive denials may be found in the notes. At 18¹⁹ 'the high priest', in view of 18²⁴, is apparently Annas. He asks in general terms about the Lord's disciples and His teaching. The specific question about the Lord's Person and office, raised by the Jewish tribunal at this point in the other gospels, would hardly be in place here, because in John it has been already dealt with (to give one example only, at 10²²⁻³⁹), and at 19⁷ the Jews show that in fact they know His answer to it. The Lord's reply in 18²⁰, ²¹ is particularly appropriate in John, since in this gospel there has been from the first no concealment in the Lord's revelation of Himself; and teaching about His Person and office, and about His mission from and relation to the Father, has been given openly throughout the ministry. When, as a result of His words, He is treated with violence [18²²], His reply in 18²³, as at 8⁴⁶, is unanswerable. He is not being thus treated because He is an evil-doer; the use of violence has only shown the officer's weakness.

In connexion with 18²⁷ attention may be drawn to the fact that no mention is made of any emotional reaction on the part of those concerned in the action of chs. 18 and 19, except for Pilate's fear [19⁸].

In 18²⁸ the word 'Praetorium' [R.V. mg] denotes the Roman procurator's official residence at Jerusalem, to which he came, from his normal residence at Caesarea on the coast, in order to prevent disturbances during the Jewish festivals; and St. John implies (although his statement here is not entirely free from difficulty) that the Jews would have incurred ceremonial defilement by entering this Gentile house and so would have been unable to eat their passover. Since, however, he makes clear that, having ranged themselves under 'the ruler of the world', they are about to allow no moral scruples to prevent them from achieving their purpose, the justice of the Lord's words in Mt. 23^{24} becomes evident, that in straining out the gnat they swallow the camel.

At 3$^{16,\ 17}$ we learned that God's purpose in giving His only Son was that all who received and welcomed Him should have eternal life, the divine purpose being thus positive, not negative: the salvation, not the condemnation of the world (cf. 12^{47b}). But the coming of the Son brings with it light, in this case perfect, flawless light; and therefore anyone who finds himself unable or unwilling to face or meet that light, will instinctively put himself in opposition to it; and since the light itself, identical with Jesus Christ [8^{12}], cannot compromise with deliberate, wilful imperfection, condemnation or judgement is self-incurred, and at once, by those who thus put themselves in opposition. This truth may be illustrated by ch. 9, where the Lord in 9$^{39-41}$ ratifies the condemnation (and therefore the blindness), which the Pharisees, by their condemnation of the enlightened beggar, have already passed upon themselves.

In 12$^{31-33}$ we read of a judgement or condemnation of this world in connexion with the Lord's coming death; and we shall therefore now be prepared for the same interpretation of the final trial scene, that before Pilate, as of that in ch. 9. The light, which has come into the world and is embodied in Pilate's Prisoner, will show, by Pilate's response to and treatment of it, where Pilate stands. Since the Prisoner is in truth the unchanging and unswerving Judge, Pilate will inevitably pass on himself a sentence of acquittal or of condemnation, which the Prisoner, the Lord, will ratify.

The reader, from his knowledge of chs. 2 to 12, especially 11$^{47-53}$, is already aware that the Jews, with the Pharisees and the chief priests at their head, have ranged themselves on the side of the world; in their case the die is already cast. They have, however, failed in their repeated attempts to destroy the Lord, and now seek to enlist against Him the help of the secular tribunal, that is, the State, which derives its authority from no earthly source [19^{11}, Rom. 13^1]. Thus the Lord, who in chs. 2 to 12 has not come into direct contact with the occupying power, the secular authority, now stands before the representative of the Roman emperor; and the event is treated much more fully by St. John than by St. Matthew or St. Mark, of whose brief narratives that in John may be regarded, if we wish, as an explanatory expansion.

It is sometimes thought that the purpose of the account in John, which, like that in Luke, strongly emphasizes Pilate's conviction of the Lord's innocence, is to prove that the Roman empire had nothing to fear from the activity and the preaching of the Church. But although the record in John does make clear the nature of the Lord's authority and shows that it need not come into conflict with the civil authority, yet the narrative also describes a prolonged struggle between the secular authority, represented by Pilate, and the Jews, who in this case represent 'the world', and shows how and why the secular authority is in the end borne down by and yields to the pressure of the world. St. John's story thus reveals how, by the cross, the whole world, including the State, is brought under the judgement of God [Rom. 3¹⁹].

Owing to the Jews' religious scruples which, it should be noticed, are respected by the occupying power, the scene in 18²⁸ to 19¹⁶ alternates between the interior of the Praetorium, where Pilate is in the presence of Him who bears witness to the truth [18³⁷], and the exterior, where Pilate is exposed to the pressure and relentless determination of the Jews, with the chief priests and their officials at their head [19⁶]. Outwardly and inwardly, therefore, Pilate is in a strait betwixt the two, and sooner or later he must decide between them; and the successive stages by which he is led to his fatal decision are clearly marked.

Regarding, then, Pilate as representing the authority which we call the State, we find that the latter at the outset proceeds altogether correctly. To the State the Prisoner is simply 'this man' [18²⁹], and Pilate asks what charge is brought against Him. The Jews reply vaguely and at first bring no specific charge (we may perhaps recall 8⁴⁶), but appear to arrogate to themselves the right to decide who is a wrongdoer and who should therefore be delivered to the State for judgement. Pilate sees in their words an opportunity to avoid the responsibility for a decision, and invites them to deal with the Prisoner according to their own, the Jewish, Law. The Jews decline the invitation, saying that they must have recourse to the State for the sentence of death, which they demand. Since there is no decisive evidence, apart from this passage, that the Jews could not, for religious offences, pronounce and execute the death sentence (by stoning, as in Acts 7⁵⁸; cf. Jn. 8⁵⁹, 10³¹), it seems probable that, as 18³³ suggests, they seek here to achieve the Lord's death by means of a political charge, on the ground of His claiming a (revolutionary) kingship. Both 6¹⁵ and 12¹², ¹³ suggest that evidence of a kind could be produced, to show that there was or had been a movement to force kingship on Him; and by making use of this evidence and thus throwing the responsibility for His condemnation on the occupying power, the chief priests would not only escape danger of criticism by their own countrymen for crushing One in whom some saw a possible national leader, but also would hand the Prisoner over to Pilate on the most dangerous charge conceivable. They do not reveal until 19⁷ that any religious question is involved; and by that time matters have gone too far to enable Pilate to draw back. In 18³² St. John notes that the coming condemnation of the Lord by the gentile authority, and therefore His death by crucifixion as opposed to stoning, will be no accident, but will be in accordance with His own words in 3¹⁴, 8²⁸, 12³². Thus the Jews unconsciously fulfil the divine purpose, which is to show the Lord, lifted up from the earth upon the cross, in the act of His fullest exaltation, that is, in the greatest manifestation of His love for men.

Accordingly, if Pilate, representing the State, does not adhere to the position which he took in 18³¹, and decline to interfere, he will be forced to decide between the Prisoner and the Jews, here representing the world, which for its own reasons [3¹⁹, 7⁷] has determined to have the Lord removed. The reader at this point should once more bear in mind the teaching of this gospel that everyone into whose presence the Lord comes cannot but make a decision, *ipso facto* and forthwith (in respect of his own person, and also of his work and office, whatever these may be), and thereby find or place himself either on the right hand or on the left hand of the Lord (cf. Mt. 25³¹⁻⁴⁶).

The next stage therefore is the first private dialogue between the Prisoner and the procurator, and it takes the form of an inquiry into the nature of the Jewish kingship which, as we may reasonably suppose Pilate by this time to have heard, the Prisoner is alleged to claim. The Lord in reply asks whether Pilate is personally interested in raising the question, or whether, as procurator, he is merely repeating the charge which he has heard. Pilate's answer repudiates any personal interest in Jewish problems, and demands the Prisoner's account of His actions. The Lord now implies that a kingship does belong to Him, but makes clear that it has no secular or political origin or quality. Pilate had inquired about actions; it should be clear that the Lord's kingship is of the character ascribed by Him to it, from the fact that, were it of this world, His 'officials' (as opposed to the officials of the chief priests; cf. 18³, and R.V. mg on 18³⁶) would have used violence to prevent His falling into the hands of the Jews (cf. 18¹⁰⋅ ¹¹); but this they did not do. When Pilate presses the Lord on this admission of kingship, the Lord points out that not He but Pilate was the first to use the word 'king'. The account which the Lord, speaking to the gentile Pilate, Himself gives of the matter is that the purpose of His birth and of His coming into the world was that He should bear witness to the truth. Every individual who belongs to truth listens and is obedient to Him. (If, then, Pilate will listen to the Lord's voice, he will recognize, both as a man and as procurator, in what sense the Prisoner is a king, and will acknowledge His kingship—cf. 9³⁸— without loss, to the State, of its authority.) Pilate, however, abruptly closes the conversation; in neither capacity is he interested in talk of truth. Hence the position now reached, before Pilate goes out for the second time, is that he will take the side neither of accusers [18³⁵] nor of Accused [18³⁸], and that he seeks, as before, to avoid the responsibility of a decision.

But the question arises, now more urgently than ever, whether such a position is possible, in, and in face of, the presence of the Lord [15²²]. It is true that, although the Lord's kingship and authority do not or need not come into political conflict with the State, yet secular authority is in the hands of men; and since the Lord's presence and voice leave no one where he was before, men in consequence, whether they themselves and others know it or not, forthwith stand for Him or against Him. And Pilate, representing the State, has rejected the possibility of recognition of the truth, offered to him in 18³⁷. After this, will he be able, in his own strength (cf. 15⁵ᵉⁿᵈ), to act with justice?

Leaving the Lord within, Pilate goes out and addresses the Jews. He finds no crime in the Prisoner, but since in fact, as we have seen, he has already made his choice, he does not act as his words to the Jews in 18³⁸ᵇ show that he ought to act, but, still seeking to avoid a decision of his own, he makes a suggestion to the Jews, by which, through their choice, the Prisoner may be freed. There is the passover custom that he should release a prisoner to them; and since he has found the Prisoner's claim to kingship empty and absurd (such is the implication of Pilate's words in 18³⁹), would the Jews not like the Prisoner to be the object of Pilate's clemency this year? So far, however, from bringing the matter to a close, Pilate's suggestion now makes his position still more difficult; for he has admitted the Lord's innocence, and now the Jews, rejecting his suggestion, request the release of Barabbas, confessedly a brigand.

The unreliability of the Jews, who, it must once more be remembered, here represent the world, thus becomes completely manifest. They delivered up the Lord on the ground of unspecified wrongdoing [18³⁰]; and now they demand the release of a criminal. And Pilate cannot now draw back; he must decide between the Prisoner and the Jews, who have already shown that their object is the Prisoner's death. Pilate, however, makes a fresh attempt, short of complete surrender, to accommodate the Jews. Although he has asserted and will assert again that he finds the Prisoner guilty of no crime, he now has Him scourged, and his soldiers, by their treatment of the Lord, ridicule His claim to kingship; and in this condition, a caricature of royalty indeed, Pilate presents Him to the Jews; the very sight of the Prisoner in this state should be enough to prove how ludicrous in such a case is any suggestion of royalty or kingship. Will not this be sufficient, to satisfy their hatred (cf. 15²⁴)?

It will be noticed that to Pilate the Prisoner is still 'the man' [19⁵], as at 18²⁹, although He is now shown in ludicrous guise, in view of His alleged claim to Jewish kingship. The reader, however, knowing that the term 'the Son of man' (a semitic expression which Pilate would not use) means 'man', will recall the earlier statement in 3¹³ about the descent of the Son of man from heaven, and in this mock presentation of the Lord, the King of truth, will see an example of the lowest depth of His condescension for man's sake, immediately before His final exaltation on the cross.

Events quickly dispelled any hopes which Pilate may have entertained of the effect to be produced upon the Jews and their leaders by his mocking presentation of the Lord; and for the first time in this gospel we meet with a direct, unequivocal reference to that form of death which awaits the Lord. Pilate's concession to the Jews at 19¹ has only led to a more direct attack upon his weakness; and since crucifixion was a Roman, not a Jewish, punishment, his answer in 19⁶ to the shout of 'Crucify!' cannot have the same meaning as his words in 18³¹, except in so far as it is an attempt to avoid responsibility, but must be regarded as a petulant refusal to condemn the Prisoner.

But the Jews have further cards to play; and in view of Pilate's repeated assertion of the Prisoner's innocence they bring forward an explicit charge of His offence against religion. The Lord has claimed divine Sonship, and they appeal to their law which prescribes death for blasphemy [Lev. 24¹⁶]. Possibly the Roman principle should be borne in mind, that the occupying power should show itself well disposed to the religious scruples of the population.

The Jews' revelation, however, that the Prisoner claims a divine Sonship has an unexpected effect upon Pilate, and gives him to pause; and he retires again within for a second examination of the Prisoner. The Jews' determined demeanour has already caused him disquiet; and now he is afraid also of the Prisoner, whose bearing, we may assume, has had some effect upon him and therefore perhaps makes the Jews' assertion especially unwelcome. He seeks therefore, as in 18³³⁻³⁸, so now in 19⁹⁻¹¹ to hear the Prisoner's own account, this time about His origin. The reader, however, has long since learned that knowledge of the answer to this question cannot be obtained in this way (see pp. 168, 325), and the Lord is silent. When Pilate, seeking to persuade the Prisoner to answer, points out that His fate rests entirely in his hands, the Lord, disregarding the matter of His own condemnation or release, reminds Pilate that the authority of the State is derived not from 'the world', but 'from above'; it is divinely given.[1] This second inquiry, therefore, is no longer concerned with the Person and office or kingship of the Prisoner; with regard to these Pilate has already made his choice [18³⁵, ³⁸]; the subject is now the authority and the responsibility of the State, which are derived not from any earthly source, but 'from above' [19¹¹]; and the issue, shortly to be decided, is whether a representative of the State who, like Pilate

---

[1] We may compare Socrates' refusal, in deference to the authority of the State and the obedience therefore due to it, to avail himself of escape from the condemnation passed upon him, although he considered it unjust.

in 18³⁸, has in the presence of the Lord put aside, in his personal capacity, the invitation to listen to the voice of truth, can in his official capacity fulfil the duties of his office rightly. But, whatever Pilate's official decision may be, there is clearly a difference between his position and that of the Jews. The world, here represented by the Jews, is moved by personal hatred of the Lord, and seeks by any means to force the secular authority to join with it against Him. But the State, here represented by Pilate, has, as such, no personal interest in the case; it does not hate the Lord. Even if, by yielding to the world, it acts unjustly and so becomes unfaithful to its office, its responsibility is less than that of those who brought it to this pass; theirs therefore is the greater sin. And not only so, but the world, in addition to its personal hatred, has sought, for its own purposes, to misuse and therefore to degrade the supreme secular authority, that is, the State.

19¹²ᵃ shows that Pilate understands what has been said to him, and when, in consequence, he seeks all the more to make a stand and to set his Prisoner free, the Jews find it necessary to play their last card; the Lord, they say, by claiming kingship has refused obedience to the Roman emperor; if therefore Pilate releases Him, Pilate is unfaithful to his lord.

Pilate now knows that he must give his decision, and also what it will be, since his fear of God, as stirred in him by the words and the demeanour of the Prisoner, is not strong enough to overcome his fear of the Jews, that is, the world. He will, however, in the very moment of his humiliation, have what revenge he can upon those who have brought him to this pass. He therefore himself takes his place upon the judgement-seat, from which his decision will be given, and then once more brings the two parties, face to face, before him. Since both the scene and the time are of supreme importance, the former is mentioned in both Greek and Hebrew, and the latter both in its religious and its all-but-complete significance (see pp. 234, 354–5). On the previous occasion [19⁴⁻⁷] Pilate mocked the Prisoner; but now, in his hatred of the Jews for the indignity which they have brought upon him, he mocks the Jews; here, in the Person of the scourged, mishandled, outraged Jesus let them see their King, and the reader who recalls St. John's comment at 11⁵¹ on Caiaphas' words in 11⁵⁰, may think that here Pilate also unconsciously speaks more truly than he knows; cf. his action in 19¹⁹⁻²². The Jews respond by demanding, with increased vigour, the Prisoner's crucifixion; and finally, in answer to Pilate's inquiry whether they really wish him, as a Roman, to punish in this way one who at least claims to be their King, the chief priests acknowledge no king but the Roman emperor.

Since the Jews were perhaps the most patriotic nation that the world has ever known, and since two outstanding features of this patriotism were, first, their claim to be the peculiar and chosen people of God and, secondly, their hopefulness in expectation of their coming messianic king, in these words they forfeit their most cherished privileges, and also involuntarily reveal their utter condemnation; their unbelief in the Lord has led them to repudiate themselves. As for Pilate, since he closed his ears to the implied invitation of the Lord in 18³⁷, he has become the cat's-paw of the Jews, and is unable to obey the divine claim, resident in his office, that he should act aright; he therefore becomes the servant and accomplice of the world, and, in delivering the Lord to crucifixion, carries out its will.

A condemned prisoner was required to carry his cross to the place of execution; St. John therefore describes a normal procedure. But, since the tradition that Simon of Cyrene was 'impressed' to bear the Lord's cross was widely spread in the early Church, being mentioned in the three other gospels, together with a special personal note about him in Mk. 15²¹, St. John has perhaps some special reason for his language here. It is noticeable that this is the first time that the word 'cross' occurs in John, whereas in the other gospels the expression 'to take up' or 'to bear the cross' has already been used during the ministry. Thus in Lk. 14²⁷ the Lord requires of the would-be disciple that he should 'bear his own cross and come after' the Lord. Since, however, at Lk. 23²⁶ it is the Lord's cross which is laid on Simon, 'to carry it behind Jesus', is it possible that St. John wishes to emphasize that, whatever may have been the outward circumstance, the Lord in truth bore His own cross, and alone? As early as 1²⁹ the reader learnt that He is 'the Lamb of God, who removes the sin of the world'; and He carries out this work unaided, since He alone can achieve it [3¹³⁻¹⁶]; it is a divine act [5¹⁹]; and whatever may have been the facts about the bearing of the cross of wood, no man can lighten the Lord's burden for Him, or share His achievement with Him.¹

---

¹ It is unlikely that St. John's language is due to a—probably later—Docetic heresy that Simon of Cyrene, not the Lord, was crucified. On the other hand it

It was customary that the ground of condemnation should be publicly displayed, and no doubt Pilate's purpose in thus wording the inscription on the cross, and in refusing to withdraw it, was to revenge himself upon the Jews for the way in which they had forced his hand. But the reader will perceive also great significance in Pilate's action. For the title placed by the gentile procurator above the crucified and dying 'King of the Jews' suggests on the one hand the price paid by the Jews for the rejection of their King, namely the condemnation and destruction of Judaism and of its age-long hopes. On the other hand the reader knows that, precisely because of the crucifixion, the Lord is King indeed; the cross is the manner of His exaltation and glorification; to those who understand and believe, it offers a new and 'better hope, through which they may draw near to God' [Heb. 7¹⁹]. The note, found in John only, that the title was written in three languages hints that the Lord's death is an event affecting all mankind; the King—and Judge—of the Jews is the Saviour of the world [4⁴²; cf. 12²⁰, ²³, ³²].

The action of the four soldiers [19²³, ²⁴] in the distribution of the Lord's garments among themselves by an appeal to chance is recorded in the other gospels also; but St. John alone mentions the Lord's seamless undergarment, confining the throw of dice to it; and he alone explicitly quotes Ps. 22¹⁸ here (following the LXX). Both ancient and modern[1] interpreters have suggested that in St. John's allusion to the seamless robe, which immediately covered the Lord's body, we may see a picture of the indivisible unity (cf. 1 Cor. 1¹³) of believers who form His body, the Church—this unity being contrasted with the division, or rent, mentioned three times in the central section of this gospel [7⁴³, 9¹⁶, 10¹⁹] as existing among the Jews, in consequence of the Lord's presence and teaching.

As regards 19²⁵⁻²⁷, if, as is probable, 19²⁵ describes the presence of four women by the cross, they may form the believing counterpart of the four unbelieving soldiers; and an obvious lesson of the passage will be that the members of the Church 'should have the same care one for another' [1 Cor. 12²⁵]. The verses, however, may also convey a deeper teaching, only to be grasped if other passages in this gospel are kept in mind.

is possible that St. John sees a parallel between the picture of Isaac in Gen. 22⁶ and that of the Lord here.

    [1] Cf. Hoskyns and Davey, *The Fourth Gospel*, 2nd ed., p. 529.

The Lord's mother has been mentioned previously in John only in 2¹⁻¹²; and His words there, it was suggested in the exposition at that point, imply that, when His hour does come, a bond of union will be forged between Him and her, stronger than that of physical relationship (cf. Mt. 12⁴⁶⁻⁵⁰). The reader knows that the Lord's hour has now come [12²³, 13¹, 17¹], and he will also recall two passages in chs. 13 to 16, where the Lord explains to the disciples the meaning of the forthcoming events of chs. 18 to 20. First, in 13⁸ the washing of the disciples' feet is said to give them a 'part' or share with Him; through the re-creation which it bestows they will be enabled to receive the Spirit, which is to be a result of His death [7³⁷⁻³⁹]. Secondly, in 16²¹ the Lord reminds the disciples that a woman in travail is bound to have sorrow, because her hour is come; but that her memory of the physical distress is overcome in the joy of delivery, because a man has been born into the world. The use in 16²¹ of the word 'hour', and of 'man' where we might have expected 'child' perhaps gives us the right to use 16²¹, as well as 2¹⁻¹², for the interpretation of 19²⁵⁻²⁷. The joy of the Lord's mother at her Son's birth had assuredly been great and pure indeed; but after her present sorrow (cf. Lk. 2³⁵) a still greater and purer joy awaits her, in the new and permanent relationship to be formed between her Son and herself, as a result of His death and resurrection. The reader will also notice that immediately after 19²⁵⁻²⁷ the Lord knows that His work is done; all has now been completed and accomplished. If, then, we put all these considerations together, it becomes possible that the Lord's mother and the beloved disciple, who from that hour takes her 'to his own', represent the Church and its members, now, in the 'new creation', endowed with the Holy Spirit. See further on 19³⁴.

If it be asked why both at 2⁴ and at 19²⁶ the Lord addresses His mother as 'Woman', rather than 'Mother', we need to remember St. John's purpose. He is concerned with spiritual relationships in the future more than with physical relationships in the past, and with these relationships as they affect those for whom the Lord is giving His life, rather than as they affect Himself.

'After this', the two opening words of 19²⁸, which occur also at 2¹², 11⁷˙ ¹¹, probably connect this section closely with 19²³⁻²⁷. (The words 'after these things', which occur eight times in John, perhaps imply a longer or a vaguer interval of time.) If so, the words 'that the scripture might be accomplished' may best be taken with the clause which precedes them. The action of the soldiers, on the one hand, and the union, on the other hand, of His mother and the beloved disciple by the Lord, together complete all things of which the scripture, which may also be described as the will of God, required fulfilment. If, however, it is preferred to link the words with the clause which follows, rather than with that which precedes, we trace in 19²⁸, ²⁹ a clear reference to Ps. 69²¹ᵇ (LXX 68²²), which 'they'—presumably the soldiers—now unconsciously fulfil.

Difficulty has been felt about the mention of a bunch of hyssop, which is a small, flexible plant, as the means by which the sponge was brought to the Lord's mouth, and the suggestion has been made that we should follow a late manuscript and read 'on a lance' or 'javelin', the Greek for which is 'hyssos'. But possibly, by an allusion to hyssop here, St. John wishes to remind his readers, who know that the Lord is both the Lamb of God [1²⁹, ³⁶] and the door [10⁷], that in accordance with Exod. 12²² hyssop, dipped in the blood of the paschal lamb, was sprinkled on the doors of Jewish dwellings during the passover night and thus ensured the safety of the inhabitants (cf. also Heb. 9¹⁹).

Certain resemblances between 4¹⁻⁴² and 19²⁸⁻³⁰ suggest that the former passage may be used to interpret St. John's meaning here in his reference to the Lord's thirst. At 4⁷ the Lord, wearied with His journey, asks for a draught of water, but proceeds to show that He Himself has living water to give, which will become in the recipient a springing fountain, leading to eternal life; and at 4³⁴ He tells the disciples that His food consists in doing the will and in finishing the work of the Father. Similarly here the Lord, knowing that all is now finished, says, 'I thirst'. And just as in ch. 4 His thirst was on one side slaked by the response of the Samaritans, so His present thirst, in its deepest meaning, is to be slaked by the response of those, represented by His mother and the beloved disciple in the previous section, for whom He has thus proved His love to the uttermost [13¹], to the gift offered in and by His death.

As regards the physical side of His thirst, either in well-meant pity or in mockery (if, as we are told, the draught mentioned would aggravate the thirst), sour wine is offered and the Lord receives it. In the record of the last supper in Mk. 14²⁵ the Lord assures the disciples that He will no more drink wine, 'until that day when

I drink it new in the kingdom of God'. Part of the purpose of this vow of abstinence seems to have been to certify and make clear to them that the time of preparation was now all but over, and that fulfilment, and therefore the kingdom of God, was more than ever close at hand. It would be in accordance with St. John's method if, knowing this earlier saying, he thus reminds the reader that the Lord's exaltation or glorification is achieved, and the kingdom of God fully revealed, at the moment when He receives the draught now offered to Him; and His final word, sealing His assurance in 19²⁸ that all has now been brought to completion, forthwith follows. His mission, in obedience to His Father's will, has been accomplished and is now finished.

In recording that the Lord bowed or inclined His head, St. John probably describes an action corresponding to the word just uttered. His work complete, the Son of man can now rest (cf. 9⁴); at length He has where to lay His head [Mt. 8²⁰, Lk. 9⁵⁸], the same Greek verb being used as here. The last words are literally 'handed over the spirit', and may merely be equivalent to the description of the Lord's death in the synoptists. But the expression is remarkable, and in view of such passages as 7³⁷⁻³⁹ it may imply that, the Lord's glorification being now complete, the dispensation of the Spirit, to be recorded in 20²¹⁻²³, is forthwith made possible as the result of His self-oblation and consequent exaltation.

The Lord's work is finished, but the world continues on its way, and in 19³¹⁻³⁷ the Jews, by their request to Pilate, are once more the indirect and unconscious cause of the fulfilment of scripture; in this case it is through the piercing of the Lord's side [19³⁴], an event to which, as 19³⁵ shows, St. John attaches great significance.

We have seen that chs. 18 to 20 describe the historical events, the religious significance of which was made clear in the Lord's actions and words in chs. 13 to 17. The Lord there showed that it is His purpose to bestow upon His disciples, and through them upon others, nothing less than a participation in the life which He has from the Father, with all that this implies. Through the destruction of the shrine of His physical life, which He has consecrated and offered for their sakes [17¹⁹⁻²¹], a new shrine will arise [2¹⁹], in which a spiritual and true worship will be offered to the Father [4²¹⁻²⁴]. In connexion with 19²⁵⁻²⁷ it was suggested that this new shrine is there set before us in the persons of the Lord's mother and the beloved disciple. Mary, the Lord's physical mother, now becomes, at the Lord's bidding and as a result of His work, the spiritual mother of all those who are or are to be reborn in Him, these being represented at the moment by the beloved disciple who with her stands beneath the cross and takes the Lord's place as her son. If St. John's thought is being correctly followed, we are not, it seems, to understand 19^{27} as implying that the new son at once takes his new mother away. The hour mentioned is likely to be the hour of the Lord's death, and until this has taken place, and for some time after, they remain at the foot of the cross; and to them primarily, when the Lord inclines His head to rest, in the peace of His union with the Father and of His accomplished work, He hands over the new dispensation of Spirit. Just as the original dispensation was effected [Gen. 1^2] by the creative activity of the spirit of God, so in this new dispensation, effected by the Lord's death, they are re-created and reborn;[1] and in the blood and water which descends both literally and spiritually upon them from above, when the Lord's side is pierced [19^{34}], they receive this new birth. This new birth, or birth from above, in and by which the kingdom of God is revealed [3^3], was explained in 3^5 as birth by water and spirit; and in 6^{53-56} a similar stress was laid on reception of the Lord's flesh and blood, signifying His death, as an essential for participation in His life, a reference to the spirit as the life-giving power being added in 6^{63} (cf. 1 Jn. 5^{6-8}); nor would St. John's readers forget that water and blood are the two principal elements in the two sacraments by which the benefits of the Lord's life and death are imparted to believers.

The importance attached by St. John to the event described in 19^{34} is shown by the following verse. The words 'he that hath seen hath borne witness' recall such passages as 1^{34} or 3^{11}; but there the witness given is to spiritual truth; here—and here only in this gospel—witness is adduced to an external, historical event. The identity, however, of the person or persons mentioned in this verse is uncertain. If, as may be the case, the whole verse refers to one person only, that person may be the beloved disciple (whether regarded as also the writer of the gospel, or not). But another

[1] This interpretation of Mary's part as the mother of believers gains support from patristic writings which describe her as the new Eve. Whereas the first Eve was the mother of a race which through sin lost its first status with God, Mary, the second and new Eve, is the mother of all who through her Son's work are freed from sin and abide in Him.

possibility is that in 19³⁵ᵇ appeal is made, in support of the witness given in 19³⁵ᵃ, to another person described in the Greek by a demonstrative pronoun (' "he" knoweth'); and in this case the pronoun may refer to the writer of the gospel (regarded as other than the beloved disciple), or to the Lord Himself. In any case the witness thus given is regarded as of great importance, because the life of the Lord's 'new creation', the Church, depends on the Lord's life and death and on the results, here described, which flowed therefrom. St. John wishes his readers both to know that the event of 19³⁴ occurred, and also to perceive its significance for themselves. With the last words of 19³⁵, cf. 20³¹; and on the two following verses consult the notes.

All four gospels mention Joseph of Arimathaea in connexion with the deposition of the Lord's body from the cross, but only St. John mentions the help given by Nicodemus, whom we now meet for the third and last time in John. With him therefore the reader is already acquainted; but since Joseph has not appeared before, the nature of his previous discipleship is described, and the joint action of the two men suggests that a transformation has now taken place in them, as a result of the Lord's death. The amount of spices brought by Nicodemus is immense, and although 19⁴¹, ⁴² may imply that the burial was carried out rapidly, there is no suggestion in John that it was provisional or incomplete. Apart, no doubt, from the great wealth of myrrh and aloes, it seems to have closely resembled that of Lazarus [11⁴⁴].

It is remarkable that in John the Lord gives Himself up in a garden [18¹⁻¹², ²⁶], and the scene of His crucifixion is said to have been close to the garden where He was buried and where, therefore, the resurrection took place [19⁴¹, ⁴², 20¹⁻¹⁰], and finally in 20¹⁵ Mary Magdalene at the tomb at first supposes, when the risen Lord speaks to her, that she is in the presence of the gardener. If those are right who trace in St. John's thought a connexion and contrast between the Lord's mother and Eve (see p. 320, note), we may also be justified in seeing the same connexion and contrast between the gardens here mentioned and the garden of Eden, though it should perhaps be added that the Greek word used by St. John is not the same as that used in the LXX for the garden of Eden. 'By emphasizing that the great deeds by which Christian redemption was effected took place in a garden, St. John suggests that the events which caused the original fall are here reversed,

and once again the garden of Eden is open to men.'¹ Whereas
in the first garden Satan in the form of the serpent was the cause
of man's fall [Gen. 3], in the second garden(s) Satan in the person
of Judas, himself 'a devil' [6⁷⁰, ⁷¹] and 'the son of perdition' [17¹²],
fails to achieve his purpose, since the Lord's death, to all appearance a result of the betrayal, is in truth His deliberate self-oblation
[10¹¹⁻¹⁸] on behalf of men, and therefore the means of the new
creation, in which the true Eden is made available; and in this
Eden Satan, the prince of the world, has no place [12³¹]. Mary,
then, was not wholly mistaken in thinking that He who addressed
her in 20¹⁵ was the Keeper of the garden. In the obvious sense of
the term, and as she used it, she was mistaken; but she also, like
Caiaphas [11⁴⁹⁻⁵²] and Pilate [19⁵, ¹⁴], spoke more truly than she
knew.

NOTES TO SECTION 7d.   18¹–19⁴²

18¹. 'the brook (wady) Kidron'. R.V. text is probably more correct than
R.V. mg, the word 'kidron' in Hebrew meaning 'dark', just as an English
stream may be called 'Blackwater' (cf. 2 Sam. 15²³, 1 Kings 2³⁷).

18². 'which betrayed him'. At 13¹¹, here, and 18⁵ the Greek has the
present participle, this being used in these three cases because (1) the
'hour' has come; contrast 6⁶⁴; (2) at 13¹¹ the thought is present to Judas
(cf. 13²), and in 18¹⁻¹¹ this thought is being translated into action.

18³. St. John alone mentions, in this context, (1) the presence of a
Roman officer and Roman soldiers [18¹²]; they, being gentiles, will conduct
the Lord into the Praetorium [18²⁸]; the reader is thus reminded, at the
outset of the action, of the part shortly to be played in the matter by the
occupying power; (2) torches and lanterns. The reader recalls that Judas,
who conducts the party, has identified himself with darkness [13³⁰] rather
than with the light of the world (cf. 1⁵ R.V. mg, 11⁹, ¹⁰).

A 'band' or cohort of Roman soldiers usually consisted of either 600 or
200 men. The word translated 'officers' here and at 18¹², ¹⁸, ²², 19⁶ refers
to the temple police, under the control of the Sanhedrin; at 18³⁶, when it
refers to the Lord's disciples, it is rendered 'servants'.

18⁴. 'went forth'. The Lord confronts them, not they Him.

18⁵. 'Jesus of Nazareth'. The expression, as used here, only occurs
again in John at 19¹⁹, where it forms part of the inscription on the cross;
the Greek at 1⁴⁵ is not quite the same. The emphasis is solely on the
Person of the Lord, without reference to His office or function; but in
His reply, identical in form with His reply elsewhere, e.g. at 8⁵⁸, the
reader will perceive His claim to divinity.

¹ Sir Edwyn Hoskyns in *J.T.S.*, April 1920, pp. 210–18.

18⁸, ⁹. In 16³² the Lord had warned the disciples that very soon they would be scattered and would leave Him alone, the reference being, no doubt, to the moment of His arrest; and according to Mk. 14⁵⁰ this is what did now happen. But at 18¹ St. John twice emphasizes the union of the Lord and His disciples, and they had formed the principal subject of His prayer, e.g. 17¹¹, ¹²; accordingly here, if they leave Him, it is only at His direction and with His consent. He will only give Himself up if they go free (cf. 10¹¹⁻¹⁵).

It is sometimes thought strange that there should be a reference here, where the question is one of external liberty, to 17¹² or 6³⁹, where the reference is clearly to a deeper, spiritual liberty. But (1) St. John is always prone to see the outward, however seemingly trivial, as a sign or parable of the inward; and (2) this scene in the garden is the beginning of the final contest between the light of the world [8¹²] and its apparent ruler, the devil. Since the hope of the world, humanly speaking, depends on these eleven men who are to carry on their Lord's work, it must be shown that He is supreme, and that, whatever their momentary defection may have been, they remain in His keeping [10²⁸].

18¹⁰. St. John and St. Luke agree in the detail of the *right* ear; St. John alone records the names Simon Peter and Malchus in connexion with this incident.

18¹¹. 18¹¹ᵃ recalls Jer. 47⁶, and 18¹¹ᵇ both recalls Is. 51²² and probably also shows St. John's knowledge of the prayer of the Lord in Gethsemane (cf. Mk. 14³⁶). The equivalent for the earlier gospels' record of the Lord's distress in Gethsemane is found in John at 12²⁷, ²⁸; as we have already seen, the last time in this gospel when there is a reference to distress on the Lord's part is when He reveals the coming action of one of the disciples, at 13²¹. His words in 18¹¹ᵇ, in justification of His non-resistance, are superficially different from His words to the same purpose on this occasion in Mt. 26⁵²⁻⁵⁴, each saying being characteristic of the record of His teaching in the first and fourth gospels respectively; but, rightly considered, they both express the same attitude on His part.

18¹³. In the four passion narratives St. John alone mentions Annas. He had been high priest from A.D. 6 to 15, when he was deposed by the Roman procurator who preceded Pilate. He was succeeded by his five sons in succession, but, between the first and the second, also by Joseph Caiaphas (according to John his son-in-law), who held the office from A.D. 18 to 36. Annas, however, seems still to have been called high priest [Lk. 3², Acts 4⁶]. The word, when used in the plural, describes all ex-high priests.

18¹⁴. Both here and at 11⁵⁰, to which 18¹⁴ looks back, the word for 'people' probably means the people of God. To Caiaphas this meant the Jewish people; but it is noticeable that the Lord has just given Himself up, on condition that His disciples go free [18⁸, ⁹]; in other words, He gives Himself to bonds and death, in order that His (true) people may go free and live.

18¹⁵. 'another disciple'. See p. 274.

18¹⁷. The variations in the four gospels as regards those who drew attention to Peter before His denials are shown in the following table.

1. The first denial. All agree that in this case it was a maid; in John it is added that she kept the door of the courtyard.
2. The second denial. Matthew, another maid. Mark, the maid already mentioned. Luke, 'another' (man). John, 'they' (i.e. the servants and officers by the fire [18¹⁸]).
3. The third denial. Matthew, Mark, 'those who stood there'. Luke, 'another' (man). John, 'one of the servants of the high priest', a kinsman of Malchus.

18²², ²³. In view of mistaken attempts to understand the teaching of the sermon on the mount too literally, a comparison of Mt. 5³⁹ with these verses is sometimes valuable. When the Lord Himself is struck, He does not turn the other cheek, but utters a gentle and dignified remonstrance.

18²⁴. The omission from this gospel of all details of the trial before Caiaphas [18²⁴, ²⁸] probably explains why in more than one text 18²⁴ is placed in or immediately after 18¹³. In this way the high priest mentioned in 18¹⁹, ²² becomes Caiaphas, not Annas.

18²⁹. It is assumed to be well known to the readers of this gospel that Pontius Pilate was the Roman procurator, before whom the Lord was brought. He had been appointed to his office, the government of that part of the imperial province of Syria which included Judaea, Samaria, and Idumaea, by the Emperor Tiberius in A.D. 26, and his duties were both administrative and military. In theory he was subordinate to the governor of the province of Syria, but in practice his authority within his jurisdiction was absolute, except where Roman citizens were concerned. It was, however, the Romans' custom to grant a large measure of self-government to the native communities, and in the case of the Jews, in spite of their riotous turbulence, this conciliatory policy was carried to unusual lengths, so that the government of Judaea was exceptionally difficult. Pilate held office for ten years, during which, although the peace was not actually broken, he was engaged in almost continuous quarrels with the Jews. Our authorities depict him as obstinate, tactless, and headstrong (cf. Lk. 13¹). On one occasion he used such violence in suppressing an armed gathering in Samaria that the inhabitants appealed to the governor of the province of Syria, who ordered Pilate to go to Rome, to defend his conduct before the emperor's council; but before Pilate arrived, the Emperor Tiberius died, in A.D. 37; and nothing more is known for certain about the procurator.

18³⁶. The word 'kingdom' occurs elsewhere in John only at 3³, ⁵, where teaching is given that the kingdom of God can only be seen and entered by those who undergo spiritual rebirth.

18³⁷. In 18³⁶ the Lord has declared that His Kingdom does not derive or originate from this world. In 18³⁷ He adds that the purpose of His birth and entrance into the world was to bear witness to the truth. Clearly, therefore, although even now men can be 'of the truth', it belongs to that which is 'above' [19¹¹], to a higher order of being than is capable of full realization in this world.

18³⁹. This custom is only known from the evidence of the four gospels.

18⁴⁰. 'cried out'. The very strong Greek verb used four times[1] in this passage [18⁴⁰, 19⁶, ¹², ¹⁵] implies here not only passionate clamour but perhaps also possession by supernatural, in this case demonic, power. It is also used, remarkably, at 11⁴³, 12¹³; see notes there.

'again'. If the word is given its full meaning, it is not clear what previous passage is in mind; and it is sometimes thought that St. John thus shows himself to be following a source which he has abbreviated. (Curiously enough, the same problem arises at Mk. 15¹³, where the context is the same.) The Greek word, however, not only is often used as a very light and unemphatic particle, but can also have a negative sense, 'on the other hand', e.g. Lk. 6⁴³, 2 Cor. 10⁷, 1 Jn. 2⁸.

'a robber'. The meaning is perhaps best conveyed by the rendering 'brigand', or 'gangster'. It is also used in Matthew and Mark of the two men crucified together with the Lord, and in all the three earlier gospels in the Lord's protest to those who had come to arrest Him in Gethsemane, 'Are ye come out as against a brigand . . .?' [Mk. 14⁴⁸ and parallels].

19¹. Scourging normally took place after condemnation, forming the immediate preliminary to crucifixion, and such is the place assigned to the scourging of the Lord in Matthew and Mark. In Luke the scourging is not narrated, but Pilate, persuaded of the Lord's innocence of any capital crime, proposes, as a sop to His accusers, to have Him scourged and then released [Lk. 23¹⁶, ²²]. In John, however, the scourging, followed by the soldiers' mockery, takes place here, Pilate's motive being the same as that ascribed to him in Luke.

19⁷. 'because he made himself the Son of God' (cf. 5¹⁸, 10³³). In the term, however, as used here, the reference is no doubt to divine sonship as understood in various ways in the Hellenistic world at the time. The expression would therefore be intelligible to Pilate.

19⁹. This is the last occasion in John when the question is raised of the Lord's origin. (The reader will do well to study all the passages in this gospel in which the word 'whence' occurs.) The question is similar to that of the Lord's authority, as raised in the earlier gospels [Mk. 11²⁷⁻³³, and parallels]. On that occasion also the Lord declines to answer—unless His questioners will first say whether the mission and task of John, prophet and baptist, was 'from heaven, or from men'. Only if they admit that it was the former, can He go on to reveal His own still greater authority and mission.

19¹². The meaning is probably not temporal, since Pilate has already sought to release the Lord [18³⁸, ³⁹, 19⁴, ⁶], but 'for this reason'. Pilate has appreciated the meaning of the Lord's words.

19¹³. The Greek verb translated 'sat down' can also be used transitively; and if it is so rendered here, the meaning will be that Pilate set the Lord upon the judgement-seat; and there is evidence of a tradition in the second century that (not Pilate, but) the Jews placed the Lord in this position. It would be in accordance with St. John's method (cf. ch. 9), if he has here used language to be understood most naturally according to the R.V. translation, but capable also of a meaning which would remind

¹ The correct reading in 19¹² is probably *ekraugasan*, not *ekrazon*.

readers who at this moment is truly Judge (cf. 5²⁷, 9³⁹), and who the judged.

'the judgement-seat'. The reference is said to be to a portable judgement-seat, brought from within the Praetorium for the occasion.

'Gabbatha'. The word does not occur elsewhere, and its meaning is uncertain.

19¹⁴. On 19¹⁴ᵃ see pp. 354–5. The words 'it was about the sixth hour' occur also at 4⁶; see p. 122. Just as the first half of 19¹⁴ speaks of the imminence of the passover (and the reader will recall that the Christian passover is the crucified Lord [1 Cor. 5⁷]), so may not these words, besides being a note of time, strike also the note of the imminence of culmination? As at 4⁶ the Lord asks for a draught of water, but a moment later reveals that He Himself offers living water, itself the gift of God, so here, although as a result of Pilate's decision now on the point of being made He will soon experience thirst [19²⁸], yet not only will His desire be satisfied (cf. 4³²⁻³⁴ with 19³⁰), but after His work is completed water will issue from His side [19³⁴], and His promise in 7³⁷, ³⁸ will be fulfilled, as St. John suggests in 7³⁹, with which cf. 20²².

19¹⁵. To the previous shout of 'Crucify!' in 19⁶ the Jews now add a cry which, besides the translation of R.V., can also mean 'lift up', 'raise', the verb being that used in 1²⁹ of the Lord who, as the Lamb of God, lifts or removes the sin of the world. If we recall all that has been said in John of the exaltation (a different Greek word) of the Lord upon the cross, we may think it possible that the Jews, in thus crying 'Hoist Him up! Hoist Him up!', unconsciously ask for His exaltation as the Son of man [3¹⁴, 8²⁸, 12³², ³⁴].

19¹⁶. 'unto them', that is, the Jews, although of course the sentence will be carried out by Roman soldiers [19²³]. The State, its justice destroyed and its authority bruised, for fear of men and from the self-interest of its representative, hands back the Lord to those who placed Him in its hands [18³⁰, ³⁵, 19¹¹].

19¹⁷. The Hebrew word 'Golgotha', the Greek word 'Kranion', and the Latin word 'calvaria' all mean 'a skull', probably because a slight elevation in the ground here bore some resemblance to a human head.

19¹⁹. All four gospels record that a title (Latin *titulus*) was placed on the cross, and in all four the title includes the words 'the King of the Jews'; but in no gospel is the wording exactly identical with that in any other.

19²⁵. A comparison with the details given in the earlier gospels suggests that the sister of the Lord's mother may be Salome, the mother of James and John; and Mary the wife of Clopas may be the mother of the other James and of Joses. Mary Magdalene is mentioned here for the first time in John; see also 20¹⁻¹⁸.

19³¹. 'the Preparation'. See pp. 354–5. According to Deut. 21²², ²³ bodies of criminals who have been executed must be removed from the gibbet and buried before sunset, to avoid defilement of the land; and it was particularly desirable to carry out the law in the present case, because the coming day was not only a sabbath, but sabbath in passover-week.

19³⁶. The Greek of the quotation in this verse does not agree exactly with either the Hebrew or the LXX of any Old Testament passage. Those who support the interpretation, offered in the exposition, of 1²⁹, ³⁶ are likely to see in the quotation here a free rendering of Ex. 12⁴⁶ (cf. Num. 9¹²), and thus to find at the end, as well as at the beginning, of this gospel a reference to the Lord as the true paschal Lamb. On this view the quotation is extremely pertinent, since the paschal lamb of the old covenant, being an oblation to Yahweh, had to be free from defect or mutilation; and in this ordinance St. John, according to the interpretation suggested here, sees a foreshadowing of the manner of the death of the true paschal Lamb, in contrast to that of those who were crucified with Him. On the other hand the quotation may equally well (and, so far as the Greek is concerned, perhaps more probably) be a free rendering of Ps. 34²⁰; but in this case there is no especial suitability in the quotation, except that there is a comparison between the Lord and 'the righteous' of the Old Testament Psalter. It is true that this is also the case in the two previous events [19²⁴, ²⁸], regarded as fulfilments of scripture, in this chapter; but in these the references are to Ps. 22 and Ps. 69 respectively, which are indeed 'psalms of the suffering righteous'; and Ps. 34 is not such. The most that can be said is that this psalm clearly was familiar in the early Church, being quoted in 1 Pet. 3¹⁰⁻¹², and was in mind in such passages as Heb. 6⁵, 1 Pet. 2³. Once more it may be that St. John is willing for his readers to see in 19³²⁻³⁴ a fulfilment of both passages.

19³⁷. The reference here is certainly to Zech. 12¹⁰. As in Rev. 1⁷, the Greek here is nearer to the Hebrew, than to the LXX, of Zech. 12¹⁰. The last chapters of Zechariah have many prophecies of the coming day of the Lord, and it is in accordance with the teaching of this gospel that the event anticipated in Zech. 12¹⁰ is here regarded as fulfilled, when those present saw the pierced body of the Lord upon the cross, whereas Rev. 1⁷, in its allusion to Zech. 12¹⁰, still looks to the future for the fulfilment of the prophecy.

19³⁹. With the immense amount of spices cf. the prodigious supply of wine implied in 2⁶⁻⁸.

19⁴⁰. The Lord's body is both bound in linen cloths and embalmed, and in this state is laid in a tomb [19⁴²]. But whereas at 11⁴⁴ Lazarus came forth from the cave with hands and feet still bound and swathed in grave-clothes, and sight still obscured by the napkin tied round his head, and needed human help before he could go free, in the case of the Lord the linen cloths and the napkin are found, two days later, to have been left behind in the tomb; nor is there then any mention of the spices which had been enclosed in them, in order to preserve the body.

19⁴¹. 'wherein was never man yet laid'. So Lk. 23⁵³; and cf. also Mk. 11².

SECTION 7 e.   20¹⁻³¹ *The Lord's resurrection, and the conclusion of the original gospel*

2O Now on the first *day* of the week cometh Mary Magdalene early, while it was yet dark, unto the tomb, and seeth the stone taken away
2 from the tomb. She runneth therefore, and cometh to Simon Peter, and to the other disciple, whom Jesus loved, and saith unto them, They have taken away the Lord out of the tomb, and we know not where they
3 have laid him. Peter therefore went forth, and the other disciple, and
4 they went toward the tomb. And they ran both together: and the other
5 disciple outran Peter, and came first to the tomb; and stooping and
6 looking in, he seeth the linen cloths lying; yet entered he not in. Simon Peter therefore also cometh, following him, and entered into the tomb;
7 and he beholdeth the linen cloths lying, and the napkin, that was upon his head, not lying with the linen cloths, but rolled up in a place by
8 itself. Then entered in therefore the other disciple also, which came first
9 to the tomb, and he saw, and believed. For as yet they knew not the
10 scripture, that he must rise again from the dead. So the disciples went away again unto their own home.

11   But Mary was standing without at the tomb weeping: so, as she wept,
12 she stooped and looked into the tomb; and she beholdeth two angels in white sitting, one at the head, and one at the feet, where the body of
13 Jesus had lain. And they say unto her, Woman, why weepest thou? She saith unto them, Because they have taken away my Lord, and I know
14 not where they have laid him. When she had thus said, she turned herself back, and beholdeth Jesus standing, and knew not that it was
15 Jesus. Jesus saith unto her, Woman, why weepest thou? whom seekest thou? She, supposing him to be the gardener, saith unto him, Sir, if thou hast borne him hence, tell me where thou hast laid him, and I will
16 take him away. Jesus saith unto her, Mary. She turneth herself, and
17 saith unto him in Hebrew, Rabboni; which is to say, ¹Master. Jesus saith to her, ²Touch me not; for I am not yet ascended unto the Father: but go unto my brethren, and say to them, I ascend unto my Father
18 and your Father, and my God and your God. Mary Magdalene cometh and telleth the disciples, I have seen the Lord; and *how that* he had said these things unto her.

19   When therefore it was evening, on that day, the first *day* of the week, and when the doors were shut where the disciples were, for fear of the Jews, Jesus came and stood in the midst, and saith unto them, Peace *be*
20 unto you. And when he had said this, he shewed unto them his hands and his side. The disciples therefore were glad, when they saw the Lord.
21 Jesus therefore said to them again, Peace *be* unto you: as the Father hath

---

¹ *Or* Teacher   ² *Or* Take not hold on me

22 sent me, even so send I you. And when he had said this, he breathed on
23 them, and saith unto them, Receive ye the ¹Holy Ghost: whose soever
sins ye forgive, they are forgiven unto them; whose soever *sins* ye retain,
they are retained.

24   But Thomas, one of the twelve, called ²Didymus, was not with them
25 when Jesus came. The other disciples therefore said unto him, We have
seen the Lord. But he said unto them, Except I shall see in his hands
the print of the nails, and put my finger into the print of the nails, and
put my hand into his side, I will not believe.

26   And after eight days again his disciples were within, and Thomas
with them. Jesus cometh, the doors being shut, and stood in the midst,
27 and said, Peace *be* unto you. Then saith he to Thomas, Reach hither
thy finger, and see my hands; and reach *hither* thy hand, and put it into
28 my side: and be not faithless, but believing. Thomas answered and said
29 unto him, My Lord and my God. Jesus saith unto him, Because thou
hast seen me, ³thou hast believed: blessed *are* they that have not seen,
and *yet* have believed.

30   Many other signs therefore did Jesus in the presence of the disciples,
31 which are not written in this book: but these are written, that ye may
believe that Jesus is the Christ, the Son of God; and that believing ye
may have life in his name.

¹ *Or* Holy Spirit   ² *That is* Twin.   ³ *Or* hast thou believed?

EXPOSITION OF SECTION 7e. 20¹⁻³¹

According to St. Mark, in the thrice repeated warning [8³¹, 9³¹,
10³³], given by the Lord to the disciples during the ministry, of the
destiny awaiting the Son of man, although the final note is in each
case that of resurrection, the emphasis is on the suffering and death
which must precede it; and in the conclusions of all the first three
gospels the Lord's resurrection is regarded as being to a large
extent a reversal of the passion, and at first causes astonishment
and fear, and can hardly be believed. But when we consider the
nature of St. John's gospel, in which the Lord during the ministry
has revealed Himself as the resurrection and the life, and the cross,
as interpreted by St. John, marks not only the last stage of His
'descent' but also His glorification, it should not surprise us that
the evangelist is not concerned in ch. 20 to dwell upon the Lord's
resurrection as forming primarily a reversal of the passion. He
expects his readers to have learned by this time the secret which he

has gradually unfolded to them in the first nineteen chapters of his gospel, the secret, namely, that the Lord at the moment and in the fact of the laying down of His life has revealed the glory of the Father, and therefore His own oneness with the Father, to the fullest possible degree. If one moment of His revelation of the Father in the days of His flesh is to be distinguished from another, then at the moment of His death, more than at any other, He has glorified the Father, and His return to the Father has at least begun (cf. 6⁶²).

But even if the reader is fortunate enough to be already fully assured of the spiritual truth of the secret thus taught by St. John, the latter will not allow him to forget that the Christian religion is one of divine incarnation, and that its truths must be found to prevail in the realm of flesh and blood, subject as these are to space and time, as well as in the realm of spirit. For this reason the return of the Lord in the flesh to His disciples, and the fulfilment of His promises to them [14¹⁸, ¹⁹, 16⁷, ¹⁶⁻²²], must find their place in St. John's record, as matters of history which actually took place. Hence the two points on which St. John lays emphasis in his resurrection narrative are, first, the resumption by the Lord of personal relations and intercourse with those who had followed Him during the ministry[1] and, secondly, the identity of the Lord's risen body with the body which suffered and was laid in the tomb. At His first reunion with the disciples after the resurrection He shows to them His hands and His side [20²⁰] and, at the second, St. Thomas is invited to satisfy himself absolutely on this point [20²⁷].

Not that there is no change. In this chapter, as also in ch. 21, more obviously than elsewhere in this gospel, we seem to be hovering between the outward and the inward, the seen and the unseen, the temporal and the eternal. Thus Mary Magdalene does not at first recognize her Master by sight or by His voice, but only when He utters her name [20¹⁴⁻¹⁶; we should perhaps compare 20¹⁹, ²⁰, and certainly 21⁴, ⁷]; and the Lord twice comes to His disciples through closed doors [20¹⁹, ²⁶]. He is indeed the same Lord as of

---

[1] It is perhaps noticeable that the first reunion is with an individual, a woman who according to the tradition of the Church held no position of authority in it but had long ministered to the Lord [Lk. 8²] and was deeply beholden to Him [Mk. 16⁹]. The first reunion is thus in the highest degree personal; and it is followed, not preceded, by the reunion with the Apostles, their commission, and the bestowal on them of the Holy Spirit and of their authority.

old; but His followers have now to learn to know Him in a new way.

Again, the Lord's return to the Father, although there is a sense, as we have seen, in which it can truly be said to have occurred at the moment and as the result of His death, is none the less also a process, even after His resurrection; nor is His reunion with His followers at once complete. Indeed, the fulfilment of the Lord's return to the Father, and the fulfilment of His reunion with His followers, are inseparable. Only when the Lord's return to the Father is complete does His reunion with His followers also become complete. For when Mary recognizes her Master, she is bidden not to touch Him, and the reason given for this command is that He is not yet ascended to the Father, although He is on His way thither [20¹⁷]. The Greek words for 'Touch me not' could also be translated 'Do not cling to me'. Whichever translation is adopted, and whether it is thought that Mary was or was not doing either of these things, the Lord's words, in the light of the rest of this chapter, show that, although she has been allowed to recognize her Master in the way described in 20¹⁴⁻¹⁶, yet intercourse with Him is in future not to depend on physical proximity, sight, or sound. For if we ask why, a week later, St. Thomas is expressly invited at 20²⁷ to do that which at 20¹⁷ was forbidden to Mary, the answer must be that it is because the Lord's ascent to the Father has meantime taken place; and this is borne out by St. John's account of the Lord's first meeting with the disciples on the evening of the first Easter day. On this occasion, which may be regarded as St. John's counterpart for the scene described in Acts 2¹⁻¹³ at Pentecost, the Lord breathes on them, that they may receive the Holy Spirit; and since it is made clear in such a passage as 15²⁶ that this gift is dependent upon the Lord's prior return to the Father, this return, although there is no suggestion of a movement in space, must now be assumed to have occurred. Hence, a week later, that which was forbidden to Mary can be allowed to St. Thomas. St. John, it seems, thus teaches the reader that since the Lord, clothed with our human nature, has now resumed His rightful place of glory [17⁵, ²⁴] at the Father's side, an immediacy of contact with Him becomes possible for disciples and believers, a contact no longer dependent, as in the days of the ministry, on external companionship or physical proximity. We are reminded of His promises in 14¹⁶⁻²⁰, 16¹⁶⁻²². The words 'clothed with our

human nature', however, must never be forgotten. Only because
the Lord became incarnate for our sakes is contact with Him
possible in His ascended life. St. John's teaching in ch. 20,
therefore, is parallel to the sacramental teaching in ch. 6.

Thus, according to St. John, from one point of view the Lord's
incarnation, death, resurrection, ascension, and bestowal of the
Spirit are regarded as drawn together into one, each of the five
features therein including and requiring all the others; but from
another point of view each may be regarded as a distinctive event,
the five together forming a connected temporal process, with a
beginning (incarnation and ministry), a middle (crucifixion and
resurrection), and an end (ascension and bestowal of the Spirit).

The words in 20¹, 'while it was yet dark', seem to be at variance
with those in Mk. 16², 'when the sun was risen'. Is it possible that
the contradiction is due to the different content of the two sections?
For whereas in Mk. 16¹⁻⁸ everything tells of the divine love and
triumph, so strongly indeed that the women cannot endure the
light revealed to them, in John 20¹⁻¹⁰ on the other hand (although
in John, as in Mark, the stone is seen to have been removed from
the tomb) there is no angelic message nor, with the exception of
the beloved disciple [20⁸], do those who come realize at first, it
seems, the significance of the state in which they find the tomb
[20⁹, ¹¹]; and even he, apparently, still has much to learn [20⁹].

The outrunning of St. Peter by the beloved disciple and the
realization, at present by the latter only, of the significance of the
condition of the tomb, are in accordance with the other passages
where the two men are mentioned together (see p. 342). We are
perhaps to understand that a natural reverence and reserve at first
prevent the beloved disciple from entering the tomb; only when
his companion, who is of a different temperament, has entered,
does he follow. Both indeed now see that, although the Lord's
body is not there, yet the state of the grave-clothes and of the head-
covering shows that there has been no act of violence or dis-
arrangement in the tomb; all is in order; Mary's assumption [20²],
therefore, cannot be correct; and the evidence is enough for the
beloved disciple, who is therefore the first to believe in his Lord's
resurrection, although, like St. Peter, he is still unaware of its
necessity in accordance with scripture.

The emphasis laid in this gospel upon the empty tomb should
be noticed. In John not only does a woman (or women, 20²) go to

the tomb, but also Simon Peter and the beloved disciple; and the two latter assure themselves both of its emptiness and of the state of the grave-clothes.

At 20¹¹ we revert to Mary, whose attention is concentrated on the tomb, nor does the vision of celestial beings within it assuage her distress or her anxiety to know where to find the body of her Lord. Only when she turns away from the tomb and when the Lord addresses her by name, does she know and acknowledge her Master (cf. 10³, ¹⁴, ²⁷). With regard to the charge at once laid upon her, it is significant that only here [20¹⁷] in this gospel, immediately after the resurrection, does the Lord speak of His disciples as His 'brethren'; we may compare Mt. 28¹⁰. Having shared in their humanity, He now takes that humanity with Him in His ascent to the Father, though the disciples must never forget that, whereas His Sonship to the Father is by nature and right, theirs is only by adoption and grace, in and through Him; and therefore He speaks of 'my Father and your Father', not of 'our Father'.

The sending of the Son into the world by the Father has been repeatedly emphasized in this gospel; and now that, with the completion of the Son's work, the hour of the dispensation of the Spirit has come (contrast 7³⁹), He in turn [20²¹] sends His disciples (cf. 17¹⁸). As He has represented the Father in the world, so they are to represent their Lord, whose peace [20¹⁹, ²¹; cf. 14²⁷, 16³³] and joy [20²⁰; cf. 15¹¹, 16²⁰⁻²⁴, 17¹³] are now therefore theirs. And just as God breathed into Adam the breath of life and he became a living being [Gen. 2⁷], so the Lord now breathes on the disciples, and they receive the 'new creation'; and finally, as the recipients of the Spirit, they are endowed with His prerogative to grant or to withhold the forgiveness of sins (cf. Mt. 9⁶).

In 20²⁰ St. John has already emphasized that the Lord, who manifests Himself to the disciples after the resurrection, is the same Lord with whom they companied in the days of His ministry. This emphasis receives further and final expression in the manifestation granted, a week later, to St. Thomas [20²⁶⁻²⁹]. True to his disposition [11¹⁶, 14⁵], this doggedly loyal but intensely literal-minded disciple demands the most tangible and external proofs of the resurrection of his Lord, before he will 'believe'. When, however, the opportunity is offered, it seems that he has no wish or need to avail himself of it, but renounces his former demand in a complete confession of faith, giving, in his last three words, the same honour to the Son as to the Father [5²³]. His words (the last confession, we should notice, in the original form of this gospel, when it ended at 20³¹) thus recall the declaration, with which the book began, that 'the Word was God' [1¹]. The Lord's reply suggests that the manifestations granted to the original disciples after the resurrection, and occurring at particular moments and in particular places, are now to be regarded as at an end. They were at the time no doubt essential; without them the apostles could not have carried out one of their chief tasks, that of bearing witness to the physical resurrection of the Lord [Acts 1²², 2³², 4³³]. But such manifestations were temporary only, and should now have fulfilled their purpose; and in His final words [20²⁹] the Lord commends those whose discipleship is based not, as in the case of St. Thomas, on the external sight which in his case has led to faith, but on faith only, a faith which, as we have seen (pp. 24–25, 301), is not to be distinguished from knowledge and which bestows eternal life [6⁴⁷]. Thus the Lord's words in 20²⁹, the last beatitude as they have been called, would come charged with especial relevance and value to those many disciples who, not having themselves been eye-witnesses, first read this gospel; and they should so come also to all disciples through the centuries.

NOTES TO SECTION 7e. 20¹⁻³¹

20¹, ². Although Mary only is mentioned in 20¹, her words in 20² seem to imply, in agreement with the other gospels, that she had not come alone to the tomb. The stone, first mentioned in Matthew and Mark in connexion with the burial, is in John (as in Luke) here mentioned for the first time.

20¹⁻¹⁰. We notice the same relative absence from these verses of any reference to the emotions of fear and astonishment (in contrast, e.g., with Mk. 16¹⁻⁸) as in the earlier chapters of John. The only signs of emotion in ch. 20 are that Mary weeps [20¹¹], and the disciples are glad [20²⁰]; but this is very different from the other records at this point.

20⁹. 'they knew not the scripture'. See note on 2²².

20¹⁴. 'she . . . knew not that it was Jesus', as at 21⁴. This unawareness of the Lord, in spite of His presence, recalls 1²⁶, 'in the midst of you standeth one whom ye know not'.

20¹⁶. Cf. 10³, ⁴. 'Rabboni', which strictly means 'my Teacher', is found in the N.T. only here and at Mk. 10⁵¹; but it is said to be little different in meaning from 'Rabbi', and therefore to be adequately interpreted by the Greek word for 'Teacher', R.V. mg.

20^{17}. 'I am not yet ascended . . . I ascend'. The same verb was used at 3^{13}, where it was closely connected with the reference to the 'lifting up' of the Son of man in 3^{14}; and a distinctive feature of the teaching of this gospel has been that the Lord's 'ascent' took place when He was lifted up upon the cross (cf. 8^{28}, $12^{32, 34}$). In so far, therefore, as the passion now lies in the past and the 'lifting up' has taken place, it may cause surprise that we meet once more the words 'not yet' in this connexion, because the Lord's 'hour', which during the ministry is said, more than once, to have not yet come [2^4, 7^{30}, 8^{20}], came, as we know, in and with the passion [12^{23}, 13^1, 17^1]. But the Lord's death was not only His 'ascent' to the Father; it was also, as St. Mark in particular emphasizes, the moment of His greatest 'descent', for the sake of men; and St. John in ch. 20 seems to wish to teach the reader that His return thereafter to the Father, like the ministry itself,[1] is also to be regarded as a process, of which the successive stages are resurrection, ascension, and the gift of the Holy Spirit.

'my brethren'. Hitherto in this gospel, when the Lord's brethren have been mentioned, the reference has been to His physical kinsmen [2^{12}, $7^{3, 5, 10}$]; now, however, the reference is to His disciples, no longer His bondservants, but His friends who share His knowledge of the Father [15^{15}].

20^{19}. 'the disciples'. In spite of the extreme importance of this occasion, as that of the first reunion of the Lord with His disciples after the resurrection and of His bestowal on them of the Holy Spirit and of their authority, it is not possible to say with certainty whether only the ten apostles are to be regarded as having been present, or whether there were others with them. The fact that, when the absence of Thomas from this first reunion is mentioned at 20^{24}, he is there described as 'one of the twelve', might seem to suggest the presence only of the rest of the eleven. On the other hand, if this occasion is identical with that recorded in Lk. 24^{33} ff., St. Luke there speaks of others also as present. But the uncertainty is not confined to this occasion. Throughout all four gospels, when the disciples are mentioned, it is often difficult to say whether the reference is only to the twelve or also includes a larger whole; but the difficulty becomes less formidable if it is agreed that, even when only an inner circle of disciples is addressed as, presumably, at the last supper, this inner circle is always representative of the whole body of discipleship, present and future.

'Peace be unto you'. These words are a normal Hebrew greeting (cf. 1 Sam. 25^6), and may be so regarded here and at 20^{26}. But the repetition of the words at 20^{21}, in closest connexion with the commission now granted to the disciples by the risen Lord, recall to the reader that at 14^{27} the Lord bequeathed His peace as a parting gift to His disciples, and that therefore His words, at any rate in 20^{21}, may be designed to remind them of this

---

[1] It is a feature of this gospel that the Lord's ministry is constantly regarded as a journey to the Father, from whom He came [3^{31}, 6^{38}, 7^{28}, 13^3, 16^{28}] and to whom He goes [7^{33}, 13^3, $14^{12, 28}$, 16^{28}]; and this, although He is never parted from the Father [$8^{16, 29}$, 16^{32}].

gift. It is noteworthy that this greeting of peace is an invariable feature of the opening words of St. Paul's epistles, and that in Eph. 2¹⁴ 'Christ Jesus' is said to be 'our peace'.

20²ᵇ. The forgiveness of sins, always a chief desire and need of those whose religious sense has been awakened (cf. Lk. 11⁴), had been part of the Lord's Gospel during His ministry [Mt. 9², Lk. 7⁴⁸], and in Christian thought has from the first been especially connected with the redemption effected by His death [1 Cor. 15³, Gal. 1⁴, Heb. 9²⁸, 1 Pet. 2²⁴]; and those who, now endowed with the Holy Spirit, the Spirit of Jesus [Acts 16⁷; cf. Jn. 14¹⁶⁻²⁰], as a body represent Him and His work in the world, receive His authority in this respect.

20²⁸. The three last words in the confession of St. Thomas show that we are concerned here with more than a recognition, on his part, of the identity of the risen Lord with the Master whom he had known before the crucifixion since, as an acknowledgement of this identity, the first two words would have sufficed.

20²⁹. The R.V. mg may be correct. In the similar sentences in 1⁵⁰, 16³¹, ³² the first clause is certainly interrogative. With the last half of the verse cf. 1 Pet. 1⁸.

20³⁰, ³¹. St. John seems here to link the events of 20¹⁻²⁹ with those, which he has narrated in the previous chapters, under the common heading of 'signs'. It would probably be a mistake to confine this designation solely to the events to which it is actually applied, e.g. those of 2¹⁻¹¹ or 6¹⁻¹⁴. The crucifixion was to St. John doubtless the greatest sign of all (cf. 12³³, 18³²); but the word 'sign' is not actually applied to it. If this is correct, it may be said that all the Lord's actions narrated in this gospel have a twofold character; on the one hand, they are objects of sight and perception, and, to some of those who witness them, no more than this; but, on the other hand, to some they convey an inner, deeper significance, leading to faith in the Author of them, and thereby to 'life in His name'.

20³¹. 'the Christ, the Son of God'. See p. 213.

IV. APPENDIX

21¹⁻²⁵ *Further manifestation of the Lord at the sea of Tiberias*

21 After these things Jesus manifested himself again to the disciples at
2 the sea of Tiberias; and he manifested *himself* on this wise. There were
together Simon Peter, and Thomas called ¹Didymus, and Nathanael of
Cana in Galilee, and the *sons* of Zebedee, and two other of his disciples.
3 Simon Peter saith unto them, I go a fishing. They say unto him, We
also come with thee. They went forth, and entered into the boat; and
4 that night they took nothing. But when day was now breaking, Jesus
stood on the beach: howbeit the disciples knew not that it was Jesus.
5 Jesus therefore saith unto them, Children, have ye aught to eat? They
6 answered him, No. And he said unto them, Cast the net on the right
side of the boat, and ye shall find. They cast therefore, and now they
7 were not able to draw it for the multitude of fishes. That disciple therefore whom Jesus loved saith unto Peter, It is the Lord. So when Simon
Peter heard that it was the Lord, he girt his coat about him (for he was
8 naked), and cast himself into the sea. But the other disciples came in the
little boat (for they were not far from the land, but about two hundred
9 cubits off), dragging the net *full* of fishes. So when they got out upon
the land, they see ²a fire of coals there, and ³fish laid thereon, and ⁴bread.
10 Jesus saith unto them, Bring of the fish which ye have now taken. Simon
11 Peter therefore went ⁵up, and drew the net to land, full of great fishes, a
hundred and fifty and three: and for all there were so many, the net
12 was not rent. Jesus saith unto them, Come *and* break your fast. And none
of the disciples durst inquire of him, Who art thou? knowing that it was
13 the Lord. Jesus cometh, and taketh the ⁶bread, and giveth them, and the
14 fish likewise. This is now the third time that Jesus was manifested to the
disciples, after that he was risen from the dead.

15 So when they had broken their fast, Jesus saith to Simon Peter,
Simon, *son* of ⁷John, ⁸lovest thou me more than these? He saith unto
him, Yea, Lord; thou knowest that I ⁹love thee. He saith unto him,
16 Feed my lambs. He saith to him again a second time, Simon, *son* of
John, ⁸lovest thou me? He saith unto him, Yea, Lord; thou knowest
17 that I ⁹love thee. He saith unto him, Tend my sheep. He saith unto
him the third time, Simon, *son* of ⁷John, ⁹lovest thou me? Peter was
grieved because he said unto him the third time, ⁹Lovest thou me?

---

¹ *That is* Twin.   ² *Gr.* a fire of charcoal.   ³ *Or* a fish   ⁴ *Or*
a loaf ·   ⁵ *Or* aboard   ⁶ *Or* loaf   ⁷ *Gr.* Joanes. *See* ch. 1. 42,
margin.   ⁸, ⁹ Love *in these places represents two different Greek words.*

And he said unto him, Lord, thou knowest all things; thou ¹knowest
18 that I ²love thee. Jesus saith unto him, Feed my sheep. Verily, verily,
I say unto thee, When thou wast young, thou girdedst thyself, and
walkedst whither thou wouldest: but when thou shalt be old, thou
shalt stretch forth thy hands, and another shall gird thee, and carry thee
19 whither thou wouldest not. Now this he spake, signifying by what
manner of death he should glorify God. And when he had spoken this,
20 he saith unto him, Follow me. Peter, turning about, seeth the disciple
whom Jesus loved following; which also leaned back on his breast at the
21 supper, and said, Lord, who is he that betrayeth thee? Peter therefore
22 seeing him saith to Jesus, Lord, ³and what shall this man do? Jesus saith
unto him, If I will that he tarry till I come, what *is that* to thee? follow
23 thou me. This saying therefore went forth among the brethren, that
that disciple should not die; yet Jesus said not unto him, that he should
not die; but, If I will that he tarry till I come, what *is that* to thee?
24 This is the disciple which beareth witness of these things, and wrote
these things: and we know that his witness is true.
25 And there are also many other things which Jesus did, the which if
they should be written every one, I suppose that even the world itself
would not contain the books that should be written.

¹ *Or* perceivest   ² *See marginal notes* ⁸ *and* ⁹ *on p. 337.*
³ *Gr.* and this man, what?

EXPOSITION OF 21¹⁻²⁵

(*a*) The draught of fishes, 21¹⁻¹⁴.
(*b*) The restoration, commission, and charge of St. Peter, the relations
  between him and the beloved disciple, and the 'tarrying' and work
  of the latter, 21¹⁵⁻²⁴.
Conclusion: the deeds of the Lord, 21²⁵.

If the exposition of the first twenty chapters of this gospel has been
upon the whole on the right lines, it is unlikely that its author did
not intend to stop at 20³⁰, ³¹; from his point of view, all has then
been said. Also certain features of ch. 21, to be noticed later,
cause some surprise, when compared with chs. 1 to 20, e.g. the
reference in 21²², ²³ to the Lord's 'coming' in a sense which is
absent from the earlier chapters.

On the other hand the chapter to which we now come (quite
apart from the fact that, like 7⁵³ to 8¹¹, it forms part of the canonical

scriptures) must be regarded, unlike 7⁵³ to 8¹¹, as forming part of the book for the following reasons:

(*a*) the textual evidence for it is all but unanimous. It is only omitted in one Syriac MS.;

(*b*) it is closely connected with chs. 1 to 20 in certain respects of both content and style. Thus, in addition to the definite links with ch. 20 at 21¹, ¹⁴, the only disciples prominent in verses 1 to 14 and 15 to 23 are St. Peter and the beloved disciple; this recalls 13²³⁻²⁶ and 20²⁻²⁰. Again, the Lord's references to lambs and sheep in 21¹⁵⁻¹⁷ recall His words in ch. 10, and His thrice repeated question to St. Peter in the same verses whether the latter loves his Lord recalls not only St. Peter's three denials but also such passages as 14¹⁵, ²¹, ²³. For small points of stylistic resemblance 21¹⁹ may be compared with 12³³, 18³², or the last five Greek words of 21² with 1³⁵. If the writer of chs. 1 to 20 did not himself add ch. 21, the addition was made by a person or persons who certainly had followed closely in his footsteps.

Before we ask why this chapter, regarded as an appendix, was added to the gospel, it is desirable to consider its contents. It may be divided into two scenes, closely connected. The first [21¹⁻¹⁴] opens with a fishing expedition of seven disciples, led by Simon Peter, at the sea of Tiberias. (The first three names are already familiar from this gospel, and the note that Nathanael was of Cana of Galilee recalls not only the previous mention of him in 1⁴⁵⁻⁵¹ but also the fact that the Lord's first sign in this gospel took place at Cana [2¹⁻¹¹; cf. also 4⁴⁶⁻⁵⁴]. On the other hand 'the (sons) of Zebedee' are now mentioned for the first time in this gospel, and St. Peter's words in 21³ are the first allusion in John to his craft, and that of James and John (cf. Mk. 1¹⁹).) The expedition is at first unsuccessful; but when at dawn the bidding of a Stranger on the beach is carried out, the catch is prodigious, and the beloved disciple is led to recognize in consequence the presence of the Lord. The disciples forthwith join Him, and He gives them bread and fish to eat, the same kinds of food, it will be remembered, as were provided for the multitude in ch. 6. The narrative, although very simply written, is marked by great reverence, and some of its details suggest that it may be intended to convey also symbolic teaching concerning the apostolic mission of the Church, and the condition, the direction of the Lord [21⁶], on which alone [21³] that mission can be successful. In the unbroken net the reader may see a picture of the undivided Church, and in the great catch of fish its world-wide mission.

The second scene [21¹⁵⁻²⁴] narrates the restoration and commission of St. Peter for his future work, together with a prophecy by the Lord of the manner of his death. His grief at his Master's thrice repeated question, and the fact that the Lord does not address him by his Christian name, as we may call 'Peter' in the light of 1⁴², suggest that the narrative in both structure and content looks back to this disciple's threefold denial of his Lord; but the chief emphasis is certainly on the commission which he now receives; he is to be the foremost guardian of his Master's flock, a stewardship to be sealed by the manner of his death to the glory of God. This part of the scene is now finished, and St. Peter, bidden to follow his Lord, is doing so, when, turning round, he sees the beloved disciple (who, it seems, needed no such order) also following. Recalling what has just been said to him about his own destiny, he presumes to inquire what the lot of the other disciple is to be. His question receives no direct answer, and its curiosity is implicitly rebuked. The form of the Lord's reply, however, gave rise, we are told, to a belief among the brethren that the beloved disciple 'should not die'; but by a repetition of the Lord's words, the misunderstanding is corrected, and it is added that the beloved disciple was the writer of 'these things' (an expression which is most naturally understood as referring to the whole or at least part of the book now ending); and the truth of his witness is guaranteed by a number of his fellow disciples.

The natural inference to be drawn from 21¹⁸⁻²⁴ is that both St. Peter and the beloved disciple lived for a considerable time after the Lord's resurrection, but that, when ch. 21 was written, both had passed away, and the beloved disciple more recently than St. Peter. If we may assume that the former was the last survivor of the original apostolic company, it is easy to understand, especially when we recall the very strong expectation, in early days, of the Lord's imminent return (cf. 1 Thess. 4¹⁵, 1 Cor. 15⁵¹), that his death had caused concern 'among the brethren', owing to the misunderstanding of the Lord's words in 21²²; and in 21²³ this misunderstanding is removed.

In the final verse of the chapter a return is made to the singular, but now in the first person; and the writer, making use, it is said, of a contemporary method of expressing 'literary insufficiency',

points out the impossibility of a complete record of the actions of
the Lord. It will be noticed that in this verse these are not described
as 'signs', as they are at 20³⁰.

We may now suggest reasons for the addition of this chapter.
Possibly attention should first be drawn to the locality, Galilee,
in which the events of ch. 21 are placed. In ch. 20 the Lord is
manifested only in Jerusalem, just as in the third gospel the manifestations are confined to Jerusalem and its neighbourhood. But
ch. 21, with its manifestation in Galilee, agrees in this respect with
the first gospel in which the principal manifestation, that to the
eleven disciples, is in Galilee (Mt. 28¹⁶⁻²⁰, as against Mt. 28⁹, ¹⁰;
and cf. also Mk. 14²⁸, 16⁷). Hence, with the addition of ch. 21,
two streams of tradition are brought together in St. John's
gospel.

But probably a stronger reason for the addition of ch. 21 is to be
found in verses 15 to 24, where for the last time we have an account
of the relations between St. Peter and the beloved disciple, and
mention is made of the very different work then lying before each
of them. These relations have already found expression in this
chapter at verse 7. There the beloved disciple is the first to realize
the presence of the Lord; and when he informs Peter, the latter
is the first to act, seeking to come forthwith to his Master. In this
verse, therefore, the same role is ascribed to each of these two
men as at 13²³⁻²⁶ and 20¹⁻⁸. The beloved disciple understands his
Lord better, and is granted greater insight, than St. Peter; the
latter is the man of action. Similarly in 21¹⁵⁻²⁴ the charge and
practical oversight of the Lord's flock are granted to St. Peter;
and he is bidden to follow his Master, and his martyrdom is
prophesied. St. Peter obeys; but when he seeks to learn the future
work of the latter too, the answer given implies only that the lot
of the beloved disciple will not be, like that of St. Peter, martyrdom; and St. Peter once more receives the command to follow.

If this interpretation is on the right lines, 21²⁴ allows us to see
what part was to be played, and no doubt in fact was played, by
the beloved disciple. His concern, as the disciple of chief spiritual
insight, was not, like that of St. Peter, to have the oversight of the
practical life of the Church; he was to remain, throughout his life,
the witness and guardian of the Lord's revelation and of the truth
of the Gospel; and although in fact he died before his Lord's
return, he became by his written word, that is, by this gospel now

completed, the permanent witness and guardian of that revelation and that truth.

NOTES TO 21¹⁻²⁵

21¹⁻¹⁴. There is certainly some connexion between this narrative and that of the draught of fishes, to which the call of the first disciples is attached, in Lk. 5¹⁻¹¹. Thus in both narratives the night-fishing has no result; success only comes when the Lord is present and His command or promise is obeyed. Since in the third gospel the Lord after His resurrection is seen by disciples only in or near Jerusalem, the story of Lk. 5¹⁻¹¹ could only find a place in the third gospel during the Lord's ministry in Galilee.

21¹. 'manifested himself'. The Greek verb here, which occurs also at 21¹⁴, is used elsewhere in the gospels with reference to the risen Lord only in Mk. 16¹², ¹⁴.

21⁵. The form of the Lord's question suggests that a negative answer is expected. If a symbolical strain in the story is admitted, a reference to 15⁵ is appropriate here. The Greek word translated 'aught to eat' really means 'something to season food', and was probably applied, in particular, to fish, as a relish to eat with bread; cf. 21⁹, ¹³.

21⁶. For the *right* as the auspicious side cf. Lk. 1¹¹, Mt. 25³³, Mk. 16⁵.

21⁷. The beloved disciple is the first to become aware of the Stranger's identity. At 13²³⁻²⁶ Peter approaches the Lord through him; at 20¹⁻¹⁰ he has, it seems, greater or quicker insight than Peter; and at 21¹⁹, ²⁰, whereas Peter receives the Lord's command to follow, the beloved disciple apparently follows, if we may so speak, instinctively; and 21²⁰⁻²² certainly contains a rebuke to Peter. In all these scenes, therefore, the beloved disciple seems to have a certain precedence of St. Peter. What was the effect upon him, in the present instance, of his realization of his Master's presence, we are not told; but St. Peter, putting on his coat, at once seeks to go to his Lord upon the beach.

21⁸. 'two hundred cubits' are roughly one hundred yards.

21¹¹. Although the other disciples had had the task of dragging the net towards the shore, it is St. Peter's act, as their leader, to go 'aboard' (R.V. mg) and bring the catch to land.

If, in the light of the story as a whole, the reader thinks that a symbolical motive probably lies behind the mention of the precise extent of the catch, the following attempts to account for the number 153 may be mentioned:

(a) The belief seems to have been held in certain circles that there were 153 different kinds of fish. St. Jerome, commenting on Ezek. 47⁹⁻¹², says, 'Writers on the nature and properties of animals, who have learned *Halieutica* in Latin as well as in Greek, among whom is the learned poet Oppianus Cilix, say that there are 153 different kinds of fishes.'[1] On this

---

[1] Quoted in Hoskyns and Davey, *The Fourth Gospel*, 2nd ed., p. 554.

view one of every kind of fish is taken in the disciples' net, the catch thus representing those 'of every tribe and tongue and people and nation' [Rev. 5⁹] purchased to God by the Lord's death.

(*b*) The number 153 is said to be of interest, for various reasons, to mathematicians. Thus it is 'the sum of the first 17 of the natural numbers, and therefore 153 dots can be arranged in the form of an equilateral triangle, with 17 dots on the base line'.[1] But it remains to be explained, in a form which will carry conviction, what bearing this has upon the number of fish here taken.

21¹³. The parallel with 6¹¹ will not escape notice; and since the meal in 6¹⁻¹³ formed the prelude to the teaching, next day, on the Lord as the bread of life, with its eucharistic reference in 6⁵³⁻⁵⁸, we are probably right to trace the same reference here too. With the verbs 'taketh' and 'giveth' cf. also Mk. 14²², ²³.

21¹⁵. 'more than these', i.e. more than these other disciples love Me. It is true that only in Mt. 26³³, Mk. 14²⁹ does St. Peter claim to possess a deeper loyalty than others to his Master; at Jn.13³⁷ he does not expressly compare himself with other men. But he has always tended to take the lead in matters affecting the disciples' relation to their Master; and this alone, in view of his exceptional fall, would be enough to account for the form of the question now put to him.

The difference in the Greek verbs used for 'to love' in verses 15 to 17 is probably not of significance.

21¹⁸, ¹⁹. In solemn assurance the Lord proceeds to tell St. Peter, in symbolic language, of the 'manner of death' by which he is to 'glorify God'. The implication in the words 'thou shalt stretch forth thy hands, and another shall gird thee', is probably death by crucifixion which, according to the tradition of the Church, was the form of death suffered by St. Peter.

'gird'. In crucifixion ropes were used, as well as, or instead of, nails.

21¹⁹. Cf. 12³³, 18³².

'Follow me'. St. Peter is now bidden, and is able, to do that which previously he wished to do, but could not [13³⁶, ³⁷].

21²², ²³. Attempts have been made to explain the word translated 'tarry' in these verses in a spiritual sense, since it is rendered elsewhere in John 'abide', e.g. 6⁵⁶, 15⁴, where it certainly has a spiritual meaning. But if the word carried this meaning here, the misunderstanding mentioned in 21²³ could not have arisen. It seems, therefore, that the reference must be to the 'parousia' of the Lord (as in 1 Jn. 2²⁸), a reference which probably does not occur as such in chs. 1 to 20.

[1] Hoskyns and Davey on 21¹⁻¹⁴.

53 ¹And they went every man unto his own house:

2 **8** But Jesus went unto the mount of Olives. And early in the morning he came again into the temple, and all the people came unto him;

3 and he sat down, and taught them. And the scribes and the Pharisees bring a woman taken in adultery; and having set her in the midst,

4 they say unto him, ²Master, this woman hath been taken in adultery,

5 in the very act. Now in the law Moses commanded us to stone such:

6 what then sayest thou of her? And this they said, ³tempting him, that they might have *whereof* to accuse him. But Jesus stooped down, and

7 with his finger wrote on the ground. But when they continued asking him, he lifted up himself, and said unto them, He that is without

8 sin among you, let him first cast a stone at her. And again he stooped

9 down, and with his finger wrote on the ground. And they, when they heard it, went out one by one, beginning from the eldest, *even* unto the last: and Jesus was left alone, and the woman, where she was, in the

10 midst. And Jesus lifted up himself, and said unto her, Woman, where

11 are they? did no man condemn thee? And she said, No man, Lord. And Jesus said, Neither do I condemn thee: go thy way; from henceforth sin no more.

¹ *Most of the ancient authorities omit John 7.53–8.11. Those which contain it vary much from each other.*   ² *Or,* Teacher   ³ *Or* trying

EXPOSITION OF 7⁵³–8¹¹

It is generally agreed that two considerable sections, and two only, in the canonical gospels, Mk. 16⁹⁻²⁰ and Jn. 7⁵³–8¹¹, did not form part of these gospels as written by the original evangelist. In each case the weight of both external and internal evidence supports this conclusion.

External evidence. The section Jn. 7⁵³–8¹¹ is omitted at this point by all the early Greek uncial MSS. except D, and by important cursive MSS. (Some of the latter place it after Lk. 21³⁸, where it is better suited to the context than here; and a few place it at the end of John.) Apart from some MSS. of the Old Latin version, the earliest evidence of the versions is against the section here; and no Greek commentator on the gospels alludes to it before the twelfth century. On the other hand, the story certainly was known at least as early as the third century. Thus, in addition to some less decisive evidence, several Old Latin MSS. contain the section at this point; and Jerome, who says, apparently with some surprise, that the passage 'is found in many Greek and Latin codices', included it here in his Vulgate version. Augustine accepted it. It might have been omitted from some texts, he implies, owing to fear that wrong conclusions might be drawn from the Lord's first words in 8[11]. It thus becomes clear that such external evidence as exists in favour of the passage is overwhelmingly 'western' in character; and its inclusion by Jerome as part of Jn. 7 and 8 may have played an important part in its final acceptance as part of this gospel.

Internal evidence. This points even more strongly to the conclusion that the section was not part of the original text of John. Thus the character of the story and also the style and the vocabulary (e.g. the expressions 'the Mount of Olives' and 'the scribes', and the particles used) are more in keeping with the earlier gospels than with John; and certain resemblances to St. Luke's gospel are especially striking. Again, the opening words 7[53], 8[1, 2] suggest agreement with the earlier tradition Mt. 21[17], Mk. 11[11, 12, 19, 20, 27], Lk. 21[37, 38], 22[39], that during the days at Jerusalem the Lord left the city each evening, and returned next morning to the temple; but as this passage stands in John, the occasion is 'the feast of tabernacles' [7[2]]; and a consideration of the immediate context on each side will show that the passage is ill adapted to its present position. Finally, 'the various readings are more numerous than in any other part of the New Testament', a fact which suggests that the section at first had a more uncertain and varied transmission than the rest of John.

The first definite allusion to the story—but not as certainly confirming also its present position in John—is in the *Apostolic Constitutions* 2[24], a passage which may be of the third century. It is there cited as a lesson to bishops who were thought to be too severe in dealing with penitents. The suggestion has been made that the passage was a story handed down in oral tradition (we may perhaps compare the addition which is contained in D after Lk. 6[4] about the man who worked on the sabbath), and that owing to the belief that its teaching might be misunderstood it failed at first to find a definite place in the teaching and accepted writings of the Church; but as time went on and ecclesiastical discipline became less severe, it was more readily welcomed, and thus was first read in public worship and then passed into the text of the gospels. Its position at this point in John may perhaps be due to the Lord's words, close by, at 8[15], 'Ye judge after the flesh; I judge no man', and indeed to the whole contrast in chs. 7 and 8 between the Jews' sin [8[21, 24]] and the Lord's sinlessness [8[46]], in spite of which He, notwithstanding His word in 8[7], did not condemn her, whom the Jews had brought before Him.

NOTES TO 7[53]–8[11]

8[2]. 'he sat down, and taught them'. Similarly Mt. 5[1, 2], 13[1, 2], Mk. 9[35], Lk. 5[3]; but in John the Lord stands, when teaching in public [7[37], 10[23]].

8[6a] makes clear that, as often in similar stories in the synoptists, the Lord's opinion was sought not in order to obtain His help in reaching a decision, but to put Him, in the presence of the people, in a difficulty, owing to His known merciful disposition to individual sinners, and His readiness, in certain cases, to reinterpret the Law, which in respect of the offence alleged laid down the punishment of death (although it seems that death by stoning was only prescribed in the case of a betrothed virgin).

8[6b]. This is the only occasion, in the canonical gospels, on which the Lord is recorded as writing; and although we cannot know what He wrote, it is permissible to consider the reason for His actions here, on which the text lays stress. These may have been only to show that He declined to give the opinion asked of Him; but it is also possible that He was unwilling to have dealings with, or to look in the face, men who, in their eagerness to put Him in a difficulty [8[6]], were prepared to act, with no hesitation or sense of shame,[1] as they had acted towards this woman [8[3, 4]].

An interesting suggestion, however, may be mentioned, in making which Dr. T. W. Manson builds on a comment on this passage by Professor J. Jeremias.[2] The latter, who holds that at the time of the Lord's ministry the Jewish authorities had no power to inflict capital punishment (cf. Jn. 18[31]), thinks that the question here put to the Lord by the scribes and the Pharisees has the same purpose as the question put to Him in Mt. 22[15-22] about paying tribute to Caesar, namely, to put Him in a difficulty. If He agrees that the woman should be put to death, He can be charged with usurping the power of the Roman procurator; if He disagrees, He contravenes the law of Moses.

Starting from this, Dr. Manson explains the Lord's action in writing on the ground by reference to a well-known practice in Roman criminal law, in accordance with which the presiding judge first wrote down the sentence and then read it aloud from the written record. Dr. Manson

---

[1] See J. R. Seeley, *Ecce Homo*, ch. 9.
[2] See *ZNW* 1950–1, pp. 145–50 and 1952–3, pp. 255 f.

thinks that the Lord by His action says in effect, 'You are inviting me to usurp the functions of the procurator. Very well, I will do so; and I will do it in the regular Roman way.' He then stoops down and appears to write down the sentence, after which He reads it out: 'whoever among you is without sin, let him be the first to cast a stone at her.' The Lord defeats His adversaries by adopting the form of pronouncing sentence in the Roman manner, but by act and word He ensures that it cannot be carried out.

8⁷. In order to bring the scene to a close, the Lord is finally constrained to speak. The best commentary on His words is Rom. 2¹; in the sight of God only one who is free from sin (of any kind) is competent to execute the divine action of judgement or acquittal.

8⁹⁻¹¹. The readings in these verses vary considerably, but all teach the same lesson, namely, that in face of the Lord's challenge none of the woman's accusers could act. And when the Lord and the offender are left alone and He faces her, His final word is neither of condemnation nor of forgiveness, but a charge to forsake her former way of life.]

APPENDED NOTE

The Lord the true passover feast

St. Paul's words in 1 Cor. 5⁷, 'For our passover also hath been sacrificed, even Christ', are evidence that at an early date the Church saw a connexion between the sacrifice of the lamb (or other animal) at the passover feast, and the sacrifice of the Lord upon the cross.

It has been pointed out (*a*) that the Lord's death is kept in view, explicitly or implicitly, in each of the six sections of the ministry, and not only in the seventh section, the passion narrative itself (p. 19); and (*b*) that St. John mentions two[1] passovers [2¹³, 6⁴], as well as the passover of the passion (p. 176). It may be added here that the words 'the passover' occur in this gospel ten times, seven of which refer to the passover when the Lord died.

Anyone who studies St. John's gospel for long is likely to be impressed, not only by the extreme care with which it is written, a care extending to the smallest details, but also by the subtlety and elusiveness of the author. A passage which in itself, and at first sight, may seem to have a plain and obvious meaning and no more, will perhaps be found, when studied more closely and brought into connexion with other passages of the gospel and, above all, with the thought and teaching of the book as a whole, to take on, in addition to the plain and obvious sense, a meaning or meanings of a deeper sort, with religious implications which only gradually become apparent.

The problem for examination in this note is whether St. John regarded the Jewish paschal symbolism as of religious value in its application to the Lord; and if at times attention is paid to matters which seem no more than trifling, it is hoped that the references above to the evangelist's care in composition, and to his elusiveness and subtlety, will be kept in mind. We begin by examining those passages in which the words 'the passover' occurs, or in which there is a clear reference to the passover.

(*a*) 2¹³, 'And the passover of the Jews was at hand, and Jesus went up to Jerusalem.'

---

[1] Some patristic evidence might suggest that the words 'the passover' in 6⁴ should be omitted; but the manuscript evidence is strongly in their favour, and the reading can scarcely be regarded as really doubtful.

On this occasion, so far as going up to attend the feast is concerned, there is no difference between the Lord's action and that of others. (We may contrast His action in 7^{2-10} ,when He goes up 'as it were in secret' at the Feast of Tabernacles.) But after His arrival, at this His first visit to Jerusalem during the ministry, He takes violent action in the temple and speaks, in language which the Jews fail to understand, of its destruction and His own replacement of it, as the seat of the worship of God. In 2^{21} St. John says that the Lord was speaking of the shrine of His body, and in 2^{22} he adds that, after the Lord was raised from the dead, His disciples remembered His words.

(*b*) 2^{23}, 'Now when he was in Jerusalem at the passover, at the feast, many believed on his name.'

The Lord is still in Jerusalem, and the reference in 2^{23} is to the same passover as that mentioned in 2^{13}, but there is now a slight difference in the terms used. The two expressions 'at the passover, at the feast' (the Greek prepositions used are the same in each case, a point obscured in the R.V.) should be noticed. They can, of course, be regarded as synonymous, the second being merely a description of the first in different wording, and no more. But in view of St. John's extreme care in the use of language, the reader may possibly be justified in questioning whether 'the feast' here means only 'the passover of the Jews' [2^{13}], or whether, after the reference to the Lord's death and resurrection, he should be prepared to begin to suspect a possible deeper reference also.

(*c*) In 4^{45} there is a final reference to this first passover, although the words 'the passover' do not occur. Possibly two points about the reference here should be noticed. (1) We read that the Galilaeans made the Lord welcome, because they had seen all the things that He did in Jerusalem at the feast. But in 2^{23-25} it was made clear that the belief which on that occasion the Lord's signs aroused in many was far from perfect in His sight [cf. 4^{48}]. (2) In the last words of 4^{45} it is explained that the Galilaeans 'also went unto the feast'. The reader will not forget that a few days previously the Lord has spoken of the coming of an hour when, in place of the worship at Jerusalem [4^{21}], a 'true worship' would be offered to the Father; indeed the hour of this true worship was not only future, but already present [4^{23}].

(*d*) 6^4, 'Now the passover, the feast of the Jews, was at hand.'

Passing over the unnamed feast (according to the best readings) at 5¹, we come to the second passover of the ministry. The verse may of course be a chronological note and no more. But since the scene of 6¹⁻¹⁵ is laid on the far side of the sea of Galilee, there seems no obvious reason why the passover should be mentioned here, unless St. John wishes the reader to see a connexion between the associations evoked by the thought of 'the passover, the feast of the Jews', and the events and teaching of this chapter.

In 6¹⁻¹⁵ the Lord satisfies the physical needs of the multitude, and His action is explicitly described as a 'sign' (see pp. 165–6). In the first part of the teaching, next day, on the bread of life [6²⁵⁻⁴⁰], when the Lord is asked for a sign [6³⁰] and is reminded of the manna granted to the fathers in the wilderness, He replies that the gift of the manna was temporary only ('gave'), whereas 'the true bread from heaven', of which He is about to speak, is a permanent gift ('giveth') from His Father. When the hearers ask that this bread may be given to them at all times, the Lord directs their thoughts to Himself. He is the living bread which gives life; and His words in 6³⁵ imply that He is not only food, but drink, since He satisfies thirst, as well as hunger. It is, however, at once emphasized that the recipient of His gift must 'believe' [6³⁶].

The second part of the teaching [6⁴¹⁻⁵⁹] is introduced by the difficulty, felt by the Jews, that one of such lowly status as the Lord should describe Himself as bread come down from heaven. The Lord does not deal directly with the difficulty, but again contrasts the manna eaten by the fathers in the wilderness with His gift, which is Himself and, unlike the manna, saves from death; and emphasis is once more laid upon belief [6⁴⁷]. A further step, however, is taken at 6⁵¹, when the Lord reveals that the living bread from heaven which gives eternal life is His flesh; and in the following verses [6⁵³⁻⁵⁸] He describes His flesh as true food, and His blood as true drink, bestowing eternal life, here and hereafter, on the recipient. In consequence many disciples leave Him; and although the twelve remain, they are warned that one of their own number 'is a devil'.

The parallel between this scene in Galilee in the middle of the ministry and the events and teaching at the last supper in Jerusalem on the night before the Lord's death is unmistakable. On that occasion the Lord, alone with the twelve, declared His coming betrayal by a disciple and gave to them His body and blood, under the forms of bread and wine. On that occasion also 'the passover, the feast of the Jews', according to a tradition followed, in part at any rate, in the other gospels, was being eaten; according to St. John, it was due to be eaten on the following evening, the Lord having died on the cross on the next afternoon, at the time when the lambs were being put to death in the temple in preparation for the paschal meal that evening. The conclusion seems to be justified that in the teaching of St. John the sacrificial thoughts connected both with the paschal lamb and with the last supper in immediate anticipation of the Lord's death are not to be confined to the Lord's last hours in Jerusalem (although only then does the consummation of the sacrifice take place), but are to be extended to His Person as such and to His ministry as a whole.

(e) 11$^{54-57}$, 'Jesus therefore walked no more openly among the Jews, but departed thence into the country near to the wilderness, into a city called Ephraim; and there he tarried with the disciples. Now the passover of the Jews was at hand: and many went up to Jerusalem out of the country before the passover, to purify themselves. They sought therefore for Jesus, and spake one with another, as they stood in the temple, What think ye? That he will not come to the feast? Now the chief priests and the Pharisees had given commandment, that, if any man knew where he was, he should shew it, that they might take him.'

The only other passage where we find the precise words 'the passover of the Jews was at hand' is 2^{13}, when the Lord went up (from Galilee) early in the ministry. But now He does not go up from the 'city called Ephraim' with the 'many' who 'went up to Jerusalem out of the country before the passover'. Their purpose, we read, was 'to purify themselves', according to Jewish rites (cf. 2^6, 3^{25}, with the context in each case); the Lord's disciples, who at present remain with Him in the country [11^{54}], are to be cleansed or purified in other ways [13$^{1-11}$, 15^3].

If the suggestion is correct, that St. John is gradually training the reader to grasp that the Lord is, and will be shown to be at this passover, the true paschal Lamb, his mention of the search for the Lord (cf. 7^{11}), and the questioning in the temple whether He will or will not come to the feast, become very apposite, and not least the desire of the authorities for information of His whereabouts, 'that they might take him'—and, we may add, put Him to death.

(f) 12^1, 'Jesus therefore six days before the passover came to

Bethany, where Lazarus was, whom Jesus raised from the dead.'

The reader should ask himself whether the reference here is to the coming Jewish passover or to the coming sacrifice of the true passover [1 Cor. 5⁷]. He is not likely to find it easy to decide the question; and it would be in accordance with St. John's method that this should be so. In any case, the reader should notice that of His own act the Lord now returns to a place of danger [11⁷· ⁸], where He had shown Himself stronger than death [11⁴³· ⁴⁴] and in consequence had Himself been proscribed for death [11⁵³].

(*g*) 12²⁰, 'Now there were certain Greeks among those that went up to worship at the feast'.

Whether these Greeks are to be regarded as proselytes or not, they are certainly not Jews, and represent the first-fruits of those throughout the world (cf. 12¹⁹), who wish to come in contact with the Lord. I have sought elsewhere[1] to show that the cleansing of the temple by the Lord, which in Mark is the first step in the events at Jerusalem leading to His death, had special reference to the court of the gentiles. Here the gentiles should have been able to enjoy certain restricted rights of worship; but of these the Jewish authorities had allowed them to be robbed. If these considerations are kept in mind here, where on hearing of the arrival of the Greeks the Lord at once speaks of the arrival of His 'hour', and of His death [12²³⁻³²], the reader who is inclined to understand the words 'the feast' primarily at any rate as a reference to the Jewish passover may also feel that he should keep in view its further meaning too. And this is still more likely to be the case, if he considers the Lord's teaching in 4²¹⁻²⁴ in connexion with the Greeks' purpose in coming 'to worship at the feast.'

(*h*) 13¹· ², 'Now before the feast of the passover. . . . And during supper. . . .'

These opening words introduce chs. 13 to 17, in which the Lord first cleanses or purifies the disciples, then completes their instruction, in the course of which He says that He has made known to them all things heard by Him from His Father [15¹⁵], and finally in ch. 17 takes them with Him into the Father's presence. At this meal, therefore, which, however, is not the paschal meal (see below), He gives Himself, and all that He is or has, to them. With regard to the significance of the words quoted above from 13¹, see p. 234.

---

[1] *The Gospel Message of St. Mark*, pp. 60–69.

(*i*) 13²⁹, 'Buy what things we have need of for the feast.'

In John the last supper is not the paschal meal; according to this gospel the passover was due to be eaten on the following day, and the Lord dies at the time (Friday afternoon) when the lambs were being put to death in the temple in preparation for the paschal meal that evening. Hence in this command to Judas, which some of the disciples think may have been the import of the Lord's words to him in 13²⁷, the reference can only be to the Jewish passover, to fulfil the ordinances of which money is needed. If the deeper meaning of 'the feast' were in view, this would not be the case (cf. Is. 55¹).

(*j*) 18²⁸, 'They lead Jesus therefore from Caiaphas into the palace: and it was early; and they themselves entered not into the palace, that they might not be defiled, but might eat the passover.'

The Lord, although a Jew, is led, no doubt by the Roman soldiery mentioned in 18³, on to unhallowed ground, where the chief priests and officers of the Jews [18¹², 19⁶] do not follow Him, in order that they may escape defilement and so may be able to eat the passover. Here, therefore, the reference is clearly to the Jewish feast, and to that only.

(*k*) 18³⁹, 'Ye have a custom, that I should release unto you one at the passover.' Here, too, the meaning is unambiguous.

(*l*) 19¹⁴, 'Now it was the Preparation of the passover: it was about the sixth hour.'

Literally, 'it was Preparation of the passover'; here and at 19³¹ there is no article before the Greek word rendered 'Preparation'. This is also the case at Mk. 15⁴², where we might translate, 'it was preparation-day, that is, the day before sabbath'; i.e. it was a Friday. The Greek word without the article had indeed become among the Jews a technical term for Friday, and the Christians took it over; this day of the week is still thus named in the Greek Orthodox calendar. Hence, if it is thought that the reference here is only to the Jewish festival, the sentence may mean 'it was preparation-day of the passover', i.e. the day before the beginning, at sunset on that evening, of the festival; or, perhaps less probably, 'it was preparation-day of passover-week', the whole festival, which lasted a week, being here called the passover; or the sentence may refer, in a less technical sense, to the final preparations for the sacrifice, that afternoon, of the paschal lambs in the temple. But if the reader considers the context in this final mention of the passover in this gospel, he may think that St. John wishes him to see, in the events now being narrated, a reference also to the last stage in the preparations for the sacrifice of the true passover. For not only is this the last scene before the Lord's condemnation to the cross [19¹⁶], but there is unquestionably a parallelism, which has a bearing on the matter, both in the note of time and in some other respects, between this passage and ch. 4; see pp. 122, 318.

We have now examined all St. John's references to the passover; but two further notes of time in this gospel may suitably be considered also, since they contain further reference to the 'Preparation'.

19³¹, 'The Jews therefore, because it was the Preparation, that the bodies should not remain on the cross upon the sabbath (for the day of that sabbath was a high *day*), asked of Pilate that their legs might be broken, and *that* they might be taken away.'

According to Deut. 21²², ²³, if a criminal had been hanged, his body must not remain all night upon the gibbet, but must be buried before sunset the same day. And according to Exod. 12¹⁶, on the first day of the passover festival no work must be done, because the people were to present themselves before Yahweh in the temple on that day. Since therefore in this particular year the first day of the passover feast (according to this gospel) was to coincide with the weekly sabbath, it would indeed be a great day (the Greek word translated 'high' in R.V. is literally 'great'.) But the reader is aware that for other reasons this particular sabbath day of rest was to be great, indeed unique.

19⁴², 'There then because of the Jews' Preparation (for the tomb was nigh at hand) they laid Jesus'.

The use of the Greek article here (unlike 19¹⁴, ³¹) before 'Preparation' suggests that the word, as used in this verse, is not merely an equivalent for Friday, whatever may have been the case before; and the addition 'of the Jews' is even more significant, because their Preparation is now the only one which can be mentioned; for the evangelist and his readers, there is no more Preparation; all has been completed [19³⁰]. He who is now laid in the tomb is He who is, in consequence, to be alive for evermore [10¹⁷, ¹⁸].

Before proceeding further, the reader is asked to consider whether he finds it probable that the thought of the Lord as the true paschal Lamb pervades this gospel or not, since his judgement on this point is likely to have a strong, if not a decisive, influence in his understanding of two passages, one at the beginning and one at the end of this gospel, which it remains to consider in this connexion. In 1[29] the Baptist, at his first encounter with the Lord, bears witness to Him in the words, 'Behold, the Lamb of God, which taketh away the sin of the world'; and he repeats the first part of the witness at 1[36]. And at 19[36], after the Lord's death and the piercing of His side, we read, 'For these things came to pass, that the scripture might be fulfilled, A bone of him shall not be broken.'

These passages have usually been understood in the light of 1 Cor. 5[7]; that is to say, in both the Lord is regarded as the true paschal Lamb. This interpretation, however, has been recently reviewed and rejected by Dr. C. H. Dodd,[1] who holds that 'paschal allusions in the gospel [of John] are by no means clear or certain'. While allowing that 'other ideas may be in some measure combined' in the expression 'the Lamb of God', he understands it as 'in its first intention, probably a messianic title', and the whole phrase in 1[29] as meaning 'God's Messiah, who makes an end of sin'. 'To make an end of sin', he says, 'is a function of the Jewish Messiah, quite apart from any thought of a redemptive death.' Similarly, in discussing the reference to the Old Testament in 19[36], which has usually been regarded as an inexact quotation of Exod. 12[46] or Num. 9[12], both of which passages refer to the paschal lamb, he decides that it is more probably a free citation of Ps. 34[20], which deals with the sufferings of the righteous man and his deliverance.

If, then, Professor Dodd's view is correct, Christian thought has poured into these passages a wealth of religious interpretation and devotion, which the evangelist at any rate did not intend them to bear. The matter is one of great complexity; but after considering to the best of my ability the difficulties which can be urged against the paschal interpretation of the passages, I still think that the 'reduced' interpretation which Dr. Dodd offers is, if not improbable, at least unproven; and I believe that the attitude of the individual reader is likely to be decided by his opinion on the prior question, whether St. John's gospel does or does not show evidence of the influence of the passover festival on the interpretation of the Lord's Person and, above all, of His death.

[1] *The Interpretation of the Fourth Gospel*, pp. 233–8, 424, 428.

INDEX OF BIBLICAL REFERENCES

SUBJECT INDEX